DILEMMAS OF GROWTH
IN
PREWAR JAPAN

This is the sixth and last volume in a series published by Princeton University Press for the Conference on Modern Japan of the Association for Asian Studies, Inc. The others in the series are:

Changing Japanese Attitudes Toward Modernization, edited by Marius B. Jansen (1965)

The State and Economic Enterprise in Japan, edited by William W. Lockwood (1965)

Aspects of Social Change in Modern Japan, edited by R. P. Dore (1967)

Political Development in Modern Japan, edited by Robert E. Ward (1968)

Tradition and Modernization in Japanese Culture, edited by Donald H. Shively (1971)

STUDIES IN THE MODERNIZATION OF JAPAN

Dilemmas
of Growth
in Prewar Japan

Edited by

JAMES WILLIAM MORLEY

CONTRIBUTORS

GEORGE M. BECKMANN   JAMES WILLIAM MORLEY
JAMES B. CROWLEY   TETSUO NAJITA
R. P. DORE   TSUTOMU ŌUCHI
PETER DUUS   HUGH T. PATRICK
KENTARŌ HAYASHI   EDWIN O. REISCHAUER
CHIHIRO HOSOYA   ROBERT M. SPAULDING, JR.
AKIRA IRIYE   ARTHUR E. TIEDEMANN

PRINCETON UNIVERSITY PRESS

PRINCETON, NEW JERSEY

L C Card: 79-155964

ISBN 0-691-00018-2 (paperback edn.)

ISBN 0-691-03074-x (hardcover edn.)

First PRINCETON PAPERBACK Edition, 1974

Second printing, 1974

This book has been set in Linotype Granjon

Printed in the United States of America

by Princeton University Press, Princeton, New Jersey

Contents

CONTENTS

FOREWORD

Scholarly studies of Japan have had a truly remarkable growth in the United States and other English-speaking countries in the years following World War II. To some extent this has been the natural result of the popular boom of interest in Japan stimulated by the war and its aftermath and by the increased opportunities which Westerners have had to associate with the Japanese people. But it is more directly the result of the spread of academic programs devoted to Japan and particularly the growing number of specialists trained to handle the Japanese language.

In the fall of 1958 a group of scholars gathered at the University of Michigan to seek some means of bringing together in more systematic fashion the results of the widely scattered studies of Japan which had begun to appear in the years since the end of the war. The Conference on Modern Japan which resulted from this meeting was dedicated both to the pooling of existing scholarly findings and to the possibility of stimulating new ideas and approaches to the study of modern Japan. Subsequently the Conference received a generous grant from the Ford Foundation for the support of a series of five annual seminars devoted to as many aspects of the history of Japan's modern development. Later the number of seminars was expanded to six.

The Conference on Modern Japan existed from 1959 to 1969 as a special project of the Association for Asian Studies. The Conference was guided by an executive committee consisting of Ronald P. Dore, Marius B. Jansen, William W. Lockwood, Donald H. Shively, Robert E. Ward, and John W. Hall (chairman). James W. Morley subsequently joined this group as the leader of the sixth seminar. Each member of the executive committee was made responsible for the organization of a separate seminar devoted to his particular field of specialization and for the publication of the proceedings of his seminar.

Although the subject of modernization *in the abstract* was

not of primary concern to the Conference, conceptual problems were inevitably of interest to the entire series of seminars. For this reason, two less formal discussions on the theory of modernization were planned as part of the Conference's program. The first of these, organized by John Hall, was held in Japan during the summer of 1960. The report on this discussion, now commonly known as the "Hakone Conference," is included in the first volume of published proceedings. A second informal meeting, held in Bermuda in January 1967, was devoted to a review of the contributions to theory made by the first five seminars. Two results of this meeting were the establishment of the Social Science Research Council–American Council of Learned Societies' Joint Committee on Japanese Studies and the drafting of plans for a new series of seminars which will place more emphasis upon the comparative dimensions of Japanese studies.

The present volume, edited by Professor James W. Morley, is the sixth and last in the series published for the Conference on Modern Japan by the Princeton University Press. The other five volumes, which have already appeared, are: *Changing Japanese Attitudes Toward Modernization*, edited by Marius B. Jansen; *The State and Economic Enterprise in Japan*, edited by William W. Lockwood; *Aspects of Social Change in Modern Japan*, edited by Ronald P. Dore; *Political Development in Modern Japan*, edited by Robert E. Ward; and *Tradition and Modernization in Japanese Culture*, edited by Donald H. Shively.

As their titles suggest, the annual seminars have adopted broad themes so as to include a wide variety of scholars working within each of several major fields of interest. Within these broad fields, however, the seminar chairmen have focused on specific problems recommended either because they had received the most attention from Japanese specialists or because they seemed most likely to contribute to a fuller understanding of the modernization of Japan. We trust, as a consequence, that the six volumes taken together will prove both representative of the current scholarship on Japan and comprehensive in their coverage of one of the most fascinating stories of national development in modern history.

The sixth seminar of the Conference on Modern Japan met in Puerto Rico in January 1968 under the chairmanship of Professor James W. Morley. The theme, "Dilemmas of Growth in Prewar Japan" grew out of questions that had been raised in the previous meetings of the Conference and served to direct attention to some of the political, economic, and foreign policy problems faced by Japan during the 1930's and 1940's. In all, twenty Japanese, American, and English scholars participated in the seminar. In addition to the authors of the papers contained in this volume, the following individuals were present: Professors Tamotsu Fujino, Kyushu University; John W. Hall, Yale University; Marius B. Jansen, Princeton University; William W. Lockwood, Princeton University; Donald H. Shively, Harvard University; and Mutsurō Sugii, Dōshisha University. All contributed most usefully to the discussion, and the editor and authors would like to express their gratitude to them. Professor Shumpei Okamoto, Temple University, and Mr. John Campbell served as *rapporteurs*.

The sixth and final seminar in the Conference on Modern Japan series had two features which served as bridges to the new series being organized by the Joint Committee on Japanese Studies. By concentrating on a specific theme within a fairly narrow time band, and by including more Japanese participants than the previous seminars, it moved toward the kind of problem focus and more truly binational exchange which will characterize the new series.

JOHN WHITNEY HALL

DILEMMAS OF GROWTH
IN
PREWAR JAPAN

CHAPTER I

Introduction: Choice and Consequence

JAMES WILLIAM MORLEY

Back to Hakone

EVER since the preliminary seminar was held in Hakone in 1960, participants in the Conference on Modern Japan have been troubled by the relationship between democratic values and the historic process of modernization. Kawashima Takeyoshi raised the issue at the start, insisting that the desire for democracy has played an "important role" in providing the "motive force" for modernizing Japan.[1] Certainly one cannot deny its presence. At the first seminar, in Bermuda, Marius Jansen reflected on the appeal of individualistic values to intellectuals early in the Meiji period;[2] and in the present volume Tetsuo Najita and Peter Duus show how important egalitarian, populist values were in the thought of others who backed parliamentary politics in the Taishō period. The depth of the attachment to democracy of most of Japan's prewar leaders is not, however, very impressive. To most participants in the Conference, the motive for modernization that has seemed dominant in Japan is that set forth by Jansen: the ambition to secure Japan's independence and to make Japan the equal of any nation in the world.[3] Scratch a modernizer and find a nationalist.

[1] Kawashima Takeyoshi, "Kindai Nihon no shakaigakuteki kenkyū" [Sociological Studies of Modern Japan], in *Shisō* [Thought], no. 442 (April 1961), 484-85; as quoted by John Whitney Hall, "Changing Conceptions of the Modernization of Japan," in Marius B. Jansen, ed., *Changing Japanese Attitudes Toward Modernization* (Princeton, 1965), p. 28.

[2] Marius B. Jansen, "Changing Japanese Attitudes Toward Modernization," in Jansen, *op.cit.*, chap. II.

[3] *Ibid.*, especially p. 65.

3

John Hall concludes from this motive that there was no viable liberal alternative to the bureaucratic structure of power erected in the late nineteenth century. More than this, he and a number of others have been impressed with what they feel is the extraordinary efficacy of the prewar imperial, oligarchic, and bureaucratic attitudes and institutions for the advancement of Japan's modernization—at least in the Meiji period.[4]

This difference of opinion about the role of democracy stems in large part from differences in definition, both of the concept of modernization and of the scholar's role in society. Kawashima contends that any definition of modernization which does not include "the values of 'democracy' or the social and political structure which goes under the name of 'democracy' " has little meaning. There would seem to be three assumptions in this definition: (1) that democracy is an integral part of the good society that the Japanese have been and are striving for; (2) that scholars should take an active part in that struggle;[5] and therefore, (3) that problems for analysis should be framed and concepts like modernization defined so as to be useful for that struggle.

For a number of reasons this approach did not appeal to most of the Western participants at Hakone. One reason, I think, was the feeling that the concept of democracy had become so confused in the emotional polemics between liberalists, pro-

[4] John Whitney Hall, "A Monarch for Modern Japan," in Robert E. Ward, ed., *Political Development in Modern Japan* (Princeton, 1968), chap. II, especially pp. 49-51. See also Roger F. Hackett, "Political Modernization and the Meiji *Genrō*," *ibid.*, chap III; Kurt Steiner, "Popular Political Participation and Political Development in Japan: The Rural Level," *ibid.*, chap. VII; Robert A. Scalapino, "Elections and Political Modernization in Prewar Japan," *ibid.*, chap. VIII; and Bernard S. Silberman, "Structural and Functional Differentiation in the Political Modernization of Japan," *ibid.*, chap. X.

[5] As Tōyama Shigeki stated at Hakone: "The greatest concern of scholars . . . has been with the problem of how to democratize the politics and thought of our country"; as quoted by Hall, "Changing Conceptions of the Modernization of Japan," in Jansen, *op.cit.*, p. 39.

gressives, and Marxist-Leninists in Japan, that an attempt—at least at that time—to define modernization in terms of democratization would have consigned the concept of modernization to the graveyard of ideological controversy before it was possible to see if it could have any new life of its own. Moreover, and more fundamentally, the problem consciousness of the Western participants was different. They were being stimulated, not so much by the hopes and frustrations natural to their Japanese colleagues living within Japanese society, as by currents in the West, two in particular: an overwhelming consciousness of change throughout the world and the desire for a more objective, more universal social science.

At Hakone, Edwin O. Reischauer described this great "transformation" as shaping not just Japan, but all countries in the world. Indeed, he suggested, it had been doing so for several centuries, affecting nations that were profoundly different in many ways and drawing them along in certain apparently similar directions.[6] Was it possible to formulate a concept that could be applied to this global transformation, a concept neither so vague that it obscured essentials, nor so restrictive that it excluded most examples? Benjamin Schwartz thought that it could, and most Western participants agreed.[7] This led in turn to a search for a definition that was value-free, that is, free of the value preferences of the observer, a definition that would make the concept of modernization useful for analyzing not just the dynamics of Japanese life, but a large number of changing societies with such different value systems and developmental characteristics as, for example, Japan, the Soviet Union, the United States, India, or Ghana.

Concepts of course are tools for intellectual analysis; they are not more or less correct, but more or less useful, depending on

[6] Edwin O. Reischauer, "An Approach to the Study of Modernization" (Hakone Conference Paper, mimeo.), pp. 1-2; quoted in Jansen, *op.cit.*, p. 16.

[7] Hall, "Changing Conceptions of the Modernization of Japan," in Jansen, *op.cit.*, p. 29.

their power to help explain the phenomenon under consideration. In this case, the value-free concept of modernization has
proved to be extraordinarily useful. It has led to new insights
by inviting comparisons between the Japanese experience and
that of such different countries as China, India, and Germany.[8]
It has stimulated the search for certain long-continuing pressures relevant to the modern transformation—such as, for example, the drive for more and more education, or the high
propensity to save, or the sophistication of the bureaucracy—
that have been influential from at least Tokugawa times to the
present, through periods of very different political orientations.[9]
It has also permitted the recognition of the fact, as already
noted above, that certain antidemocratic political institutions
and values, paricularly in the Meiji period, exerted an obviously positive influence on Japan's modernization.

But the questions about democracy raised at Hakone by
Kawashima, Tōyama, and others have surfaced repeatedly at
subsequent seminars of the Conference. Various participants
have been unable to suppress the feeling that, when history has
run its course, the processes of modernization will be seen as
incompatible with political forms and ideas other than democracy. John W. Bennett, for example, argues that Japan's economic and social transformation has closely resembled that of

[8] Hellmut Wilhelm, "Chinese Confucianism on the Eve of the Great
Encounter," in Jansen, *op.cit.,* chap. VIII; Stephen N. Hay, "Western
and Indigenous Elements in Modern Indian Thought: The Case of
Rammohun Roy," *ibid.,* chap. IX; Reinhard Bendix, "Preconditions of
Development: A Comparison of Japan and Germany," in R. P. Dore,
ed., *Aspects of Social Change in Modern Japan* (Princeton, 1967), chap.
I; and Hayashi Kentarō's essay in the present volume (Chapter XII).

[9] See, for example, R. P. Dore, "The Legacy of Tokugawa Education,"
in Jansen, *op.cit.,* chap. III; Herbert Passin, "Modernization and the Japanese Intellectual: Some Comparative Observations," *ibid.,* chap. XIII;
E. Sydney Crawcour, "The Tokugawa Heritage," in William W. Lockwood, ed., *The State and Economic Enterprise in Japan* (Princeton,
1965), chap. I, pp. 29-33; and Robert E. Ward, "Japan: The Continuity
of Modernization," in Lucian W. Pye and Sidney Verba, eds., *Political
Culture and Political Development* (Princeton, 1965), chap. II.

the advanced countries in Europe and North America, and that for "industrialized societies of this type" democracy is the natural political concomitant.[10] His formulation leaves open the possibility of a typology of modernization for industrialized societies of some other type, societies that would not require democratic politics; but Robert E. Ward puts the thesis more broadly, albeit hesitantly, suggesting again the possibility "that in a secular sense liberalizing tendencies are inherent in the modernizing process and that even political systems as authoritarian as Meiji are not in the long run immune to the effect."[11]

This raises an even more fundamental question about the concept of modernization than that of its relevance to democracy: to what extent is the process of modernization best conceived of as choice-free as well as value-free? To what extent is it defined as a process with an inevitable result, or at least one so universally desired as to seem inevitable, and to what extent is it better understood to have alternative courses depending on human choice? A minimum deterministic definition has appealed to some. Ward, for example, in commenting on what he feels are eight "essential elements of politically developed societies," suggests that four of these are needed in some "minimal quantity and combination" for the process to "go critical," that is, to "acquire a capacity for sustained and self-generating political change or development that is so characteristic of all modern societies."[12] Ward restricts his comments to the political sphere, but Bennett seems inclined to find the "modernizing" changes in both the society and the economy to be proceeding not only on sustained courses, but also on courses which must inevitably be compatible and therefore presumably part of the same self-generating process.

The argument for indeterminacy has been put equally as strongly. Ardath W. Burks addresses himself to the relationship

[10] John W. Bennett, "Japanese Economic Growth: Background for Social Change," in Dore, *op.cit.*, chap. XIII, p. 413.

[11] Ward, "Epilogue," in Ward, *op.cit.*, chap. XV, p. 588.

[12] Ward, "Introduction," *ibid.*, chap. I.

between the political and the social and economic subsystems, insisting on the "relative autonomy of political decision-making." His remarks carry implications beyond Ward's toward a position that political development itself remains to the end indeterminate, the product of specific human choice.[13] In the economic sphere, Kazushi Ohkawa and Henry Rosovsky also take up the problem, rejecting the idea that there is any necessary "law" of development or any such thing as "self-sustained growth."[14] The history of Japan shows, they argue, that economic progress can stop as well as go: "a series of alternative paths was open to the economy at almost any time." Instead of talking about "stages" through which Japan had to pass, they prefer to talk about "phases" through which it did pass. Harry T. Oshima follows this up with a critique of Meiji economic policy, suggesting that the growth rate could have been accelerated and future political strains reduced if the Meiji leaders had spent less on the state administration and the military and more on the economy, particularly agriculture.[15] And Reinhard Bendix concludes, following Schumpeter, that there are greater varieties of political, social, and economic forms compatible with each other than is immediately apparent from our parochial experience.[16]

These citations from the preliminary discussion at Hakone and the five succeeding seminars are not meant to suggest that problems of broad social theory have dominated the deliberations of the Conference, but they do show a deep and continuing concern for the broader meaning of history. They testify also to the fact that some of the questions raised at Hakone

[13] Ardath W. Burks, "The Politics of Japan's Modernization: The Autonomy of Choice," *ibid.*, chap. XIV, p. 537.

[14] Kazushi Ohkawa and Henry Rosovsky, "A Century of Japanese Economic Growth," in Lockwood, *op.cit.*, chap. II, pp. 49-50.

[15] Harry T. Oshima, "Meiji Fiscal Policy and Agricultural Progress," *ibid.*, chap. VIII, pp. 380-81.

[16] Reinhard Bendix, "Preconditions of Development: A Comparison of Japan and Germany," in Dore, *op.cit.*, p. 31.

about democracy, value, and choice remain deeply relevant to the search for a useful and generally accepted concept of modernization.

It was to turn more directly to these questions that a sixth seminar was held in Puerto Rico in January 1968. The earlier seminars, having been organized largely along disciplinary lines, had tended to emphasize the long flow of the modernization process, the deep continuities in separate spheres of life—intellectual, economic, political, social and cultural. At the same time, partly as a result of having tried too hard to look at the secular trends from the late Tokugawa to the present, the Conference had inevitably become impressed with the extraordinary overall success of various phases of the modernization effort in Japan and therefore had devoted considerable effort to trying to explain why things had gone so well.

On the other hand, the discussion of favorable trends frequently lapsed when reference was made to the 1920's and 1930's, everyone recognizing that, for reasons of which they were not sure and in ways they found difficult to define, something in that period had gone wrong. As R. P. Dore points out in this volume, many of the processes of modernization which had been set in motion in earlier periods and which seemed to hold such promise for a peaceful, orderly, more satisfying society, continued during that period to shape Japan in even more "modern" directions—more education, bigger cities, and the like. But, at the same time, certain other processes faltered, and no one could deny that the peaceful evolution of society was increasingly thwarted by the intensification of social, economic, and political strains, the rise of revolutionary protest movements, the spread of violence, and the intensification of repression until war finally brought Japan to collapse. Was this tragedy necessary? Could an interdisciplinary band of pathfinders concerned about the process of modernization shed any light in that dark valley of Japanese experience? Could a study of that valley lead in turn to a clearer understanding of the modernization process?

Back to the Interwar Period

The road to the interwar period is already strewn with the monuments of conflicting historical interpretations. Some appreciation of the strengths and weaknesses of their positions is necessary before one attempts to plot another course.

On one side stands the judgment of the Allied governments that defeated Japan in the Pacific War: Japan's tragedy was entirely of Japan's own making. According to the International Military Tribunal for the Far East, Japan's difficulties had been caused in the first instance by a group of twenty-eight "criminals" who had conspired to wage "aggressive war."[17] These included some of the highest military and civil officials of the realm, but not the emperor. The "criminals" were tried and convicted in 1948, the evidence for the charge having been spread on the records of the tribunal. Secondly, according to the Basic Initial Post-Surrender Directive, this "conspiracy" was supported by the elite in nearly all areas of Japanese life. All persons who had held "key positions of high responsibility since 1937" were suspected of advocating "militarism and militant nationalism"; hence, the purge.[18] In the third instance, judging from the reforms required by this same document, the fault lay broadly with the political and social structure of the nation which produced this elite and induced the people to follow it. Specifically, this means that the fault lay in the "feudal and authoritarian tendencies" of the government, which the Constitution of 1947 was designed to correct; in the "military machine," which was dissolved and which included not only the armed forces, but also the munitions industry, the "ultra nationalistic," terroristic, and secret patriotic societies, the religious institutions, such as established Shinto, which were seen as "cloaks" for militaristic movements, and militaristic in-

[17] International Military Tribunal for the Far East, *Judgment of the IMTFE, November 1948* (1948).

[18] Supreme Commander for the Allied Powers, Government Section, *Political Reorientation of Japan, September 1945 to September 1948: Report* (Washington, D.C., 1949), II, 429-39.

struction in the schools and propaganda in the mass media; and in the antidemocratic forces in society. Antidemocratic forces were identified especially as the lack of protection for "individual liberties and civil rights," the lack of "democratic political parties" and of democratic organizations in labor, industry, and agriculture, the concentration of income and the ownership of the means of production and trade in a few hands, and the lack of information about and appreciation of democracies in the educational system and mass media.

Since 1948 neither the conspiracy thesis nor the blanket indictment of Japan's wartime leaders has received much support from Western writers. Robert J. C. Butow perhaps comes closest in his *Tojo and the Coming of the War* (1961), where he conveys the impression that for Tōjō the conviction may have been justified, but his approval is partial at most: in his *Japan's Decision to Surrender* (1954) he exonerates others. Richard Storry, who also relies heavily on the trial materials in his *Double Patriots* (1957), directly challenges the plot thesis, but he does not completely deny it when he concludes that the plots and the "incidents" which he describes in the prewar period "conformed very broadly—with the possible exception of the Ketsumeidan affair—to the same general design." On the other hand, most Western writers have been noncommittal, following the lead of the general historians, like Hugh Borton, Edwin O. Reischauer, and W. G. Beasley, who have treated the period in broad summary fashion, stressing trends rather than personalities and simply reporting the verdict of the trial and the conduct of the purge without commenting directly on their validity.[19] James B. Crowley is frankly revisionist. In his *Japan's Quest for Autonomy* (1966) he declares that in the period from 1932 to 1938 Japan's "political and military leaders," including presumably those held for trial, not only were not engaged in

[19] Hugh Borton, *Japan's Modern Century* (New York, 1955), pp. 420-21; Edwin O. Reischauer, *Japan: Past and Present* (New York, rev. 1964), p. 228; and W. G. Beasley, *The Modern History of Japan* (New York, 1963), pp. 281-82.

any conspiracy, but also "did not perceive problems and devise politics in terms of a Pacific War. . . . They were honorable men, loyal servants of the Throne; they sought what their predecessors had sought, security and prosperity."[20]

In Japan, the staunchest supporters of the Allied indictment have been the orthodox Marxist-Leninists, the so-called Kōzaha or Lectures faction, who have consistently championed the classic 1927 and 1932 theses of the Japan Communist party. To be sure, they have largely passed over the fate of the individuals accused at the trial and the charge of conspiracy. Indeed, the two leading works of this school, the *Shōwashi* (History of the Shōwa Era, 1955) by Tōyama, Imai Sei'ichi, and Fujiwara Akira, and the *Nihon kindaishi* (Modern History of Japan, 1957) by Inoue Kiyoshi, do little more than mention the "conspirators" by name; but, they leave no doubt of their condemnation, not only of those tried, but also of the entire Japanese elite who were purged broadside.

It is not surprising that these works have been criticized as "history without people" and have not yet found a grateful acceptance by most Japanese. The war was a personal thing, a time of grief through which all Japanese have passed, either in their own experience or vicariously in the experience of their fathers and brothers. Surely there is fault somewhere, but, in a land where group responsibility, the virtue of loyalty, and a consciousness of fate have been so interwoven in the sensibilities of the people, there has been a deeply felt demand for an attitude more humane than that of the victors or the Marxist-Leninists, and for a more humane history, one to be sure that will not deny the wrong paths taken, but one which will also build a bridge over the great gulf of defeat, so that surviving Japanese can live with themselves and so that future generations can look back on their ancestors with love and pride or, at the very least, understanding.

It is to try to meet these deep demands, naturally unfelt in

[20] James B. Crowley, *Japan's Quest for Autonomy* (Princeton, 1966), pp. xvi-xvii.

the Western world, that a whole body of memoirs and apologist literature is being written. The defense in such works has usually been of three kinds: one, that certain of the individuals accused, usually the civil officials, did not do what they are accused of having done, that is, that they were improperly charged with championing war when actually they were working for peace; two, that the indictment virtually ignores the heart of the problem, motivation, and that in this vital area those officials who sought only to defend the state loyally and those subjects who followed their call to liberate the rest of Asia idealistically, that is, the bulk of the Japanese people, are blameless; or three, that there was no guilt because there was no choice, that the path to war was set by the Meiji Restoration and the men who came after simply did what history demanded of them.

The civilians accused seemed particularly wronged. The dissident opinions of Justices Bernard V. A. Roling and R. M. Pal were widely circulated.[21] The Foreign Ministry, in its carefully documented *Shūsen shiroku* (The Historical Record of the Termination of the War, 1952), edited by Kurihara Ken, described the efforts for peace made by former foreign ministers Tōgō, Shigemitsu, and others. In 1955 it also issued the two-volume *Nihon gaikō nempyō narabini shuyō bunsho* (Diplomatic Chronology and Major Documents), again under Kurihara's editorship, to provide archival materials to permit scholars to reach more objective judgments. Tōgō and Shigemitsu themselves sought to clear their names by publishing their own memoirs.[22]

---

[21] International Military Tribunal for the Far East, *Judgment of the Honorable Mr. Justice Pal, Member from India* (1948); and IMTFE, *Opinion of Mr. Justice Roling, Member from the Netherlands, 12 November 1948* (1948).

[22] Shigenori Tōgō, *The Cause of Japan [Jidai no ichimen]* (Tokyo, 1952; New York, 1956), trans. Fumihiko Tōgō and Ben Bruce Blakeney; Mamoru Shigemitsu, *Japan and Her Destiny: My Struggle for Peace [Shōwa no dōran]* (Tokyo, 1952; New York, 1958), trans. Oswald White.

Some of these same themes are struck by the liberalists, those who believed in civil rights and parliamentary politics during the prewar and wartime periods and who are the "new conservatives" of today. One of their leading representatives, Takeyama Michio, internationally known for his reflective novel on the wartime period, *Harp of Burma* (1964), writes in his *Shōwa no seishinshi* (A History of the Spirit of the Shōwa Era, 1956) that it is not enough to judge men by what they do. If one is to judge fairly, one must probe deeper into their minds and lay bare their views of the world and their motives; and if one does this for the men on trial for war guilt, one finds that many of the civil bureaucrats, including Tōgō and Hirota, served in the government not to promote aggression, but to work for peace.[23] Such sincere "patriotism," he pleads, should be praised, not condemned. There were aggressive elements all right—the young renovationist officers—but the trial was wrong in asserting that even such men "conspired" to produce the war. They simply did not have the power to bring about such a result.

Others have gone beyond this position to assert that not only do these civil bureaucrats deserve better treatment from their countrymen, but so do the officers of the military establishment in general. Efforts at re-evaluating the role of the military have been delayed, no doubt due in part to the difficulties in assembling relevant source materials and in part to the postwar climate which has been so pacifist. But now they too are receiving new attention as Inaba Masao of the War History Office and others are making available significant archives of military, naval, and private papers for selected scholars to examine and in part to publish. The results to date, notably the *Taiheiyō sensō e no michi* (Road to the Pacific War, 1962-63), have been attacked by the progressives and Marxist-Leninists for their

[23] Takeyama Michio, *Shōwa no seishinshi* [A History of the Spirit of the Shōwa Era] (Tokyo, 1956), p. 2; also available in an English translation by John A. Harrison as *The Spirit of Our Times* (Gainesville, 1958).

failure to proceed from the premise that all of Japan's wartime military leaders were aggressive imperialists. Indeed, they do not. Judging from the commentaries appended to each volume, it seems clear that the intent of the editor, Tsunoda Jun, is to demonstrate that by and large Japan's military were acting as competent and loyal officers should to defend Japan's interests against the hostile actions of the Western powers. The essays do not, however, add up to any consistent defense of the military since each of the contributors follows his own lights, sticking close to the "facts" he has found without attempting to fit these into an overall pattern.

Others have gone further, not just to defend the loyalty of the officials who served the state, but to reaffirm the dream of pan-Asian liberation, in whose name the Pacific War was fought. This is to be expected from the emotional ideologues of the wartime frenzy, a leading exponent of which is Hayashi Fusao. A young proletarian writer of the 1920's who was jailed for his radicalism in 1930, Hayashi underwent a change in viewpoint, emerging in 1932 as a champion of right-wing emotional populism whose hero he found in the antiestablishment rebel and expansionist of the Meiji period, Saigō Takamori. In spite of the catastrophes of defeat and occupation and in spite of the hostilities the war engendered in the hearts of most Asians, in 1965 Hayashi returned to the same theme, publishing *Daitōa sensō kōteiron* (In Defense of the Greater East Asia War). Here he reaffirms the Pacific War as the final, glorious act of a one hundred years' war for the liberation of Asia and calls for the absolution of the right-wing fanatics and activists who roused the nation to arms: leaders of the Amur River Society like Tōyama Mitsuru and Uchida Ryōhei, and radical theorists like Ōkawa Shūmei, who was released from the war crimes trial for insanity, and Kita Ikki, who was murdered in 1936. They, he proclaims, are the very essence of the Japanese spirit and worthy successors to the great Saigō.

The call of the old ideals is heard not only by the revolutionary Right. It echoes also in the memories of the progressive and

INTRODUCTION: CHOICE AND CONSEQUENCE

Marxist-Leninist pan-Asianists who roundly denounce Hayashi, but cannot themselves shake off a feeling of ambiguity about the war. As Takeuchi Yoshimi argued in 1959 in "Kindai no chōkoku" (Transcendence of Modernity), the Greater East Asia War was not only a "colonial aggressive war" as the Marxists say; but, in the sense that it was an effort by Japan to oppose the imperialism of the Western powers, it was also a "war against imperialism."[24] In a round-table discussion in December 1963 on the significance of the Great East Asian Co-Prosperity Sphere, Takeuchi, Yamada Munemutsu, Hashikawa Bunsō, and Tsurumi Shunsuke, found no problem in denouncing the war against China as "imperialist" and "aggressive," but the war against the Western powers, the so-called Pacific or Greater East Asia War, was, they felt, a bit different.[25] They recall being stirred themselves by the appeal for the liberation of Asia from Western colonialism; and while they now concede that it was largely the efforts of the colonial peoples themselves which broke the bonds of imperialism, they take pride in believing that it was Japan's war which "gave them the chance." Oda Makoto agrees, saying that you have only to look at the results of Japan's war to see that, unlike Germany's, it did in fact "serve the liberation of Asia and Africa."[26] Therefore, while Japan's leaders are to be condemned for their aggressive intent, the effects of the war were not all bad, the vision of liberation which captivated the Japanese people was a true vision, and the people are blameless for

[24] Takeuchi Yoshimi, "Kindai no chōkoku" [Transcendence of Modernity], in *Kindai Nihon shisōshi kōza* [Lectures on the History of Thought in Modern Japan], VII (Tokyo, 1959).

[25] Yamada Munemutsu, Takeuchi Yoshimi, Hashikawa Bunzō, and Tsurumi Shunsuke, "Daitōa kyōeiken no rinen to genjitsu" [The Idea and the Reality of the Great East Asian Co-Prosperity Sphere], in *Shisō no kagaku* [The Science of Thought], December 1963, pp. 2-19.

[26] Oda Makoto, "Shimin to shite no jikaku" [Consciousness of Being a Citizen], in *Gendai no me* [Contemporary Outlook], May 1965; as cited in Inoue Kiyoshi, *Sengo Nihon no rekishi* [History of Postwar Japan] (Tokyo, 1966), chap. I.

16

having followed it. Indeed, they argue, it is just this vision of Asian solidarity which Japan should be following today.

An outstanding exponent of the defense of fatalism is Ueyama Shumpei. Writing in *Chūō kōron* (The Central Review) in September 1961, Ueyama argues that the coming of the war was determined by the mid-nineteenth-century decision to open the country and modernize it.[27] That decision which, he says, was taken in order to prevent Japan's reduction as a colony by the Western powers, "implied by almost logical necessity the pursuit of a course of development from the dissolution of feudalism to the industrial revolution, from the industrial revolution to aggression, and from aggression against underdeveloped countries to collision with the advanced countries." The logical necessity, of course, is the Marxist dialectic, interpreted here simplistically as driving men through the stages of capitalism, imperialism, and war whether they will it or not.

The second explanation for the war given by the Allied governments, namely, the "feudal and authoritarian" character of the Japanese social structure, has received more support. It was, after all, largely the outgrowth of prewar and wartime Western analyses like those of E. H. Norman, Robert K. Reischauer, Hugh Borton, and Hugh Byas, which have remained influential in Western thinking; and these in turn were in large part derived from the two leading trends of Japanese historical thinking at the time, the Marxist for Norman, and the liberalist for Reischauer and Borton. But the eclectic, pragmatic character of the Post-Surrender Directive deprives it of a clear thesis, so that, while Japanese progressives and Marxist-Leninists basically agree with its conclusions, except for its

[27] Ueyama Shumpei, "Daitōa sensō no shisōshiteki igi" [The Significance for the History of Thought of the Greater East Asia War], in *Chūō kōron* [Central Review], September 1961. This essay has since been republished in a volume of Ueyama's collected articles, entitled *Dai-Tōa sensō no imi* [The Meaning of the Greater East Asia War] (Tokyo, 1964).

light treatment of the civilian bureaucracy, they have preferred to build their own interpretations of the origins of the war on their own theoretical scaffolds. Others, including the liberalists, find the pragmatic approach of the directive's analysis attractive, but prefer to change the emphasis or to concentrate exclusively on one particular phase or another.

The keystone of the orthodox Marxist-Leninist analysis of prewar Japanese society is the concept of absolutism, which Hattori Shisō is said to have adapted in the late 1920's from Kautsky's study of *Class Conflict in Revolutionary France* in an effort to verify the propositions advanced in the 1927 Japanese Communist party thesis.[28] Absolutism is held by the Marxist-Leninists to be a form of state power which stands on a balance of class forces: the feudal lords and the landlord class on the one hand, the rising bourgeoisie on the other, a situation which may occur in the period of transition from feudalism to capitalism. By playing one class off against the other, it is argued, the absolute monarch is enabled to build a united dictatorial state, whose standing army and civilian bureaucracy he uses to promote the interests of both classes. The landlord and bourgeois classes had achieved just such an equilibrium in Japan in 1868, Hattori suggested, and the peculiar Meiji state, which was erected over them, came to play precisely the absolutist role predicted by the model.

This concept of the total state-society structure, commonly referred to as the emperor system or *Tennōsei*, has been immensely stimulating to Hattori's fellow Marxist-Leninists. For them, as well as for him, however, the problem continues to be how to apply it in detail, within the framework of the Marxian categories of thought, to the actual historical situation in Japan.

[28] Tōyama Shigeki, *Meiji ishin* [The Meiji Restoration] (Tokyo, 1951), pp. 13-16, where he summarizes the Marxist debates on the nature of capitalism; and p. 23, note 1, where he comments on Hattori Shisō, *Meiji ishinshi* [History of the Meiji Restoration] (Tokyo, 1928). I am grateful also to David Titus for sharing his knowledge of Marxist historiography with me.

This in turn was complicated by the felt necessity to make such academic applications into guides for practical social action. The result has been a ferment of Marxist historiography that now stretches over forty years along two paths, the one defined broadly by the so-called Kōzaha or Lectures faction, which is the orthodox line ôf the Japanese Communist party, and the other by the so-called Rōnōha or Labor-Farmer faction, which broke from the party in 1927.

While there are many variations now, most Lectures faction historians, like Inoue mentioned above, follow Hattori rather closely, agreeing that the Meiji Restoration was brought about by a coalition of landlords, bourgeoisie, and certain ex-samurai, who did not complete a bourgeois democratic revolution, but a partial revolution that enabled them to establish the absolute state described by Hattori, chiefly on the basis of a "semi-feudal land system" and a "semi-colonial capitalism," plagued intrinsically with a host of "feudal remnants."[29] In fact, the required bourgeois democratic revolution, they argue, has yet to be fought. Throughout most of the Meiji period the fundamental support for the emperor system, they say, was the "semi-feudal landlord class." Gradually, however, after about 1900, the commercialized landlords and the big bourgeoisie came into their own, ushering in the stage of monopoly capitalism that, because it grew by exploiting the tenant farmers and the proletariat, thereby constricted its domestic market and was driven to imperialism in order to despoil the resources of others. As always, however, imperialism only intensified the general crisis, which set in in earnest after World War I. Panic followed panic and revolutionary threat followed revolutionary threat until in 1937, in a final effort to save themselves, the doomed rulers instituted an even more repressive regime. This resembled European fascism in being designed as a final effort of

[29] Even in spite of the reforms of the Occupation, this faction argues that the emperor system remains fundamentally unchanged to this day. See *Nihon shihonshugi kōza* [Lectures on Japanese Capitalism] (Tokyo, 1953-55), I-XI.

monopoly capitalism to suppress the revolutionary forces, but it differed from European fascism in that it retained important feudal remnants, represented particularly by the semi-feudal landlord class, partially in whose interest the absolute state was being administered. It was then a unique semi-capitalist, semi-feudal autocracy best called imperial fascism, a cruel Japanese form of dictatorship which drove Japan to war. The fullest development of this theme for the immediate prewar and war-time period is to be found in the *Shōwashi* of Tōyama, Imai, and Fujiwara previously referred to.

The Labor-Farmer faction scholars, while not quarreling with Hattori's theoretical conception of absolutism, have generally taken exception to his application of the concept on the ground that class balance and absolutism are more character-istic of the Tokugawa than the Meiji period. Capitalism, they say, was in fact much further advanced in late Tokugawa than the Lectures faction acknowledges; it had even penetrated agri-culture. As a result, the Labor-Farmer scholars argue, the Res-toration was "in essence a bourgeois revolution" and, although the emperor system remained as "an institutional remnant of absolutism," political power also became in essence bourgeois.[30] This means that as the modern era wore on, the emperor and his civil and military bureaucracy were not independent feudal elements manipulating, as they served, the landlords and the bourgeoisie; rather, they were simply the tools of the bour-geoisie whose desperate effort to save themselves from the gen-eral crisis of capitalism in the late 1930's must be recognized as just as purely fascist as the regimes of their counterparts in Germany and Italy.

While the Marxist-Leninist schools have dominated Japanese historical scholarship for more than a generation, their interpre-tations are not uncontested: their theses have in fact been the object of more discussion than the Allied indictment. Liberal-ists like Takeyama contend that it is ridiculous to assert that

[30] See, for example, Yamakawa Hitoshi, *Nihon minshu kakumei ron* [An Essay on Japan's Democratic Revolution] (Tokyo, 1947), p. 12.

the same classes, the feudal landlords and the merchants, who
are alleged to have ruled Japan in the mid-nineteenth century,
continued to rule Japan in the 1930's.[31] It is ridiculous, he says,
to try to find the roots of the renovationist thought of the 1930's
in the feudalistic thinking of the Mito School. It is ridiculous
to call the "democratic" parties and party leaders of the 1920's
"forerunners" of fascism when all they were doing was loyally
trying to defend the interests of Japan. It is ridiculous to call
the emperor system of the 1930's fascist if by that one means
the emperor, the zaibatsu, the military, the parties, and all the
other leadership groups, when it was precisely these groups that
the young assassins of the early 1930's set out to destroy.

Rejecting the Marxist framework as well as the conspiracy
and purge indictments of the Allied powers, Takeyama argues
that the period of the 1930's and the war was not one of fascism.
There was no single will, he argues, no dictator, no single party
control; all was done legally and with widespread public support. Rather, the 1930's should be seen simply as a time of militarism, when "military men of the revolutionary clique" came
to power, neither by conspiratorial planning nor by historical
inevitability, but rather step by step. They took advantage of
such institutional weaknesses as the independence of the supreme command; they were aided by the concessive attitude of
the zaibatsu, the parties, public opinion, and the intelligentsia;
and they were inspired, as were most Japanese of the period,
by the "spirit" of the age itself. This spirit was tormented by
the disruptions and confusions brought on by the process of
modernization and by the international environment and demanded a fundamental change in the country's basic social,
political, and economic structure.

With slight variations, this is also the contention of Nakamura Kikuo,[32] and indeed of such humanistic Marxists as
Nezu Masashi. In his *Hihan Nihon gendaishi* (A Critical His-

[31] Takeyama, *op.cit.*, p. 3.

[32] Nakamura Kikuo, *Shōwa seijishi* [A Political History of the Shōwa
Era] (Tokyo, 1958), pp. 26-32.

tory of Contemporary Japan, 1958), Nezu calls for less arid theory and more "common sense."[33] The "ruling classes" are not always "reactionary," he declares, and "the people" are not always "progressive." In fact, "if we include all the battles from the Manchurian Incident to the Great War, except for a few critics, the nation admired the aggression of the military . . . and thought to take advantage of it to make money and get ahead." "Labor" and "the masses," after all, were as riddled with "feudal elements," he contends, as were the "rulers."

As a man who, in his student days, had personally been caught up in the enthusiasms of the democratic movement of the 1910's and 1920's, Nezu is unwilling to join the Marxist-Leninists in writing off that movement as superficial and its leaders as simple, albeit unwilling, tools of the absolutist, imperialist state.[34] No, he says, Premier Hara, for example, was opposed to the military; he twice refused an aristocratic title; he devoted himself to party rule; and in all he was probably closer to the people of the time than were the socialists. As for theorists like Yoshino Sakuzō and Minobe Tatsukichi, they stood not for absolutism, but for the conversion of the emperor system into a bourgeois, constitutional monarchy of the English style; and so successful were they in propagating these ideas that only by terror were the military and the bureaucracy able to prevent their success. Moreover, not all of the bureaucrats are to be condemned either, for there were those like Shidehara and Makino and Abe, for example, who sought to prevent the military takeover of Japan's diplomacy and gave their lives not to war, but to peace.[35]

Nezu also calls for a more balanced assessment of the emperor's role.[36] He agrees with the Marxist-Leninists that the emperor should be held responsible for not intervening to prevent the Manchurian incident, the China incident and the Pacific

---

[33] Nezu Masashi, *Hihan Nihon gendaishi* [A Critical History of Contemporary Japan] (Tokyo, 1958), pp. 5-6.

[34] *Ibid.*, pp. 23-100.   [35] *Ibid.*, pp. 101-18.

[36] *Ibid.*, pp. 135, 142, and 161-74.

War, but at the same time he feels it only fair to recognize that the emperor did act to put down the February 26th incident in 1936 and did act to end the Pacific War in 1945, so that his role was not one of unmitigated reaction on the side of absolutism and imperialism. And finally, he takes up the right-wing ideologues, particularly Kita Ikki, and the revolutionary officers of 1936.[37] He accepts the same thesis as does Inoue, namely that the origins of the mutiny are to be found primarily in the intramilitary struggle between the Imperial Way faction or Kōdōha which revolted, and the Control faction or Tōseiha, which put the revolution down. However, Inoue's charge that Kita was the "leader" of the mutiny, calling for the violent establishment of a dictatorship by the military for the sake of the military and the capitalists, he finds unacceptable. If this were so, he asks, why was Kita condemned to death rather than glorified by the powers that ruled?

Scholars like Takeyama, Nakamura, and Nezu are building on the prewar analyses of Yoshino Sakuzō and other liberalists, whose thought has been so congenial to and so well represented in the wartime and immediate postwar writing of Western historians, notably Robert K. and Edwin O. Reischauer and Hugh Borton, who write of the 1920's as a significant era of parliamentary or at least semiparliamentary politics that was frustrated in the 1930's by the rise of militarism. A bit more eclectic is Robert O. Scalapino, who, while he uses the customary liberalist periodization and terminology, has at the same time borrowed from the Marxists. He begins his standard work on *Democracy and Party Movement in Prewar Japan: The Failure of the First Attempt* with a catalogue of "feudal remnants" from the Tokugawa period,[38] reminiscent of Japanese Lectures faction literature, and proceeds to an explanation of the failure of parliamentary parties to seize and hold power in the prewar years in terms of their being forced to ally with and

[37] *Ibid.*, pp. 144-59.
[38] Robert O. Scalapino, *Democracy and Party Movement in Prewar Japan: The Failure of the First Attempt* (Berkeley, 1953), chap. I.

finally sell out to the bureaucracy because of the late development of a capitalistic class.[39]

Between the Marxist-Leninists and the liberalists, there ranges a varied school of writers who may perhaps be best described by the vague term of progressives: men who sympathize with the elements wanting fundamental change in society but do not accept their discipline. One of the most influential has been the political scientist–historian, Maruyama Masao. Although his approach shows traces particularly of Marxian and Weberian influences, his intention is to carve out his own science of society centering on intellectual history. In his two-volume collection of essays, entitled *Gendai seiji no shisō to kōdō* (Thought and Behavior in Contemporary Politics), Maruyama criticizes the Marxists for what he terms "reductionism," that is, trying to reduce the complexity of history to an analysis of the class structure.[40] On the other hand, he does not deny the importance of class, or the utility of the concept that modern Japanese society has been divided between two large class groupings, the reactionary rulers and the progressive people, or the fascism of the regime, instituted by the reactionary rulers of the 1930's, that forced Japan into an imperialist war. But his explanation of the process of fascistization is his own.[41] Utilizing the same thesis mentioned above—that the army of the 1930's was torn by a conflict between two factions, the Imperial Way faction led by Araki Sadao and inspired by Kita Ikki, and the Control faction led by Nagata Tetsuzan and others, and that the February 26th incident in 1936 represented the victory of the Control faction over the Imperial Way faction—Maruyama adapts it to his own theory of fascist devel-

[39] *Ibid.*, chap. VII, particularly pp. 290-93.

[40] Masao Maruyama, *Thought and Behaviour in Modern Japanese Politics*, ed. Ivan Morris (London, 1963), chap. 6. This volume is a translation of selected essays originally published in a variety of Japanese journals, then collected in *Gendai seiji no shisō to kōdō* (Tokyo, 1957-59) and reissued with some additions under the same title in 1965. The citations here and below are to the English language edition.

[41] *Ibid.*, chap. 2.

24

opment in Japan. The Imperial Way faction, he argues, repre-sented a revolutionary mass movement, one which was "sub-jectively" directed against the ruling classes, but which, if suc-cessful, would "objectively" have resulted in a "fascist" restruc-turing of the state "from below." The alleged victory of the Control faction in 1936, he contends, represents a victory of the ruling classes over this revolutionary movement, one which resulted in the institution of "fascism from above." His empha-sis on the importance of the right-wing thought of the period and his account of its historical origins is also his own.[42] These and others of his views, including those about the multiplicity of political power in Japan, the peculiarities of leadership types, and the irrationality of Japan's military, are now influential in Western as well as Japanese discourse.

Another Progressive scholar whose interpretations have had wide influence is E. Herbert Norman. Norman borrowed from both schools of Marxist-Leninist interpretation, but relied par-ticularly strongly on the Lectures faction. The Restoration, he argues, was essentially a "political compromise of merchants with feudal elements . . . [which] . . . has enabled the former feudal leaders and the feudal outlook to exercise far greater influence than in most other modern societies."[43] He stresses the growing together rather than the competition that most Japa-nese Marxists see in the so-called ruling classes, but he con-cludes that the by-product in any case was the same: the crea-tion of a "centralized, absolute state," manned by a "quasi-independent" bureaucracy, "which in its origins showed a marked feudal coloring." He hesitates, however, to apply the term fascist, even imperial fascist, to the authoritarian regime evolving in the late 1930's. "Contemporary Japan," he writes in 1940, "has some of the earmarks of fascism, but it lacks the destructive full-blown features of a fascist dictatorship."[44] The

[42] *Ibid.*

[43] E. H. Norman, *Japan's Emergence as a Modern State* (New York, 1940), p. 5.

[44] *Ibid.*, p. 206.

bureaucracy, he argues, was simply too strong to be taken over: just as it had "gradually snuffed out all signs of genuine democratic activity," represented most effectively by the labor and the socialist parties, so it had also succeeded in "blocking the victory of the outright fascist forces."

There is no lack of breadth in the various approaches to the problems of the 1920's and 1930's. The difficulty is that none is fully satisfying. The Allied charge of conspiracy is obviously too gross an oversimplification of history and unfair to various of the individuals accused. The Allied condemnation of the entire elite, excluding the bureaucracy, is not a defensible conclusion based on factual knowledge or any but the crudest social theory and most pressing political expediency.

The Marxist-Leninist explanations do indeed leave out of the equation the role played by the real mass of society, which cannot be subsumed under the minorities of either repressive or progressive classes that the Marxist-Leninists claim to be the engines of history. They do indeed overemphasize social structure to such an extreme that the social process itself goes largely unexplained. They do indeed so ignore the role of human consciousness and choice that their theories are difficult to relate to the world of human experience. And by the time one sufficiently qualifies Japanese "absolutism" and "fascism" with the alleged peculiarities of the emperor system, one is left with an explanation in which nothing is clear, where in all areas in which Japan might be compared with other nations, Japan is always somehow "semi-"—in short, as mysteriously unique and unfathomable as the traditionalists have always claimed.

The liberalists, one must admit, are the most satisfying in their humane and democratic values and in their discussion of men and events in terms with which the participants themselves and contemporary observers can readily identify; but, the fudging "semi-quasi" syndrome of terminology is all too common here too, and the fundamental questions of social causation are all too often glossed over.

26

The Relevance of Modernization

For the concept of modernization to be useful in illuminating the dark places of the interwar period more convincingly than the interpretations now current, the precise problems that concern us need to be set forth clearly. First of all, to what extent did certain fundamental processes which are generally acknowledged to be integral to a value-free concept of modernization—such as, for example, economic trends toward greater productivity, social trends toward greater equality and individuation, intellectual trends toward greater rationality and secularization, and political trends toward an administrative state structure—continue during this period?

The answer so far appears to be mixed. According to Ohkawa and Rosovsky, as confirmed in this volume by Patrick, economic growth continued, but not uniformly.[45] The rate itself fluctuated widely, falling in the 1920's to the lowest point since the 1890's and soaring in the 1930's to the highest; and the imbalance between the modern industrial and the traditional agricultural sectors became even more pronounced. In the social sphere, Dore summarizes the third seminar's findings as indicating movement throughout the modern period toward greater equality, but not so clearly toward individuation.[46] Intellectually, the flight to utopian radicalism, as illustrated in this volume by Duus, Najita, and Beckmann, and to renovationism as described below by Crowley, would seem to confirm a retreat from rational, secular thought, at least among a number of social critics.[47] And in the political sphere, while the government continued to grow in size and area of activity, and while the people continued to become more and more involved with its processes, modernization did not proceed unambiguously. Spaulding points out in this volume, for example, a

[45] Ohkawa and Rosovsky, *op.cit.*, pp. 66-83; Patrick, Chapter VII.

[46] Dore, "Introduction," in Dore, *op.cit.*, p. 22.

[47] Crowley's own evaluation of the thought of the *Shōwa Kenkyūkai* members is somewhat different. See his essay in this volume (Chapter IX).

growing politicization of the bureaucracy as the 1930's wore on, and Hosoya delineates a growing irrationality in the decision-making process.

The inquiry so far is incomplete, but there is enough evidence to suggest that even using a restricted, value-free definition of modernization, Japan in the interwar period could be called only partially modern. While in certain spheres modernizing trends continued, in others, as Hosoya points out, they seem to have undergone "retrogression." Still other spheres seem to have been immune to the process. This being the case, to what extent are these trends responsible for the heightening of violence which swept Japan in the 1920's and 1930's and for which the government found no more satisfactory answers than repression and war?

The answer would seem to be that they were very largely responsible, responsible in the sense that they set up many of the most serious dilemmas Japan then had to face. There were dilemmas of priorities in economic development; for example, how to give priority to industry without excessively depriving agriculture? There were dilemmas of social order, such as how to secure the full participation of the rural areas in the life of the nation without dissolving what was felt to be the stabilizer of social values, the hamlet? There were political dilemmas, such as that involving the leadership succession: to whom could the management of the nation be turned over after the passing of the original oligarchy when the institutions for channeling the newly emerging forces had not yet become fully legitimized? There were dilemmas of devising economic policies when price levels at home and abroad were seriously out of line, and dilemmas of foreign policy toward a world in which order was disintegrating. These are but a few of the problems which came to a head in this period. Some, of course, were created by external developments, but the great bulk of them stemmed from the modernization process itself.

Were such dilemmas inevitable? Only in the sense that they

sprang from precedent conditions. It might be said, for example, that once the decision was made for an oligarchy to monopolize power on a personal basis, then inevitably there would be a crisis on their passing. Or once the decision was made to mythologize the emperor in order to mobilize the nation for modernization, then inevitably there would come a time when such parochial attitudes would confront the requirements of peaceful international intercourse. Once the decision was made in early Meiji to "hold the countryside constant," then inevitably there would come a time when the isolation of the countryside would so deprive the nation of the energies of its rural people or when the depression of the villagers' living standard would so arouse them to protest, that modernization of the countryside also would have to be faced. But there is no reason to assume that all modernizing nations will face the same dilemmas. Presumably, if other modernizing societies make similar original decisions, they will tend to have similar consequences; but, if they make different original decisions, the consequences also will obviously be different. What one can suggest, however, is that from the very beginning all societies undergoing the modernization process will have to make difficult and consequential decisions about priorities of development and that from these decisions will inevitably flow a number of subsequent dilemmas which may well be so serious as to threaten the stability of the political system.

Is it inevitable that the political systems of other modernizing nations will be unable to resolve their dilemmas of growth, that is, unable to resolve them without resorting to repression and war as did Japan? There is no reason to assume so. Obviously this will depend on the exact nature of the dilemmas, the timing of their crises, and the strength and ability of the political leadership at the time. But one can say that the odds are great that if such fundamental problems are allowed to pile up, the likelihood of violence and political failure is great. As a corrective, then, to our theories of growth, we also need a pathology

29

of growth, a study of the kinds of difficulties societies are likely to encounter as a result of various choices made in the growth process. In this aspect as well as in its healthy aspects, Japan's modernization is a rewarding object of study.

PART ONE

Political and Military

CHAPTER II

The Bureaucracy as a Political Force, 1920-45

ROBERT M. SPAULDING, JR.

IN MOST accounts of Japanese political history after World War I, the central theme has been the capture and manipulation of the Cabinet by political parties and later by the military services. Historical analysis has centered on the character and purpose of these two groups: Were the party leaders pioneering democrats or hypocritical spoilsmen; the military officers, reckless plotters or maligned patriots? Other elite institutions and groups are either ignored or treated as static components of the environment. Passing references to the pluralism of the political system have not attracted much attention to the Privy Council, the House of Peers, the zaibatsu, or the civil service.

In the case of the civil service, this neglect can be plausibly explained. Unlike the military services, which flaunted their legal independence and their ability to coerce Cabinets, the civil service was by law subordinate to the Cabinet, and by choice and tradition a silent service not given to public revelation of its opinions or its disagreements with titular superiors. In general, bureaucrats were noticed only when they ceased to be bureaucrats and became Cabinet ministers.[1] Those who remained in subordinate positions were seen merely as a faceless crowd of underlings performing routine functions upon command.

Yet we can hardly assume that what is inconspicuous must be inconsequential. Since Japanese legal forms have seldom coincided with political realities, is it possible that bureaucrats

---

[1] Under Japanese law, Cabinet ministers and privy councilors were technically part of the civil service, but throughout this chapter, they are excluded from the meaning of such terms as *bureaucracy, civil service, career service,* and *career bureaucrats.*

possessed autonomous political power distinguishable from that of the Cabinet? Were they content simply to await instructions and meekly comply? If they wanted to oppose policy decisions or to initiate legislation, did they have the ability to do so? The purpose of this paper is to explore such questions in order to evaluate the power of the civil service in the period between the two world wars, and to see how and by whom that power was used.

Structure of the Civil Service

The civil bureaucracy was much larger than is generally recognized. At the end of 1928, it totaled (for Japan proper) at least 1,300,000 people, not counting several categories about which little information is available. Even this conservative figure was then four times the combined strength of the army and navy, and roughly five percent of the employed population. Most of the 1,300,000 belonged to one of three large categories: 421,464 *konin, yonin,* and other "employees"; 382,893 *riin* paid from local-government funds; and approximately 482,000 hannin civil officials (*hannin bunkan*) and "treated officials" (*taigū kanri*) of comparable rank. Above these three large groups was the civilian counterpart of the army and navy officer corps: the elite corps of 12,864 "higher civil officials" (*kōtō bunkan*), subdivided into shinnin, chokunin, and sōnin ranks according to appointment protocol.[2]

The hannin and higher officials comprised what might be called the classified civil service, divided into numbered grades within each protocol level except the highest (shinnin). There

[2] Cabinet Statistical Bureau, *Dai Nihon Teikoku tōkei nenkan* [Statistical Yearbook of the Japanese Empire] (1929 edn.), pp. 394-403; and Education Ministry, *Gakusei hachijūnenshi* [Eighty-year History of the School System] (Tokyo, 1954), pp. 1092-93. These sources omit some types of "treated officials," women in the Imperial Household Ministry, and apparently the 135,991 employees of government factories (see *Jiji nenkan* [Jiji Yearbook], 1931 edn., p. 360).

was also an important functional division based chiefly on method of recruitment. Men came to positions in the classified service by three avenues: screening, examination, or free appointment. These were associated respectively with technical, administrative, and policy offices. There were intricate restrictions on movement from one category to another.

Screening (*senkō*) usually consisted of a review of documentary evidence of educational or other qualifications, and was used for selecting all kinds of "technical" officials (from engineers to medical doctors), other officials "needing special knowledge and skills," and teachers in national government schools. Examinations included the decentralized Ordinary Examinations (*Futsū shiken*) for hannin positions, and the unified administrative, judicial, and diplomatic Higher Examinations (*Kōtō shiken*) for sōnin appointments. "Free appointment" (*jiyū nin'yō*) was an unofficial term indicating exemption from educational and experience qualifications, from examinations, and from restrictions on rank of initial appointment.

For twenty years after the Restoration of 1868, all offices in the classified civil service were open to free appointment. Many of the men appointed then were generically indistinguishable from their Tokugawa predecessors. They qualified for office in the traditional way—by inheriting appropriate rank within a privileged social class and by having influential friends in government. However, Ōkubo, Ōkuma, Itō, and other Restoration leaders recruited many younger men whose education and initiative impressed them, regardless of geographic or feudal considerations. Such men are a transitional type between traditional bureaucrats who qualified by ascription and modern bureaucrats who qualify by achievements subject to impersonal verification. Between 1884 and 1900, screening and examination regulations were gradually instituted, and by 1900 free appointment was confined to shinnin posts (Cabinet ministers, ambassadors, a few others), the chokunin chief Cabinet secretary, diplomatic ministers, and sōnin confidential secretaries to Cabinet members.[3]

The Locus of Power

How these differences in rank, function, and recruitment affected bureaucratic power is, of course, partly dependent on a definition of power. The unclassified employees were a negligible political factor despite their great number. Lacking the legal protection of tenure, they had little power even in disputes over pay and working conditions, except in those rare instances when their dissatisfaction was shared by bureaucrats of higher rank. The *riin* were not of much more consequence in national terms, though as low-ranking members of prefectural and municipal government staffs they might possess local influence.

The political role of hannin officials is more difficult to evaluate. For most Japanese, political power was personified not by the remote and seldom-seen elite of the Diet, Cabinet, and higher civil service but by the ubiquitous civil police, the clerks in the tax offices, and perhaps the public school principals and teachers. Most of these were hannin officials,[4] and their impact on the daily life of the ordinary citizen was indeed profound.

The police, for example, had operational responsibility for a bewildering variety of government programs and policies in addition to public safety, traffic control, and criminal investiga-

---

[3] I have discussed this evolution of recruitment methods in *Imperial Japan's Higher Civil Service Examinations* (Princeton, 1967), pp. 51-120, 307-17.

[4] Patrolmen (who constituted about ninety percent of the civil police force) and primary school teachers, along with several other groups, were technically neither officials nor employees. They belonged to a curious category which reflected the special genius of Japanese administrative law: officials who were not officials but were accorded "treatment" as if they were. In legal jargon, they were *kanri taigūsha* (persons treated as officials) or simply *taigū kanri* (treated officials) assimilated to hannin rank.

tion and apprehension. They enforced economic controls, discouraged unionism, inspected factories, censored publications, licensed commercial enterprises, arranged for public welfare aid, supervised druggists and public baths, controlled public gatherings, managed flood control and fire prevention, maintained surveillance of people suspected of "dangerous thoughts," and did countless other things that brought government close to the daily life of every Japanese.

Nevertheless, the police, the tax-collectors, and other low-ranking officials were political agents, not principals. They carried out instructions from above, and their responsiveness to higher authority was probably superior to that of the rest of the civil service and certainly superior to that of the army. What is uncertain is the extent to which instructions to officials in the field were influenced by hannin officials in the central government ministries. Nearly all statutes originated in the executive branch—not only the numerous imperial and ministry ordinances, but also ninety-one percent of all laws enacted by the Diet under the Meiji Constitution (1890-1947).[5]

From the meager evidence available, it appears that the first drafts of most laws and ordinances were prepared by low-ranking officials and that many of these were of hannin rank. But drafts were usually initiated on instructions from an official of the higher civil service, and in any event they were always subject to revision, rejection, or approval by higher officials.[6] The

[5] House of Representatives, *Gikai seido shichijūnenshi: Teikoku Gikai gian tō kemmeiroku* [A Seventy-year History of the Diet System: A List of Bills presented in the Imperial Diet] (Tokyo, 1963), appendix.

[6] See Kawanaka Nikō, *Gendai no kanryōsei* [Contemporary Bureaucracy] (Tokyo, 1962), pp. 13-24, esp. p. 21. However, Tsuji Kiyoaki, "Decision-Making in the Japanese Government: A Study of Ringisei," in Robert E. Ward, ed., *Political Development in Modern Japan* (Princeton, 1968), pp. 463, 467-68, contends not only that the function of drafting was monopolized by "permanently low-grade administrators" who had not passed the Higher Examinations (i.e., hannin officials), but also that higher officials felt unable either to issue instructions (rather than

37

role of hannin officials, whether in field agencies or in Cabinet ministries, was comparable to that of their counterparts in the military services, the non-commissioned officers of the army and navy. Though hannin influence was no doubt enhanced by procedures that tended to disperse responsibility, the higher civil service was clearly the center of bureaucratic power.

Four Determinants

By 1920, influence and status within the civil service were determined largely by the cumulative consequences of four decisions made in the last decades of the nineteenth century. The first of these was a decision in 1886 that the classified service would have two career ladders rather than one. During the first eighteen years after the Restoration, there had been no barrier to promotion from hannin to sōnin rank. Many bureaucrats of the transitional type began as hannin clerks (*zoku*) and rose to sōnin and later to chokunin positions. The unity of the career ladder was symbolized by the designation of grades in a continuous numerical sequence from highest chokunin to lowest hannin grade. Signs of the reconsideration of this policy were evident by the early 1880's, notably in the use of the legally anomalous euphemism "quasi-sōnin rank" (*jun-sōnin*) for appointments below sōnin level that were expected to lead to sōnin posts. By 1886, the government had decided to apply to the civil service the distinction already made in the military services between noncommissioned and commissioned officers, and the official grades were renumbered accordingly. Under the appointment ordinances of 1887 and later years, teachers and technical personnel chosen by screening could still move from hannin to sōnin posts, but for all other officials there were sep-

---

suggestions) to these hannin officials or to alter their drafts. He offers no evidence to support this implausible assertion. If it were true, one would be hard pressed to explain why such powerful hannin officials did not push through an ordinance eliminating the formidable legal barriers to their own promotion into the higher civil service.

arate hannin and sōnin recruitment systems with little movement from one to other.[7]

A second major determinant was the Meiji oligarchs' conclusion that, in Yamagata's words, "administration is ... a single
specialized technique."[8] It was therefore to be separated from
all other functions and performed by an elite corps of administrators trained in law, chosen through highly competitive examinations, and aided by technically-trained subordinates. The
latter were not trained for administration and therefore were
not often chosen for administrative positions. In the laconic
metaphor of one prominent examination man, "the task of a
cormorant should not be given to a crow."[9] Exceptions to this
dichotomy were infrequent and concentrated in a few atypical
agencies such as the Railway Ministry, at least until after the
beginning of the third war with China in 1937.

The third determinant was a very narrow definition of "policy" offices—that is, of offices open to free appointment. All
shinnin and chokunin positions were in this category before
1899, when Yamagata removed nearly all chokunin administrative offices from the free list and imposed strict rules of eligibility for appointment. He said, in effect, that vice ministers,
bureau chiefs, and prefectural governors were not policy offi-

[7] The most common exceptions were purely technical. Men who
passed the Higher Examinations after 1893 usually served a few months
as hannin clerks while awaiting a sōnin vacancy, and a few men passed
the examinations while serving as hannin clerks. Most career hannin
officials, however, were eligible for promotion to sōnin posts only after
serving at least five years in the top half of the hannin pay scale, and
then only to sōnin posts separated (in rank and pay ceilings) from
those open to examination men.

[8] This concept was written into law by Itō in the appointment ordinances of 1887 and 1893. The quoted phrase is from Yamagata's "statement of reasons" for the 1899 appointment ordinance (about which Itō
had misgivings). It was thus actually a rationalization for the third
determinant described here, but applies more accurately to the second.

[9] Kanamori Tokujirō, "Kanri saiyō seido zakkan" [On the Bureaucratic Appointment System], Hōritsu jihō, II:7 (July 1930), 132. Kanamori was then a counselor in the Cabinet Legislative Bureau.

cials but simply administrators, and therefore must be chosen by promotion from the ranks of career sōnin administrators. Under the 1899 ordinance, appointments to these offices were, with minor exceptions, closed to anyone who had neither held chokunin rank for at least one year before 1899 nor reached the highest sōnin rank as an administrator. Access to the highest sōnin rank was carefully regulated by ordinances that imposed limits on the grade of first appointment in the higher civil service, on rapidity of promotion to each higher grade, and on transfer from a technical office to an administrative office.

The fourth determinant was in some ways the most important: beginning in 1900 the Privy Council had the power to veto any change in civil service statutes. At Yamagata's request, this power was conferred by an "imperial message" (*gosatasho*) committing the emperor to refer to the council any Cabinet proposal to amend a civil service ordinance. This was an ingenious device because it was extralegal. Cabinets governed by creating, changing, or rescinding imperial ordinances, but since there was neither precedent nor procedure for repudiating a supposedly personal expression of sovereign will, the "message" conferring the veto power was never successfully challenged. Although Yamagata's chief objective was to perpetuate the restrictions on chokunin appointments, later Cabinets found it even harder to persuade the Privy Council to relax sōnin rules.

A Redistribution of Power

By 1920, the barrier between hannin and sōnin ranks, the dichotomy between administrative and technical offices, the narrow definition of policy offices, and the Privy Council's control over changes in civil service rules had produced a substantial redistribution of power within the Japanese political system. First, effective (though not total) control of the managerial echelons of the career civil service passed to a well-defined group of bureaucrats of a new type, the examination men. Second, the Cabinet's power to control the career service was so weakened that the two became separate components in the political balance of power.

The sōnin and chokunin ordinances of 1893 and 1899, respectively, gave examination men an almost complete monopoly of all subsequent appointments to administrative posts in the higher civil service. As men appointed before those dates retired or died, examination men moved up the promotion ladder to replace them. The percentage of bureau chiefs who were examination-qualified rose from thirty-three percent in 1910 to eighty-two percent in 1920. The first vice ministers chosen from the ranks of examination men were appointed in 1912, and every vice minister of the Foreign, Home, Finance, Education, Commerce, Communications, Overseas, Welfare, Greater East Asia, and Munitions ministries between 1918 and 1945 was an examination man.

The difference between transitional and examination bureaucrats is easily exaggerated but nonetheless real. Many of the later transitional bureaucrats—those who became sōnin administrators in the 1880's and early 1890's—had the same scholastic background as most examination men: that is, they were graduates of a law college, most often that of Tokyo Imperial University. However, they had not been required to overcome the formidable barrier of the Higher Examinations, which, in most years after 1893 stopped about ninety percent of all applicants, including a majority of those from Tokyo Imperial University. These extremely high rates of failure had a profound effect on the civil service, first by improving the caliber of men selected for administrative posts and secondly by creating a distinctive esprit de corps among those selected.

Men who had won appointment through the Higher Examinations felt a special sense of achievement which the civil service ordinances recognized with substantial rewards: preferential salary scales, greater lateral and vertical mobility and optimum prospects for eventual promotion to section chief, bureau chief, or vice ministerial rank. They also felt a commitment to the civil service that was more lasting and more impersonal than that of their predecessors. Status achieved with so much difficulty was not as readily abandoned. Moreover, since the ordinances restricted not only first appointments but also the reappointment of former officials, even the transitional bureaucrats began to think twice before resigning. The result was a career service much more selective and much more stable than the early Meiji bureaucracy—and well aware of its elite position.

The requirement that most chokunin positions be filled by promoting senior sōnin administrators gave examination men a powerful incentive, and disqualified most of their competitors. It also gave chokunin officials a new outlook: instead of being the lowest "policy" officials they became the highest career men, without in fact losing their voice in policy-making. Having risen from the ranks of examination men, they felt a group loyalty that at least equalled and often outweighed their loyalty to the transient ministers above them. In short, the appointment system made examination men the most privileged and protected group in the bureaucracy and substantially weakened the Cabinet's power to control subordinate officials.

Of course, this did not mean that career men and Cabinet ministers were natural enemies, or that the former were in a constant state of insurrection. In most situations, obedience was indicated not only by traditional ethics but also by individual and collective self-interest. Insubordination was contagious and likely to get out of hand: the career official who disobeyed his superior always had to worry that he might be inviting disobedience among his own subordinates. Another consideration was perhaps still more compelling. Even under the Yamagata rules, the number of men eligible for selection as section or bureau chief, prefectural governor, vice minister, or minister always far exceeded the number of positions available, and a reputation for troublemaking was obviously a disadvantage in competing for such promotions. Finally, the ability of the executive branch of government to act or to prevent action was clearly greater if the Cabinet and the career service were united than if they were not. The advantages of cooperation were beyond dispute.

Nevertheless, when there was a conflict of interests or attitudes between the Cabinet (or one minister) and career bureaucrats, the latter were always able and often willing to offer substantial resistance. Such conflicts were uncommon before 1918, because men of similar experience and purpose—generally transitional bureaucrats—occupied most of the senior appointive positions in the government. But as the career service became more homogeneous in origin and outlook, Cabinet ministers became more heterogeneous. The great increase, after World War I, in the number of party politicians and military officers appointed to the Cabinet placed new strains on relations between the Cabinet and bureaucracy. Disagreement between "policy" officials—that is, the Cabinet—and the career service became more frequent and more open than before. Since the Cabinet was legally the highest echelon of a unified civil service, any such disagreement was by definition a breach of official discipline. In everyday language, it was usually described by the term made famous in the feudal indiscipline of the fourteenth century: *gekokujō*, "the low oppress the high" —though it can be argued that the name is appropriate only when the will of the subordinate prevails.

Gekokujō was not merely indiscipline or insubordination. Indeed, it was most successful, and therefore most important, when it did not involve public disobedience at all. The career civil service was often able to induce Cabinet ministers to adopt or advocate in their own names policies and decisions initiated by their subordinates. The popular impression that *gekokujō* of this kind in the civil service was much more common in the period of party Cabinets than thereafter is clearly erroneous. If anything, complaints about indiscipline were more common after than during the party era. One reason for this was the achievement of a compromise which satisfied neither politicians nor bureaucrats but proved reasonably effective.

The Parties and the Bureaucracy

Seiyūkai leaders tried, both in the First Yamamoto Cabinet in 1913 and more insistently in the Hara Cabinet after 1918, to overturn the Yamagata ordinances and restore all chokunin positions to the free-appointment list. The most they were able to achieve, after strenuous battles with the Privy Council, was the right to appoint noncareer men to a small number of the most clearly "political" offices at the highest sub-Cabinet levels. Even these hard-won gains were short-lived because the anti-Seiyūkai parties preferred a different strategy. Instead of placing politicians in offices that were integral parts of the civil service command structure, as the Seiyūkai proposed, Ōkuma and his political heirs in the Kenseikai created new offices (parliamentary vice ministers and counselors) that were grafted onto the structure but outside the formal chain of command. The result was that the free appointment of administrative vice ministers was restored in 1913 but abolished again in 1914, restored again in 1920 and once more abolished in 1924. The same fate overtook most of the other Seiyūkai additions to the free-appointment list, either in 1924 or under the Saitō Cabinet in 1934.

Both major parties discovered, however, that there were other and more effective means of securing a measure of control over the career service. Bureau chiefs and prefectural governors had to be chosen from the ranks of career bureaucrats, but even a limited power of choice gave the Cabinet some leverage. Incumbent officials who proved wholly unwilling to cooperate with a party Cabinet could be transferred to less desirable positions or suspended. This fact and its corollary—the power of a Cabinet controlled by the opposing party to reinstate men transferred or suspended by its predecessor—produced a tacit alignment of many career bureaucrats, especially in the Home Ministry, with one or the other party. They usually did not become party members, but they did make peace with a party and in some instances worked actively in behalf of the party's electoral interests.

Career men who did not follow this route were usually quite scornful of those who did. In the traditional view, not only of bureaucrats but also of many historians, association with a political party amounted almost to a blood taint, permanently transforming the career bureaucrat into a "party man," regardless of any other consideration. Thus, many writers have implied that a choice between one career bureaucrat and another for appointment as bureau chief or governor was a routine personnel transfer when made by a nonparty Cabinet, but part of a notorious spoils system when made by a party Cabinet.

Moreover, the ability of party Cabinets to obtain bureaucratic cooperation through the power to select, transfer, or suspend must be weighed in the balance with an extraordinary fact that is seldom recognized: party Cabinets often chose examination men even for positions open to free appointment. The free list included administrative vice ministers in 1913-14 and in 1920-24, and the superintendent-general of the Metropolitan Police Board and the Home Ministry's police bureau chief in 1913-14 and in 1920-34. Yet twenty-three of the thirty vice ministers, and all of the senior police officials, appointed in these periods were examination men. Willingness to cooperate may explain many or most of the choices made by party Cabinets for career offices; it is obviously not a sufficient explanation for appointing career men rather than party members to policy offices on the free list.

Senior examination men had two important advantages. Having served as administrators in many sections and bureaus of a ministry, they knew the work and procedures of the ministry much better than any outsider, better even than a technical official, whose experience was always much more narrowly specialized. For the same reason, they were well acquainted with the other personnel of the ministry, knew the abilities and shortcomings of these colleagues, and usually could count on support or cooperation from them. Conversely, a businessman or politician appointed to an office on the free list often found that he knew few if any of his subordinates and little or nothing about their duties and methods. The need for governmental experience and the need for maintaining good relations with the career staff thus caused many Cabinets to choose examination men even for offices open to outsiders.

Advice and Consent

The second of these considerations seems also to have induced many Cabinets and Cabinet-makers to consult—or to regret not having consulted—senior bureaucrats on even the highest-level appointments. Though proof of this is not easily found, a few suggestive examples can be documented. In 1940 Konoe chose a business leader (Kobayashi Ichizō) as commerce minister on the advice of Commerce Vice Minister Kishi Nobusuke, who mistakenly thought that the new minister would be an obliging figurehead to rubberstamp Kishi's own economic proposals and to absorb any public criticism of these.[10] On the other hand, Prime Minister Kiyoura Keigo, a career bureaucrat himself, did not consult Foreign Vice Minister Matsudaira Tsuneo in choosing a zaibatsu official (Fujimura Yoshirō) to be foreign minister in 1924. Matsudaira and other career diplomats complained so forcefully that Kiyoura was constrained to assign Fujimura instead to the lowly Communications Ministry and substitute career diplomat Matsui Keishirō as foreign minister.[11]

A much more complex situation in 1936 involved Privy Council President Hiranuma Kiichirō and a mixed trio of career diplomats, Hirota Kōki, Honda Kumatarō, and Arita Hachirō. Hiranuma asked Prime Minister Hirota to appoint

[10] Yabe Teiji, Konoe Fumimaro [A Biography of Konoe Fumimaro] (Tokyo, 1952), II, 122; Yoshimoto Shigeyoshi, Kishi Nobusuke den [A Biography of Kishi Nobusuke] (Tokyo, 1957), pp. 106-107.

[11] Inoue Masaaki, Hakushaku Kiyoura Keigo den [A Biography of Kiyoura Keigo] (Tokyo, 1935), II, 268-70.

Honda (then in retirement) to a Privy Council vacancy. Hirota was willing but Foreign Minister Arita had other ideas. He protested first to Hirota and then to Prince Sainoji's ubiquitous agent, Harada Kumao. Calling Honda "a man who may do anything when displeased," Arita accused him of aggravating the London Naval Treaty dispute, and said that having him in the Privy Council would "create endless difficulties for the Foreign Ministry."[12] Honda was not appointed.

In the same year, 1936, Commerce Minister Ogawa Gōtarō asked outgoing Vice Minister Yoshino Shinji who should be chosen to succeed him. Yoshino's answer reveals the considerations a career bureaucrat felt were relevant. Nonbureaucrats were legally ineligible, but it seems not to have occurred to Yoshino that some career man in another ministry—perhaps Finance or Foreign Affairs—might be a useful choice as vice minister of commerce. For him, the choice could only be among the Commerce Ministry's six bureau chiefs. Of these, Commerce Bureau Chief Murase Naokai was "senior" and Patent Bureau Chief Takeuchi Kakichi was "next senior." However, Murase had left the ministry to spend eight years in the Cabinet Legislative Bureau, returning to Commerce in 1934. Therefore, Takeuchi should take precedence over Murase as "next in line" (*juntō*) to become vice minister. Ogawa followed Yoshino's advice.

This episode illustrates four important characteristics of higher civil service career patterns: the preference for staying within the boundaries of a single ministry, the tendency for those who (like Murase) left a ministry to return someday to the fold, the emphasis on seniority as a qualification for promotion, and the preferment of one kind of seniority over another. Although Takeuchi was the oldest of the six bureau chiefs and had been a bureau chief longer than any of the others, neither fact made him senior. Yoshino considered Murase to be senior because he had graduated from law school

---

[12] Harada Kumao, *Saionji-kō to seikyoku* [Saionji Memoirs] (Tokyo, 1951), V, 100-101, 105.

one year before Takeuchi. It was only his temporary "desertion" of the ministry that dropped Murase to second in line.[13]

It has been suggested above that critics who picture examination men as robots controlled from below rely too much on an equation of responsibility for drafting with responsibility for deciding. The same caveat must, of course, be applied to any generalization about the relative power of senior career men and Cabinet ministers. There is, however, one important difference. Unlike career bureaucrats, whether at the hannin level or in the higher civil service, a Cabinet minister could expect to remain in office for only a comparatively short time. This meant that his wishes could often be frustrated by simple procrastination or stalling by his career subordinates. It also meant that he often knew much less about the work of his ministry than career officials did, and consequently that he had little choice but to rely upon their judgment and advice. It is hardly surprising that the Cabinet ministers whose control was strongest and least often challenged were those who knew most about the functions of their ministries.

The distinction between harmony and control must be emphasized. Many Cabinet ministers achieved harmony without control; very few achieved control without harmony, and then usually for only a short time. A minister could obtain cooperation from career subordinates either by knowing as much

[13] All six bureau chiefs were examination men. Murase and two others had passed the Higher Examinations in the year preceding their graduation, two had passed in the year of graduation, and the sixth (Takeuchi) a year after graduation. Passing before graduation made it easier to obtain the first sōnin appointment, but thereafter the year of examination was less significant than the year of graduation. Yoshino may not have been entirely impartial in applying his criteria of seniority. He admits that Murase was considered neutral in commerce politics while Takeuchi was a member of "the Yoshino faction," whose influence Ogawa wished to curtail; Yoshino was therefore somewhat surprised that Ogawa followed his advice and promoted Takeuchi. See Yoshino, "Nihon shihonshugi no ayumi" [The Path of Japanese Capitalism], Part 47, in *Ekonomisuto*, 22 November 1960, p. 59.

about the ministry's work as they did, or by doing as they advised; in the former case he controlled decisions, and in the latter he did not. The pattern of relations was determined by several independent variables: the minister's knowledge or experience, how he acquired it, the kind of functions assigned to the ministry, the extent of personal factionalism and ideological or philosophical disagreements, and of course the personalities of all the men involved.

A minister who had been a career bureaucrat possessed undeniable advantages in dealing with career subordinates. Yet, if assigned to head a ministry other than the one in which he had served, even an examination man was handicapped, both by insufficient familiarity with the work involved and by his consciousness of being considered an "outsider." Kido Kōichi, for example, felt that as home minister in the Hiranuma Cabinet he had to move cautiously in making personnel changes because he "had come from the outside"—that is, from a career in the Commerce and Imperial Household ministries.[14] In the Second Konoe Cabinet, Commerce Minister Kobayashi Ichizō was both forceful and well-qualified but ran into formidable difficulties with his subordinates, partly because he was a businessman rather than a bureaucrat and partly because he and Vice Minister Kishi Nobusuke held irreconcilable views on economic policy. Conversely, there were other ministers who were experienced but irresolute, or resolute but inexperienced.

Thus the balance of power between career men and their Cabinet chief shifted frequently, within each ministry and within the government as a whole. Although the cleavage between the career service and the Cabinet grew out of Yama-

---

[14] Postwar memorandum by Kido commenting on his diary, in Kido Nikki Kenkyū Kai, ed., *Kido Kōichi kankei bunsho* [Kido Kōichi Papers] (Tokyo, 1966), p. 118. Characteristically, Kido said that "coming from the outside" enabled him to see the need for personnel changes more clearly than the Home Ministry career men did; but he also makes it plain that he acted only after careful consultation with them, and that he was relieved when they offered no objections.

gata's effort to hamstring party Cabinets by barring party men from subministerial posts, it was not simply or primarily a confrontation between bureaucrats and politicians. These categories were never mutually exclusive, and ministers of impeccably bureaucratic origin often came into sharp conflict with career officials, whereas some party ministers got along well with their career subordinates. The experiences of two members of the First Konoe Cabinet illustrate a few of the many patterns of conflict and compatibility that can be found in the period between the two world wars.

Konoe's first agriculture minister, Count Arima Yoriyasu (1884-1957), was married to an imperial princess and was himself the heir of a daimyo who claimed imperial ancestry. After graduating from the agricultural faculty of Tokyo Imperial University in 1910 with rather low grades, Arima spent six unhappy years as a hannin technical official in the Agriculture Ministry, resigning in 1917 because of discrimination against technical personnel in rank, pay, and promotion. He then taught agriculture for six years, and was associated with Kagawa Toyohiko and others in the farm co-operative movement, retaining a lifelong interest in agriculture. Elected to the House of Representatives in 1924 on the Seiyūkai ticket, he inherited his father's title in 1927 and served in the House of Peers from 1929 to 1940, becoming a close friend of such men as Prince Konoe and Marquis Kido Kōichi. Under the Saitō Cabinet of 1932-34 he was parliamentary vice minister for agriculture, and in 1938 Konoe appointed him to the Cabinet.

Despite his knowledge of agriculture and his friendship with the prime minister, Arima found that he did not control the Agriculture Ministry. In later years he wrote bitterly that he had been "mistaken in thinking that by becoming the minister one became the head. . . . The head consists of the bureaucrats who are vice minister, bureau chiefs, and section chiefs. The [administrative] vice minister is the head and the minister the headdress, . . . used only when the head considers it necessary. The minister's function is to secure appropriation of as much as possible of the money requested in the Ministry's budget. . . . [My agricultural] knowledge and experience were not needed as Minister. . . . [I] was used when the head required, and was expected to hang quietly on the hatrack when not needed."[15]

One of Arima's colleagues in the First Konoe Cabinet was Yoshino Shinji (b. 1888), a blood brother but hardly an ideological disciple of Yoshino Sakuzō. As Commerce Minister, Yoshino had none of the difficulties Arima felt so keenly. He was a career bureaucrat who placed second from the top in the 1912 Higher Examinations and ranked first in his class at Tokyo Imperial University. Before entering the Cabinet he had spent twenty-three years in the Commerce Ministry (originally Agriculture-Commerce, later Commerce-Industry), becoming vice minister at the early age of forty-three and serving an almost unprecedented term of five years in that post. Considered one of the ablest career men in the government, he was so influential that some suggested it was not a case of "the Commerce Ministry's Yoshino" but of "Yoshino's Commerce Ministry."

Yoshino had served under twenty commerce ministers and had been vice minister under ministers from both major political parties. In later years, though conceding that he "did not have very high regard for party men" in general, he spoke highly of at least five under whom he had served: Takahashi Korekiyo, Nakahashi Tokugorō and Maeda Yonezō of the Seiyūkai, and Kōno Hironaka and Machida Chūji of the anti-Seiyūkai parties. His reason is very revealing: "each of these was a man of real power within his party and came to office without the sordid thought of personal gain."[16] The implication is surely that Yoshino respected politicians who brought

---

[15] Arima Yoriyasu, *Nanajūnen no kaisō* [Reminiscences of Seventy Years] (Tokyo, 1953), pp. 191-93, 283.

[16] Yoshino Shinji, "Nihon shihonshugi no ayumi" [The Path of Japanese Capitalism], Parts 13 and 18, in *Ekonomisuto*, 29 March 1960, p. 61; and 17 May 1960, p. 61.

political strength to the ministry instead of trying to acquire strength from it (either politically or financially).

It is also noteworthy that despite their long careers in the civil service and government banks, and his favorable opinion of them, Yoshino thought of both Nakahashi and Takahashi as "party men" (*seitōjin*). Most career bureaucrats seem to have felt that party membership took precedence over all other affiliations, and tended to efface the "proper" bureaucratic attitude. Though obviously unacceptable as a universal proposition, this belief undoubtedly contributed to the difficulties some ex-bureaucrats[17] encountered as members of party Cabinets. Few bureaucrats realized, until experiencing it themselves, that appointment to the Cabinet was likely to give one a new perspective—whether party membership was involved or not.

The Pay Disputes of 1929-31

This point is exemplified by two vehement controversies involving party leaders who had been career bureaucrats of great distinction. Hamaguchi Osachi had the honor of being the first examination man to become prime minister, and the misfortune to suffer ignominious defeat in a major battle with the civil service. Coming to power in July 1929, the Hamaguchi Cabinet decided that among other economies it would have to reduce all civil service salaries by ten percent, beginning on the first day of 1930. This was announced on October 15, 1929, bringing an immediate wave of public protests: first from procurators in the Tokyo courts, next from judges, then from officials of the Railway and Overseas ministries. The protests were supported not only by members of the conservative House of Peers but also by the socialist Japan Masses party (*Nihon Taishūtō*). After only four days, the Cabinet capitulated and

[17] As used in this chapter (see note 1), the word *bureaucrat* has a narrower meaning than either the Japanese legal term *kanri* (which included all Cabinet ministers, as well as the civil service proper) or the popular term *kanryō* (which included those Cabinet ministers who had been in the civil service proper).

announced cancellation of the pay cut. It was a complete and humiliating defeat for a prime minister who a few months later would display unusual courage in forcing both the navy and the Privy Council to accept the London Naval Treaty of 1930.

But as the depression worsened, the Second Wakatsuki Cabinet revived the Hamaguchi plan with one important change: the cuts would be graduated so that low-ranking officials would lose less than ten percent. This modification did not soften bureaucratic anger; on the contrary, the 1931 protest movement was far more widespread and vehement than that of 1929. Organized resistance began in the Railway Ministry on May 19, 1931, spread quickly to the Communications, Justice, Agriculture, Commerce, and Foreign Affairs ministries and to the Governments-General of Korea and Taiwan. Personnel of the Railway Ministry hurled charges of bad faith against Railway Minister Egi Tasuku (one of two examination men in the Cabinet), and adopted a public "resolution of nonconfidence" in him. Railway employees threatened to call a general strike, and in several ministries there were mass resignations of officials of the classified service.

Like Hamaguchi, Wakatsuki was a career bureaucrat. His first response to the protest movement was to declare that when all the people were suffering, civil servants must make sacrifices too. This had little effect. The controversy was complicated by a constitutional dispute over the Cabinet's plan to override by executive ordinance a law which specified that "a judge shall not, against his will, . . . have his salary lowered."[18] After nine days of argument and mass meetings, the Cabinet

[18] Article 73 of the Court Structure Law of 1890. One prominent law professor, Sasaki Sōichi of Kyoto Imperial University, supported the Cabinet by arguing that a salary reduction by ordinance, though illegal if applied only to one judge, was legal if applied to all judges. This curious reasoning was sharply challenged by Minobe Tatsukichi; see Ugata Junzō, "Kempō to gyōseihō no ichinen" [Constitutional and Administrative Laws], *Hōritsu jihō*, III (1931), 996-1001.

achieved a Pyrrhic victory that made substantial concessions to judges and railway employees, and exempted from the pay cut all personnel receiving less than 100 yen a month. The press concluded that the Cabinet had managed to save some face but not much money.

The 1929 and 1931 pay disputes illustrated how far bureaucrats could or would go in meeting a threat to their personal interests—they would oppose a cut not only in base salaries but also in various allowances and such status symbols as the government limousines assigned to bureau chiefs. The reaction probably also reflected a feeling that career bureaucrats like Hamaguchi, Wakatsuki, and Egi had betrayed a loyalty owed to the bureaucracy as a group. However, two other facts of considerable political significance are explicit in these confrontations between the Cabinet and civil service. Bureaucratic action crossed hierarchic boundaries (within ministries) but stayed within ministry boundaries. These two patterns are major additions to what has already been said about distinctions within the supposedly monolithic bureaucracy.

Joint Action and Sectionalism

Despite a strong consciousness of differences in rank, most of the protest groups in 1929 and 1931 included unclassified employees, hannin officials, and higher civil servants—even section and bureau chiefs. One is reminded of Albert Craig's observation that in the vertical cleavage of late Tokugawa society "it was easier for samurai to join with peasants of their own han than with samurai of other han."[19] Of course, this was not always true either of Tokugawa dissidents or of modern bureaucrats, but the fact that it was true at any time is rather startling. Since (because of their extremely low pay) employees and hannin clerks would have been hardest hit by the 1929 plan, and since they were the chief beneficiaries of the 1931

[19] *Chōshū in the Meiji Restoration* (Cambridge, 1961), p. 358. The analogy is not meant to imply that the bureaucrats in either 1929 or 1931 were "feudalistic" in any acceptable meaning of that term.

concessions, one might suppose that this was *gekokujō* within *gekokujō*: lower bureaucrats manipulating higher bureaucrats in order to overpower the highest of all, the Cabinet ministers.

However, it is more likely that sōnin and chokunin officials were willing "victims" who used discontent in the lower ranks to justify actions that were hardly warranted by the prospective injury to their own interests. A particularly suspicious example was the 1931 protest movement in the Commerce Ministry, which began only after the larger ministries had reached compromise agreements with their personnel. The leader of the Commerce protest was Kishi Nobusuke, then a sōnin official of the highest (third) grade, with rank and pay equivalent to that of an army colonel. He induced lower-ranking sōnin and hannin personnel to give him their signed resignations, for use as a club against Commerce Minister Sakurauchi Yukio, a leader of the ruling party. This involved far more risk for his subordinates than for Kishi, who (as one biographer incautiously admits) had "made many business contacts in his job" and would have had little difficulty finding a lucrative position outside the government.

Kishi's admiring biographers[20] picture him as leading a kind of heroic class war of the poor against the rich, despite a "reluctance" to defy his superiors. The evidence suggests that his motives were less altruistic. Rejecting all compromises until his followers urged him to accept one, Kishi returned their resignations and submitted his own, saying that as leader of the insurrection he had "clearly violated the Official Disciplinary Regulations." This was a classic use of the tactics the Japanese call *haragei*. Having obvious reason to fear a renewed rebellion if Kishi were ousted, the minister and parliamentary vice minister were forced to implore him not to resign. Kishi had adroitly built for himself a strong following within the min-

---

[20] Yoshimoto Shigeyoshi, *Kishi Nobusuke den* (Tokyo, 1957), pp. 85-88; and Dan Kurzman, *Kishi and Japan* (New York, 1960), pp. 110-11. Kurzman erroneously assigns these events to 1929 instead of 1931.

istry and had also developed confidence in his ability to defy superior officials with impunity. The 1931 episode was only the first of many in which Kishi was to act with arrogant insubordination toward ministers who were not career bureaucrats.

The other characteristic of the 1929 and 1931 disputes was sectionalism. The civil service had rarely been as united on any issue as it was on resisting the pay cuts. Even so, the personnel of each ministry met and acted separately. Though there may have been interministry consultation in private, all public action stayed within ministry boundaries. Men of the several ministries acted simultaneously but separately, not jointly. Officials of each ministry held their own meetings, passed their own resolutions, made their own demands on their respective ministers. While truly collective action might have been more successful in 1931, the point is that even when their vital personal interests were at stake bureaucrats felt a strong identification with a particular ministry rather than with the civil service as a whole, or with a rank grouping across ministry lines.

Individual career records also reflect this compartmentalization. Transfers from one ministry to another, though perfectly feasible under law, were in practice uncommon. When they did occur, they were often either temporary or more technical than real—for example, mass movement of personnel in the infrequent instances where two ministries were merged, one ministry was split in two, or a bureau was shifted to a different ministry. These were transfers of functions, with personnel accompanying the functions, rather than personnel moving from one function to another.[21] A career bureaucrat's ties to his original ministry were likely to remain strong even after he left the civil service proper, as can be seen for example in Marquis

[21] A variation of this kind of transfer was the assignment of men from several ministries to a new agency responsible to the Cabinet as a whole, or to the prime minister. Whether or not the agency itself was temporary, many of the men assigned to it considered themselves to be "representatives" from their original ministry, planned to return to it eventually, and frequently did so.

Kido Kōichi's contacts with former colleagues in the Agriculture Ministry after he moved to the imperial palace staff.

Consequences of Sectionalism

The effect of sectionalism or interministry compartmentalization on bureaucratic power was ambivalent and unpredictable. On the one hand, it tended to unite the personnel of each ministry in a group loyalty that softened the divisive effects of rank differences and personal-clique factionalism (which was always somewhere in evidence, though less pervasive than among the transitional bureaucrats of the late nineteenth century). This unity gave the group as a whole and its senior men as individuals considerable bargaining power with a minister or a divided Cabinet. On the other hand, compartmentalization invited jurisdictional disputes and reduced bureaucratic ability to resist either a united Cabinet or the military services.

Most career men undoubtedly regarded sectionalism as "normal" and inherent in the Japanese concept of constitutional government. They thought of the executive branch as a confederation of autonomous ministries. The Cabinet was not so much an organ of state as a summit conference in which each minister's primary duty was to represent the career men of the ministry he temporarily headed. For a minister to subordinate the interests of his bureaucratic "constituents" to those of his colleagues or those of the prime minister (who was only *primus inter pares*) amounted to a kind of dereliction of duty. To resist a "collectivization" of the Cabinet, career men sought to keep their respective ministers in line by persuasion, procrastination, passive noncooperation, or if necessary outright disobedience, usually in connection with the drafting of statutes and policy statements.

In addition, the career bureaucracy erected its own collectivity as a restraint on Cabinet collectivization. This was the vice-ministerial conference (*jikan kaigi*), through which nearly all matters passed before consideration by the ministerial conference (*kakugi*), that is, by the Cabinet. The vice-ministerial conference was usually routine, but on occasion it provided a line of defense in a hierarchical dispute between the Cabinet and bureaucracy or a forum for discussing (though probably not settling) a sectional dispute between ministries.

While most career men seem to have considered sectionalism a source of bureaucratic strength, not weakness, they also saw the impossibility of an absolute separation of functions. Every ministry's work affected and was affected by the work of some other ministry, in one way or another. Moreover, while sectional loyalty may have fostered jurisdictional disputes, it did not prevent joint or collective action to resolve disagreements or to avoid them.

Though poorly documented, informal collaboration among bureaucrats of different ministries appears to have been very common. It took innumerable forms, ranging from office visits and telephone conversations to ostensibly social gatherings and golf foursomes. The Harada and Kido diaries record an incredible number of meetings, consultations, talks, and intrigues involving bureaucrats of section-chief rank and above, as well as nonbureaucrats of many kinds. Reading these accounts, one wonders whether any man in public life ever dined alone, and whether any dinner conversation strayed far from political matters. If, as seems likely, Kido and Harada were exceptional only in the number and variety of men they talked with, it is reasonable to conclude that bureaucratic sectionalism was significantly alleviated by informal consultation by bureaucrats among themselves and with business and political men.

Formal institutions for interministry collaboration and compromise included (in addition to the vice-ministerial conferences) numerous official committees, the seconding system, and Cabinet agencies. As of July 1, 1939, for example, there were 134 standing committees in the central government, with a total of 5,177 members—chiefly career men, including most vice ministers, bureau chiefs, and section chiefs.[22] Each such

[22] Figures are from a count of names in the 1939 official personnel register, *Shokuinroku*. "Committee" is here used generically to include

committee was formally created by an imperial ordinance and made responsible to a specific Cabinet minister but nearly always included personnel from several ministries. There were, for example, the Finance Ministry's Tariff Re-evaluation Committee with members from six other ministries, and the Agriculture Ministry's Farm & Forestry Insurance Examination Committee with members from four other ministries.

The fairly loose link between ministries through the committee system was supplemented by the seconding system, in which a bureaucrat from one ministry was assigned temporarily to another. This usually involved career men (including technicians) below the rank of section chief. The Planning Board, for example, had, in addition to its own career personnel, a number of men on loan from every other ministry except Justice. Most of the traditional ministries had at least a few such borrowed personnel, who retained their main appointment (*honkan*) in one ministry while being seconded by concurrent appointment (*kennin*) to another. Some worked full or nearly full time in the seconded post; others worked there only part-time or intermittently. (Seconding was also used to link two bureaus within a ministry.)

Unlike the committee and seconding systems, which involved the temporary sharing of personnel by two or more ministries, the creation of Cabinet agencies involved assignment of a permanent staff (possibly augmented by seconded personnel). Cabinet agencies were supposed to perform functions not clearly allocable to a single ministry, to coordinate functions shared by two or more ministers, or to do both these things.

---

79 *iinkai*, 51 *kai*, 2 *kaigi*, and 2 *in* whose members held full-time appointments in a permanent subdivision of a ministry (bureau, division, section, etc.). The membership figure includes *iin, rinji iin*, and *kanji*, but not clerks. Net membership was substantially smaller, since men of high rank often held concurrent appointments to several committees. As extreme examples, in 1939 the finance vice minister was a member of 50 committees in 8 ministries, and the budget bureau chief a member of 40 in 10 ministries.

Administrative law recognized two types of Cabinet agencies: those responsible to all the ministers collectively, and those responsible to the prime minister as head of the Cabinet. Politically, however, this distinction was much less important than functional differences among the Cabinet agencies.

At one extreme were the apolitical Decorations, Pensions, Printing, and Statistical bureaus, whose functions the various ministries were quite content to forgo. A middle category included the Cabinet Secretariat and Legislative Bureau, whose indispensability was recognized by all ministries. At the other extreme were the Manchurian Affairs Bureau, Planning Board, Asian Development Board, Information Bureau, and Board of Technology, which either deprived the ministries of important functions they did not wish to relinquish, or possessed powers of "coordination" which tended to become powers of intervention or supervision. Significantly, the agencies in the first and second categories were as old as the Cabinet system, whereas those in the third category came into existence between 1934 and 1942, at the insistence of the army.

Creation of a new Cabinet agency almost invariably increased the number of higher civil service positions, both at supervisory levels and below. Since such an agency was initially staffed by the transfer of career men from various ministries, its creation brought immediate promotion to some and improved prospects for most of the others. Nevertheless, establishment of each of the third-category boards and bureaus mentioned above was strenuously resisted by examination men who objected to interference with ministerial autonomy by Cabinet superagencies. Unfortunately for them, creation of these agencies was supported not only by the army but also by some examination men.

The Revisionist Bureaucrats

The emergence of such atypical examination men substantially altered the pattern of bureaucratic power in the 1930's, especially after 1937. They have traditionally been known in English as "new bureaucrats," and in Japanese as "young," "new," "new-new," "reform," "super," or "super-super bureau-crats" (*seinen kanryō, shinkanryō, shin-shinkanryō, kakushin kanryō, chōkanryō,* or *chō-chōkanryō*). Many Japanese writers use some or all of these terms synonymously. Others propose distinctions but disagree on what they should be.[23] The impor-tance of subtypes and the criteria for differentiating them need not concern us here. For present purposes it is sufficient to un-derstand how the men referred to by these names differed from other bureaucrats. In general, what set them apart was their determination to change the status quo—in one or more of several ways, some contradictory. To emphasize this charac-teristic, and to escape the ambiguities of the older terms, I pro-pose the generic name "revisionist bureaucrats."

Not all young bureaucrats in the 1930's were revisionists, by any means, and not all revisionists were young. The most in-fluential were career examination men in their forties, already well established in government. What is involved is not the advent of a new generation or a change in recruitment rules, but a change in methods and purposes. As already indicated, revisionists were atypical in supporting the creation of Cabinet superagencies—which soon became their strongholds. They were also much more willing than other bureaucrats to act in concert across ministry boundaries, and across the line between the civil and military services. And though quantification is impossible, they seemed to be much more uninhibited in re-

[23] For example, in *Nihon kindaishi jiten* [Dictionary of Modern Japanese History] (Tokyo, 1958), pp. 79, 285, Asada Mitsuteru attempt-ed a chronological distinction between *shinkanryō* (active in 1932-37) and *kakushin kanryō* (1937-45), but left vague the substantive differ-ence (if any) between them. Ishida Takeshi, *Kindai Nihon seiji kōzō no kenkyū* [A Study of the Political Structure of Modern Japan] (Tokyo, 1956), pp. 35, 246-48, 252-54, 260-61, contrasted "ideological right-wing bureaucrats" (*kannen uyokuteki kanryō*) and "controlled-economy bureaucrats" (which he variously called *kakushin kanryō* and *tōsei kanryō*), using the term *shinkanryō* in ways that suggested some-times his first category, sometimes his second, sometimes both. Aside from the incompatibility of the Asada and Ishida classifications, a serious objection to both is that the supposed types overlap substantially.

sorting to *gekokujō* tactics, both in promoting their legislative ideas and in influencing appointments to senior posts above them.

All revisionists felt a general commitment to change the existing order—political, social, economic, or all three—for the purpose of increasing the nation's spiritual and military strength. They advocated either ideological purification, state control of the economy, or both. Most were strident chauvinists, with a history of involvement with political groups in their university days, often groups of the Left rather than the Right. They usually supported army policies, at least those not involving domestic violence. Many were consciously or latently anti-capitalist, though they rarely had any clear notion of a substitute for capitalism. Even those whose chief objective was not a controlled economy but spiritual rectification had usually been strongly influenced by economic considerations, especially by the plight of farmers after World War I.

Individuals contrived rather bizarre combinations of such ideas. Statements made in July 1936 by a young revisionist from the Foreign Ministry are a striking example. He remarked that university graduates of the 1920's, when Communist influence on the campus was great, were now the vanguard of Japanese fascism (in which he seemed to include himself). Communist thought, he said, had given him social awareness, and he used the Hegelian term *aufheben* in claiming that the "new-new bureaucrats" had achieved a synthesis of thought above the level of materialism. But "the eradication of communism from the world" should be the goal of Japanese foreign policy—which must be reformed "on a moral foundation . . . a foundation of Japanese ideals as manifested in the Three Sacred Treasures" of the imperial regalia. Yet he also believed that "the most necessary of all the steps that Japan should now take is the complete cancellation of farm debts."[24]

[24] "Seinen kanri, shain wa nani o kangaete iru ka" [What Are Young Bureaucrats and Company Officials Thinking?], *Bungei shunjū* XIV:

The Spread of Revisionism

While leftist influence in the 1920's was starting this young diplomat on his evolution to chauvinist revisionism, rightist influence was permeating a group of older men who were to become the first revisionist bureaucrats. Public awareness of the importance of this group can be dated almost to the hour. It began when newspaper reporters in May 1932 greeted with disbelieving laughter the announcement that Gotō Fumio would be a member of the new Cabinet headed by Admiral Saitō Makoto.[25] Gotō was then forty-eight; the average age of the other ministers was sixty-three. Without having attained vice-ministerial rank, he had retired from the civil service two years earlier to accept a lifetime appointment to the House of Peers. However, he was still very much the leader of a potent clique of Home Ministry career officials who were newly alarmed by revival of the Communist party's hard-line attack on the emperor system (in the 1932 theses).[26] The press began calling these men "new bureaucrats," but it was the elevation of their leader to Cabinet rank that made them conspicuous.

Moreover, the fact that Gotō became agriculture minister, not home minister, soon drew attention to a more significant dimension of revisionism. Among Agriculture Ministry bureaucrats, led by Vice Minister Ishiguro Tadaatsu, Gotō found a receptive audience for his ideas about farm relief. He was supported also by Army Minister General Araki Sadao, who began to take an active public interest in farm village prob-

---

7 (July 1936), 216-40. This is the record of a roundtable discussion by five unnamed revisionist bureaucrats and two young zaibatsu officials. The remarks cited above are those of "Bureaucrat D" on pp. 226-28, 234-35, 238.

[25] For one reporter's recollections, see Morikawa Musei, "Kanryō no antō: Naimu Shō no maki" [Bureaucratic Feuds: The Home Ministry], *Nippon hyōron*, XIII: 3 (March 1938), 175-76.

[26] The circumstances of this revival are discussed by Professor Beckmann in Chapter V.

lems.[27] Gotō, Araki, and Foreign Minister Hirota had long been associated with the Golden Pheasant Academy (Kinkei Gakuin, founded in 1926), where they and other bureaucrats, along with Colonel Hashimoto Kingorō and other extremist army officers of the Sakurakai, attended lectures by Yasuoka Masaatsu on the Confucian philosophy of Wang Yang-ming (Ōyōmei).[28] Gotō, Araki, Hirota, and Konoe Fumimaro were also sponsors of Yasuoka's Kokuikai or National Prestige Maintenance Association (1932-34), which included many revisionist bureaucrats, especially from the Home Ministry.

The early revisionists under Gotō had close connections not only with Araki and Hashimoto but also with a different kind of army leader, General Nagata Tetsuzan. One important link with Nagata was the shadowy Breakfast Society, of which so many conflicting accounts have been given.[29] Meetings under

[27] Maruyama Masao comments that the Gotō-Araki collaboration led "the military as a whole . . . to take a more positive interest in the question of the villages." See his *Thought and Behaviour in Modern Japanese Politics* (London, 1963), pp. 65-66.

[28] Gotō's interest in Ōyōmei thought was directly relevant to his revisionist program of farm relief, since the leading classical exponents of Ōyōmei in Japan, Nakae Tōju (1608-48) and Kumazawa Banzan (1619-91), had also been concerned with farm problems. Ōyōmei thought also influenced Nakano Seigō, as shown in Professor Najita's paper in this volume (Chapter X). Until the end of 1931, Nakano was a member of the Minseitō, a party with which Gotō (although a career bureaucrat) had close connections. In September 1940, Nakano and Gotō became directors of Konoe's Imperial Rule Assistance Association (Taisei Yokusan Kai), along with Colonel Hashimoto Kingorō and six other men. Gotō was later managing director (1942-43) and vice-president (1943-44) of the IRAA under Tōjō.

[29] The Japanese name is usually recorded as Asameshikai (also read Asahankai or Chōhankai) but the Kido diary often gives it as Chōsankai or Chōshokukai, varying the second character. In the innumerable published accounts (including some from 1935), the organizer or chief sponsor of the group is variously identified as Harada, Inoue Saburō (son of Katsura Tarō, adopted grandson of Inoue Kaoru), Izawa, Karasawa, Kido, Konoe, or Nagata. The Kido diary records numerous meet-

that name were held about once a week from the end of 1931 until the summer of 1935, for private discussion of current political problems. Participants, at one time or another, included men of four different types: (a) politically active, titled peers like Harada Kumao, Kido Kōichi, and Konoe Fumimaro; (b) active and retired bureaucrats, such as the Home Ministry's Izawa Takio, Gotō Fumio, Karasawa Toshiki, and Yoshida Shigeru, and the Foreign Ministry's Tani Masayuki; (c) such army officers as General Nagata, Colonel Inoue Saburō, and Lieutenant Colonel Suzuki Teiichi; and (d) senior zaibatsu officials like Ikeda Seihin.

If the Saitō Cabinet in 1932 brought revisionist bureaucrats to prominence, the Okada Cabinet in 1934 seemed to give them command of the government. Okada entrusted formation of the Cabinet to Gotō Fumio, who became home minister (and in effect deputy prime minister). Five other bureaucratic members of the Kokui Kai received major appointments: Hirota as foreign minister, Fujii Masanobu as finance minister, Kawada Isao as chief Cabinet secretary, Karasawa Toshiki as police bureau chief, and Yoshida Shigeru as social affairs bureau chief. All these men were described as "new bureaucrats,"

---

ings of the group, nearly always at Harada's Tokyo residence, but few of these are mentioned in the Harada diary. Many of the participants named most often by other writers are included only infrequently in Kido's lists of those present. A possible explanation is that there were other meetings which Kido either missed or refrained from recording. Two cashiered army officers charged in a July 1935 handbill that Harada, Kido, Gotō, Karasawa, Nagata, and others held secret meetings of the Asameshi Kai at a *machiai* in Tsukiji (text quoted in Hata Ikuhiko, *Gun fuashizumu undōshi* [A History of the Military Fascist Movement] [Tokyo, 1962], pp. 281-82). Though disagreeing on important details, the published accounts agree on so many other points that it seems improbable that they could refer to different groups using the same rather indistinctive name. There seems to be no direct connection between the Asameshi Kai of 1932-35 and that of 1937-40, attended by Konoe's associates (including Kaya Okinori, Wada Hirō, and other revisionist bureaucrats).

that is, revisionists.[30] When their appointments attracted unwelcome attention to the Kokui Kai, that society was dissolved in order to quell rumors about its influence; its members, of course, retained their offices.

It is often said that in the four years between the attempted coups d'etat of May 15, 1932 and February 26, 1936, the Saitō and Okada Cabinets exalted bureaucratic power to a zenith from which the army soon displaced it. This is superficially plausible but on the whole rather misleading. In the first place, the true measure of bureaucratic power is not how many ex-bureaucrats sat in the Cabinet but how much voice bureaucrats collectively possessed in deciding policy and shaping legislation. The power of the civil service was not dependent upon (and not necessarily enhanced by) having bureaucrats elevated to Cabinet posts. Without much more detailed knowledge than we now have about the origins of specific laws and ordinances, we cannot easily compare bureaucratic power under different Cabinets, but there is considerable doubt that it was significantly greater from 1932 to 1936 than in many previous years. In any event, how should bureaucratic power be measured when the bureaucracy is sharply divided, as in the disputes over farm relief appropriations under the Saitō Cabinet and the Minobe "organ theory" under the Okada Cabinet?

Secondly, the traditional account of these Cabinets overlooks the critical distinction between the power of revisionist bureau-

[30] Of the six men named, Karasawa (then forty-three) was the youngest and Hirota (then fifty-six) the oldest. Today there is some dissent from the classification of Hirota as a "new bureaucrat," because of his age and his disagreement with some of the later revisionist diplomats. However, these terms defy precise definition, and have always been loosely used. Unlike the rebellious "young officers," who were identifiable by age and behavior, the "new bureaucrats" were often identifiable only by association or the intuition of reporters. Moreover, the men called revisionists in this paper can be divided into several subtypes; the differences among these seem more significant to some observers than to others.

crats and the power of the higher civil service as a whole. Despite the sudden eminence of their leaders in the Saitō and Okada Cabinets, revisionists were still a small minority within the bureaucracy, and in many ministries their presence exacerbated the factionalism that already existed. Their power from 1932 to 1936 has been exaggerated, as some of them observed with regret in a secret paper prepared in December 1936 by the Shōwa Research Society (Shōwa Kenkyū Kai).[31] The real significance of the Saitō and Okada Cabinets in this regard is that they breached the wall between the civil and military services. This undermined the power of the bureaucracy as a whole, but created unique opportunities for revisionists willing to collaborate with the army.

Military Penetration of the Civil Service

The decision to admit active-duty military officers to positions in the heart of the higher civil service was closely connected with the subsequent growth in number and influence of revisionist bureaucrats; the consequences of these twin developments can hardly be overemphasized. Until after the conquest of Manchuria, Japan's civil and military services were rather strictly separated. Army and navy flag officers served in free-appointment shinnin posts as Cabinet ministers and colonial governors-general. But military officers appointed to any other civil service positions were automatically placed on the inactive list; such appointments were therefore extremely rare.

In 1932, the Saitō Cabinet gave the army undivided control in Manchuria by combining three posts in a personal union: the commander of the Kwantung Army became concurrently

---

[31] Text in *Kido Kōichi, op.cit.*, p. 235. This society (to which Kido belonged but which he says he never attended) was active from 1935 to 1940. Formed by Konoe's close friend Gotō Ryūnosuke, it included several prominent advocates of a state-controlled economy from the ranks of revisionist bureaucrats, and a larger number of nonbureaucrats of various types. See Chapter IX.

Japanese ambassador to the puppet government and governor-general of the railway zone and leased territory. This ended the appointment of civilian governors-general in Kwantung, and set a precedent for appointing other military men to ambassadorial posts. Yet it required no special legislation, because all three posts were of shinnin rank and therefore open to free appointment.

However, as ambassador and governor-general the Kwantung commander was still technically subject to instructions from the Foreign and Overseas ministries. The army was determined to eliminate these civilian voices in Manchurian affairs. The Foreign Ministry, headed by one revisionist bureaucrat (Hirota) and represented in Manchuria by another (Embassy Counselor Tani Masayuki), offered little resistance. The defense of civilian interests was left to the Overseas Ministry, politically the weakest of all the ministries. With the melodramatic support of a delegation of protesting civil policemen from Kwantung, the Overseas Ministry achieved the remarkable feat of blocking Cabinet approval of the army's demands until the end of 1934. The Okada Cabinet then agreed to strip the Foreign and Overseas ministries of virtually all powers relating to Manchuria and the leased territory.

These powers were not transferred outright to the Army Ministry, but assigned to a new Cabinet agency, the Manchurian Affairs Bureau (Tai-Man Jimu Kyoku)—with the army minister serving concurrently as chief of this bureau, commanding a staff composed of revisionist bureaucrats and army field- and company-grade officers. To avoid having to modify the inactive duty rule, the Okada Cabinet revived a legal fiction that General Tanaka had used on one occasion in 1927: the military officers were not "appointed" but merely "assigned" (*ho*) to civil service posts, and thus remained on active duty.

Soon even this subterfuge was discarded. In the spring of 1935, the Okada Cabinet created the Cabinet Investigation Bureau (Naikaku Chōsa Kyoku), and authorized the formal appointment of active-duty military officers to civilian positions

68

in it.[32] The first such appointment went to Army Lieutenant Colonel Suzuki Teiichi, long a close associate of prominent revisionist bureaucrats. By this time, there were revisionists throughout the government, even in such improbable places as the Communications Ministry. The Cabinet Investigation Bureau and its much more powerful heir, the Planning Board (created in 1937 by the First Konoe Cabinet), became the revisionist stronghold and seedbed, drawing together such men as Yoshida Shigeru and Nakamura Keinosuke from the Home Ministry, Matsui Haruo from the Resources Bureau, Wada Hirō from Agriculture, and Okumura Kiwao from Communications. Aoki Kazuo of Finance, having pleased the army as vice chief of the Manchurian Affairs Bureau, was the army's choice in 1937 as vice chief (later chief) of the Planning Board.

Between 1938 and 1940, revisionist ranks were augmented by the return to Japan of a number of career bureaucrats whose political fortunes had profited enormously from temporary service in Manchuria and collaboration with Tōjō Hideki while he was the Kwantung Army military police chief and later chief of staff. This important group included Hoshino Naoki, Matsuoka Yōsuke, Kishi Nobusuke, Shiina Etsuzaburō, Ōhashi Chūichi, and Minobe Yōji (nephew of Tatsukichi).[33] The power of these men was made plain in the Second Konoe Cabinet, which included Tōjō as army minister, Matsuoka as foreign minister, and Hoshino as president of the planning board, with Kishi and Ōhashi as vice ministers of commerce and foreign affairs, Shiina as a commerce bureau chief, and Minobe as a planning board staff member.

[32] Ishikawa Junkichi, Sōgō kokusaku to kyōiku kaikakuan: Naikaku Shingikai, Naikaku Chōsa Kyoku kiroku [General National Plan and Educational Reform: The Records of the Cabinet Deliberative Council and the Cabinet Investigation Bureau] (Tokyo, 1962), pp. 38-39, 138-40.

[33] Tōjō, Hoshino, Matsuoka, Kishi, and Ayukawa Gisuke were the "2 ki, 3 suke" who ruled Manchuria, a term derived from the fact that two had names ending in ki and the other three in suke. Ayukawa was president of the Manchurian Heavy Industry Development Company and leader of the army's "new zaibatsu."

Revisionists and the Army

The military and civilian revisionists were a powerful combination, cemented together not only by shared attitudes and objectives but also by interdependence: neither group was strong enough to rule alone. Disunity, however, was a persistent problem, arising both from chronic factionalism within each group and from the mutual mistrust that civilians and soldiers could never wholly suppress. This was more than a suspicion of motives; it was also a fear of being exploited.

The most unbridled expressions of mistrust came from army officers of the Imperial Way faction. Their propaganda always put the bureaucracy high on the list of their enemies, and by 1935 they no longer regarded revisionist bureaucrats as exceptions to the rule. Shortly before the February 1936 insurrection, one of the ringleaders of that coup called the new bureaucrats counter-revolutionaries who were feigning friendship for the army in order to use its strength for selfish bureaucratic purposes.[34] In a striking historical analogy, he likened the new bureaucrats of the 1930's to the advocates of *kōbu gattai* in the 1860's. In other words, the latter had sought civilian help to save a corrupt military regime and stave off the Meiji Restoration; the revisionists were seeking military help to save a corrupt civilian regime and avert the Shōwa Restoration which the army dissidents were demanding. To justify such indictments, the rebels postulated a lack of true "reform" spirit among the revisionists, but their real grievance was revisionist collaboration with army officers of the Control faction. Civilians in the Breakfast Society, for example, were openly accused of conspiring with General Nagata in the 1935 ouster of General Mazaki Jinzaburō.

[34] *Gendaishi shiryō* [Source Materials on Modern Japanese History] (Tokyo, 1964), V (*Kokkashugi undō* [Nationalist Movements], II), 770-71. The provenance of this document, written shortly before the 1936 rebellion, is explained in *ibid.*, pp. xlii-xlv and 774. Part of it, including the passage cited above, was published in the March 1936 issue of *Nippon hyōron*.

Civilian bureaucrats, whether revisionist or not, undoubtedly felt more at ease with army officers not committed to the violent tactics of the Imperial Way faction, but the triumph of such officers in 1936 did not eliminate mistrust or friction. In fact, their ascendancy seemed to make them more intransigent, more confident that they could get civilian cooperation on their own terms and by their own methods, however tactless. In July 1936, a self-proclaimed "new-new bureaucrat" from the Foreign Ministry was asked whether it were not true that since formation of the Hirota Cabinet, military interference had paralyzed the Foreign Ministry. He agreed that this was true, but added that other ministries were under similar duress. Mentioning three laws which the Home Ministry had just pushed through the Diet with some difficulty, he declared that none was genuinely the idea of the Home Ministry, that at least one was wholly a product of military coercion, and that the army was even interfering with the police.[35]

One may conjecture that this young revisionist objected less to what the army wanted than to the humiliation of being forced to comply. Even so, his resentment was real enough to induce other comments that sound very startling on the lips of a revisionist. Political parties, he said, had "not yet been given a real chance" in Japan and could never make progress as long as civilians were barred from serving as army and navy ministers. Moreover, when the military could "grab the first appropriations, and make official pronouncements even on diplomatic policy . . . and domestic administrative problems," the result was "creation of a separate Cabinet within the Cabinet."[36]

Coming only a few months after the greatest of the military

[35] "Seinen kanri, shain wa nani o kangaete iru ka," *Bungei shunjū*, XIV:7 (July 1936), 228. The speaker is the same "Bureaucrat D" quoted previously (see note 24). The censor has deleted the words *military* and *army* throughout and substituted blank circles (*fuseji*), but the meaning is indisputably clear.

[36] *Ibid.*, p. 239.

uprisings, these are remarkably blunt statements (even under the cloak of anonymity), and the comment about political parties is too charitable to be representative of revisionist opinion. Nonetheless, Foreign Ministry officials—even revisionists—had special cause for resentment of military meddling. The army was not content simply to usurp diplomatic functions; it seemed bent on destroying the Foreign Ministry. In Manchuria the army demoted the puppet government's foreign ministry to the status of a Cabinet bureau; in Japan it sought to do the same thing by stages, stripping the Foreign Ministry of responsibility first for Manchuria, then for the rest of China, finally for all of Asia.

The first step, creation of the Cabinet Manchurian Affairs Bureau in 1934, was accepted by Foreign Minister Hirota with scarcely a murmur. The second step, establishment of the Asian Development Board in 1938, was strongly resisted not only by Hirota but also by his successor, General Ugaki Kazushige— to Prime Minister Konoe's anger and astonishment. The third step, creation of the Greater East Asia Ministry in 1942, was bitterly resented by career diplomats. Some of these happened to be privy councilors, and their resistance reduced Tōjō to pounding the table in rage, heedless of the emperor's presence, in order to coerce the council into approving.[37]

Surprisingly, the army lost one major dispute with the Foreign Ministry despite support from the Cabinet and revisionists in other key agencies. Beginning in 1936, the army had wanted to separate the Foreign Ministry's Trade Bureau and make it the nucleus of an independent Trade Ministry. It was tacitly understood that career men in the bureau would retain posi-

[37] Okada Keisuke, *Okada Keisuke kaikoroku* [Okada Keisuke Memoirs] (Tokyo, 1950), pp. 96-99; Okada Taishō Kiroku Hensan Kai, ed., *Okada Keisuke* [A Biography of Okada Keisuke] (Tokyo, 1956), pp. 251-58; Harada Kumao, *op.cit.*, IV, 13-15, 25, 39-44, 59-83, 91-92, 95-103, 131; Yabe Teiji, *op.cit.*, II, 539-56; Fukai Eigo, *Sūmitsuin jūyōgiji oboegaki* [Notes on the Minutes of the Privy Council] (Tokyo, 1953), pp. 251-68.

tions in the new ministry, and many in fact would be promoted. Nevertheless, they steadfastly opposed the army plan, and it made little progress until 1939, when General Abe Nobuyuki became prime minister, with Admiral Nomura Kichisaburō as foreign minister. Under army pressure, the Trade-Ministry proposal was revived by two prominent revisionist bureaucrats, Planning Board President Aoki Kazuo and Cabinet Legislative Bureau Chief Karasawa Toshiki, formerly of the Finance and Home ministries respectively. When the Cabinet approved the proposal, Trade Bureau Chief Matsushima Shikao and more than a hundred other foreign service officials resigned in protest. The Cabinet capitulated; both the resignations and the Trade Ministry ordinance were withdrawn, and the army abandoned its plan.[38]

An even more massive dispute between the military and civil services resulted from army and navy efforts to create a Cabinet Personnel Bureau to control civilian appointments and promotions. This was formally proposed to Prime Minister Hirota on September 21, 1936 in a memorandum from Army Minister Terauchi Hisaichi and Navy Minister Nagano Osami. Three weeks later the army released the memorandum to the press, evidently to intensify the pressure on the Cabinet. One can imagine the apoplectic fury with which the military services would have greeted a similar proposal from two civilian ministers for Cabinet control over military appointments and promotions. Aside from the fact that civilian personnel matters were none of the military's business, Terauchi and Nagano seemed to go out of their way to antagonize the civilian ministries. In the same memorandum, they called for abolition of the Overseas Ministry, consolidation of the Agriculture and Commerce ministries, consolidation of the Railway and Communications ministries, transfer of responsibility for shrines, roads, ports,

[38] Kiba Kōsuke, *Nomura Kichisaburō* [A Biography of Nomura Kichisaburō] (Tokyo, 1961), pp. 395-96; Nagai Ryūtarō Hensan Kai, *Nagai Ryūtarō* [A Biography of Nagai Ryūtarō] (Tokyo, 1959), pp. 430-31; *Asahi nenkan* [Asahi Yearbook], 1941 edn., pp. 117-18.

and harbors from the Home Ministry to other ministries, and "improvement" of local government.[39]

The career bureaucrats of every ministry were singularly united in adamant opposition to a centralized civilian personnel bureau. One reason was undoubtedly the knowledge that in Manchuria the army had used such a bureau as its principal device for controlling the civil service. Others were simply the strong sectionalist tradition of the career service and the conviction that, while it was proper to centralize the Higher Examinations, each ministry should be autonomous in making appointments and promotions. If these reasons were not enough, the army and navy had augmented them by seeming to make a special target of the powerful Home Ministry, which controlled the appointment of prefectural governors. Quite predictably, the Home Ministry led the bureaucracy's resistance to the military plan.

Six successive Cabinets tried and failed to enact an ordinance creating a Cabinet personnel bureau. The Hirota, Hayashi, First Konoe, Hiranuma, Abe, and Yonai Cabinets tried first one and then another version of the plan, usually in conjunction with several other proposals for relaxing the restrictions on chokunin appointments and modifying the Higher Examinations. Konoe, probably more antipathetic to the bureaucracy than any other prime minister, made the most strenuous efforts. Hiranuma, however, was at best a reluctant advocate; in one version drafted for him, the "Cabinet bureau" dwindled to a mere committee in the Home Ministry. Even this was unacceptable to the career men; a vice-ministerial conference adopted a formal resolution opposing the changes.[40]

Konoe's chief Cabinet secretary, Kazami Akira, was visited

[39] The text of the memorandum is reprinted (from the Nov. 10, 1936 issue of *Tokyo asahi shimbun*) in *Nihon kokusei jiten* [Dictionary of Japanese Politics] (Tokyo, 1958), X, 264-65.

[40] Yoshitomi Shigeo, "Kanri seido no kaikaku" [Reform of the Bureaucracy], *Kōhō zasshi*, VII:4 (April 1941), 46-74; VII:5 (May 1941), 62-82.

in 1938 by "four or five young officials who were reputed to be reform-bureaucrat leaders (*kakushin kanryō no champion*)." Kazami took it for granted that they wanted him to fight vigorously for the pending changes in the personnel system. He was about to assure them of his firm resolution to do just that, when he discovered to his astonishment that they were totally opposed to the changes. Their reasons were an elaboration of Kanamori's warning that crows should not be given the task of cormorants; in their view, the crows included Konoe's "men of ability in private fields" as well as technical bureaucrats. Like nearly all prominent revisionist bureaucrats, Kazami's young visitors were examination men, and like the vice ministers of the Hiranuma Cabinet the following year, they were staunchly opposed to appointing noncareer men to chokunin positions.[41]

In 1940, in his second Cabinet, Konoe abandoned the five-year battle for a personnel bureau but revived the draft ordinance to relax chokunin appointment rules. The army, which had vigorously opposed such an ordinance throughout the period of party Cabinets, now cynically endorsed it on the ground that collapse of the parties had eliminated the danger of a spoils system. Although the Privy Council remained very much opposed, the war atmosphere made it reluctant to resist Cabinet demands. On January 6, 1941, an imperial ordinance opened all chokunin offices to relatively unrestricted appointment, subject only to approval by a special screening committee of high officials chosen by the Cabinet.

Within the next three years, the army pushed through most of its plans for structural change in the government. Yet it made surprisingly little use of the liberalized appointment rules. At the end of 1943, after Tōjō's second major reorganization, two-thirds of all bureaus were still headed by examination men. In four important ministries—Home, Finance, Foreign Affairs, and Greater East Asia—all bureau chiefs were

[41] Kazami Akira, *Konoe naikaku* [The Konoe Cabinet] (Tokyo, 1951), p. 153.

examination men. Very few crows had been admitted to the ranks of the cormorants. The army used the Konoe ordinance chiefly to bring military officers and career technicians into bureau-chief positions in the new Munitions and Transportation ministries and the Board of Technology.

A Balance Sheet

Thus even at the zenith of their power, military Cabinets governed as party Cabinets had governed—by informal coalitions or working agreements with career civilian bureaucrats, chiefly examination men. Time did not fundamentally alter the mutual dependence that held such coalitions together. Each Cabinet, whether led by party politicians or by military officers, discovered that essential managerial skills and detailed knowledge of governmental problems could rarely be found outside the career bureaucracy. Conversely, the competition among career men for advancement to better posts or higher rank gave each Cabinet some leverage in obtaining bureaucratic cooperation.

However, the character of the coalition did change substantially after 1932, and the changes bear upon a central question about the political role of the bureaucracy: Did bureaucrats impel or impede Japan's movement toward the Right in the 1930's? Of course, there were always some who liked and some who disliked the army's plans, and within each group there were always some who acted and some who did not, some who were zealous and some who were apathetic. The overt collaborators may have included secret resisters, saying one thing while meaning another. But how significant was any of this? The following conclusions are offered with the caveat that individual exceptions are to be expected.

First, it is evident that the bureaucracy did not offer strong philosophical or ideological resistance to the trend toward military control of national policy, domestic or foreign. The bureaucratic elite, trained in law schools and recruited through examinations on law, was alarmed and repelled by the lawlessness of army and navy extremists from 1930 to 1936, but relieved and largely placated by the army's switch to constitutional methods after the 1936 rebellion. Precisely because they were thoroughly indoctrinated in the legal concepts of the Meiji system, career bureaucrats accepted the one-way barrier between the civil and military services, which allowed military officers to serve in nonmilitary positions but prevented civilian intervention in matters of military "command." Nothing in the career bureaucrat's education, experience, or view of history predisposed him to regard military Cabinets as inherently pernicious or less desirable than party Cabinets.

Empathy between the civil and military services was minimal, but they shared two attitudes. Each accepted within limits the other's proud self-image of imperial stewards of the national interest, an elite based on achievement and selfless dedication. Each retained a visceral conviction that party politicians were venal and self-seeking spokesmen for special and sectional interests, so that party government was at best a divisive aberration from Japanese tradition. When bureaucrats resisted army proposals, they did so not because of a philosophical commitment to civilian rule but because of some threat to bureaucratic interests or sense of fitness, as in the controversies over superbureaus, relaxation of appointment rules, and dismemberment of the Foreign Ministry.

Secondly, after 1936 revisionist bureaucrats played a major and probably indispensable role in moving Japan toward the Right. Though many of them seem just as opportunistic as some bureaucrats who earlier collaborated with party Cabinets, they also had an ideological commitment not apparent in the period of party rule. There was a difference, not in the quality of the men who collaborated, but in the quality of their collaboration. Revisionists were important not simply because they shared the army's desire for basic changes in Japanese society, but because they were capable of defining the changes more concretely and planning them more effectively than could most military officers. A contemporary observer noted that, when

Gotō Fumio "and General Araki and their respective disciples met in that famous Fukui conference in the fall of 1933, it was the bureaucrats who held the upper hand because they had precise plans and the army did not."[42]

Although bureaucratic power was often used negatively, to prevent action or to protect privilege, it was also used positively —especially in the superbureaus created specifically as planning agencies. Official secrecy and the diffusion of formal responsibility make it extraordinarily difficult to identify the prime movers behind major laws, ordinances, and policy decisions, so that very few case studies exist. Nevertheless, there is considerable evidence that revisionist bureaucrats were the chief architects of the historic economic control measures enacted after 1936. The far-reaching Electric Power Control Law and National Mobilization Law of 1938 are important examples.[43]

Finally, it appears that opportunities for obstructionism or passive resistance within the civil service declined after 1936. This can be attributed partly to external pressures felt by all Japanese. Unlike the political parties, the army was able both to act decisively and to make its program seem unavoidable and even desirable. Support of the army became an imperative act of patriotism. Yet it seems likely that this difficulty could have been surmounted at least occasionally by career bureaucrats skilled in exploiting the intricacies of coalition rule in a pluralist system. The more serious inhibitions were internal and peculiar to the bureaucracy: the emergence of revisionists as a fifth column supporting the army, the creation of superbureaus like the Planning Board, the opening of civil service positions to military officers on active duty, and eventually the sweeping relaxation of eligibility rules for chokunin positions.

These four developments, though all disruptive of the bureaucratic order, tended to produce not less but more conformity. The first two breached the walls of sectionalism and made

---

[42] Minoru Uchida, "Japan as a Totalitarian State," *Amerasia* (May 1938), p. 135.

[43] Ishikawa, *op.cit.*, pp. 91-96, 106-107, 136-38, 1661-68.

it easier to enact economic controls and other legislation cutting across ministry boundaries. The last two did not actually bring large numbers of nonbureaucrats into the higher civil service, but they were a constant reminder to career men that recalcitrants had become much more vulnerable to replacement. In abstract terms, the second and fourth of these developments might be considered salutary. It is hard to defend sectionalism, or to deny that the superbureaus facilitated the integration and rationalizing of decision-making, or to oppose absolutely the infusion of qualified outsiders into a career bureaucracy. But under the circumstances prevailing in Japan in the 1930's, the effect was to make the government more authoritarian by subverting some of the checks and balances of the pluralist system.

This assessment is more critical of the bureaucracy, and especially of the revisionists, than was the judgment offered at the end of 1939 by E. Herbert Norman. Commenting that "it might not be an exaggeration to say that the key to understanding Japanese political life is given to whoever appreciates fully the historical role and actual position of the bureaucracy," Norman concluded that "this almost anonymous but experienced bureaucracy has gradually snuffed out all signs of genuine democratic activity, but on the other hand . . . has blocked the victory of outright fascist forces."[44]

In the hindsight of three decades, Norman's interpretation seems to misplace both praise and blame. "Genuine democratic activity" in prewar Japan was hampered less by bureaucratic elitism than by military terrorism, the shortcomings of all the political parties, and the insuperable constitutional obstacles to responsible government. That bureaucrats had much to do with diverting the totalitarian movement into constitutional channels is probably true, but terrorists of the early 1930's and legalists of the late 1930's might both be regarded as "outright fascist forces," differing more in tactics than in objectives. On the whole, the revisionist-military coalition found legal procedures

[44] E. Herbert Norman, *Japan's Emergence as a Modern State* (New York, 1940), p. 206.

more often a help than a hindrance, because they tended to disarm, confound, and conciliate potential dissenters within the plural elite, including the career bureaucracy. Revisionist bureaucrats brought to the coalition both legalistic ingenuity and much of the substantive thought that shaped Japan's course after 1936.

CHAPTER III

Retrogression in Japan's Foreign Policy Decision-Making Process

CHIHIRO HOSOYA

ALTHOUGH the problem of modernization has increasingly attracted the attention of social scientists in various fields since the Hakone Conference, this does not mean that there were no academic controversies or studies dealing with the problem before 1960. On the contrary, the social changes in the modern world, which the term "modernization" attempts to designate, have been the object of serious study for a long time and even the term itself does not sound as fresh and modern as it once did.

To account for the increasing tendency to pay more attention to the modernization problem and to view it in a broader perspective, it might be useful to refer to two recent developments. First, since 1967 as many as twenty-three joint research groups, composed of social scientists from most of the major universities, have been engaged in exploring various aspects of the modernization process in Japan, with financial assistance from the government. Secondly, modernization in Japan was the main theme of a meeting of the Conference on Modern Japan which brought together about eighty participants representing sixteen countries, including the Soviet Union and Czechoslovakia, in Fukuoka in September 1967. It would seem that the Hakone Conference provided the kind of intellectual stimulus which has aroused much new academic interest in the modernization problem.

In spite of the increased interest, the concept of modernization continues to be ambiguous; some use it in the sense of the development of capitalism and others in the sense of industrialization or westernization. When one looks at the list of subjects to be taken up by the joint research groups to which I referred, he can quickly detect this lack of common understanding. Also, it must be noted that there is a serious argument among the Marxist historians, who tend to equate modernization with the development of capitalism, as to whether or not the modernization theory is one deliberately constructed to challenge the theory advocating the progress of human society from feudalism through capitalism to socialism.

Here, I do not want to argue about the concept of "modernization," but I do want to provide a historical context for the question of how modernization relates to the foreign policy decision-making process of Japan in the 1930's. This question can be dealt with in various ways. For example, one could analyze Japan's imperial policy in the 1930's as an inevitable product of the modernization of Japanese society since the Meiji period, or one could explain Japanese expansionism as reflecting a "distortion" in the modernization of Japan.

I shall explore the modernization of foreign policy decision-making as an aspect of political modernization in Japan. In other words, I shall assume three characteristics of foreign policy decision-making to be indices of its modernization and will attempt to analyze them in the case of Japan in the 1930's. The first such characteristic is an increasing popular interest in foreign policy decision-making and a demand for democratic control over it. This might be called the popularization aspect of foreign policy decision-making. The second characteristic is the prevalence of rational thinking in both the setting and achieving of goals in foreign policy. This might be called the rationalization aspect. The third characteristic is integration within the foreign policy decision-making structure, or the integration aspect. Judged according to these standards, Japan in the 1930's was in an era of retrogression. Perhaps I should say a few words about retrogression. In my observation, it frequently occurs in periods of political modernization even though the developmental process is operative in the long run. Political modernization seems to follow a spiral or zigzag line. In this sense, it is somewhat different from social or economic modernization, which both tend to follow a fairly straight line, with repetitions of progress and stagnation. Japan in the 1930's witnessed modernization in various fields, resulting, for example, in greater urbanization, more widespread literacy, the growth of mass communication networks, and an annual increase of 5.5 percent in the gross national product during the period from 1931 to 1938. At the same time, however, Japan experienced retrogression in some aspects of political modernization.

A Decline in the Popularization of International Affairs

With the modernization of various aspects of a society—such as the growth of an extensive and penetrative network of mass communication, the spread of a public educational system, and an increasing flow of international trade and travel—a growth of popular interest in international affairs can also be observed. The general public in a modern society is not only stimulated to pay attention to international affairs, but also provided with a great deal of information about the outside world. This tendency is striking when compared with the state of affairs prevailing in the days of "court diplomacy," in the seventeenth or eighteenth centuries, when the general public was neither interested in nor informed about international affairs.

An increasing public interest in international affairs naturally leads to a rising desire to get the popular view expressed in the process of foreign policy making. The people become more active in communicating their views on foreign affairs, either directly to the decision-makers, or indirectly through leaders and members of the legislature. It can be asserted that in foreign affairs the ratio of the attentive public to the mass public has been increased in a modern society.[1] In addition, the government leaders in a modern state tend to pay increasingly more attention to public attitudes toward foreign affairs

[1] Gabriel Almond, *The American People and Foreign Policy* (New York, 1961), p. 228.

and to expect more support from the public in carrying on foreign policy.

Two limited problems of the popularization aspect of the foreign policy decision-making process in Japan in the 1930's were a change in the role played by the Diet and a change in the government's attitude toward the public.

During the period of the Siberian Intervention from 1918 to 1922, Japan's military activities in Siberia were severely criticized in the Diet.[2] The cause of the military expedition itself was subject to criticism: WHY did the government keep soldiers in Siberia after having already fulfilled the announced aim of the expedition? It appeared that the Diet found it obligatory to voice views critical of the government's foreign policy, whether special military problems or basic questions of ways and means were involved or not. The Shantung expedition, from 1927 to 1928, created another target for a strong attack on the government by members of the Diet.[3] The military activities were severely criticized for causing an extensive anti-Japanese movement in China and for seriously damaging Sino-Japanese relations.

A change in the attitude of Diet members toward the government's foreign policy became noticeable in the years following the Manchurian incident. First, military operations on the continent tended to be discussed in the Diet much less frequently. This did not, however, mean that Diet members had stopped raising critical opinions on the government's handling

[2] See, e.g., the interpellations of Katō Sadakichi, March 7, 1919 and Feb. 24, 1920 on the Diet floor, in *Dainippon Teikoku Gikai-shi* [History of the Imperial Diet of Great Japan] (Tokyo, 1930), XI, 1241-42, 1823; see also the somewhat more lengthy interpellation of Masaki Shōzō, January 26, 1920, in *ibid.*, pp. 1662-71. Also, *Gikai seido shichi-jū-nen-shi* [Seventy Years of Parliamentary Government] (Tokyo, 1962), vol. II: *Teikoku Gikai-shi* [A History of the Imperial Diet]; part I, *passim.*

[3] See, e.g., The criticism of Nagai Ryūtarō on the Diet floor, in *Shūgiin giji sōkkiroku* [Diet Records], January 23, 1929. Also, *Gikai seido Shichi-jū-nen-shi*, vol. III: *Teikoku Gikai-shi*, part 2, p. 227.

of foreign policy. To cite some examples, Ashida Hitoshi criticized Japan's Manchurian policy in the Diet in January 1933 as follows: "Japan's foreign policy has not been formulated on the basis of the general will of the nation, but instead has been steered by the military."[4] Both "military diplomacy" and "secret diplomacy" were under sharp attack in the Diet in those days. Even as late as February 1937, Uehara Etsujirō severely criticized the way in which the government had conducted a secret deal with Germany to conclude the Anti-Comintern Pact, and he strongly advocated open diplomacy under the leadership of the Foreign Ministry.[5]

Then, with the beginning of the China War, the Diet changed its attitude remarkably. Criticism was directed toward technical points of policy or toward the "weak-kneed" attitude of the Foreign Ministry. The majority in the Diet encouraged the government to carry out its China policy with strong determination and declined to question its aim or draw attention to "military diplomacy." Saitō Takao, who was exceptional in February 1940 in raising severe criticism against Japan's policy in China, was doomed to quit the Diet.[6]

A change also occurred in the government's attitude toward the public in regard to foreign affairs during the 1930's. A close examination of policy statements made by foreign ministers and premiers in the Diet reveals that government leaders in the 1920's, including Foreign Minister Shidehara Kijūrō, had taken the approach of presenting basic principles of foreign policy to the Diet and to the people with a view to asking for their support for actions the Japanese government intended to take.

[4] For Ashida's remarks, see *Shūgiin giji sokkiroku* [Diet Records], January 21-25, 1933. Also, *Gikai seido shichi-jū-nen-shi*, III, 400.

[5] For Uehara's complaint, see *Shūgiin giji sokkiroku* [Diet Records], February 25, 27, and 28, 1937. Also *Gikai seido shichi-jū-nen-shi*, III, 562-63.

[6] *Tokyo Asahi Shimbun*, February 3, 1940, p. 6; *ibid.*, February 4, 1940, p. 6; also, for a fuller discussion, see Shiraki Masayuki, *Nihon seitō-shi: Shōwa-hen* [The History of Japanese Political Parties: The Shōwa Period] (Tokyo, 1949), pp. 290-94.

Such efforts gradually diminished in the 1930's; official statements were filled with descriptive explanations about actions the government had already taken and developments which had taken place in foreign affairs. The fact that statements had become couched in enigmatic terms and expressions difficult for the public to understand indicates that the leaders had become indifferent about popular reaction to their policy and felt that popular support was not essential.

The Rise of the Irrational Kōdō Policy

There has been much argument among Japanese historians concerning the difference or similarity between the so-called Shidehara policy and the Tanaka policy in the 1920's.[7] I am not inclined to stress their difference, but would rather devote my attention to their similarity. This is not to say that I do not subscribe to the view, often presented by the Marxist historians, that the Shidehara and the Tanaka policies only represent different aspects of Japanese imperialism and that their difference is merely related to the strategy or means to achieve expansion in China. Rather, their difference appears to me to be much less outstanding than the difference between Japan's foreign policy in the 1920's and the so-called Kōdō or Imperial Way policy in the 1930's, a difference which can best be explained in terms of changes in both the rationality of diplomatic thinking and the values operative in the decision-making process.

In his inaugural address to the Diet on July 1, 1924, Foreign Minister Shidehara Kijūrō clearly defined the issues confronting Japan in her relations with neighboring countries, such as the United States, the Soviet Union, and China, and he stated Japan's major objective in terms of preserving her economic

---

[7] For a discussion of this debate and the more representative theses, see Usui Katsumi, "Taishō-Shōwa shoki no gaikō" [Foreign Policy in the Taishō and Early Shōwa Periods], in Nihon Rekishi Gakkai, ed., *Nihon-shi no mondai-ten* [Some Problems in Japanese History] (Tokyo, 1965), pp. 372-75.

interests in China.[8] As was indicated in this address, Shidehara's conduct of foreign affairs was characterized by his rational thinking in setting goals and considering alternative actions. Realizing the folly of opposing the rise of Chinese nationalism, and calculating the international surroundings to be rather unfavorable to Japan, he felt it reasonable to seek a *modus vivendi* with the right-wing leaders of the Chinese Nationalists, without intervening forcefully in their domestic strife, and to maintain as much as possible a concerted action with the Western powers. Shidehara's concept of diplomacy was expressed in his lecture before an audience at Keiō University on October 19, 1928, when he said that a statesman must be able to make the distinction between a practical policy and an impractical one and to clearly understand that conducting diplomacy is quite different from playing tricks.[9] He further stressed that an essential task for diplomacy was to develop economic relations between countries.

Although he was more determined to safeguard Japan's special position in Manchuria and more prepared to employ armed force to attain that objective, Premier Tanaka Giichi was essentially not much different from Shidehara in his conception of Japan's China policy. The main concern of the Tanaka policy was the matter of economic interests, as well as national security, and threats to the country were perceived as coming from two directions: Chinese nationalism and international Communism. Tanaka was realistic, like Shidehara, in formulating his China policy within the framework of the "Washington system," conscious of the relative strength of Japan *vis-à-vis* other powers involved in Asian politics. His recognition of the importance of maintaining good relations with other powers led him

[8] For the full text of Foreign Minister Shidehara's inaugural address, see Shidehara Heiwa Zaidan [Shidehara Peace Foundation], comp., *Shidehara Kijūrō* [A Biography of Shidehara Kijūrō] (Tokyo, 1955), pp. 262-66.

[9] For the full text of the Keiō Address, see *ibid.*, pp. 367-69.

to send two former foreign ministers, Gotō Shimpei and Uchida Yasuya, as special envoys to the Soviet Union and to the Western countries (including England and the United States) respectively.

In the years following the Manchurian incident such political values as expansionism, national prestige, and "national mission," increasingly took precedence over economic values in the process of foreign policy decision-making. More emphasis was placed on an independent course of action to achieve the national goal of expansion, rather than on international cooperation. The new direction of Japan's foreign affairs was very evident in the announcement to withdraw from the League of Nations in March 1933 and in the signing of the Anti-Comintern Pact in November 1936.

By taking these actions, Japan alienated all those powers who were playing an active part in Asian politics. A lack of rational thinking was readily apparent in the choice of such courses of action. This lack caused a drastic deterioration in Japan's international position, resulting in her isolation from the surrounding nations. It might be said that if Japan had really been determined to eliminate the influence of the Anglo-American powers in Asia, she should have joined hands with the Soviet Union; or that if she felt it most essential to strengthen her position against the threat of international communism, she should have been more cautious about maintaining a cooperative policy with the Anglo-American powers.

In the days following the Manchurian incident, Japan experienced not only a change in foreign policy but also a change in outlook or approach to international affairs. This new approach, known as the Kōdō policy, was marked by the following characteristics: 1) the pursuit of economic interests as a national goal was degraded; 2) positive interference in the domestic affairs of China was supported, provided that it was not designed to attain Japan's selfish interests; 3) the consciousness of a confrontation with the Western powers, rather than cooperation with them, was assumed to underlie Japan's foreign

88

policy; and 4) the resort to force to realize international justice was accepted.

At first supported by the right wing and the military, Kōdō thinking gradually gained influence among Foreign Service officers and led to the creation of a group called the *Kakushin-ha* or Renovation faction within the Foreign Ministry.[10] To elucidate the cardinal principles and points of the Kōdō policy, Nimiya Takeo, an active member of the *Kakushinha*, wrote a 152-page booklet in 1936 entitled "The Guiding Principles Characterizing Japan's Diplomacy," which was to provide an ideological basis for the conduct of Japan's expansion policy in the late 1930's.[11]

Exponents of the Kōdō policy found it essential to promote as a national ideal the propagation of Japan's "Imperial Way" in other countries and to accept as a national task the elimination of Western influence in Asia. These ideals of foreign policy were assumed to have existed throughout the long history of the Japanese nation, and so were to be realized regardless of the sacrifices. There was not much concern as to how to implement these ideals or whether it was practicable to do so

[10] For a brief outline of the formation of the *Kakushinha* in the Foreign Ministry in 1932-33, see Nihon Kokusai Seiji Gakkai, Taiheiyō Sensō Genin Kenkyū-bu, comp., *Taiheyō sensō e no michi* [The Road to the Pacific War] (hereafter referred to as *TSM*), 7 vols. (Tokyo, 1963), V, 3-15. The faction grew up around the leadership of Shiratori Toshio, then chief information officer in the ministry and later special adviser to the ministry. The main strength of the faction was the group of younger civil servants who had entered the ministry in 1932-33. As noted below, the faction's leaders were instrumental in the consummation of the Tripartite Alliance and were influential in foreign affairs generally in the time of Matsuoka Yōsuke.

[11] "Nihon koyū no gaikō shidō genri kōryō." This booklet, extracts of which are quoted in *TSM*, V, 9, was said to have been read by the youth of the day. Nimiya served overseas in California, New York, Holland, and Italy in the Foreign Service, and in the Research Bureau of the Foreign Ministry, one of the sections heavily staffed with *Kakushinha* activists. He was long active in right-wing youth movements and continued to publish after the war.

at all. The questions of what reaction might be expected from other nations in the course of executing the Kōdō policy or what means were available for carrying out such a policy were only secondary.

Shiratori Toshio, leader of the _Kakushinha_ in the Foreign Ministry, was quite active in advocating the Kōdō policy, giving public lectures and writing articles with such statements as these:

> Although the Kōdō policy is similar to the imperialistic policy followed by Western Powers, the former is quite different in essence from the latter since the Kōdō policy is aimed at mutual benefits, while the other, at self-expansion merely for its own interests.

> Japan's continental policy is essentially based on its efforts to realize a cultural mission. No other cases are comparable in world history to Japan's present venture, which is designed to reconstruct human society and to regenerate modern civilization.[12]

The impact of Kōdō thinking on the actual conduct of foreign policy gradually became noticeable in the 1930's. As early as April 1934, Foreign Minister Hirota Kōki declared, in the so-called Amō Statement, that Japan had a mission to maintain peace and order in Asia and that the nation was determined to carry out this task regardless of the attitude of other countries.[13]

[12] See Shiratori's article on the Kōdō policy in Shiratori Toshio, _Kokusai Nihon no chii_ [The Status of Japan in the World] (Tokyo, 1938), pp. 145-55.

[13] The "Amō Seimei," so called because it was first enunciated by Foreign Ministry Information Officer Amō Eiji, in an off-the-record press conference April 17, 1934. The text was made public in Japan on April 18, 1934 (_Tokyo Asahi Shimbun_, p. 6) only after the foreign reaction made disclosure inevitable. For an American discussion of the statement and its implications, see Dorothy Borg, "The Amau Doctrine," _The United States and the Far Eastern Crisis of 1933-1938_ (Cambridge, Mass., 1964), pp. 46-99. For a Japanese interpretation, see

CHIHIRO HOSOYA

It became more and more apparent that the ideology of the Kōdō policy was increasingly influential in the formulation of Japan's foreign policy, when the Konoe Cabinet made the following announcement on November 3, 1938, to define the goal of Japan's China policy in terms of establishing a new order:[14]

What Japan seeks is the establishment of a new order which will insure the permanent stability of East Asia. . . . This new order has for its foundation a tripartite relationship of mutual aid and coordination between Japan, Manchukuo and China in political, economic, cultural and other fields. Its object is to secure international justice, to perfect the joint defence against communism, and to create a new culture and realize a close economic cohesion throughout East Asia. This indeed is the way to contribute toward the stabilization of East Asia and the progress of the world. What Japan desires of China is that that country share in the task of bringing about this new order. . . . The establishment of a new order in East Asia is in complete conformity with the very spirit in which the Empire was founded; to achieve such a task is the exalted responsibility with which our present generation is trusted.

Deeply convinced that Japan should carry out the divine task of establishing a new order, the *Kakushinha* saw as inevitable Japan's strengthening its ties with the Axis powers, whose declared purpose was to set up a "new order" in Europe and to eradicate Communist influence there. The *Kakushinha* were outstanding in the late 1930's for their efforts to actualize the

Tamura Kōsaku, *Taiheiyō sensō gaikō-shi* [The Diplomatic History of the Pacific War] (Tokyo, 1966), pp. 89-93.

[14] For the original text of this statement, see "Tōa no shinchitsujo kensetsu e" [Toward a New Order in East Asia], *Tokyo Asahi Shimbun*, November 3, 1938, p. 6; and the related reportage, "Makoto no ikusa wa ima hajimareri" [The Real Battle Has Just Begun] and "Ichigatsu seimei ni han-sezu" [No Contradiction of the January Declaration], *Tokyo Asahi Shimbun*, November 4, 1938.

Tripartite Alliance and to get their leader, Shiratori, appointed foreign minister.[15]

It was not Shiratori, however, but Matsuoka Yōsuke, who in July 1940 was given the opportunity to steer the course of Japan's foreign policy with the support of the *Kakushinha*. Matsuoka's diplomacy was most representative of Kōdō policy in its orientation to ideology, strong sense of mission, and lack of rational calculation, believing that one must depend on divine inspiration rather than on rational calculation in making crucial decisions. Foreign Minister Matsuoka went so far as to conclude the military alliance with Germany and Italy without a careful examination of the repercussions it would bring from other countries and from the United States in particular. "One cannot obtain a tiger's cub unless he braves the tiger's den," was the phrase he would often use to express his willingness to take great risks regardless of the situation.

In Matsuoka's view, Japan was destined to create a new world where each country would be able to find its own proper place, and for this purpose Japan was obligated to assist in dissolving the current order, one full of injustice resulting from the control of the Western powers. He was further convinced that the only way to attain this goal was to make other nations understand the Imperial Way and follow Japan's lead. The most important thing for Japan to do, he believed with undoubted sincerity, was to propagate her Imperial Way throughout the world.

Matsuoka's lack of rationality in making foreign policy decisions was vividly demonstrated by his seeking a four-power entente among Japan, Germany, Italy, and the Soviet Union when, in the fall of 1940, there was no apparent likelihood that such an alignment could be accomplished. Even as late as March 1941, he made a visit to the Axis powers and the Soviet Union in the hope that he might find a way of realizing this

[15] See my article, "Sangoku dōmei to Nisso chūritsu jōyaku" [The Tripartite Alliance and the Soviet-Japanese Neutrality Pact], *TSM*, V, 159-331 *passim*.

entente. Matsuoka diplomacy was too compulsively driven by the desire to establish a new order to take much account of the relevant factors of the international environment.

As I have written elsewhere, the Japanese military leaders did not feel entirely confident of gaining a victory in the fall of 1941, when they decided to go to war with the United States.[16] It is well known that War Minister Tōjō Hideki argued for the decision to go to war by stating to Premier Konoe Fumimaro that "sometimes a man has to jump, with his eyes closed, from the veranda of Kiyomizu Temple."

Taking such a risk, with slight chance of success, must be judged an irrational act from a Western point of view. However, for the Japanese leaders who were filled with a sense of mission and who visualized an inevitable struggle in carrying out this mission, the risk of war was regarded as an alternative which might have to be taken. Perhaps it could be said that Japan's decision to go to war with the United States was not unrelated to the increasing influence of the Kōdō policy after the Manchurian incident.

The Disintegration of the Decision-Making Structure

With the growing interdependence of states in the modern world, the external issues confronting them, as well as the external information they receive, have increased prodigiously in both number and variety. Under such circumstances, modern states tend to magnify the institution which copes with foreign affairs and to expand its specialized organizations and the number of specially trained personnel. This leads to an increased number of levels in the decision-making hierarchy at which voluminous information must be screened and relayed, and it multiplies the steps necessary to decide on even minor issues. There is then an increasing tendency on the part of key deci-

[16] "Twenty-five Years After Pearl Harbor: A New Look at Japan's Decision for War," in Grant K. Goodman, ed., *Imperial Japan and Asia*, Occasional Papers of the East Asian Institute, Columbia University (New York, 1967), pp. 52-64.

sion-makers to delegate a part of their power to lower echelons. In other words, decentralization is a characteristic of the decision-making structure of a modern state.

As decentralization proceeds, there is a tendency for interdepartmental and intersectional conflicts to develop, since various organs within the decision-making structure tend to perceive an issue from different points of view and to advocate their own interests. A greater effort is necessary to coordinate the various activities involved in the decision-making process; especially to resolve serious conflicts arising between the civilian and the military sectors. Thus, in any modern state there is a growing need to reinforce the power held by key decision-makers and to centralize it in order to achieve a unity of national will and resolve serious conflicts. However paradoxical it may sound, centralization is another trait of the modern decision-making structure: it can be assumed that both centrifugal and centripetal forces are at work within such a structure.

Now, let us look at the foreign policy decision-making structure of Japan in the 1930's. Balance between centrifugal and centripetal forces was lost in favor of the former. The integrative power maintained by the key decision-makers had weakened for several reasons, and as a result the disintegrative movement gained momentum. It is partly due to the fact that no strong political leaders or groups, corresponding to the senior statesmen of the Chōshū clique during the Meiji and Taishō eras, appeared on the scene, while the military voice in foreign affairs became stronger as a result of extended military involvement on the continent.

In a modern state where there is a need to coordinate the views and interests of specialized agencies, and in particular the military and the civilian sectors, there is a tendency to rely more on an impersonal system of controls to maintain integration than on the personal authority and prestige attached to a particular decision-maker. Japan in the 1930's had lost such influential leaders as Itō Hirobumi, Yamagata Aritomo, Hara Takashi, and Tanaka Giichi, and found herself facing the

94

need to create an impersonal system of controls to accommodate civil-military conflicts.

Regardless of the changing situation, there had been little attempt to integrate the foreign policy decision-making structure. Instead, "the right of supreme command" was invoked with increasing frequency to hamper Cabinet efforts to exert control over the military. In particular, the army was so strong in asserting its position in the formulation and conduct of Japan's China policy that it was prevailing over the Foreign Ministry. Further, it often took an independent action in China regardless of the attitude of the Cabinet. The result was a dual policy, with the Cabinet engaging in one and the army pursuing another.

As an attempt to secure integration within the government, an inner cabinet emerged in the form of the Four- and Five-Minister Conferences. This institution served the purpose, to some extent, of attaining unity of national will; but it often proved that it was not powerful enough to overrule the opposition raised by the service minister when the problems were serious. This was exemplified by the controversy about strengthening the Anti-Comintern Pact. It was said that Premier Hiranuma Kiichirō held the Five-Minister Conferences more than seventy times in the period from January to August 1939 in an effort to reach an agreement on whether or not Japan should conclude a military alliance with the Axis powers, but due to the premier's failure to reconcile the views of the war minister with those of the foreign and the navy ministers, the government could not decide on any alternative.[17]

The establishment of the Liaison Conference late in 1937 represented the most significant attempt to coordinate the views of the government and the military. It did not last long, but was revived in November 1940 to work as the supreme body for making decisions on major foreign policies. It was composed of key Cabinet members representing the government

[17] For the role of the Five-Minister Conferences and Hiranuma's role in the Anti-Comintern Pact, see *TSM*, V, 107-136.

and the chiefs and vice-chiefs of staff representing the High Command. On account of its composition and because the most embarrassing questions tended to arise between the government and the High Command, the Liaison Conference was intended to be more effective in integrating the decision-making activities of the nation than such inner Cabinet systems as the Four- or Five-Minister Conferences.

The Liaison Conference was involved in discussing most of the relevant issues of foreign affairs confronting Japan during the critical days of 1941. The records for the conference, which are available, thanks to the writings of General Sugiyama Gen, chief of army staff, tell us that it certainly served the purpose of coordinating policies proposed by the government and the High Command.[18]

It had been customary for the High Command to communicate its views on questions of foreign affairs through the service ministers to the government, although it sometimes happened that a chief of staff communicated his opinion directly to the emperor, side-stepping the government, as in the case of the London Naval Treaty controversy in 1930.[19] Even in the Five-Minister Conferences, the service ministers often found it difficult to express their views clearly or to commit themselves to a particular policy proposed by the government without first conferring with the High Command. It often happened that the service ministers, having supported the government's stand in the conference, were later subjected to severe criticism from the High Command and forced to revise their position. There were a number of cases where the High Command tried to execute its own policy in disregard of the government's stand. Even as late as September 1940, Major General Tominaga

---

[18] For an English translation of the Army High Command transcripts of these conferences see Nobutaka Ike, ed., *Japan's Decision for War* (Stanford, 1967); for the Japanese originals see Headquarters of the General Staff, ed., *Sugiyama memo* [Sugiyama Memorandum] (Tokyo, 1967), I, 139-570.

[19] *TSM*, I, 88-91.

Kyōji, chief of the first section of the Army General Staff, sent an order to the operational forces to invade North Indochina in contradiction to a decision made in a Four-Minister Conference.[20]

To be sure, the Liaison Conference was instrumental in bringing the controversy between the government and the military out into the open and in finding a compromise for their conflict. It enabled the civilian ministers to discuss foreign affairs with the chiefs of staff, and it enabled the premier to exert more control over the military if he were so determined. The opening of a communication channel between the premier and the chiefs of staff in such a fashion must have had a good effect on the integration of decision-making. In fact, it might be assumed that it produced a more cautious attitude on the part of the General Staff, restraining it from taking independent action without the government's sanction.

The conference was, however, not so strong as to be able to settle any serious government-military conflicts pertaining to strategic and foreign policy problems. Its conduct often revealed that its function was to provide a liaison rather than to integrate. That the premier was powerless to impose his will against strong military opposition was demonstrated in the downfall of the Konoe Cabinet in October 1941. Although he was most anxious to continue negotiations with the United States and was even prepared to compromise and make many concessions, Konoe failed to persuade the army leaders to follow his lead.

In the decision-making structure of Japan in the 1930's disintegrative forces were operative both horizontally and vertically, not only at the top of the hierarchy, but also at the middle level. The long-standing rivalry between the army and the navy, often intensified by problems of budget allocation and national defense programs, developed into such a serious confrontation when the problem of the Axis alliance came up in the summer of 1939 that the navy even took steps to guard the

[20] *TSM*, VI, 219-44.

Ministry of the Navy building for fear of being attacked by the army.

Also, within the army serious conflicts between the General Staff and the War Ministry arose concerning Japan's foreign policy. Although an *ad hoc* institution called the Section and Bureau Chiefs Conference had been entrusted with the task of coordinating their different views, it was not always successful in finding a real compromise.

The Foreign Ministry exhibited a similar tendency toward disunity, largely due to the rise of the *Kakushinha*. Terasaki Tarō, director of the Bureau for American Affairs, confessed in his memoirs that when he was engaged in the 1941 negotiations between Japan and the United States, he felt isolated by the cool attitudes of his colleagues and worried about being interrupted by them, particularly those representing the *Kakushinha*.[21] He did not even show other senior officials the cables transmitted from Washington, and he performed his tasks chiefly in collaboration with a few of his subordinates.

An example of the vertical disintegrative forces at work within the decision-making structure in prewar Japan is the importance accorded to middle-grade officers and officials.[22] They not only performed the ordinary functions of selecting and transmitting information to the decision-makers and giving opinions on alternative courses of action, but also formulated the substance of crucial decisions and sometimes even went so far as to press such decisions on the decision-makers for their approval.

It was through talks among the middle-grade officers within each service and at joint staff meetings that the substance of important national programs was formulated—such as the "Essentials for Coping with the Current Situation," in July 1940,

---

[21] Terazaki Tarō, "Omoi-izuru mama ni" [As I Recall] (Tokyo, March, 1967); published as the final issue of *Reimei*, the house organ of the Terazaki Gaiji Mondai Kenkyūsho [Terazaki Foreign Affairs Research Institute].

[22] See my essay, "Twenty-five years After Pearl Harbor," *op.cit.*

which formed the basis for Japan's policy of moving southward; and the "Essentials for Executing the National Purpose of the Empire," in September 1941, which specified that Japan should go to war with the United States, if diplomatic negotiations failed.[23] It is well known that the middle-grade officers of both services, as well as the *Kakushinha* of the Foreign Ministry, were very active from 1938 to 1940 in their efforts to press a military alliance with the Axis powers on the decision-makers. Furthermore, it is fair to assume that the determination to go to war with the United States was first crystallized among the middle-grade officers of the navy, in particular those composing the First Committee, and that then the military decision-makers were gradually persuaded to move in this direction.[24]

The senior officers not wanting to be accused of being "weaklings" or "degenerates," often seemed to be psychologically vulnerable to strong policies proposed by their subordinates. They understood that a good boss should quietly trust his subordinates to manage affairs. In comparison with other modern countries, prewar Japan allowed middle-grade officers to occupy a much more influential position within the government's decision-making machinery, and so the decentralization pattern became more pronounced.

Disintegration in the Communications System

Disintegration was also to be found in the communications aspect of foreign policy decision-making in prewar Japan. Here I would particularly like to comment on the communications system between the government and its ambassadors abroad.

Generally speaking, an ambassador is expected to perform

[23] "Sekai jōsei no sui-i ni tomonau jikyoku shori yōkō," in the Foreign Ministry of Japan, ed., *Nihon gaikō nempyō narabini shuyō bunshō* [Chronology and Principal Documents of Japanese Foreign Policy] (Tokyo, 1955), pp. 437-38; and "Teikoku kokusaku suikō yōryō," *ibid.*, pp. 544-45. The latter is translated into English in Ike, *op.cit.*, pp. 135-36.

[24] See *TSM*, VII, 204-213.

two major functions: namely, to negotiate and to transmit messages. As a transmitter he receives and sends messages in two directions; that is, from his home government to the government to which he is accredited, and vice versa. In prewar Japan there were several cases in which an ambassador greatly overemphasized his role as negotiator and underestimated that of transmitter. An ambassador whose previous career had been military tended to look upon his diplomatic profession as being devoted primarily to pursuing a certain national purpose through negotiation or machination. He would give only a secondary priority to acting as a communicator for his government. With such a perception of his role, an ambassador might deliver his government's messages in his own way, sometimes disregarding his instructions, or he might send a message to his government in such a way as to create a distorted image of foreign affairs. Let me offer two outstanding examples of this.

THE CASE OF AMBASSADOR ŌSHIMA HIROSHI

It is widely known that Ōshima was very pro-German and had been most active in promoting Japan's military alliance with Germany. While serving as a military attaché in Berlin, then Major-General Ōshima took initiatives in a secret negotiation which led to the Anti-Comintern Pact. He finally succeeded in securing the approval of the Japanese government to conclude the pact.[25]

After becoming ambassador to Germany in the fall of 1938, Ōshima, who was determined to realize a military alliance with Germany, carried on talks with German Foreign Minister Ribbentrop regardless of the Japanese government's attitude. Dur-

[25] See *TSM*, V, 17-21; and Gaimushō Hyakunen-shi Hensan Iinkai, ed., *Gaimushō no hyakunen* [100 Years of the Foreign Ministry] (Tokyo, 1969), II, 389-400, for Ōshima's activities in Germany, meetings with Ribbentrop, etc. Ōshima was military attaché to the embassy in Berlin from 1934 to 1938. A constant advocate of Japanese-German alliance, he was appointed ambassador to Berlin in October 1938 after resigning in October 1939. He was reposted to Berlin in February 1941.

ing the course of these talks he gave a pledge, without instructions from his government, that Japan was prepared to apply the military alliance not only to the Soviet Union, but also to Britain and France. Whether the alliance should be directed only against the Soviet Union, or should include Britain and France as well, became a very controversial problem and caused heated discussion among the members of the Five-Minister Conferences.

Although Foreign Minister Arita Hachirō supported the strengthening of the Anti-Comintern Pact in principle, he had never sent an instruction to Ambassador Ōshima to lend Japan's approval to a proposal that the pact be extended to include Britain and France. The Five-Minister Conferences of the Hiranuma Cabinet found a new formula of compromise in January 1939—after the Konoe Cabinet had resigned because of disunity on the alliance question. Accordingly, Foreign Minister Arita sent new instructions to Ōshima to the effect that "Japan would not render military assistance if Germany and Italy were attacked by countries other than the Soviet Union unless these countries turned communistic." Clearly, the new instructions did not give Ōshima any authority to accept an all-out alliance with Germany; they were intended to communicate the Japanese government's view that the main objective of the alliance should be confined to the Soviet Union. Lest Ōshima decode his message wrongly, Arita took the unusual step of sending a special mission to Berlin headed by Minister Itō Nobufumi to confirm this new instruction.

Despite Arita's efforts to communicate Japan's real intentions, Ambassador Ōshima, dissatisfied with the government's policy, did not faithfully follow the government's instruction, but instead proceeded to express an official willingness to accept the German proposal for the alliance.[26]

---

[26] For details on the lack of communication between Arita and Ōshima over the question of strengthening the Anti-Comintern Pact, see *Gaimushō no hyakunen*, II, 402-432; and *TSM*, V, 60-136.

THE CASE OF AMBASSADOR NOMURA[27]

The way in which Ambassador Nomura Kichisaburō behaved during the course of Japanese-American talks in 1941 reveals another defect in the communications system within the Japanese decision-making machinery. Unlike Ōshima, Nomura was engaged in a peace mission dedicated to averting a war against the United States. He was, however, so strongly convinced that the national destiny hinged on a reconciliation with the United States that he discounted the value of transmitting precisely correct messages to and from his home government. In this respect, he exhibited a behavioral pattern similar to that of Ōshima.

Believing it necessary to improve the psychological atmosphere between the two nations as a first step toward settling a long-standing feud, Nomura advocated following a "soft line" policy and making concessions on the Japanese side. In this respect, his diplomatic posture toward the United States was different from that of the foreign minister Matsuoka Yōsuke. Matsuoka advocated a "hard line" policy designed to exert pressure on the United States in such a way as to demonstrate the strength of Japan's position and to convince the United States of the advantages of compromise.

The communications system between Nomura and his government became very dysfunctional when Matsuoka served as foreign minister. Nomura engaged in informal talks with United States Secretary of State Cordell Hull in April 1941, without Matsuoka's knowledge, and proceeded to deliver to Tokyo a "draft proposal agreed upon by Japan and the United States on April 16."

Nomura's report gave Japanese leaders the impression that the "draft proposal" was initially submitted by the United States government, and thus reflected their official thinking

[27] For details of the Nomura-Hull negotiations, see Nomura's memoirs [*Beikoku ni tsukai shite*] (Tokyo, 1946), *passim*; and *Gaimushō no hyakunen*, II, 536-622.

about Japanese-American accommodation. Furthermore, Nomura did not mention in his report "a statement of four basic principles" that Cordell Hull had emphasized should underlie any agreement between the two countries. While talking with Nomura on April 16, Hull went on to communicate his government's feeling that "we have in no sense reached the stage of negotiations; that we are only exploring in a purely preliminary and unofficial way what action might pave the way for negotiations later."

Nomura did not communicate the real position of the United States government to Tokyo and as a result the Japanese decision-makers painted a rather rosy picture of the prospects for negotiations between Japan and the United States. The optimistic reaction of the Japanese leaders to the "draft proposal" was best exemplified by the following remarks made by the emperor to Marquis Kido Kōichi: "It is beyond expectation that the American president has carried the talk so far as to commit himself in this fashion; it may be judged as an outcome of the Tripartite Pact. Forbearance has proved to be most needed in everything."

Later on, Nomura failed to send his government some important messages, which reflected the American attitude toward negotiations, because he feared that these messages might discourage further talks. There is no evidence that an oral statement which Hull gave Nomura on May 16, with a view of making "certain preliminary comments" on the Japanese official proposal of May 12, was ever transmitted to Matsuoka. Moreover, Nomura held up a relevant document entitled "Oral Explanation for Suggested Amendments to the Japanese Draft," which he had received from the Department of State on May 31, until Matsuoka demanded to see it on June 9, having been informed of its existence through military channels.

Nomura played a kind of match-maker role in the way he handled messages between the two governments. He did not relay an oral statement to Hull, which Matsuoka had instructed him to do on May 7, because, he said, "there were many things in it that 'were wrong'"; he therefore summarized its substance in his own words. As to the instruction of May 13 in which Matsuoka intended to clarify Japan's strong posture by specifying the prerequisites for successful negotiations, there is no evidence that Nomura acted on it. Again, in June there were several instances in which he delivered "new Japanese proposals" to the United States government without any instructions from Tokyo.

Nomura's failure to perform faithfully the function of a communicator between the two governments led each country to a distorted image of the other's intention. While in the case of the United States government, "magic" enabled it to correct the impressions Nomura sought to give, the Japanese government was not so fortunate. For some time, Matsuoka did not realize that Nomura was holding up the unpalatable messages, so that his "hard line" diplomacy was being sabotaged on the spot. When he did become aware of it, Matsuoka exploded in a strong letter to Premier Konoe on July 17, saying that Nomura's manner of conducting negotiations was just like "pounding the Americans' sesame seeds for them" and that this had seriously hampered progress in the Japanese negotiations with the United States.

When Admiral Toyoda Teijirō succeeded Matsuoka as foreign minister, he took several steps to improve the communications between Tokyo and Washington. He made more effective use of a channel between himself and Ambassador Joseph C. Grew in Tokyo and had professional diplomats from the Japanese embassy in Washington sit in with Nomura whenever he met with Hull. In spite of such steps, defects still remained in the communications system. The "Konoe Message" of September 27, which made a significant formal proposal for a summit conference with President Franklin D. Roosevelt, was conveyed by Nomura to the United States government in words slightly different from those of the original sent from Tokyo. In addition Nomura handed a "Japanese Proposal" to

Cordell Hull on September 4 which stipulated "withdrawal of Japanese armed forces from Chinese territory as promptly as possible with the restoration of peace, and within a period of two years"; this was without instructions from Tokyo. At the time, the question of withdrawing Japanese armed forces from China constituted the most difficult of all questions for which the decision-makers in Tokyo sought a consensus.

It is well known that Japan committed a vital error in handing an ultimatum to the United States government in such a way that its notification came after Japan had opened hostilities in Hawaii. The defects in the communications system which I have described seem to me to be closely related to this disgraceful incident.

CHAPTER IV

The Failure of Military Expansionism

AKIRA IRIYE

IN THE 1920's Japan tried peaceful expansionism and failed. If the nation was to continue to grow, military means must now be employed; the use of force would enable the nation to achieve ends which the "economic diplomacy" of the 1920's had not been able to obtain—such was the reasoning behind the militaristic adventures of the 1930's.[1]

In discussing Japanese militarism after the Manchurian incident, it is useful to view it as the antithesis not of pacifism but of peaceful expansionism. Militarism triumphed not as a goal but as a means for obtaining the same ends which the diplomacy of the preceding era had unsuccessfully sought. By the early 1930's there was almost universal consensus that the peaceful, economic diplomacy of the 1920's had brought no benefits to Japan and that in fact it had been powerless even to safeguard the nation's existing rights and interests. The whole orientation of postwar Japanese policy could be attacked and the fundamental assumptions underlying peaceful expansionism questioned. Without such questioning, it would be difficult to account for the general enthusiasm with which the bold military initiatives taken after 1931 were greeted. What united the military, the nationalistic groups, and the bulk of the intellectuals was the shared perception of the 1920's as a decade of futile attempts at peaceful expansion through international cooperation.

Certain images about the previous decade that were held by the proponents and defenders of the new order were central to

[1] Elsewhere I have discussed the peaceful expansionism of the 1920's. See Akira Iriye, "The Failure of Economic Expansionism, 1918-1931," paper presented at the Conference on Taishō Japan, held at Duke University, January 23-26, 1969.

their thinking. It is immaterial whether such images were accurate or realistic. What is important is that these perceptions defined a reality which the militaristic expansionists endeavored to overcome by means of their own strategy. The economic diplomacy of the 1920's had been based on a set of assumptions about the nature of the postwar world. What the men of the succeeding decade did was to challenge these assumptions and substitute for them their own ideas about the world.

Were the assumptions held during the 1930's more accurate reflections of the realities of international relations than those common in the preceding decade? In the end both peaceful expansionism and military expansionism failed, and these failures constitute an important aspect of the story of the "dilemmas of growth" in modern Japan. The study of the ideology of military expansionism provides one way of examining changing attitudes toward growth in modern Japan and the relationship between domestic factors and forces external to the country.

Because the initiative to reorient foreign policy in the 1930's was undertaken by the military, and because military decisions were at the core of national politics, it will be meaningful to analyze military perceptions of the world in the decade preceding Pearl Harbor. One way to do this is to examine memoranda, minutes of conferences, diaries, and other military writings to see how they tried to relate Japanese military action to the policies of other powers. Their writings almost invariably include "estimates of the international situation," "developments in foreign countries," and similar entries. By examining these writings it is possible to evaluate how the exponents of forceful expansionism visualized the world, sought to predict changes in international affairs, and called for corresponding responses by Japan.

It is, of course, doubtful that one can speak of the Japanese military as a generic collective term, any more than one can generalize about the civilian bureaucracies or business interests. Differences between the army and the navy, between service ministries and general staffs, and between sections within each of these, were always of great significance, and some of them will be noted below. However, this essay is not a study in decision-making or in institutional history. Rather, it seeks to look at one aspect of the dilemmas of growth in prewar Japan by examining some of the ideas constituting the ideological structure of military expansionism. Since the failure of peaceful expansionism was fundamentally a failure to develop a realistic conceptual model of international relations, it is germane to ask if military expansionism was based on any more workable assumptions.

Continental Expansion

The justification of the use of force was naturally the starting point of military expansionism. It was derived from the belief that, given such "objective" conditions as the disproportionately superior material strength of the Western countries, their exclusive trade and immigration policies, and Chinese nationalism, Japanese interest could not realistically be predicated upon the goodwill of these nations. If Japan was to grow, the necessity for which was never questioned, the nation must be prepared to use force. A Kwantung Army memo written just before the Mukden incident noted that the policy of gradualism in Manchuria had failed and that there could be no successful execution of a China policy without the resolution to use force. "If we win the war it should not matter what the world thinks of us." At a time when alien ideologies permeated Japanese society and when there were unprecedented economic difficulties, only a decisive blow in defense of national interests would enable the nation to attain its goals.[2]

Force, however, must be used selectively. An indiscriminate resort to military measures would complicate strategic and diplomatic questions and defeat the very purpose for which force was employed. It was thus imperative to scrutinize carefully

[2] *Gendaishi shiryō* [Source Materials on Modern Japanese History] (hereafter cited as *GS*), VII (Tokyo, 1964), 162-63.

trends in the policies and strategies of other powers. The successful execution of military expansion depended upon an accurate analysis of these trends as well as a realistic evaluation of the probable responses to Japanese action that must be expected from foreign countries. It was particularly important to prevent an eventuality in which Japan was caught off guard and compelled to wage war against antagonists who were not of Japan's own choosing.

In 1931 a major decision was made—to use force in Manchuria—and the military judged correctly that war with other countries would not be involved. Yet they remained extremely sensitive to the possibilities of foreign intervention and actual conflict with third powers. Numerous memoranda, "judgments on current developments," and "evaluations of the international situation" written at the time give evidence of the intensity of this concern and the acute awareness of these possibilities. There was virtual unanimity in army writings during the period from 1931 to 1937 that the Manchurian incident would eventuate in hostilities with the Soviet Union. For instance, in the spring of 1932, Colonel Itagaki Seishirō wrote that "war with the Soviet Union in the future is unavoidable. . . . If the Soviet Union should decisively intervene against our policy in Manchuria and Mongolia or persist in its communist propaganda despite our protests, we must be prepared to settle the Soviet question fundamentally."[3] Much of the Japanese army's strategic planning at this time was based on the assumption that conflict with Russia was impending. This necessitated the avoidance of open hostilities with the Chinese government. Instead, it was considered desirable to persuade China to pool resources with Japan to prepare against the Soviet Union.[4]

This is not to say that Russia was the army's sole concern. The General Staff conceded that in the event of hostilities with

[3] *Ibid.*, pp. 172-79.

[4] See Akira Iriye, "Japan's Foreign Policies Between World Wars—Sources and Interpretations," *Journal of Asian Studies*, XXVI (August 1967), 678-79.

Russia there was a possibility of intervention by the United States, Britain, and China, either individually or jointly. An August 1936 memorandum from the second (operations) section noted that the opening of conflict with these powers would make the prosecution of the Russian war extremely difficult. Such a possibility, however, could not be ruled out. It was hoped that Japanese diplomacy would effectively check American and British intervention, but in the meantime the armed forces developed their strategic plans against them.[5]

The army was in part indulging in a self-fulfilling prophesy when it visualized conflict with the Anglo-American nations. According to some Kwantung Army strategists, it was because of their belief in the inevitability of war with these countries that they had taken radical steps to expand forcefully into Manchuria. In Ishiwara Kanji's words, "the coming war with the Anglo-American nations will be mankind's last war, to be fought for the unification of world civilization." Japan was to prepare for the war by creating an "East Asian union" to liberate Asia from the West. The use of force was justified by the ends, but even so Japanese military action would be met by Western obstruction. "War will come," Ishiwara wrote in 1933, "when our national policy of establishing the East Asian union is obstructed by an enemy. Whether the enemy be America, Russia, or Britain, the war will be a protracted one."[6] It is evident that pan-Asianism was both a justification for forceful expansion and a cause for anxiety when the military tried to relate their action in Manchuria to the attitudes of other powers.

It is interesting to note, however, that the military tended to think of these various possibilities in terms of separate stages. On most occasions army strategists talked of war against the United States as a possibility after the anticipated war with the

[5] Nīhon Kokusaī Seiji Gakkaī, Taiheiyō sensō genin kenkyūbu, comp., *Taiheiyō sensō e no michi* [Road to the Pacific War] (hereafter cited as *TSM*), VIII (Tokyo, 1963), 227-31.

[6] *GS*, VIII (Tokyo, 1964), 666.

Soviet Union which, in turn, was viewed as a likely sequel to some settlement of the conflict in China. For instance, a General Staff memorandum of June 1936 stated that as soon as Japan, Manchuria, and north China could jointly complete military preparations, positive steps must be taken to cripple Soviet power in East Asia. The next step was to expel British influence from East Asia, liberating the colonial peoples and forcefully occupying Australia and New Zealand. Then, as the final target, preparations should be made to fight against the United States.[7] Similarly, in the same memorandum of 1933 quoted above, General Ishiwara made it clear that he envisaged conflict with the West as an inevitability after the establishment of Japanese hegemony over China. In his words, "It should be our basic national defense policy first to establish control over China quickly and skillfully, then to create a self-sufficient economic bloc encompassing Japan, China, and Manchukuo, and finally to use force against the Soviet army and the American and British navies to protect our East Asian union."[8]

Such thinking expressed the complacent optimism of Ishiwara and others that Japan would proceed according to the set stages of her plan while her potential adversaries meekly sat back and watched the inevitable unfolding of the drama. This optimism existed side by side with the more alarmist perception of Western policies. Both reflected the reluctance to face the possibility of simultaneous warfare with China and the Western powers, especially the United States and Britain. While conflict with the Soviet Union before the settling of the Manchurian crisis could not be ruled out, it was generally held extremely undesirable to open hostilities with the Anglo-American nations. The persistence of the stage theory may be taken as evidence that in the Japanese military's perception of the situation at this time it was possible to avoid such an eventuality.

The belief that forceful expansion on the continent of Asia

[7] *TSM*, VIII, 224.   [8] *GS*, VIII, 666.

would not necessarily be penalized by the military might of Britain and the United States became strengthened as these countries failed to intervene, except verbally, with Japanese action. America's disapprobation, in particular, had been foreseen, but as the United States even failed to impose economic sanctions against Japan, it seemed unlikely that there would be an American-Japanese war in the immediate future so long as Japan refrained from openly attacking American possessions and vested interests in Asia. According to Colonel Itagaki, this would mean allowing American capital to enter Manchuria to an extent compatible with Japan's "management of Manchuria and Mongolia." He believed it possible to accumulate *faits accomplis* slowly and patiently so that Japanese hegemony over Manchuria would be established without incurring the open hostility of the United States.[9] Given the record of American foreign policy throughout most of the 1930's, it would be difficult to fault Itagaki's judgment. There might be war in the future, as dictated by pan-Asianism, but not in the immediate future as an outgrowth of the Manchurian incident, so long as Japan behaved discreetly and proceeded piecemeal.

The outbreak of the Sino-Japanese War in 1937 did not alter such perceptions of international affairs. It is surprising that the war with China brought about little change in the army's view of Japan's relations with China, the Soviet Union, and the United States. Army Ministry, General Staff, and Kwantung Army memoranda continued to enunciate clichés about "cooperation and co-prosperity among Japan, Manchukuo, and China."[10] They also visualized conflict with Russia as a distinct possibility, a sequel to or part of the Chinese war. The army remained hopeful that somehow the Chinese would recognize and appreciate the ideal of "harmony and cooperation" between Japan, Manchukuo, and China, so that the three could work together in a joint struggle against communism. Toward the end of the year the General Staff reiterated that "our basic

[9] *GS*, VII, 178.   [10] *GS*, IX (Tokyo, 1964), 44.

national defense plan is still directed toward the Soviet Union."[11] Moreover, as the war in China dragged on, it came to be expected that open hostilities with Russia might come at any moment, before the settlement of the Chinese conflict. The war-direction section of the General Staff defined the goal for military planning during the period from 1938 to 1941 as national mobilization in preparation for simultaneous warfare against China and the Soviet Union.[12] On November 18, 1938, the army supreme command adopted a strategic decision which stated, "We must carry on our war with China and at the same time strengthen our defense capabilities with a view to preparing the nation for war against both the Soviet Union and China."[13]

Pan-Asianism, too, persisted after 1937. It became an instrument for the moral justification of the Sino-Japanese War, but its essentially self-fulfilling nature had not changed. The war was defined as aimed at "the construction of a morally oriented culture in East Asia."[14] "The expulsion of Europe and America [from Asia]," exclaimed a November 1937 memorandum, "is a common concern of Japan and China." The two peoples had a joint mission to liberate themselves from Western influence, whether democratic or Communist.[15] As earlier, pan-Asianism envisaged the establishment of imperial self-sufficiency. In a paper written in the early spring of 1938, General Staff officers defined "the national defense sphere" in terms of three areas: the core area (Japan, Manchukuo, North China), the self-sufficiency area (Indochina, the Dutch East Indies), and the supplementary area (India, Australia). The core area was the "foundation of our national existence," and its security had to be the cardinal objective of all strategy. This necessitated preparedness against the Soviet Union. Japan should also undertake the defense of the self-sufficiency area, and this would re-

[11] Horiba Kazuo, *Shina jihen sensō shidō-shi* [Direction of the War with China] (Tokyo, 1962), p. 116.

[12] *Ibid.*, p. 143.   [13] *TSM*, VIII, 20.

[14] Horiba, *op.cit.*, pp. 191ff.   [15] *Ibid.*, pp. 133-34.

quire "adjustments" in Japanese relations with Britain and the United States.[16]

Again as earlier, the army's view of the United States was cautiously optimistic. Pan-Asianist thoughts were essentially vague generalities that were not related to any kind of conflict with America in the near future. The above memorandum pointed out that the establishment of a new East Asian order would take thirty to fifty years, and at any event it was asserted as imperative that Japan first settle the war with China and then concern itself with the possible conflict with the Soviet Union, to be ultimately followed by probable changes in Japanese relations with the Anglo-American countries.

Because of their overriding concern with China and the Soviet Union, Japanese army leaders continued to warn against precipitous involvement in an American conflict. In October 1937 the Kwantung Army insisted that Japan should maintain good relations with America by proposing a bilateral agreement on the Pacific and on economic and cultural cooperation in general. Japan should also honor American rights in such areas as Kwantung and the Philippines.[17] Two months later, the Supreme Headquarters' army division drafted a basic guideline for the conduct of the war and stated: "Our diplomatic efforts should focus on maintaining friendly relations with the United States. We must try especially to promote economic cooperation, so necessary for carrying out our industrial and defense plans, and to improve American public opinion."[18] In the "General Plans for Directing the War," drafted in January 1938, the General Staff referred to "strengthening the friendship with the United States" as a necessary step for completing preparedness against the Soviet Union. Certain rights and concessions in Manchuria and north China might be granted to America, and the two countries might collaborate economically to establish "intimate and unseparable" relations.[19] In the following July, the War Ministry reaffirmed the

[16] *Ibid.*, pp. 150ff.
[18] *Ibid.*, p. 55.
[17] *GS*, IX, 47.
[19] *Ibid.*, p. 240.

army's position that the fundamental national policy was to frustrate the Soviet Union's "aggressive designs in East Asia" and that it was essential to have the United States "maintain at least a neutral attitude but if possible take a pro-Japanese stand." It was also desirable to strengthen friendly economic relations between the two countries through Japan's protection of American rights and interests in China and an expansion of American trade with and investment in Japan.[20]

It can be seen that the exponents of military expansionism believed it was within their power to prevent a crisis with the United States and even to sustain "friendly" relations with that country. So long as Japanese military action did not openly violate American rights and interests, there seemed to be no reason why the Chinese war should develop into an American war. In fact some hoped that the United States might be induced to act as a mediator in the Sino-Japanese War. In the "Plans for Ending the War," written by the operations section of the General Staff in the late summer of 1938, it was asserted that the United States seemed to be in the best position to offer good offices to terminate the hostilities. Although such intervention would tend to increase American influence in East Asia, it was argued that the risk was worth taking in view of the likelihood of an impending conflict with the Soviet Union.[21]

As in the period before 1937, the military's cautious optimism *vis-à-vis* the United States, the view that America would not provoke war with Japan but would be desirous of playing a role in terminating the hostilities in Asia, was not unjustified. General Ishiwara reminisced somewhat later that the Japanese army had been "certain the United States would not intervene, since it had not intervened in the Manchurian incident."[22] While American policy was not clear-cut, the fact remains that for about a year after the outbreak of the Sino-Japanese War the United States pursued an extremely cautious policy in East Asia, fearful of inviting an open clash with Japan. The State

[20] *Ibid.*, pp. 263-65.   [21] *Ibid.*, p. 274.
[22] *Ibid.*, p. 317.

Department periodically protested against Japan's violations of the open door, but it was unwilling to go a step farther and adopt military or economic measures which could be taken as evidence of its pro-Chinese stand. America's response to the Sino-Japanese War was such as to convince Japan's military expansionists of the soundness of their perception of international affairs. They had used force on the continent of Asia and had achieved substantial goals without incurring forceful resistance on the part of Russia or the Western powers. They expected war with Russia, but so long as they limited their strategy to a Soviet war they were hopeful that normal relations could be maintained with the Anglo-American nations. As late as November 1938, when the Konoe Cabinet was proclaiming a new order to East Asia under Japanese hegemony, the army supreme command reiterated its belief that Japanese-American amity should and could be maintained.[23]

Changes in the International Situation

Horiba Kazuo, chief of the war-direction section of the General Staff in 1938 and 1939, wrote afterwards that the beginning of the Pacific War "signified the failure of the Sino-Japanese War."[24] Until the East Asian crisis was merged with the European crisis and Japan was drawn into the vortex of international politics, Japan's military expansionists had been generally successful in preventing open conflict with the Western nations. Their estimates of world affairs had not been very wrong. From late 1938 on, however, the Japanese perceived so many and such vast changes in international affairs that they were led to view the Chinese war as part of the developing global conflict. But they were never able to establish a clear conceptual relationship between the two, with the result that they lost their freedom of choice, which had been emphasized so strongly, and ended up by waging two simultaneous wars and forfeiting the fruits of military expansionism.

[23] Horiba, *op.cit.*, pp. 210-11.   [24] *Ibid.*, p. 40.

A speech made by Vice Chief of Staff Nakajima Tetsurō in April 1939 to the commanders of the army divisions is a good example of the attitude emerging at this time. Because of rapid developments in Europe, he said, the world could expect a radical transformation in 1941 or 1942. Japan, therefore, must build up sufficient strength to be able to adjust herself to this situation. Then he solemnly declared: "Our nation faces two great tasks: the settlement of the China incident, and military preparedness to enable the nation to adjust itself to the impending changes in international relations. Both these objectives must be pursued simultaneously." Since the war in China and the general development of the international situation were intimately linked, he said, Japan must adapt her strategy in China accordingly.[25] Such remarks revealed concern and fascination with the developing tension in the world. Instead of isolating the nation from this tension, there was now a readiness to consider deeper involvement in world affairs. How the Chinese war could be related to world affairs was the big question about which much was spoken but little was settled.

Some saw in changing world conditions an opportunity to settle the Sino-Japanese War speedily. A General Staff memorandum of May 1939 pointed out that "it should be rather easy, in view of developments abroad and inside China, to seize an opportunity" to seek third-power mediation in the war. Germany and Italy could be utilized in this connection, the paper noted, although it might be more advantageous to turn first to the United States. If an Axis alliance was concluded, "our European policy and East Asian policy could be linked and settled simultaneously."[26] As seen here, the idea of a German alliance was the link by which a growing number of army leaders came to relate the Chinese war to the European crisis. According to a paper written by the Supreme Headquarters' army division in the same month, an Axis alliance would serve to terminate the Sino-Japanese War by means of the

[25] *GS*, IX, 559-60.   [26] *Ibid.*, pp. 561-62.

German and Italian diversion of British and French resources.[27]

There was, however, another way in which the Japanese perception of the European crisis established a connection between it and the Chinese war. The Japanese were now less sensitive to the danger of their involvement with Western nations before the Chinese war was settled. They saw the Chinese war as only a prelude to the impending world war, and thus it seemed less important to keep the two separate. Put in another way, military expansionists were now less reluctant to undertake forceful action elsewhere, even before the goals of the first undertaking on the continent of Asia had been achieved. The General Staff memorandum mentioned above declared that "the defeat of the Soviet Union and Britain is the basic strategic goal in the next world war." It was hoped that such warfare would not come until 1942 or 1943, when the nation would be better prepared, and that a German alliance would restrain Russia, Britain, and France, and serve to postpone the outbreak of the war. But even if war should come before 1942, the alliance would be of use in curtailing British assistance to China and enabling Japan to push either northward or southward. As is evident in such thinking, the army was not necessarily visualizing conflict with Britain or Russia as a sequel to the Chinese war. Instead, conflict with Britain was envisaged as a distinct possibility as part of the global conflagration, which was seen as likely to develop, not out of the Sino-Japanese War, but from changes in European politics.

Curiously enough, even those who came to talk of armed conflict with Britain and France remained quiescent about Japanese-American relations. It was still considered possible to maintain normal relations between the two countries. For one thing, the faith that there was no cause for conflict with the United States in China persisted. Army Minister Itagaki, for instance, asserted that the Soviet Union and Britain were the major obstacles to the successful prosecution of the war in

[27] *GS*, X (Tokyo, 1964), 276-79.

China, implying that the United States would continue to take a neutral attitude.[28] At the same time, it was well known that the administration and development of the Japanese-occupied areas in China depended upon the supply of raw materials and machinery from the United States.[29] To some spokesmen at least, such a fact provided evidence why the two nations could and should cooperate economically. At any event, economic sanctions were "a matter of degree," as an operations-section memorandum noted. Unless and until America resolved to go to war against Japan to help China, it was thought unlikely that America would resort to total economic sanctions.[30] To such optimism, which went back to the early part of the 1930's, the army added the belief that the global war which it was visualizing would find the United States uninvolved. Even in the event of the Axis powers' fighting against Britain, France, and the Soviet Union, conflict with America was envisaged only as a remote possibility—a conflict which Japan's pan-Asianism dictated but which its military leaders relegated to the realm of the distant future. "The United States does not seem positive about entering the world war," stated Itagaki. Japan's alliance with Germany, far from inviting American retaliation, could probably guarantee continued American aloofness from European politics.[31] To make doubly certain that this was the case, the army suggested from time to time that America be informed that it was not an object of the contemplated German alliance.[32]

Here we see the beginning of the wishful thinking that was to characterize the Japanese military attitude toward the United States until December 1941. Perception and reality began to diverge rapidly as the military sought to conceptualize the way in which the East Asian conflict was related to the European crisis and postulate Japan's own involvement in affairs beyond East Asia. It should have been clear to them that the United

---

[28] *Ibid.*, p. 270.
[30] *GS*, X, 278.
[32] *Ibid.*, p. 208.

[29] *GS*, IX, xxxii-xxxvii.
[31] *Ibid.*, pp. 270-71.

States was also starting to involve herself in the European crisis and was becoming extremely sensitive to possible connections between German aggressiveness and Japanese expansionism. Despite the continued stance of neutrality and isolation, American public opinion was turning decisively against these two countries, and policy makers were taking certain steps to work out coordinate responses with China and Great Britain. Global strategy was evolving. A new meaning was given to the East Asian crisis; the Sino-Japanese conflict was no longer a war between two belligerents but part of the global crisis involving democratic and peace-loving countries on one hand and aggressive totalitarian states on the other. Starting with the embargo of airplanes to Japan in July 1938, the American government gradually increased its pressure on Japan and assistance to China. A climax was reached in July 1939 when Washington announced the intention to abrogate the Japanese-American commercial treaty as of January 1940.

These moves made little practical impression on Japan's military expansionists. A July 13, 1939, memorandum from the General Staff insisted that economic cooperation with the United States would serve to strengthen ties between the two countries so that the Chinese Nationalists would be impressed by the futility of further resisting Japan.[33] This was two weeks before America's notification of the abrogation of the commercial treaty. Not to be daunted even by this evidence of American policy, an army memo of August 1, confidently stated, "We must try to guide developing circumstances with a view ultimately to having the United States cooperate with us and contribute to the settlement of the [China] incident."[34] It can be seen that in the Japanese view the result of the globalization of the East Asian crisis was merely the production of the illusion that America would help Japan settle the Chinese war. Such a view was given impetus by the failure of a German alliance to materialize. The army's immediate response to the

[33] *GS*, IX, 568-69.   [34] *Ibid.*, p. 570.

conclusion of the Nazi-Soviet pact was to stress, once again, the policy of "cooperation with all the powers" rather than reliance on an Axis alliance to solve the Asian crisis. Although war with the Soviet Union and Great Britain could still be visualized, this was likely to be postponed for a number of years. Instead, it seemed possible that a "moral" alliance with Germany and Italy, economic cooperation with Britain and the United States, or a border agreement with Russia might be achieved.[35]

With the outbreak of war in Europe, the Japanese army talked once again of "the new international situation" and of the need to adjust national strategy accordingly, but the illusion persisted that the Chinese war could be ended without further foreign complications. A memorandum of October 30, written by the war-direction section of the General Staff, postulated seven possible courses of action open to the Japanese military, all but one of which envisaged a settlement of the Sino-Japanese War on the basis of the "merging," under Japanese encouragement, of the Chiang Kai-shek and Wang Ching-wei factions. Only the seventh alternative was the continuation and expansion of the war as part of the developing international crisis. As for the larger implications of the European war, the memorandum asserted, "We must try to adjust ourselves to the new situation, rearrange our international relations so as to settle the [China] incident, utilize the powers' mutual jealousies, and in particular induce Britain, the Soviet Union, and others to limit their assistance to Chungking and instead cooperate with us in settling the war."[36] The army's view of Japanese-American relations also remained basically unchanged. It generally supported the Foreign Ministry's effort to improve relations with the United States by protecting American rights in China and negotiating a new commercial treaty.[37]

Obviously, with the United States slowly but unmistakably shaking herself loose from her neutrality and persisting in her

[35] *Ibid.*, pp. 574-75. [36] Horiba, *op.cit.*, pp. 309-10.
[37] *TSM*, V (Tokyo, 1963), 163-64.

refusal to recognize the fruits of Japanese expansionism, such an attitude contributed to the further widening of the gap between perception and reality.

Southern Expansion and Japanese-American Relations

By the end of 1939, then, the Japanese picture of the international system was at variance with reality. Japan's continental expansionists envisaged a world which tolerated their action so long as they did not openly challenge the status quo outside of China. Changes in the international situation, far from altering the basic orientation of this thinking, served to reinforce the conviction that conditions were favorable to the speedy conclusion of the Chinese war. The inability to visualize Japanese-American relations in a state of crisis epitomized the illusion.

Even so, had the expansionists continued to confine their action to China, open conflict with the Anglo-American nations would have been postponed indefinitely. The war with China would have dragged on, but a simultaneous war with a group of Western powers would not have developed. That this was in fact what happened was due to a conscious decision to widen the sphere of Japanese expansion to include Southeast Asia. More fundamental than this decision, however, was the image of a world which tolerated such expansionism. This image was in turn related to the geopolitical notion of the world as divided into a few "pan-regions." The dream of pan-Asianism was to be put into effect, since the time seemed to be approaching when Asia would in fact be rid of Western influence and left to Asians under Japanese hegemony. Whereas the peaceful expansionists of the 1920's had envisaged an economically interdependent, open international society and failed to promote their goals, the military expansionists of the 1930's visualized a divided world, which they felt was emerging and which would best serve Japan's interests.

The trouble, of course, was that the Western nations, in particular Britain and the United States, did not accept such a definition of the situation. For them Asia was not synonymous with Asians, but was an arena for a global struggle between freedom and dictatorship, the outcome of which was of the utmost importance for the future of mankind. These Western powers would not acquiesce in a Japanese hegemony any more than they would tolerate a German conquest of Europe. The United States would deepen its commitment to the maintenance of the status quo in Southeast Asia, and the status quo was based on the continued presence of Western rights and interests. Far from countenancing what the Japanese took to be the trend toward regional autonomy, America would keep Southeast Asia tied to the rest of the world, and the United States itself would become an Asian power to keep Japan from speaking for all Asians.

Some of this was well recognized by Japan's policy makers and military strategists, and the possibility of war with the United States kept them from undertaking expansion into southern Indochina until the summer of 1941. What is notable is the way in which considerations of southern expansion affected the course of war in China. It was a great tragedy that certain images about the Chinese war and the powers' responses to it had become fixed and that deliberations on policy toward Southeast Asia were therefore conducted with little regard to the Chinese situation. In other words, the view persisted that the powers would tolerate Japanese action in China. Because of this, the southern expansion tended to be considered on its own merit; Japan would undertake it as soon as international conditions were favorable, while the Chinese war would settle itself sooner or later. This assumption was a fundamental flaw since China would have been part of the new Asian order the Japanese were trying to create, and if some Western powers opposed the scheme, there was no reason why they should not have disapproved of Japanese action in China itself. Through a process of feed-back, Western support of China increased the more the Japanese threatened to invade Southeast Asia. Thus, in the final analysis, a failure to establish a clear conceptual connection between the war in China and the premeditated expansion southward was at the root of the failure of Japan's military expansionism.

In considering southern expansion, the military believed either that the war in China would somehow be settled before the thrust southward was undertaken, or that the invasion of Southeast Asia would not interfere with the prosecution of the Chinese war. The navy on the whole took the second position, while the army fluctuated between the two, but in either case complacency *vis-à-vis* China persisted until 1941.

It was the navy, of course, that had been most eager for southern expansion. Japan's basic naval strategy, as the Navy Ministry noted in 1935, was "to control the western Pacific, protect the lines of communication at sea that are necessary for national existence and expansion, and become the stabilizing force in East Asia."[38] Such a policy dictated the primacy of a southern orientation in military strategy, with the implication that the United States and Great Britain, rather than China and the Soviet Union, would be the likely enemies. In the mid-1930's, with the naval disarmament treaties abrogated and the army intent upon extending its sphere of influence into northern China, the navy began stressing the need for a southern advance and preparedness against the United States.[39] It should be noted that the navy distinguished Japan's involvement on the continent of Asia from naval conflict in the South Seas and that war with the United States was postulated only in connection with this second eventuality. The Sino-Japanese War did not change this orientation. The navy, like the army, was convinced that the war could be terminated speedily.

It was in the spring of 1940, after the successful German offensive, that the navy came to visualize the southern advance as a strategic goal for the near future. The war in China was far from being over, but the navy showed a readiness to consider action which could lead to simultaneous wars with America and China. "The time for action has finally come," declared

---

[38] *GS*, XII (Tokyo, 1965), p. 86.
[39] *TSM*, VI (Tokyo, 1963), 148-50.

an exponent of southern expansionism. "Japan must once again become a maritime nation and expand its navy, not hesitating to go to war with England and America."[40] The opportunity seemed to have arrived to seize Indochina and then other areas in Southeast Asia so as to establish Japanese hegemony in the area, which would give the nation strategic advantages in the anticipated conflict with the British and American navies.[41] From this time on the navy became so preoccupied with Southeast Asia, Britain, and the United States that one finds less and less reference to the question of China by naval spokesmen.

Army strategists kept China very much on their minds, but they, too, became infected with an urge to expand southward. Intelligence officers were dispatched to Southeast Asia in June 1940, and a southern section was created within the intelligence division of the General Staff.[42] The problem of the relationship between continental and southern expansion remained, but generally speaking in 1940 and well into 1941 the army continued to believe that the southern advance would be undertaken after the Chinese war had been settled, or at least in such a way as to hasten that eventuality. In a famous decision, made on May 18, 1940, the General Staff and the War Ministry agreed that the war in China should be brought to a conclusion by the end of the year. The basic motive behind this decision was the increasing interest in expansion in the South Seas—the "long-term war" in the army's jargon.[43] Germany's successful campaigns in May and June strengthened the conviction that Japan must quickly settle the Chinese war in order to expand southward. In July, in drafting the basic military policy for the new Konoe Cabinet, the army supreme command asserted that Japan "should quickly settle the China incident and then, improving conditions both domestic and external, seize an oppor-

[40] *TSM*, VII (Tokyo, 1963), 16ff.

[41] *GS*, X, 369-71.

[42] Tanemura Sakō, *Daihonei kimitsu nisshi* [Secret Diary of the Imperial Headquarters] (Tokyo, 1952), pp. 14-15.

[43] *GS*, IX, 594-95.

tune moment to solve the southern question."[44] When, around this time, the crucial "Basic Principles for Coping with the Changing International Situation" were drawn up, the army asserted time and again that it was "logical" first to finish the Chinese war and then strike southward. However, the southern advance might be undertaken even before the settlement of the war if a favorable opportunity presented itself, such as a German invasion of the British Isles.[45] It was difficult to pass up what appeared to be an impending and spectacular opportunity for expansion southward. All the same, the army was hopeful that this would not cause prolongation and deterioration of the conflict with China. A strategic plan for Southeast Asia drafted by the operations section of the General Staff noted the desirability of at least maintaining the status quo in China as a precondition for launching military action in the south.[46] At the very least, it was argued that Japanese control over French Indochina and the British colonies would cut off Chungking's only supply routes and serve to bring the latter more easily to its knees.[47]

What is notable about these arguments is the army's continued optimism about settling the Sino-Japanese War without incurring the intervention of a third power. This can best be seen in the persisting belief that war with America was unlikely in the near future. The army insisted that in the event of a southern advance the initial attack should be upon the European colonies. As for the United States, "it was best not to provoke her at first . . . but expel her from East Asia after several years," according to an army memorandum written in the summer of 1940.[48] It seemed possible to avoid war with America so long as Japan confined her assault to the European colonies. In a series of memoranda written by General Koiso Kuniaki, who had

[44] *TSM*, VIII, 316-17. See also *Sugiyama memo* [Sugiyama Memorandum], I (Tokyo, 1967), 50.

[45] *GS*, X, 507. The text of "Sekai jōsei no suii ni tomonou jikyoku shori yōkō" (July 22, 1940) is printed in *TSM*, VIII, 322-23.

[46] *TSM*, VI, 178.   [47] *TSM*, VII, 41.   [48] *GS*, X, 507.

just resigned as minister of colonial affairs, it was noted that the time had come to expand the Japanese-Manchukuo-Chinese block to embrace Southeast Asia, but that the United States would not resist such an attempt by force if Japan guaranteed the security of the Philippines.[49] Such a view is remarkable for its extreme optimism which saw no open conflict with America as a result of the Sino-Japanese War even as late as 1940.

The navy, of course, was constantly aware of the possibility of war with the United States, but only as a corollary of the southern advance and not of the war in China. In a memorandum of August 1, 1940, the Navy General Staff warned that the Japanese occupation of French Indochina could bring about an American embargo on scrap iron and oil. Their supply was "a matter of life and death" for Japan. Whether Japan could prevent or overcome such an embargo was the crucial question which must be faced before the nation undertook southern expansion by force. As can be seen here, from the Japanese navy's point of view the timing of the southern advance depended ultimately on American behavior.[50] A memorandum of August 27 pointed out that forceful action should be undertaken by Japan in one of three foreseeable circumstances: a total embargo by the United States, actual or anticipated cooperation between America and Britain to defend their mutual territories and interests in the Pacific, or steps taken by either of these countries to threaten the existence of the Japanese empire directly. These three possibilities dictated Japanese response regardless of whether or not Japan was ready. On the other hand, there was a chance that the European conflict would so tie Britain and America down that Japan would enjoy freedom of action in Southeast Asia. In such an event the nation should take the initiative to use force. This memorandum made it clear that in the Japanese navy's view the southern advance was synonymous with actual or premeditated hostilities with the United States.[51] It is also evident that for the navy the question of

[49] *Ibid.*, pp. 466ff.   [50] *Ibid.*, pp. 369-71.   [51] *Ibid.*, pp. 497ff.

China was not immediately relevant. The memorandum did not once raise the question of the relationship between the Chinese war and the anticipated war in Southeast Asia.[52]

While both the army and navy supported the Axis alliance, concluded in September, and the expedition to northern Indo-china, executed in the same month, their differences remained. The army supreme command viewed the southern advance favorably because no war with America was envisaged as a result and because it did not seem to inhibit the ending of the Sino-Japanese War. The navy was not concerned with termi-nating the Chinese war as a major goal, but it hesitated to undertake military action in Southeast Asia for fear of Amer-ican retaliation. "Developments from now on," said the chief of the operations division of the Navy General Staff, "depend on when the United States completes its strategic mobilization in East Asia, and on whether or not at that point it carries out a total embargo *vis-à-vis* Japan."[53] This embargo, it may be pointed out, was visualized by the Japanese navy as an Ameri-can weapon to restrain Japan's southern advance and otherwise prevent her naval expansion; the embargo was not something the United States was expected to resort to in retaliation against Japanese policy in China. Although the United States had al-ready adopted a policy of limited economic sanctions in con-nection with the violation of American rights in China, the navy anticipated the embargo of the crucial item, fuel oil, only in the event of an actual or impending clash between Japan and America in the Pacific and the South Seas. For the navy, then, the primary concern was with the war against the Euro-pean colonies and the United States, whereas the army was concerned with the war that was going on in China and an-other that might or might not develop as a result of an advance southward. The army leadership was still confident, at the end of 1940, that war with the United States could be avoided, since neither the Chinese war nor the premeditated thrust southward

[52] See *Sugiyama memo*, I, 45.   [53] *TSM*, VII, 87.

seemed a *causa belli*, so long as Japan refrained from attacking American territories and possessions. For the navy, on the contrary, the southward advance and war with America were aspects of the same situation: they expected either both or neither.

Two Roads to Pearl Harbor

Thus there were in fact two roads to Pearl Harbor. Without going into the details of decision-making in 1941, it may be pointed out that the Japanese navy's road to war with America was a much simpler one than the army's. As early as 1940, the navy had postulated the possibility of conflict with the United States the moment the latter undertook severe economic sanctions, especially an embargo of oil, against Japan. Assuming that such a course of events was a logical possibility, the naval strategists of the section-chief level pushed ahead with specific mobilization and tactical planning. A long memorandum, which they wrote on June 5 and for which they subsequently obtained the approval of the navy minister and the chief of naval operations, asserted that Japan must immediately resolve on "war (including the United States)." This was not the same thing as an attack on American territory; rather, the writers urged military preparedness against the United States under the assumption that war was imminent. One of the specific steps recommended was the speedy occupation of Indochina and Thailand. This was particularly crucial since Japanese inaction might invite American and British advances into this area, a possibility which seemed likely in the event of America's forceful intervention in the European war. French Indochina and Thailand, the memorandum noted, "lie between the spheres of influence of Japan and the Anglo-American nations." In order to remove a threat to the Japanese empire, and as a first step toward building up a self-sufficient imperial bloc, the occupation of these countries seemed amply justified. This did not necessarily mean that there would be war between Japan and the United States—unless the latter embargoed the export of oil to Japan.[54] The risk, however, was always there, and from the navy's point of view Japan's decision to send troops to southern Indochina and America's immediate economic retaliation, in the summer of 1941, merely confirmed the logic of events.

As earlier, the navy's attitude toward the Chinese war was ambiguous and not related to strategy in Southeast Asia and Japanese-American relations. The above memorandum tried to argue that the occupation of southern Indochina and Thailand would help prosecute the Chinese war. It was also pointed out that the third powers' assistance to Chungking must be completely stopped and drastic measures, such as the declaration of war, must be taken to destroy China's will power decisively. At the same time, the memorandum supported the Hull-Nomura conversations only if they brought about a truce in China through American good offices. While the United States was recognized as an obstacle to the prosecution of the war in China, the navy did not envisage open hostilities with America on account of China. It continued to distinguish between the Sino-Japanese War and the southern advance and failed to time the latter in accordance with the progress of the former war. It was willing to consider the use of force in Southeast Asia irrespective of the course of the Hull-Nomura conversations.

The Japanese army's road to war against the United States was a much more tortuous one. Before 1941 it had not anticipated such a war as a result of either the southern advance or the Sino-Japanese War. By the spring of 1941, however, army planners had become persuaded that Japan's thrust southward might invite hostilities with the United States and that in the event of an American war Japan was quite unprepared militarily and materially. An Army Ministry study, completed on March 25, decisively concluded that Japan must avoid irritating Britain and the United States unnecessarily and should instead step up her preparedness by obtaining military resources from

[54] *TSM*, VIII, 427ff.

the Anglo-American bloc.[55] This was tantamount to scrapping the 1940 decision to take advantage of the European war by advancing southward. Instead, the army confirmed its intention of giving top priority to a successful termination of the war in China. Ironically, it was then that the prospect of conflict with the United States began to loom large in connection with the Sino-Japanese War.

In the middle of May, Ishwara Kanji gave a series of lectures at Ritsumeikan University. He reiterated his decade-long conviction that a Japanese-American war would come when Japan completed "the union of East Asia." He predicted the imminence of a global war, which would prove to be the last war humanity would have to face since it would be a war between East and West. This war, however, would come *after* the Sino-Japanese War was concluded. Japan must first finish the Chinese war and establish a pan-Asian union and then take on the ultimate adversary, the United States.[56] In such a view, typical of army thinking up to that point, no war with America was visualized as part of the war with China.

It was this optimism, coupled with pessimism about the possibility of terminating the Sino-Japanese War quickly, that finally reoriented the army's thinking. There was general agreement that the Chinese war must be settled first; in the meantime, friction with others, especially the United States, should be avoided. When such ideas were contrasted to the reality of a seemingly never-ending conflict on the Chinese mainland, it was natural that the Japanese army should have seriously entertained the possibility of settling the Chinese war through American good offices. If the United States could be induced to mediate between Japan and China, this would in fact be killing two birds with one stone. The long sought-after

[55] Hattori Takushirō, *Dai-tōa sensō zenshi* [Complete History of the Great East Asia War], new ed. (Tokyo, 1965), p. 52; *Sugiyama memo*, I, 82ff.

[56] Ishiwara Kanji, *Kokubōron* [On National Defense] (Tokyo, 1941), p. 94.

objective of terminating the Chinese war would be obtained, and the final showdown with the United States would be postponed while Japan reconstructed her preparedness program. At bottom, of course, was the by then long-established conviction that there was no basic conflict between Japan and America in China. It was believed that the United States would welcome the role of mediator if this would put an end to the East Asian crisis, even if it meant accepting certain Japanese terms for settlement, in particular the independence of Manchukuo.[57] Thus emerged what Satō Kenryō has decried as the spirit of reliance upon America to settle the China incident, reflecting the inability of the Japanese army to do so by itself.[58]

Because so much was expected of American mediation, the sense of disappointment and bitterness was profound when it became known that the United States had no interest in expediting the conclusion of the Sino-Japanese War on Japanese terms. Part of the Japanese-American difference was, of course, due to the stiff attitude of Foreign Minister Matsuoka Yōsuke, who went far beyond the army in presenting inflexible terms to the State Department. All the same, the tone and content of the American note of June 21, communicated in anticipation of the German invasion of Russia, were such as to shake the army from its short-lived delusion that peace could be restored in China through America's good offices.[59] Moreover, for the first time, the United States began to appear as the obstacle in the way of terminating the Chinese war. Since the settlement of the war was still the army's chief concern, this new evaluation of the United States meant that Japan would have to be prepared either to fight against America in order to subjugate Chungking or to find some *modus vivendi* with the United States in China in order to avoid such an eventuality. Thus for the first time Japanese-Chinese relations and Japanese-Ameri-

[57] Hattori, *op.cit.*, p. 62.

[58] Satō Kenryō, *Tōjō Hideki to Taiheiō sensō* [Tōjō Hideki and the Pacific War] (Tokyo, 1960), p. 2.

[59] Hattori, *op.cit.*, pp. 68-70.

can relations were related in army thinking. These two sets of relations would either simultaneously deteriorate or simultaneously improve. In the former instance, concurrent war against China and America had to be envisaged.

From the army's point of view, the decision to occupy southern Indochina was more an aspect of the Chinese war than the beginning of a southern advance. As Chief of Staff Sugiyama Gen stated at the crucial imperial conference of July 2: "It is extremely important at the present juncture to increase our direct pressure upon the Chungking regime and at the same time to advance southward in order to sever the link between the Chungking regime and Anglo-American power which is supporting it from behind and is instrumental in increasing Chungking's will to resist. The sending of troops to southern Indochina has been prompted by these considerations."[60] It is revealing to contrast such an explanation with that given by Naval Chief of Staff Nagano Osami, who talked about the establishment of a self-sufficient imperial system as the reason for the decision. Neither army nor navy expected an immediate American reprisal; in their view the occupation of southern Indochina did not seem likely to provoke American retaliation so long as other areas in Southeast Asia were not touched. When, nevertheless, the United States responded by freezing Japanese assets and imposing an embargo on oil export, the navy took the logical step of preparing for war in the immediate future. The army agreed.[61]

That war did not come until December was primarily due to the efforts of the nonmilitary, including Prime Minister Konoe Fumimaro and the emperor himself, to try to avoid an open clash with the United States. But it should also be noted that the army never lost sight of the war which was going on in China. It still preferred to settle that war somehow before another war began. Besides, after Hitler's invasion of the Soviet Union, the army once again had to consider possible action in

[60] *Ibid.*, pp. 83-84.   [61] *Ibid.*, p. 97.

the north. If negotiation with the United States could solve the Chinese question, the army would be able to reorient its strategy to cope with the developing international situation. By the same token, no temporary agreement with America was feasible which did not explicitly settle the question of China. This was why War Minister Tōjō Hideki balked at Konoe's effort at peace and why the Hull note of November 26 was considered a war message. The settlement of the Chinese war by Japan's complete evacuation not only from China proper but also from Manchuria was no settlement at all. Because the army had envisioned a more favorable outcome of the Chinese war, it felt it had no choice but to go to war with the United States. In the words of General Tōjō: "The stationing of troops in China is the heart of the matter. . . . To make concession after concession [to the United States] and to yield on this question is like piercing the heart and tantamount to surrender." If Japan accepted the American terms for peace, "the achievements of the China incident would be nullified, the existence of Manchukuo would be endangered, and our control over Korea would be shaken."[62] Having started the Chinese war, the army was placed in a position where it was impossible not to fight against the United States.

Conclusion

"Lacking the resolution or capacity to choose," Raymond Aaron has written, "Japan ultimately found herself in a war with China, which the Japanese armies vainly attempted to occupy, and with the United States and Great Britain, maritime powers, protecting the islands."[63] While simplistic, the observation correctly refers to the fundamental predicament of Japanese military expansionism in 1941, an inability to concentrate on either continental or southern expansion. Yet it would be misleading to attribute the simultaneous war with China

[62] *Ibid.*, p. 111.

[63] Raymond Aron, *Peace and War: A Theory of International Relations* (New York, 1966), p. 190.

and with America and Britain to Japan's lack of resolution or the capacity to choose. The Japanese image of world affairs was such that, following the changes in the international situation in 1938-39, the time seemed opportune to create a pan-Asian sphere of autonomy, of which Japanese-controlled China would be a foundation.

The decision to go to war with the United States before the end of the Chinese war was made when the Japanese army and navy came to view an impending conflict with America as inevitable. This view in turn was derived from an emerging image of the United States as a power intent upon establishing its influence in China and in Southeast Asia, thereby obstructing Japan's paths of expansion. Having accepted this image, there seemed to be no alternative but to go to war. War against China and war against America were conceptually merged as a struggle for the establishment of a free Asia.

The question is why such a view did not emerge earlier. The navy had postulated war with the United States over Southeast Asia but had separated it conceptually from the Chinese war. The army, too, had believed that the Sino-Japanese War could be solved without war with America. It was only in mid-1941 that such a war came to be visualized over both Southeast Asia and China. Japanese perception, in a sense, approximated the American view of external events. What had caused this development? Why did the army assume, before 1941, that it could settle the war in China without endangering relations with the United States, and, in 1941, that the Chinese war had become part of the larger conflict against the Anglo-American nations? Why did the navy fail to appreciate the American definition of Asia, including closer ties between China and the United States? If on the whole Japan's military expansionists correctly judged the probable responses of the other powers before 1938 and again in 1941, what accounts for the notable gap between perception and reality between the two dates? Was the Japanese inability to maintain a realistic view of the world entirely their fault, or did it reflect rapidly changing conditions defying neat definition?

These questions point up the relevance of external factors in the "dilemmas" of Japanese history in the 1930's. Certainly the proponents of military expansionism were guilty of oversimplification. Just as the architects of peaceful expansionism in the 1920's had failed to conceptualize a realistic model of international relations, the military expansionists of the subsequent decade postulated a world that was tending toward regionalism and closed economic units and they underemphasized the interrelatedness between the Chinese war, the Southeast Asian question, and American policy. The military expansionists' greatest flaw may have been their simplistic image of the 1920's; because peaceful expansionism had failed, they concluded that the whole structure of the postwar peace had been a product of wishful thinking. But they created their own dogmas for the 1930's and believed that the world would tolerate their forceful expansionism. Nothing illustrates this optimism more graphically than the oft repeated assertion that the United States would "understand" Japan's "intentions" as the latter used force to expand into the Asian continent.[64]

The world did tolerate Japanese expansion up to a point. Before 1938 there had been little inclination on the part of other powers to resist Japan's military action with force. It was the outbreak of the European war and the deadly struggle between Germany and Great Britain that involved the United States more and more deeply in the East Asian conflict, as it became more and more determined to prevent Japan from destroying the European empires. Ironically, it was the same "changes in the international situation" with which the Japanese army was so impressed and which made them optimistic about the success of their forceful expansion southward, that drove America to come to the aid of China. Changes in Europe, which were

[64] Honjō Shigeru, *Honjō nikki* [Honjō Diary] (Tokyo, 1967), p. 175.

perceived by the Japanese as an opportunity to settle the Chinese war and plan further acts of expansion, in fact served to entrench American power and influence in East Asia.

Expansion, whether peaceful or forceful, whether territorial or purely economic, had been an essential aspect of modern Japan's "growth." Modernization had been accompanied by expansionism. The problem was that the Japanese had to seek expansion in a world which was making it more and more difficult for them to do so. Having been frustrated by the meager results of peaceful expansionism in the 1920's, the nation tried another alternative, only to find that the avenue of military conquest was similarly closed.

Here certainly was a dilemma for modern Japan, but it was also a dilemma for the modern world. The world was not ready to accommodate Japan's peaceful expansion or to tolerate her military aggression, yet the belief in the imperative need to expand remained. Because the use of force ultimately provoked countermeasures and retaliation, it should not be forgotten that military expansionism was conceived of as an alternative to the more peaceful methods of the 1920's. In both decades the Japanese failed to picture the world as it existed and tended to indulge in an illusion in order to find a legitimate place for their expansionistic urge. The existence and persistence of such an illusion reveals something about the world that gave birth to it. The dilemmas of modern Japan were the world's as well as Japan's. They were an expression not only of the pathology of the modern Japanese mind but also of the inherent contradictions and irrationalities of the modern world.

CHAPTER V

The Radical Left and the Failure of Communism

GEORGE M. BECKMANN

THE history of the Japanese Communist party, especially in the period from its establishment in 1922 to the outbreak of the China incident in 1937, constitutes an important sidelight on the nature of the Japanese imperial system and of intellectual change in a society which, however conservative, was well along in the process of modernization. Japanese Communists were primary agents in the diffusion of Marxism, which became an important influence in Japanese universities and intellectual circles in the 1920's and which was the ideological basis of the first fundamental challenge to the imperial interpretation (*kōkoku shikan*) of Japanese history and modern development. Moreover, it was the major ideological factor in the Japanese student movement of that decade and was an important element in the labor and peasant movements. Yet, as a political force, the Communists could not make any substantial headway against the imperial system and those dominant interests in industry and agriculture that it tended to protect. In its challenge to the prewar power structure, the Japanese Communist party suffered one defeat after another.

Description and analysis of the prewar Japanese Communist party as a revolutionary organization tend to emphasize two major characteristics.[1] The first is the cyclical pattern of the rise and fall of party leadership and organization. There were three major cycles in the life of the party: the first Communist group and party from 1921 to 1924, the second group and party from 1925 to 1929, and the third group and party from 1930 to 1932.

[1] See George M. Beckmann and Okubo Genji, *The Japanese Communist Party, 1922-1945* (Stanford, 1968).

After the latter date, the Communist movement can no longer be considered as one led by an organized political party. Its subsequent history centers around small groups of Communists, rarely united and often in conflict with each other. Each of these cycles had its periods of hope and expectation, defeat and despair, and suppression and destruction. The second major characteristic of the prewar Japanese Communist party is, paradoxically, a kind of continuity that transcends this cyclical pattern. This continuity had its roots in ideology, particularly the strategy of the two-stage revolution, but, perhaps even more, in the undaunted commitment and determination of a small hard core of party leaders who, despite the hardship of long prison terms, refused to join the growing number of Communists and socialists who compromised with Japanese nationalism and state socialism in the 1930's. This continuity factor was to contribute to party strength and cohesion in the immediate postwar years.

The Early Marxist and Anarcho-Syndicalist Movements

The Communist challenge of the 1920's had its origin in the spread of socialist thought in Japan in the first two decades of the century. By 1906, Japanese socialists formed two groups—reformers and revolutionaries. The former were for the most part Christian Social Democrats like Abe Isoo and Katayama Sen. They exuded a kind of Tolstoian humanitarianism and advocated universal suffrage and social reform through parliamentary action. The revolutionaries were materialists who derived their ideas from German and French Marxist and anarcho-syndicalist sources. Their number included Kōtoku Shūsui, intellectual leader of the group, Sakai Toshihiko, one of the first systematic students of Marxism, and younger men like Yamakawa Hitoshi, Arahata Kanson, and Ōsugi Sakae. They sought to popularize the ideas of class struggle and direct revolutionary action by class-conscious workers. In November 1904, Kōtuku and Sakai had published Marx and Engel's *Communist Manifesto* in *Commoners' News* only to have the police immediately ban the issue. While the revolutionary socialists based their strategy on Marxist principles like class struggle, they were at the same time attracted to the tactics of anarcho-syndicalism.

The revolutionary socialists believed that the abolition of the state, the destruction of capitalism, and the formation of a free society could only be achieved by the direct action of organized workers. For the most part, they rejected action in the political field, affirming that efforts to gain universal suffrage and seek reform through the Diet were a waste of time. They insisted that the Diet would forever be the tool of the propertied class, explaining that if the hope of democracy ever became more than a delusion deceiving the people, the propertied class would use all the force and influence that comes from the possession of wealth to reduce the government to the simple function of acting as a policeman. Moreover, as anarchists, they regarded Japanese Social Democrats as corrupted by political power since they accepted the premises of the bourgeois state. In their view, the weapons of labor, the force to bring about the rejuvenation of society, were direct negotiations with employers and strikes, especially the general strike. The latter was to be the instrument for compelling the bourgeois state to abandon its place on the historical stage to the voluntary associations of the wage-earning class. The general strike would supersede all pragmatic shortrun strikes because it was part of the permanent revolutionary process. The revolutionary socialists recognized that syndicalism departed from strict anarchism in its utilization of the labor union as a necessary organizational form. In brief, anarcho-syndicalism was attractive to them, as it was to radical socialists in Europe and the United States, because it appeared to provide the shortcut to socialism. Moreover, it seemed suited to the Japanese scene where the gradual approach of the Social Democrats was making little if any headway in the face of a repressive regime. They felt that the spontaneous labor riots of 1906 and 1907 confirmed their judgment.

While Japan's socialists can be divided into two main camps, there are some dangers in such a classification, especially when characterizing particular individuals. Kōtoku and Katayama present no major problem of this kind. The former was impatient with the parliamentarianism of the Social Democrats and looked to anarcho-syndicalism's direct action by the workers. The latter, who espoused the parliamentary tactics of social democracy, was unequivocal in his condemnation of anarcho-syndicalism as a dangerous doctrine. Yamakawa, however, though strongly influenced by the ideas of Kōtoku, upheld political action as a means of developing class consciousness among workers. Tazoe Tetsuji, close to Katayama, made the strongest arguments for a parliamentary policy, criticizing direct action as woefully ineffective. Sakai, hoping to effect a compromise, advocated a combination of direct action and parliamentarianism. Classification also tends to obscure the extent to which individuals in both camps increasingly utilized Marxist ideas to support their arguments. Kōtoku and Katayama both believed that the degeneration of the working class was an inevitable result of capitalism, but Kōtoku held that the emancipation of the proletariat was contingent upon the destruction of capitalism, while Katayama believed that it could be achieved through reform. Both felt that Marxism provided a theoretical framework for analyzing existing conditions in Japanese society and for determining the general principles of strategy for the socialist movement, but not its tactics. Even Sakai, who had perhaps the deepest knowledge of Marxism of all the early Japanese socialists, could not find in it the basis for revolutionary tactics. Such an insight came only after the Russian Revolution and the popularization of Leninism in Japan.

Japan's socialists, reformers and revolutionaries alike, made little progress against the power of the Japanese state and the forces that it represented. They continued to be denied the right to organize labor and to form political organizations. Whenever they attempted to act, even if only to disseminate ideas, they suffered suppression by the state. Suppression reached its climax in 1910 when Kōtoku and his followers were arrested and charged with plotting to assassinate the Meiji emperor, the members of his family, and the ministers of state. They were quickly tried and convicted of treason without the right of appeal to a higher court. Twelve of them, including Kōtoku, were executed within three days of sentencing in January 1911, and another twelve were condemned to life in prison. Whether Kōtoku was actively involved in the plot or whether he was the victim of a government frame-up has never been resolved. In any event, Sakai, Yamakawa, Arahata, and Ōsugi escaped death only because they were already in jail. Yet, despite all kinds of difficulties, a small number of anarcho-syndicalists continued to be active and managed to keep the socialist movement alive.

Ōsugi, Arahata, and Sakai, after completing their prison terms, lay low for a while but soon resumed publishing journals in order to spread socialist ideas. Yamakawa rejoined them in 1916. These four men played key roles in continuing the development of revolutionary socialism in Japan. At first all four were devoted to the cause of anarcho-syndicalism with its emphasis on direct action by workers instead of politicians and were instrumental in its gaining a prominent position in the revival of the labor and socialist movements that began near the end of World War I. Of the four, however, three—Sakai, Yamakawa, and Arahata—were converted to Marxism-Leninism, popularized its tenets, and were leaders of the Japanese Communist party established in 1922. Ōsugi was the only one of the four to resist the Communist tide; he adhered to anarcho-syndicalism until his brutal murder by the military police in 1923.

The Appeal of Marxism-Leninism

The Russian Revolution marked the beginning of the decline of anarcho-syndicalism in Japan, although this was not clear at the time. Japan's revolutionary socialists initially explained Lenin's triumph as a victory for anarchism. Yamakawa wrote to this effect in *Shin Shakai* (New Society), and he joined with

Arahata in April 1918 to form the Labor Union Study Group and to publish *Aofuku* (Blue Uniform) in order to popularize anarcho-syndicalism. The police banned their organ in July. Later, in 1919, with Sakai, they became champions of Communism, although they could not completely divorce themselves from their anarcho-syndicalist backgrounds, especially in their opposition to the universal suffrage movement. As they studied developments in Russia in order to grasp "the realities of socialism," they began to realize that Russian communism was something very different from anarcho-syndicalism. They came to believe that communism, as the foundation of the successful Russian Revolution, would provide more practical guidelines for achieving the socialist transformation of Japanese society. As yet, however, they were hardly conscious of the theoretical and organizational contributions of Lenin. The first article in Japan on Lenin's theories was "The Political Movement and the Economic Movement" by Takabatake Motoyuki in the February 1918 issue of *Shin Shakai*. Takabatake was the first Japanese to use the term "bolshevism." Although he later shifted to the camp of national socialism, he made another important contribution to the Japanese understanding of Marxism with his complete translation of *Das Kapital*, begun in 1919 and completed in 1924.

From 1919 on, Sakai, Yamakawa, and Arahata spread revolutionary Marxist, or Bolshevist, ideas, especially among university students and to a much lesser extent among Japan's new labor leaders. The success of the Russian Revolution and the consolidation of Soviet power gave them a larger and more receptive audience. They continued to publish *Shin Shakai* and declared their conversion to bolshevism in the May 1919 issue. Later, in February 1920, they changed the name of the journal to *Shin Shakai Hyōron* (New Social Review) and began writing on the problems of Japanese society. They also published the more theoretical *Shakaishugi Kenkyū* (Studies in Socialism) from April 1919 on. Arahata who based himself in Osaka after the spring of 1920, took over the editing of *Nihon*

Rōdō Shinbun (Japan Labor News), a monthly to which Sakai and Yamakawa also contributed articles. These journals also included articles on the Soviet Union and on the emerging international Communist movement. For example, the July 1920 issue of *Shin Shakai Hyōron* contained a report on the establishment of the Third International, based on material provided by Katayama's socialist group in the United States; and the issue of *Shakaishugi Kenkyū* for the same month had a long article on the Soviet Union, explaining the consolidation of the dictatorship of the proletariat. Sakai, Yamakawa, and Arahata formed study groups—Sakai, the Friday Society; Yamakawa, the Wednesday Society; and Arahata, the Labor and Liberty Society. They were also active as lecturers among student and labor groups, although they had to contend regularly with police interference. By 1920 it is appropriate to speak of them as Communists.

Marxism was, of course, popularized by others as well, especially in university circles. One of its most prominent promoters was Professor Kawakami Hajime of Kyoto Imperial University, who began publishing *Shakai Mondai Kenkyū* (Studies on Social Questions) in January 1919 and who wrote many treatises on Marxism. Marxist ideas were also spread by new magazines like *Kaizō* (Reconstruction) and *Kaihō* (Emancipation) both of which began publication in 1919.

Sakai, Yamakawa, and Arahata were assisted in their efforts by Katayama Sen, who had been converted to communism in the United States. Katayama had entered Communist circles in New York in 1916, and, through contact with S. J. Rutgers, had met Trotsky, Bukharin, and other Russian revolutionaries. Under their influence, he gave up his belief that socialism could be achieved in Japan under the existing political system and called for revolution. The success of the Russian Revolution strengthened his commitment to communism; he saw in it the means to "liberate the oppressed masses of Japan." While his understanding of Marxism-Leninism was always very elementary, he made up for his weakness in theory with his dedication. He organized the Communist-oriented League of Japanese Socialists in America, composed largely of university students or recent graduates and vagabonds. Under Katayama's leadership, the socialist group was dedicated to assist in the establishment of an American Communist party, to work for the formation of a Japanese Communist party, and to support the objectives of the international Communist movement. To help achieve the second part of that program, Katayama sent information on communism to his old socialist comrades-in-arms in Japan in return for news of home. And in May 1919 he dispatched Kondō Eizō to Japan in order to establish direct contact with Sakai and Yamakawa, as well as Ōsugi and his followers, and to work for the establishment of a Japanese Communist party.

The timing was propitious because the Japanese modernization process, especially industrialization and urbanization, was creating new demands for fundamental changes in society. Intellectuals and emerging labor leaders called for universal suffrage as a means to achieve a balance between imperial sovereignty, party government, and democratic rights, and they called for checks on the abuses of capitalism through recognition of labor's right to organize, bargain, and strike. Some among them envisaged a revolutionary reconstruction of Japanese society. They were encouraged by the growing popular discontent which appeared to be symptomatic of a deep and widespread unrest among the Japanese people, especially the urban labor force. A few saw the Rice Riots of 1918 and the more frequent and violent strikes as foreshadowing revolution.

Japan's revolutionary intellectuals, mostly university students or recent graduates and young self-educated labor leaders, were motivated by strong humanitarian feelings and a sense of justice. They wanted a thorough reform of Japanese society for the benefit of all the people. They yearned to go beyond the objectives of liberals like Yoshino Sakuzō and of Social Democrats like Abe Isoo. They developed a sense of mission that exuded the energy and enthusiasm of youth. They were determined to build "a new, more rational society in Japan." Marxism was attractive to them because it provided the fullest explanation of the idea of progress that they had yet encountered. They were easily seduced by the Marxist proposition that through the dialectic progress was inevitable. Dialectical materialism gave them a scientific methodology for analyzing Japanese society, as well as general principles of strategy for effecting change. It explained the transition from feudalism to capitalism and from capitalism to socialism. Marxism, moreover, satisfied their desire to catch up and surpass the Western nations. These young intellectuals were emotionally challenged by the possibility of achieving socialism before any of the nations of the Western world. In addition, Marxism was compatible with Japan's modern academic synthesis. Building on the Japanese tradition of Confucian scholarship and on transplanted German idealism and scholasticism, Marxism provided a modern integrated system of philosophy. Many Japanese intellectuals believed that Marxism had made social science into a unified philosophy or system that could cut across the disciplines. As Professor Maruyama Masao has pointed out, it "provided a methodology for analyzing social phenomena in comprehensive terms" and "aroused intellectuals to study the many diverse elements that have gone into the historical background of Japan and to seek the fundamental causative factors that generated them." Unfortunately, however, as Maruyama has also noted, Marxist intellectuals "put too much faith in theoretical conceptualization. Theories were too often mistakenly identified with reality itself."[2] Lastly, Marxism appealed to their humanism. It demanded action for the good of all men rather than fulfillment of particular obligations.

Some of these intellectuals and labor leaders became Marxist-Leninists after the Russian Revolution, when the ideas of Lenin and knowledge of the transformation of Russia under Soviet leadership were disseminated throughout Japan. Along

[2] Maruyama Masao, "Japanese Thought," *Journal of Social and Political Ideas in Japan* (April 1964), p. 47.

with the older revolutionary socialists, like Sakai, Yamakawa, and Arahata, they comprised the membership of the first Japanese Communist party established in 1922. They came to believe that the strategy and tactics of communism were more flexible and realistic than those of anarcho-syndicalism. The older party leaders found it difficult, of course, to overcome their anarcho-syndicalist heritage, but the failure of the direct action tactics of anarcho-syndicalism both in Japan and abroad finally convinced them of the need for political action. They also became aware of the need for a broader socialist movement than one based just on labor. Moreover, the Russian Revolution demonstrated that Marxism-Leninism was the "science of successful revolution." Given the socialist and labor movements' record of failure in the previous several decades, Lenin's triumph had a great impact on Japan's revolutionaries, old and young alike. Marxism-Leninism's concept of the vanguard, the leadership group of the masses, strengthened and deepened the revolutionaries' sense of mission.

The Hostility of Japanese Society

Despite their exuberance and dedication, Japan's Communists never realized their goals; in fact, they never became a serious threat to the modern synthesis that was being built by Japan's dominant conservative forces. The Communists, like the Socialists, were only dissidents on the fringes of society; they never became a mass force. The dominant conservative elite guided the process of modernization and at the same time maintained the traditional Japanese value system, which helped sustain their power. Education, religion, the civil code, and social and business conduct all emphasized the virtues of loyalty, obedience, and status at the expense of freedom, individual rights, and equality. The patriarchal family system with its strong paternalism pervaded almost every political, economic, and social group, determined patterns of behavior in them, and caught up all Japanese in the web of obligation. To try to get out of this system amounted to seeking rejection by society and

thereby bringing shame on one's family. Shame was the ultimate sanction to maintain social conformity. It was a powerful
factor in the decision of many Communists and socialists to
defect from their respective movements in the 1930's. The conservative value system and patterns of behavior dominant during the modernization of Japan tended to prevent basic antag-
onisms from becoming open clashes or struggles. This collectivist ethic maintained an operative harmony and stability.

The Communists, moreover, could not overcome the powerful integrating and binding forces of modern Japanese nationalism and Confucianism, especially as ultimately expressed in
the imperial system and the person of the emperor. Their ideology was alien, and as a group they depended for support on
an alien movement and a foreign state that had long been the
enemy of Japan and was still a competitor in the East Asian
and Pacific power structure. In contrast to the other Communist movements in Asia, Japanese communism could not join
the nationalist stream. It did well for a brief period in the
early 1920's when internationalism still had some hold on
Japan's intellectuals and political leaders, but as the forces of
militarism and statism grew stronger and ultimately dominant,
nationalism swept everything before it, including important
segments of the socialist and Communist movements.

Moreover, the raw power of the state, especially the police
and the military, was something that the Communists could
not combat at all effectively. They had no civil liberties to protect them as individuals or as members of a political organization. Like the revolutionary socialists before them, they suffered constant harassment and suppression at the hands of the
dominant political elite. Genrō, party politicians, and militarists alike suppressed revolutionary socialism and communism
once their theories left the academy and became agents for
change among the masses. Arrest and dissolution were major
weapons constantly used to break Communist and Communist-
front organizations. The Communist party organization was
crushed by mass arrests in 1923, 1928, 1929, and even more reg-

ularly in the 1930's. It was simply impossible to create and maintain a large underground apparatus that could function effectively. Moreover, the state's use of police spies sowed seeds of suspicion and dissension in Communist organizations, further weakening them. After the outbreak of hostilites in China in 1937, the Japanese government no longer tolerated Marxism even as an academic theoretical system.

Beginning in 1923 the state made concessions to the moderate Left, and after 1925 it used the socialist movement as a kind of safety valve. Suppression and concession—or "whip and candy"—were symbolized best by the almost simultaneous passage by the Diet of the Peace Preservation Law and the Universal Manhood Suffrage Law in the spring of 1925. It is significant that the Peace Preservation Law was used primarily, if not almost exclusively, against communism or Communist influence.[3] The government of Japan tolerated the existence of the socialist movement even though its long range goals, to be achieved through evolution instead of revolution, were hardly less detrimental to the Japanese power structure and economic and social order than those of the Communists. The socialist movement, of course, ultimately succumbed to the state socialism of the nationalists and was in large part absorbed by it.

The Japanese Communists, like the socialists, were handicapped by the lack of a strong unified labor movement. Japanese labor was characterized by local particularism; it was therefore diffuse and weak. The lack of unity was further ac-

---

[3] Arrests and prosecutions under the Peace Preservation Law of 1925 were as follows in the period from 1928 to 1937:

1928 —	3,426	(530)	1933 — 14,624	(1285)
1929 —	4,942	(339)	1934 — 3,994	(469)
1930 —	6,124	(461)	1935 — 1,772	(113)
1931 — 10,422		(307)	1936 — 1,645	(159)
1932 — 13,938		(646)	1937 — 1,291	(210)

Committee for the Scientific Study of Thought, comp., *Tenkō* [Conversion] (Tokyo, 1959), I, 191.

centuated by personal and ideological rivalries. Moreover, the labor movement was never able to secure large-scale mass support and participation; only a small segment of the industrial labor force entered unions. In the mid-1920's, for example, only some six percent of Japan's industrial and mining workers were in unions, and these workers came largely from small and medium industries, especially metal working and printing. Major industries like textiles, railways, electrical manufacturing, and mining were hardly touched. The Japanese industrial worker simply did not break from and rebel against the paternalistic labor-management relations system. Those workers who did were generally disillusioned with unionism as a result of the constant failure of negotiations and strikes. This record of failure hung like a pall over the labor movement. The mass of Japan's industrial workers rejected political action, let alone the use of revolutionary tactics. They wanted no part of unionism or left-wing political parties.

The peasant movement, another major concern of both the Communists and socialists, suffered from similar weaknesses and difficulties. It, too, was badly split. Moreover, the peasant organizations lacked strong central leadership. Like labor unions, actual power rested with the leaders of district groups. The Communists never had sufficient manpower to work effectively in the peasant movement; nor could they risk exposure, a danger which was much greater in the countryside than in the cities. And, like the labor movement, the peasant movement was handicapped by the lack of numbers. At its peak, it had the support and participation of only some ten percent of Japan's peasant families. The Japanese agricultural community was unreceptive and actually hostile to communism and even to socialism. As George Totten has pointed out, "Though this can be attributed largely to the landowning gentry's active efforts to keep out 'unsettling' influences, it was also a reaction against industrialism which appeared to the peasants to be utlimately responsible for their woes."[4] In the final analysis, it was hardly likely that the Communists could organize a strong peasant base in a modern society. This was not China. A Communist oriented peasant movement was too easily suppressed.

In simplest terms, then, the very nature of Japanese society made it extremely difficult, if not impossible, for a Communist movement to exist, let alone operate with any degree of effectiveness. In Marxist-Leninist terms, the objective conditions were not at all favorable. But there is more to the story than that. The Japanese Communists suffered from a number of weaknesses and difficulties of the Comintern's and its own making. Again, in the jargon of Marxism-Leninism, the subjective conditions were hardly favorable either.

Difficulties Raised by Comintern Policy

From the beginning, the Comintern had a difficult time developing strategy and tactics for Japan. The immediate objective was to eliminate the vestiges of feudalism and complete the bourgeois-democratic revolution, a necessary stage in the revolutionary process. Japan did not fit either the classical European pattern of industrial societies or that of Asian peasant, colonial or semi-colonial societies. She was neither France nor China, nor was she like Russia despite very obvious superficial similarities. Compared to Russia, by the 1920's Japan was much further along in the process of modernization in some ways, yet more traditional in others. As already noted, both characteristics tended to work against the Japanese Communist movement. The situation was not helped of course by the exaggerated reports by Japanese Communists of labor and peasant unrest or by the misguided optimism of Japanese Communists in Moscow like Katayama Sen. Quite clearly, the Comintern created serious difficulties for the Japanese movement by its insistence, in the 1922 theses on the two-stage theory of revolution

[4] George Oakley Totten, III, *The Social Democratic Movement in Prewar Japan* (New Haven, 1966), p. 392.

with initial emphasis on the revolution against the absolutist imperial system and its economic base, a substantial part of which was "feudal" landlordism.[5] The Japanese Communists were put in an impossible position, given the objective conditions in which they had to operate. No movement which advocated such changes could exist under those conditions. Intellectual leaders as far apart as Yoshino Sakuzō and Yamakawa Hitoshi understood this very well and acted accordingly. That is why the first Japanese Communist party did not formally adopt the 1922 theses[6] and why, in part, the party dissolved in 1924.[7]

The life of the first Japanese Communist party was indeed a very short and unsettled one. The power of the state destroyed its organization, and the appeal to social democracy, which the party helped in part to revive, undercut its pretensions to exclusive leadership of the masses. The party itself, however, suffered from basic weaknesses. It was not a unified body with a concrete platform; it was instead an amalgam of personal factions whose members could not agree on appropriate strategy and tactics of revolution. Despite its acceptance of the Comin-

[5] Historical Materials Committee of the Japanese Communist Party, comp., *Kominterun Nihon mondai ni kansuru hōshinsho ketsugi shū* [Collection of Comintern Policies and Resolutions on Japan] (Tokyo, 1950), pp 5-11.

[6] Tateyama Takaaki, *Nihon Kyōsantō kenkyo hishi* [Secret History of the Japanese Communist Party Arrests] (Tokyo, 1929), pp. 112-21; Takase Kiyoshi, "Hiwa—Daini no taigyaku jiken" [Unknown Story— A Second High Treason Case], *Jiyū* (October 1962), pp. 128-37; and Kazama Jōkichi, *Mosukō to tsunagaru Nihon Kyōsantō no rekishi* [History of the Japanese Communist Party and Its Relations with Moscow] (Tokyo, 1951), I, 103-05.

[7] Shinobu Seizaburō, *Taishō demokurashii shi* [History of Democracy in the Taishō Period] (Tokyo, 1959), III, 1000, 1018-21; Arahata Kanson, *Kyōsantō o meguru hitobito* [People Around the Communist Party] (Tokyo, 1950), p. 46; Arahata Kanson, *Kanson Jiden* [Autobiography of Arahata Kanson] (Tokyo, 1960), pp. 461-62; and Nabeyama Sadachika, *Watakushi wa Kyōsantō o suteta* [I Left the Communist Party] (Tokyo, 1949), p. 79.

tern slogan "Into the Masses," the party had not developed to the point where it was based on mass organizations of workers and peasants. Yamakawa recognized all of this and began to search for ways in which communism could play a more effective role. He was the first of the Communist leaders to recognize that the strategy and tactics of the Comintern would not work in Japan. He saw that with the enactment of universal suffrage, communism would not be able to stand aloof from the movement to establish legal proletarian political parties. Communism, he believed, would have to join that movement and seek to influence it from within. There was simply no need for an illegal Japanese Communist party. The Japanese party's role, according to him, would have to be dependent on what actual conditions would permit. The crucial factors were the level of political consciousness among the masses, the extent to which political power was distributed among the classes, and the degree to which the Communist vanguard could formulate strategy and tactics empirically.

The Comintern could not let Yamakawaism triumph. In fact, the whole business of the party's dissolution placed the Comintern in an awkward position. The Fourth Comintern Congress in 1923 had publicized the founding of the party. The Fifth Congress, which met in June 1924, had to recognize its demise. The Comintern therefore encouraged and cajoled the Japanese Communists to reestablish the party, and its efforts were finally successful in December 1926.

The Comintern's continued advocacy of the two-stage theory of revolution was to create difficulties for some of the Japanese Communist leaders. They were disturbed by what they regarded as a basic inconsistency between growing indications of bourgeois hegemony and the call for a bourgeois-democratic revolution. They felt that the position of the bourgeoisie in the Japanese power structure should point logically to a proletarian revolution. Moreover, former Communists like Yamakawa and his followers held the same view. In fact, it was not until 1927 that the Comintern's strategy and tactics for a two-stage revolution were finally adopted by the Japanese Communist party in the slightly amended form of the 1927 theses.[8] The Comintern classified Japan as a society of medium capitalist development, a category where there were two possible strategies of revolution. In one case, such a society might not be sufficiently developed, economically and politically, to permit an immediate advance toward socialism as the basic party strategy. The revolution would therefore be a bourgeois-democratic one which would "grow over" into the socialist revolution. The other possibility was that such a society might be sufficiently advanced to permit a revolution that would be proletarian from the outset, although it would have to carry out a number of bourgeois-democratic tasks in the process. Despite her considerable industrial development, according to the Comintern's judgment reaffirmed at its Sixth Congress in 1928, Japan was not destined to have a proletarian revolution. The Comintern held to the view that Japan's chief characteristics were her semi-feudal system of agriculture and her peculiar political regime headed by a monarchy representing the interests of the landlords and bourgeoisie.[9]

The Labor-Farmer faction, or Rōnōha, organized in December 1927 under the leadership of former Communists like Yamakawa and Inomata Tsunao, hoped to overcome these difficulties by seizing on the 1927 theses' recognition of bourgeois hegemony. Its members felt that logically they could avoid the emperor issue, at least on the surface, by calling for a proletarian revolution that would by implication complete the tasks of the bourgeois-democratic stage. The Rōnōha position, as de-

[8] The full text of the 1927 theses appeared in *International Press Correspondence* (January 12, 1928), pp. 50-54. The most convenient source for the Japanese text is Ishidō Seirin and Yamabe Kentarō, eds., *Kominterun Nihon ni kansuru tēze shū* [Texts of Comintern Theses Pertaining to Japan] (Tokyo, 1961), pp. 28-45.

[9] Kermit E. McKenzie, *Comintern and World Revolution, 1928-43: The Shaping of Doctrine* (London and New York, 1964), pp. 74-75, 78.

veloped by Yamakawa and Inomata,[10] challenged the strategy
and tactics of the Japanese Communist party in two fundamental ways. First, by denying the power of feudal absolutism and
focusing on a single revolution against the bourgeoisie, they
removed the need to attack the imperial system and thereby
were able to remain for a decade a legal segment of the left-
wing movement. Yet, while legal, because of its doctrinal extremism, the Rōnōha tended to be just as isolated from the
mainstream of the left-wing movement as the Japanese Communist party. Ultimately, although it had no relationship with
international communism, it invited suppression by the authorities. Secondly, with the sole exception of Inomata, the members of the Rōnōha minimized or denied the need for a Communist party, emphasizing instead a mass party of workers and
peasants which would constitute a united front against "the
despotic, imperialist bourgeoisie." Yet the Rōnōha never became a political force because it did not develop an organization
and concrete program. It tended to represent only a point of
view, one whose influence was confined largely to intellectuals.
Yamakawa and Inomata, for example, were more interested in
theory than in practice. Without any organization, leadership,
discipline, or program, the Rōnōha was never able to develop
a foundation from which to work to achieve political unity in
the Japanese left wing. Rōnōha influence was probably more
significant in the academic community than elsewhere because
it provided an interpretation of Japan's modern development
that was attractive to many "progressives" in history and the
social sciences. The weaknesses of the Rōnōha were, however,
not apparent in 1927. At that time it represented a serious chal-

[10] Yamakawa Hitoshi, "Seijiteki tōitsu sensen e—Musan seitō gōdō
ron no konkyo" [Toward a United Political Front—The Basis of the
Argument for the Merger of the Proletarian Political Parties], pp. 2-48,
and Inomata Tsunao, "Nihon musankaikyū no ippan senryaku" [Gen-
eral Strategy of the Japanese Proletariat], pp. 118-25, both in the December, 1927 issue of Rōnō. See also in the same issue, Arahata Kanson,
"Sekutoshugi no seisan" [Liquidation of Sectarianism], pp. 88-96.

lenge to the leaders of the Japanese Communist party and to their strategy based on the two-stage theory of revolution.

Later, in 1931, under the leadership of Kazama Jōkichi, the Japanese Communist party adopted theses advocating proletarian revolution,[11] but this shift invited strong criticism from the Comintern. The Comintern branded as "erroneous" the definition of the coming Japanese revolution as a proletarian one which would include a broad scope of bourgeois-democratic tactics. This mistake, the Comintern declared, "can be attributed to underestimating the tasks of agrarian revolution and the lack of understanding of acute agrarian problems and the need to destroy landlord ownership completely." The Comintern also explained that the Japanese Communists had misinterpreted the nature of the Japanese government, minimizing the power of the imperial throne. For these reasons, the Comintern claimed, "it is proper to define the nature of the coming revolution in Japan as a bourgeois-democratic revolution with a tendency toward a forced transformation toward a socialist revolution."[12] This view became dogma once again in the 1932 theses and was not challenged by Japanese party members thereafter.

The Comintern created further difficulties for the Japanese Communist party by its preoccupation, after 1928, with the need to mobilize forces against Japanese imperialism, which posed a threat not only to China but even more to the homeland of international communism, the Soviet Union itself. This unavoidably placed the Japanese Communists athwart the path of Japanese nationalism; and as nationalism swept the country after the Manchurian incident in 1931, the Communists found themselves more and more isolated. Some of them, like the socialists, were carried along by the tide. Almost every Communist defector complained that the party had been the unwitting pawn of the Comintern. They objected to the complete subordination of the party to the Comintern and the Soviet

[11] Ishido and Yamabe, *op.cit.*, pp. 46-75.
[12] *Sekki* (July 2, 1932, special issue), II, 235-38.

Union. Japan's judicial authorities and police appealed to the patriotism of arrested Communists in order to get them to defect and return to society to play a constructive role. It is apparent that after 1932 the Comintern was increasingly disillusioned with the Japanese Communists. It continued to provide assistance and advice, but the Soviet leaders were more concerned with securing accurate intelligence reports on Japanese military developments and foreign policy moves than with fostering the party. When the popular front appeal came in 1936,[13] it was too late to create an effective mass opposition to militarism.

It is hard to avoid the conclusion that the Comintern was never able to take the long view with regard to Japan. Perhaps it felt that it could not afford that luxury. Instead, Comintern policy for Japan was precipitous. The tactics of the united front from below, for example, isolated communism from the socialist movement, especially after the 1928 decision not to support the rebuilding of the Labor-Farmer party,[14] and its strategy and tactics in general made suppression of the party apparatus more likely, if not inevitable.

Weaknesses of the Communist Party

In addition to the difficulties created by the Comintern, the tendency of Japanese Communist leaders to be more often concerned with theory than with practice made it difficult to create a mass movement. The role of the intellectual in prewar Japan was in general passive not active. The intellectual preferred the role of social critic to that of social reformer. There were some exceptions to the rule but not as many as one might

[13] Ishido and Yamabe, *op.cit.*, pp. 205-17.

[14] This shift in policy is explained in the so-called "October theses" or the "1928 theses," which appeared in *Marukusushugi* (December 1928–January 1929), pp. 70-86, under the title "Nihon no Puroretaria [to] tōmen no ninmu" [Immediate Tasks of the Japanese Proletariat]. These theses were also published as a pamphlet, *Nihon Kyōsantō tōmen kinkyū no Ninmu* [Present Urgent Tasks of the Japanese Communist Party], in December 1928.

think. Yamakawa pointed out this phenomenon early in the course of the Communist movement, but he, too, could not overcome his reluctance to play an activist role in bringing the party closer to the masses. This disability may explain in part his disavowal of the need for a vanguard party. The tendency toward inactivity was even stronger in Fukumoto Kazuo and his followers who for a time dominated the second Japanese Communist party, established in December 1926.

Fukumoto's ideas were attractive to the Communist elements who were moving in the direction of reestablishing a Japanese party. Unlike Yamakawa, whose empirical approach empha-sized the spontaneous growth of a vanguard, Fukumoto urged that a Communist party be formed. Yamakawa was more in-terested in a broad, joint-front, legal proletarian party, one based on mass support. He was, however, aware of the pitfalls of this approach and, for this reason, had already written off cooperation with the Social Democratic elements. Fukumoto accepted the need for a legal proletarian party; his major con-cern was that a vanguard be prepared to capture the legal party at the decisive time. Fukumoto's main impact on the Commu-nists was to improve their understanding of the importance of a theory of revolution, the organization of a revolutionary party, and a unifying principle for such a party. He contributed therefore to the reestablishment of the Communist party in Japan, and he paved the way for its acceptance of the strategy and tactics prepared by the Comintern. The obvious danger in Fukumoto's approach was the likelihood of the Communists' isolation from other left-wing groups, as well as the masses. His dogmatic emphasis on theoretical struggles to achieve Marxist-Leninist consciousness involved the Communists in seemingly endless, meaningless, complacent discussion almost for the sake of discussion. There was a tendency, moreover, for the Communists to rationalize any type of intragroup feud-ing in the name of consciousness and theoretical struggles to achieve "separation and unity."

There are other reasons why the party did not develop a

mass base. The preoccupation of the Japanese Communists with political matters created difficulties. Both Comintern and the party tended to exaggerate the political and class consciousness of the Japanese workers and peasants and therefore put too much emphasis on political aims and class struggle. In fairness to the Comintern and the Japanese Communist party, however, it should be pointed out that the socialists hardly fared much better. In addition to being too political, party policy was often too radical. To call for the expropriation of land, as did the party's economic program, was hardly realistic. It was simply too hot an issue. And finally, occasional lapses by party leaders into adventurism tended to alienate the masses even further.

The Japanese Communist party also suffered from a number of basic organizational weaknesses. Throughout the prewar period it was rent by factionalism based on personalities and on disagreements over issues of strategy and tactics. Moreover, there was no operative continuity of leadership and no accumulation of revolutionary experience. Because of constant arrests by the police, the Communist movement was much like a student movement which loses its leadership through graduation. Communist leaders were also lost through defection. Continuing frustration led to defeatism and generally to separation from the movement. Although replenished with new recruits, membership in the Japanese Communist party never exceeded one thousand and was usually far below that figure.

The Beginning of Defection

Defection from the Japanese Communist party was a problem in the 1920's, but at that time it was based largely on the appeal of Yamakawa's own brand of Marxism-Leninism and on recognition of the need to avoid a head-on clash with the emperor system. By the end of the decade, however, defection began to be based on acceptance of the principle that socialism could be attained under the emperor system; there was therefore no present or future need for a Japanese Communist party.

Advocates of this point of view were of course quickly expelled from the party. Their number included such key figures as Kawai Etsuzō, Mizuno Shigeo, Nakamura Yoshiaki, Sano Fumio, Murayama Toshirō, Inamura Ryūichi, Asano Akira, Toyota Sunao, Minami Kiichi, Murao Satsuo, Kadoya Hiroshi, and Koreeda Kyōji. Frustration and the resultant defeatism were also key factors in some of these later defections.

The Japanese Communist party's denunciation of the "dissolutionists" in *Red Flag* was sweeping, to say the least. In 1929, it accused them individually and collectively of making propaganda on behalf of the dissolution of the party and separation from the Comintern; of renouncing the central slogans laid down in the 1927 theses concerning abolition of the monarchy and confiscation of the lands of landlords, temples and shrines, and the government; of attempting to reduce the party program to petty bourgeois reformism; and, like the Rōnōha, of disgracing the party's revolutionary tradition. The party used strong words because it feared that the influence of the dissidents would grow. History ultimately proved this judgment to be correct. What started in a relatively small way eventually became a general movement among the ranks of the Communists.

Kawai Etsuzō provided the initial leadership for the dissidents. While in jail at Osaka, he wrote notes criticizing the Communists' frontal attack on the emperor system, a policy which decisively separated the Japanese Communist party from the socialist parties. He preferred to place emphasis on clearing the throne of corrupt elements in order to carry out systematic reform. As he began to think through this approach, he concluded that there was really no need for a Communist party or a relationship with the Comintern.[15] Mizuno Shigeo was the most important figure to follow Kawai's lead. Starting with the point that the Communist party was isolated from the masses, Mizuno formulated a more elaborate explanation of

[15] Kawai Etsuzō, "Kansō" [Thoughts], a note dated April 17, 1929, quoted in *Tenkō*, I, 153.

the need for a bold shift of strategy based on an understanding of the conditions peculiar to Japan.[16] He posed the following three questions: "Do the masses of Japan now keenly feel that they cannot advance even a step toward their liberation without abolishing the monarchy? Objectively, does the monarchy stand before the masses as a yoke and absolute obstacle to them? Is the Japanese monarchy likely to become a yoke on the masses in the future?" His own answers to these questions were in the negative, and, like Kawai, he went on to develop the basis for a socialist movement within the framework of the emperor system. He explained that the throne had been a center of national worship since ancient times and that it had never been tied to political or economic power, a situation which made the Japanese imperial household different from Czarist and other foreign monarchical systems. For this reason, Mizuno advised Communists to give up the slogans of "Abolish the monarchy" and "Confiscate the lands of the imperial household," because they tended to alienate the masses. Like many of his comrades, Mizuno also found it difficult to accept Comintern orders regarding the emancipation of the Japanese colonies. He tended to make a special case for Japan's colonialism on the ground that she was a relatively backward nation compared to England and France.

Mizuno was also highly critical of the party's leadership, from both personal and political standpoints. He first attacked what he called conduct in the "tradition of corruption and degeneration." What he criticized was the practice, even among the Japanese Communists, of seeking relaxation in brothels and *machiai* (assignation houses) and of using them as hideouts because policemen generally did not enter them. The *machiai* had a particular stigma for Communists because of their "bourgois" nature. Mizuno also criticized what he called "a com-

[16] Mizuno explained his views in a document dated May 23, 1929, and entitled "Nihon Kyōsantō dattō ni saishi tōin shokun ni" [To Party Members on the Occasion of Withdrawing from the Japanese Communist Party], cited and summarized in *Tenkō*, I, 152-57.

plete failure in political direction." He stated: "Had the party been a legal entity, its central leadership would have been rejected by the masses in the general election. Party leaders were able to keep their position simply because the party was completely illegal and because of its complete defiance of democratic centralism resulting from the abuse of illegality." He appealed to ordinary party members to display "real heroism as true Bolsheviks" and renounce the corrupt central leadership. Lastly, he called for the party's dissolution. "Here I announce to all the masses of workers and peasants of Japan that party members should resolutely dissolve the Japanese Communist party . . . and boldly advance toward the liberation movement in a renewed spirit. I express my ardent hope for a militant union with the masses." Mizuno could hardly end his argument without demanding separation from the Comintern's influence.[17]

Some of the defectors, out on bail—Asano, Kadoya, Minami, Toyota, and Murao, among others—called for the establishment

[17] Mizuno Shigeo, "Kukyō no aji" [Experience of Hard Times], in *Chūō Kōron* (March 1952), p. 151. Writing much later with the advantage of hindsight, Mizuno claimed that the relationship with the Comintern had been bothering him for some time.

I went over to China, under the Wuhan government, to represent Japan at the Far Eastern Bureau and lived for the first time with more than ten delegates from foreign countries for nearly one year. It [Far Eastern Bureau] was centered around those from the Soviet Union just like the present Far Eastern Cominform. And there I found that my sense of humanity was incompatible with communism. And I realized, after witnessing the realities of the Chinese revolution and the instructions and policies of the Comintern, that the use of any means for attaining the objectives of a certain country (Soviet Union) or a party (Russian Communist Party) is incompatible with humanism. On my return home I frankly conveyed my impressions to Watanabe Masanosuke, then chairman of the central executive committee of the Japanese Communist party. He reproached me and said, "You are after all an intellectual, and you talk such nonsense." But I did not yield. Soon I was jailed, and after some two years of serious thinking there, I chose defection in accordance with my beliefs.

of a legal party appropriate for conditions in Japan.[18] Under Mizuno's and Minami's leadership, they formed the so-called Japanese Communist Party Workers' faction (*Nihon Kyōsantō Rōdōsha*) in June 1930 in order to achieve that objective. They used the title "Workers faction," or Rōdōsha, because they attributed the collapse of the Japanese Communist party to its overemphasis on theory and intellectualism. The Rōdōsha proved, however, to have very little appeal for workers or intellectuals. It was bitterly attacked by Communists in and out of jail, and it was regarded with utmost suspicion by the socialists. Some faction members, moreover, continued to be attracted to the Japanese Communist party. Kawai and Murayama, who cooperated with the Rōdōsha, and a few faction members, like Numata Hidesato, ultimately returned to the party fold. Mizuno withdrew from all political activity. The Rōdōsha collapsed completely in July 1932, when its remaining members were forced to return to jail.[19]

The Sano-Nabeyama Defection

The most decisive case of defection occurred in 1933 in a totally unexpected quarter. It happened following the trial, in October 1932, in which the Japanese Communist party leaders were sentenced to long prison terms. On June 10, 1933, the morning dailies carried the news that "two Communist bigwigs," Sano Manabu and Nabeyama Sadachika, had defected from the party. The report was based on a statement prepared by the two party leaders in the form of a letter dated June 6, sent to their lawyers and friends. Earlier, at the end of May, they had informed the authorities of their "change of heart" in a long memorandum, which their letter summarized. Party members, in and out of jail, were stunned by the news. It seemed incredible. Even their lawyers did not believe that two

[18] Naimushō Keihokyoku [Home Ministry, Police Bureau], *Shōwa gonen ni okeru shakai undō no jōkyō, 1930* [Condition of Social Movements in 1930], p. 117.

[19] *Shakai undō no jōkyō*, 1931, pp. 77-81; and *Tenkō*, I, 157.

such "brilliant leaders" could desert the party, but after a direct confrontation they had to admit the fact. As more information became available, it was clear that their defection had been in the making for some time. Receiving sentences of life imprisonment in October 1932, they decided shortly thereafter on their course of action. The authorities quite naturally were cooperative and accommodating.[20]

In their original memorandum[21] Sano and Nabeyama explained in detail the basis of their action. They maintained that they had not repudiated their belief in the need "to free the working class from the iron chains of violent capitalism." They did, however, repudiate the Japanese Communist party, branding it as "a petty bourgeois organ, moving fast in the wrong direction." They argued that the existing party was not "a progressive factor in Japanese society." They claimed that it was

[20] Nakano Sumio, "Sano-Nabeyama tenkō no shinsō" [True Account of the Sano-Nabeyama Defection], *Kaizō* (July 1933), pp. 200-04. According to Nakano, Sano took the initiative and was joined by Nabeyama. Nakano claimed that two events were particularly upsetting to Sano, the Ōmori bank incident and the assassination of Prime Minister Inukai. News of the defection was first reported in several Tokyo newspapers on January 26, 1933, but was denied by Sano and Nabeyama. Judge Miyagi Minoru, who had presided over the Communist trial and who served as adviser to Sano and Nabeyama, believed that both men were influenced by the fact that the public trial of party leaders did not have the impact on the public that the party expected. See his "Tenkō no dōki [Motivations of Defection], *Kaizō* (July 1933), pp. 208-09.

[21] The statement was entitled "Kimpaku seru naigai no jōsei to Nihon minzoku oyobi sono rōdōsha kaikyū—sensō oyobi naibu kaizō no sekkin o mae no shite Komintan oyobi Nihon Kyōsantō o jiko hihan suru" [Intense Internal and External Conditions and the Japanese Nation and Its Working Class—Self-Criticism of the Comintern and of the Japanese Communist Party in the Face of Approaching War and Internal Reconstruction]. It is included in Shihōshō Keijikyoku [Ministry of Justice, Criminal Affairs Division], *Shisō kenkyū shiryō* [Materials for the Study of Thought], no. 36 (July 1933). A slightly different version appears in Yamamoto Katsunosuke and Arita Mitsuo, *Nihon kyōsanshugi undō shi*. [History of the Japanese Communist Movement] (Tokyo, 1950), pp. 376-81. See also *Tenkō*, I, 164-68.

instead "a negative force." In brief, Sano and Nabeyama explained that they wanted "to show the right course to the working class."

What caused them to make this shift? Their own answer to this question was rooted in the reawakening of their "national consciousness" following the Manchurian incident and in the realization that the Japanese imperial system "has been an expression of national unity and has decreased the violence of class strife within the country, bringing equilibrium to social life and ensuring a smooth transition from one class to another at times of social change." According to Sano and Nabeyama, "The emperor system of Japan, unlike czarism, has never been one of exploitation and suppression."

> The imperial household helps the clock of history to move, as in the case of the Meiji Restoration, when it overthrew the shogunate, which stood in the way of the progress of Japanese society, and played a central role in the movement to build a united Japan. The masses of the people have feelings of respect for and identification with the imperial family. The Japanese people have a sense of being a great kinship group, of which the imperial family is the head. Such natural feelings cannot be found in the case of any other monarchy at this time. To that extent the Japanese imperial family has a popular foundation. We should grasp the feeling of reverence for the imperial family, trace it to its origins, and have the same attitude as the people. With the slogan "Overthrow the Emperor System," the Communist party goes against the people and for this reason is alienated from them.

Sano and Nabeyama also claimed that the Comintern did not sufficiently understand that "the form of revolution will vary according to factors peculiar to each country."

> The Comintern has very little understanding of the historical traditions, peculiarities of social life, and social-psychological features of the Japanese nation. It cannot understand them. It

has forcefully drawn Japanese realities toward principles of class struggle based on European experience, not on Japanese peculiarities. The 1932 theses while treating the monarchy as a political organ hardly explains anything. It simply states that the monarchy plays an independent and a relatively great role and maintains an absolutist character hidden only slightly by the fake front of constitutional government and that at the same time, forming a close and lasting bloc with the upper strata of the parasitic landlord class on one hand and the greedy bourgeoisie on the other, it represents the interests of those classes.

They argued that "traditional and social-psychological factors must be taken into account in the conduct of revolution." Then what kind of revolution would Japan have? They answered: "In Japan it is natural and possible to carry out a one-country socialist revolution under the imperial family."

In Sano's case, assumption of this position had been in the making for a number of years. In the spring of 1923 he had opposed the party's adoption of the 1922 theses because the theses included an attack on the imperial system and advocated a bourgeois-democratic revolution instead of a socialist one. The position of the emperor posed a special problem for the young Japanese Communist party. On the ground that the question of the emperor was already well understood, Sano supported the efforts of the older leaders, like Sakai Toshihoko, to eliminate the provision calling for the abolition of the imperial system. Mindful of the past, such leaders warned that it might create "victims" unnecessarily. Some of the younger party members, however, had no qualms about attacking the imperial institution. In the end, the party members approved the demand for the abolition of the imperial system as a key objective, but they decided not to include it in any statement of immediate action policy. Sano also maintained that, in view of the rapidly changing conditions in Japan, the revolution would have to be a socialist one. Within the party, discussion of the nature of the coming revolution was heated, and no conclusion was reached.[22]

Although during the period of his residence in the Soviet Union, from 1923 to 1925, Sano was won over to the Comintern view regarding the need for a bourgeois-democratic revolution, he clung to the opinion that the attack against the imperial system created serious difficulties for the Japanese Communist party, especially by weakening its relationship with the masses. After his return to Japan in 1925, Sano persisted in wanting to avoid discussion of the need for a direct attack on the imperial system; he therefore tended to make the imperialist bourgeoisie the main object of revolutionary struggle in the bourgeois-democratic stage as well as in the socialist stage. The Comintern's continued advocacy of the two-stage theory of revolution created difficulties for the Japanese Communist party leaders. They were disturbed by what they regarded as the basic inconsistency between indications of bourgeois hegemony in Japan and the call for a bourgeois-democratic revolution. Sano tended to believe that since the bourgeoisie held power, the revolution should be directed against them. Therefore, the revolution should be proletarian. This was, of course, the view held by former party members like Yamakawa and his followers. Later, when Sano accepted the idea that the Japanese imperial system differed from monarchism in general, he was able to conclude that it was not a barrier to socialist revolution. The idea of revolution under the emperor was not far removed from the Rōnōha conception of socialist revolution, for the Rōnōha did not regard the emperor as central to political power.[23]

[22] See note 6 above.

[23] Writing much later, Sano described his personal struggle against his national consciousness.

My national feeling grew stronger and stronger in Shanghai, but as a believer in internationalism, I killed this feeling intellectually. After I was arrested in Shanghai in June, 1929, this feeling stopped. I felt a strong fighting spirit again. I thought that even though I would be sentenced to death, I would expand the Communist Party as much

However, the character of the revolution, implicit in Sano's and Nabeyama's statement, was more nationalist than socialist.

Today Japan belongs among the leading nations of the world. This is the result of (1) firm national unity and, as its expression, the state and the monarchy, (2) internal cohesion in social life, (3) the role of the family as the basic social unit, (4) the excellent productivity of workers, and (5) the cumulative genius of Eastern culture. Japan stands among those nations which lead, not among those which are led. The ideas of independence for the colonies and national self-determination are outdated bourgeois ideas. Weak nations like Manchuria, Formosa, and Korea should enjoy equal rights within a people's government of Japan, Manchuria, Formosa, and Korea by merging with Japan, which is economically close to them.

Japan's mission, according to Sano and Nabeyama, extended to China as well and was directed against imperialism.

The present war is being waged against the Chinese Nationalist military clique, which is the agent of European and American capital and which supports the old order. The war has the objective of liberating 400 million Chinese. It involves the expansion of the Japanese nation into a country which is remarkably backward in culture compared to Japan. It is therefore in accord with the principle of historical progress.

According to Sano and Nabeyama, the Japanese aggression in China was likely to develop into a Japanese-American war. Such

---

as possible from prison, encourage the comrades outside of prison, and propagandize in the public trial. Although I sometimes felt disillusioned about Soviet Russia and the Comintern, I forced myself to shut my eyes to it and did my best to develop the Communist Party, hoping that something good would come of it.

Nabeyama Sadachika and Sano Manabu, *Tenkō jūgonen* [Fifteen Years Since Our Defection] (Tokyo, 1949), pp. 86-87.

a war, in their opinion, would be "a progressive step because it will have as its aim the liberation of Asian nations from American and European capital." Yet, they conceded that "as a war waged by Japanese imperialists, it cannot be called a war of national liberation by Japan." They made their one-pointed socialist argument in stating that "to transform it into a war of national liberation will require internal political reform— the achievement of a government of working people." On this point, however, they said nothing more except to imply that reform would occur through the arming of the masses.

Lastly, the two defectors were also influenced by Pan-Asianism. In their words,

There are common characteristics among Asian peoples in language, culture, race, and religion. There is spiritual solidarity among them in their confrontation with Western capitalism. Their struggle for existence will inevitably be conducted against capitalism. The struggle against Western capitalism, which will develop into a war, will be a progressive one for the peoples of Asia. Japan should be the leader of Pan-Asianism and unite the peoples of the East on a class basis and join them into a greater nation. The West, reorganized by the proletariat and the East reconstructed through Pan Asianism, will finally become a unit.

Sano and Nabeyama sent a second letter, dated June 8, to their friends in and out of jail. They expressed much the same views, but they wrote in greater detail and with more feeling. When the letter was published in the July issue of *Reconstruction*, it created a sensation.[24] Sano and Nabeyama were highly critical of the failure of the Japanese Communist party to provide leadership for the proletariat. They accused the party of being alien to the working class. According to them, the party had been infiltrated by intellectuals and radical elements of the

[24] "Kyōdō hikoku ni tsuguru sho" [Letter to Our Common Defendants], *Kaizō* (July 1933), pp. 191-99.

petty bourgeoisie who had no relations with the people and who used the Communist movement to satisfy personal ambitions. Sano admitted suffering the "poison of intellectualism." Both men blamed this unfortunate situation in large part on "the political and organizational principles of the Comintern, in which we have had unlimited trust." They expanded their charge.

We now recognize that it is necessary to put the Comintern itself to criticism. We have concluded that the Comintern has grown remarkably sectarian and bureaucratic. It has become too much of an organ of the Soviet Union itself and has lost the spirit of strictness of the twenty-one articles of admission under which the vanguard of the proletariat would be united. It has played to the petty bourgeoisie of countries and has tended to make demagogic propaganda. In the case of the Communist Party of Japan, the Comintern has preferred the petty bourgeoisie who talk about revolution to strong-willed workers, has devised arbitrary strategy by confusing its wishes with the actual situation, and has been making irresponsible propaganda through obvious lies. In 1926 and the year that followed, when the Japanese Communist party experienced a flood of petty bourgeois influence within its camp, the Comintern scathingly criticized it and helped to overcome this deviation by support of the able worker members of the party. Now, however, when petty bourgeois elements are much more predominant than in those years and are causing tangible and intangible damage to the left-wing labor movement, the Comintern has not said anything about this deviation; instead, it sings the praises of the party to our consternation. The theoretical analyses by the Comintern of the recent world economic crisis and the subsequent aggravation of conditions have been sharp and worthy of attention. But the Comintern has proved to be incapable of leading, as an international revolutionary organization, the practical struggles of workers in many countries. These workers are fighting capitalism independent of the Comintern and its branches.

Sano and Nabeyama pointed out that the Comintern, having not convened a congress in five years, had continued to reject nationalistic trends developing in various countries. According to them, moreover, it made no effort to analyze this trend scientifically. They continued,

> It is understandable that the extraordinary development of the Soviet Union and the international crisis have tended to make the Comintern an agency of the Soviet state in implementing policy. But this tendency has unfortunately gone to the extreme of making "Protect the Soviet Union" the supreme and sole slogan of all national parties and of demanding the sacrifice of the interests of the working classes to that end. This is certainly not desirable for the development of a world-wide workers' movement. The Japanese Communist party appears to be one devoted more to providing a defense corps for the Soviet Union or its public opinion agency in Japan rather than to struggling for the liberation of our working class. . . . We urge the left-wing labor movement of Japan, both party and unions, to terminate relations with the Comintern and to reorganize on a new basis in order to confront impending social changes.

The two defectors went on to reiterate that the Comintern did not study Japanese particularities and that the 1932 theses were an example of its practice of applying European, particularly Russian, experience to Japan. They explained that socialism could be achieved in Japan without a conflict between "class" and "nation." They insisted, moreover, that "a higher level of internationalism will be built through the efforts to construct one-country socialism in the major parts of the world." Sano and Nabeyama also repeated their attack on the slogan "Abolish the emperor system" and their view on war and colonialism. As a final blow, they predicted the future course of Comintern-Chinese relations and of the fate of the Comintern itself.

We believe it to be only a matter of time before the comrades active in the Chinese soviet government or Chinese Communist party are in agreement with us regarding the sectarian and bureaucratic nature of the Comintern as well as its transformation into an agency of the Soviet state. With the outbreak of a world war, the Comintern will collapse completely.

Sano's and Nabeyama's ideas were quickly accepted by many of their comrades in jail, and they influenced many Communists and sympathizers on the outside. They helped pave the way for the dissolution of many left-wing cultural and intellectual organizations. Defection from the party became increasingly common. The concept of "one-country socialism" with separation from the Comintern had the effect of relieving many jailed Communists who were frustrated and defeatist because of the difficulty of continuing the movement along the line set by the Comintern. Sano and Nabeyama gave such men a new sense of revolutionary responsibility that appeared to be compatible with the peculiarities of Japanese society.

The reaction of the Communist party to all this was predictable. The central committee announced the expulsion of Sano and Nabeyama in the June 16 issue of *Red Flag*. It branded them as "betrayers, renegades, traitors, spies, provocateurs, agents of capitalism," etc. Over the next several years, issue after issue announced more expulsions with appropriate vitriolic statements. The party could hardly risk attempting to analyze the situation objectively. It tended, on the whole, to fall back on the simple explanation that petty bourgeois elements which had infiltrated the party were now disclosing their essential nature under the stresses of police suppression.[25] As

[25] *Sekki* (July 16, 1933), IV, 35; and *Sekki* (April 23, 1934), IV, 136-37.

might be expected, the Comintern also directed several blasts at the defectors, especially Sano and Nabeyama, branding them as "police provocateurs" and charging them with serving the interests of the Japanese army in particular and the imperial system in general. From Moscow, Katayama, Yamamoto, and Nosaka joined the chorus: "No one will fail to discern that their 'declaration' is nothing else but the joint work of Sano, Nabeyama, and the public prosecutor; that the latter supplied the former with the conclusions; and that the task of these 'Communists' was to color them with 'revolutionary' phraseology, sophism, demagogy, and abuse borrowed from all sorts of renegades in the past, e.g. Yamakawa, Akamatsu, the group of 'liquidators,' Trotsky, etc." They called upon Japan's workers, peasants, and revolutionary intellectuals to throw Sano, Nabeyama, and their followers out of their ranks. "No mercy, no compromise, no half-way attitude can be permitted to these criminal traitors and agents-provocateurs."[26]

The party and the Comintern could not, however, stem what was becoming a nationalist tide. The ideas of Sano and Nabeyama were quickly accepted by other Communists. Mitamura Shirō, Takahashi Sadaki, and Nakao Katsuo were the first to follow this path. They were soon joined by Sugiura Keiichi, Tanaka Seigen, Sano Hiroshi, Kazama Jōkichi, Iwao Iesada, Kawasaki Tateo, Tai Tameshichi, and Kodama Shizuko. These defectors formed a "one-country socialist group" in jail and advocated this concept during hearings in the court of appeal. In June 1934, when he was freed on bail, Nakao Katsuo joined with Nishimura Saiki to lay the foundation for a legal party movement. They formed a party central committee, drafted socialist theses, and in 1935 launched a newspaper *Nihon Seiji Shimbun* (Japan Political News) and a theoretical journal, *Zenshin* (Advance). The movement, however, gained few active participants and was consequently short-lived. It provided nothing new. As Yamakawa pointed out, the socialists were already treading the nationalist path, with some like

[26] *International Press Correspondence*, XIII (August 4, 1933), 754-56.

Akamatsu Katsumaro moving along it faster than others.[27] The authorities saw no need to ban this party's organization or suspend publication of its organs, especially when Sano and Nabeyama, the spiritual leaders, increasingly emphasized the idea of "upholding the imperial family as the central force of the Japanese nation." When Sano and Nabeyama were released from jail in 1943, they were ready to cooperate with the military and serve "the cause of the emperor." Both served with the Japanese army in Peking, and in 1944 it was rumored that the Koiso Cabinet was planning to send one of them on a secret mission to Yenan in order to initiate peace negotiations with the Chinese Communist party.[28]

The total number of Communist defectors was substantial, as the following figures indicate. At the end of July, of the 393 jailed Communists who had been convicted, 133, or approximately thirty-five percent, defected in the month following the Sano-Nabeyama announcement. Of the 741 Communists awaiting trial, 468, or approximately sixty-five percent, defected by the end of 1934.[29] According to the official source that provided the latter group of figures, motivation for defection was as follows: (1) consideration for families and close relatives, 225 persons or 47.9 percent; (2) avoidance of detention, 68 or 14.5 percent; (3) national consciousness, 65 or 13.9 percent; (4) disappointment with Communist theory, 55 or 11.7 percent; (5) personal reasons or health, 22 or 4.7 percent; (6) religious beliefs, 18 or 3.8 percent; and (7) others, 16 or 3.5 percent.[30] An

[27] Yamakawa Hitoshi, "Tenkō to sono hamon" ["Conversion" and the Stir It Creates], *Kaizō* (August 1933), pp. 86-94.

[28] *Shakai undō no jōkyō 1935*, pp. 47-48; Chalmers Johnson, *An Instance of Treason* (Stanford, 1964), p. 197.

[29] Shakai Keizai Rōdō Kenkyūjo [Center for Social, Economic, and Labor Studies], *Kindai Nihon rōdōsha undō shi* [History of the Workers' Movement in Modern Japan] (Tokyo, 1947), p. 137; and *Tenkō*, I, 192.

[30] See the attachment prepared by the ministry of justice in *Sano-Nabeyama tenkō riron no kenkyū* [A Study of the Theory of the Defection by Sano and Nabeyama], an undated mimeographed report issued by the home ministry.

important additional factor was encouragement by the authorities who were willing to suspend indictments in the case of defectors. Procurators, when dealing with ideological offenders, tended to look for a change of heart or "conversion" (*tenkō*) that would entitle the accused, after investigation and trial, to be readmitted into society as a legal subject.[31] The authorities had of course rejoiced at the defection of Sano and Nabeyama. As one high judicial official put it: "This will mean the complete ruin of the Communist party in our country. It is far better than a revision of the Peace Preservation Law."[32] By mid-1936, of 438 Communists serving sentences, 324, or seventy-four percent, had defected.[33]

Militarism and the Extinction of the Radical Left

After 1933, the efforts of the Japanese Communists to maintain any kind of national organization were repressed. The omnipresent police crushed one local group after another. It was impossible, therefore, for the Comintern to find an effective base to implement its Seventh Congress (1935) policy of a united front against Japanese militarism. Elements of the far left of the legal proletarian movement, organized under the banner of the Japan Proletarian party, led by Katō Kanjū and Suzuki Mosaburō and supported by the Rōnōha, made the only serious attempt (in 1936-1937) to create such a united front. They were, however, unable to win over the leaders of the Social Masses party, and, after the outbreak of hostilities between Japan and China in July 1937, they were destroyed by the police. As Colbert has pointed out, "After the suppression

[31] F. W. Deakin and G. R. Storry, *The Case of Richard Sorge* (New York, 1966), p. 276.

[32] Nakano Sumio, *op.cit.*, p. 204. See also *Shihō kenkyū* (March 1935), p. 22.

[33] *Tenkō*, I, 192. Sekki (July 16, 1933), IV, 35; and Sekki (April 23, 1934), IV, 136-37. *International Press Correspondence*, XIII (August 4, 1933), pp. 754-56.

of the Japan Proletarian party and its affiliated organizations, militarism, for all practical purposes, ceased to be an issue within the proletarian movement, and the statements of the Social Masses party and the trade unions, like those of other parties and groups, became even more fulsome in their praise of the holy war."[34]

The police also cracked down on the academic world during this period. Their first target was the historians and social scientists who, as Communist sympathizers, had defended the two-stage theory of revolution in their publications. The Communist Noro Eitarō mobilized them to fight the Rōnōha and its scholarly allies. In 1932-1933 he edited the famous symposium, *Nihon shihonshugi hattatsu shi kōza* (Lectures on the History of the Development of Japanese Capitalism). As a historiographical group, the academic contributors came to be called the Kōzaha. In July 1936 the police arrested Hirano Yoshitarō, Yamada Moritarō, and other Marxist scholars who took part in preparing the lectures. In all, some thirty scholars were indicted. In February 1938, the police jailed their Ronoha scholarly adversaries as well.

While the authorities were able to crush one Communist group after another, they could not break the tenacity of belief among the hard core of former party leaders. While many party members defected, this hard core did not. They were, therefore, kept in jail, even after having served the sentences set for them by the court. Under the modified Peace Preservation Law, effective March 10, 1941, the authorities had the power to detain "thought criminals" who had failed to give sufficient evidence of reform "in order to prevent further offenses by them." The revision of the law was directed mainly against the Communists. Their number included Tokuda Kyūichi, Shiga Yoshio, Miyamoto Kenji, Kasuga Shōjirō, Konno Yojirō, and Hakamada Satomi, all of whom were to play key roles in the devel-

[34] Evelyn Colbert, *The Left Wing in Japanese Politics* (New York, 1952), 51ff; see also Totten, *op.cit.*, p. 400.

opment of the Communist movement in the postwar period. Others such as Ichikawa Shōichi and Kokuryō Goichirō did not survive the hard conditions of prison life. Their comrade Nosaka Sanzō was to rejoin them after the Pacific War when the revolutionary struggle would be renewed under much more favorable conditions.

PART TWO

Economic and Social

CHAPTER VI

Rural Origins of Japanese Fascism

R. P. DORE AND TSUTOMU ŌUCHI

Definition of the Problem

IN THIS Meiji centennial year many Japanese intellectuals are, for the first time and in gingerly fashion, allowing themselves the indulgence of self-congratulatory celebration of the last century of their national history. It is fitting that it should be in this year that the Conference on Modern Japan, which has done its share to propagate the "success story" interpretation should be having its second thoughts. Clearly it was not roses, roses all the way; nor was the toil and blood and sacrifice always purposefully exacted by wise leaders for ultimate objectives of which we can all approve; nor are we inclined to transfer our congratulations to some Unseen Hand which saw to it that all should come out right in the end. Undeniably, something "went wrong" in Japan in the late 1920's and 1930's. The purpose of this chapter is to discuss how much the agricultural sector of Japanese society had to do with what went wrong; to what extent the developments of those years were determined by the overt "problems" of rural Japan —economic distress and peasant unrest—or alternatively by continuing characteristics of the rural social structure which were not perceived by contemporaries as particular sources of "problems."

First of all it would be useful to discuss briefly what we mean by "going wrong." Quite clearly, it is a moral judgement that we are making. Can one perhaps cloak the crudity of such a judgement in some such phrase as the one Eisenstadt uses to characterize the period—"breakdown of modernization"?[1] We

[1] S. N. Eisenstadt, *Modernization: Protest and Change* (Englewood Cliffs, N.J., 1966), pp. 129-34.

do not think so. Modernization is usually defined as a process which consists of—or of which significant indicators are—a "bundle" of trends of social, political, and economic change. Not all the indicative trends of modernization apparent in post-1870 Japan were reversed in the period from 1927 to 1945. Consider the following list:

Growth in GNP.

Shift in population from agriculture to industry; within agriculture an increase in productivity and commercialization;[2] within the non-agricultural sector growing productivity and a shift to heavy manufacturing.

Increasing division of labor in production and administration; increasing rationalization of bureaucratic procedures in both government and business.

Increasing accumulation of technical skills and rise in average years of schooling per capita.

Increasing national integration of culture and aspirations, erosion of regional and other particularistic loyalties.

Increasing equality of opportunity (of life chances) and equality of formal political and legal rights.

These trends continued as much in evidence after the Manchurian incident as before. The same cannot be said of other trends continuously or intermittently apparent from the nineteenth century onwards. For example:

Increasing freedom of political expression.

Increasing "tolerated diversity" of intellectual viewpoints and cultural interests.

Increasing popular control over government.

Diminishing role of violence in formal and informal power relations; increasing "civilianization."

Trends like these were reversed. By the values most of us share they are extremely important, but even by the loosest of cur-

[2] Despite the depression of agricultural incomes. See T. Ōuchi, "Agricultural Depression and Japanese Villages," *The Developing Economies,* IV (December 1967).

rent definitions they do not constitute the whole of "modernization." What happened in Japan in the 1930's is better described as a breakdown, not of modernization, but of political democratization.[3]

A Maximal Thesis

What, then, did the agrarian situation have to do with this "breakdown of political democratization"? According to some it was, indeed, the prime cause. The thesis has recently been stated with great clarity by Barrington Moore, who sees Japan and Germany as constituting a typical pattern of development determined by the particular manner in which those two countries handled the agrarian problem. Despite the differences between the two countries, the "underlying similarities" remain the "fundamental features."

Both Germany and Japan entered the industrial world at a late stage. In both countries, regimes emerged whose main policies were repression at home and expansion abroad. In both cases the main social basis for this programme was a coalition between the commercial-industrial élites (who started from a weak position) and the traditional ruling classes in the countryside, directed against the peasants and the industrial workers. Finally, in both cases, a form of rightist radicalism emerged out of the plight of the petty bourgeoisie and peasants under advancing capitalism. This right-wing radicalism provided some of the slogans for repressive regimes in both countries but was sacrificed in practice to the requirements of profit and "efficiency."[4]

This thesis is quoted for its clarity rather than for its authoritativeness. It makes its own schematic sense and as such pro-

[3] I.e., not even of "democratization" in its broader social sense. As noted above, one can plausibly argue that there were significant advances towards greater social equality and equality of opportunity. Equally, it can be argued that in the family the erosion of parental authority, for example, continued unabated.

[4] Barrington Moore Jr., *Social Origins of Dictatorship and Democracy* (London: The Penguin Press, 1967), p. 305.

vides a convenient peg, or rather a series of pegs, on which to hang a discussion. Moore's thesis is basically that industrialization without any "fundamental change" in the structure (property system, labor system) of agriculture—that is, the attempt to modernize while keeping the rural part of the social structure intact—set up strains which led directly to the events of the 1930's. Implicit in this thesis as he develops it in his book are a number of assertions or hypotheses about the causal relationships between historical events. Let us enumerate these one by one and examine the historical evidence for believing or disbelieving them.

The hold of the landlords on the villages and on their tenants depended on more than the constraint of the market situation—on some kind of extra-economic power. At first this extra-economic power was provided by the traditional legitimation of their role—by landlord paternalism and the support it received from accepted traditional values.

This much one can accept, though with reservations. The first reservation is that landlord paternalism was of much greater importance in some areas than in others. In the more commercialized districts of central Japan tenancy had already become a primarily economic, functionally specific, affectively neutral relation before the end of the nineteenth century. It was not until World War I, however, that tenancy disputes became common even in these areas, and when they did there was only a few years' time-lag before the mood of tenant militancy spread to the more paternalistic areas. Paternalism alone, therefore, was hardly an effective weapon for keeping tenants in their place.

The second reservation concerns the status gap between landlord and tenant. It is wrong to equate the Japanese landlord with, say, the British aristocrat or the German Junker or the Latin-American hacendado, as different exemplars of the category "traditional rural upper class." The Japanese equivalents, if there were any, of these latter groups—aristocratic landlords of many generations' standing whose families owed their land to conquest or patrimonial grants—were the daimyo. Some post-Meiji landlords, to be sure, did have gentry-like traditions of long standing, and even warrior pedigrees, which placed a considerable cultural distance between them and their tenants, but the majority were of quite different origins. Most were the sons or grandsons or great-grandsons of peasants who had come out better than most in the struggle for existence and acquired the land of their less fortunate, less diligent, or less provident neighbors. Others were, or were descended from, small, country merchant money-lenders. Consequently, the right of such landlords to collect rents from their tenants was not much legitimated by the noblesse of aristocratic origins or an acquired aristocratic style of life. Nor was that right only affected by the extent to which they allowed such noblesse as they did have to oblige paternalistically. It also depended in large measure on the general approbation given to the principle of private property and to the rights of land ownership in mixed village communities—communities which contained many owner-farmers, and even many tenants and part-tenants who could conceive of the possibility of one day being able to exercise those rights themselves.

The cement of any social system represents a mixture between consent and coercion. The landlords were able to continue their labor-repressive form of agriculture because their paternalism was reinforced (and this was the point of their coalition with the commercial-industrial classes) by the coercive power of the state—the police and the army.

A crucial incident for this interpretation would, of course, be the Chichibu and other riots of 1883-1884 and the dissolution of the Jiyūtō, the opposition party which drew its main support from rural areas. "Landlords" softened their opposition to the government, according to this view, because they realized that they needed the army to put down the lower orders.[5] But how many landlords were involved in the decision to dissolve the Jiyūtō? And, either then or later, how many Japanese landlords really went in fear for their lives and property and were able to sleep soundly in their beds at night only because of the comforting thought that the village policeman was not more than two miles away and that, if worst came to worst, there was always the barracks in the local prefectural town?

The answer probably is: very few, at least until the 1920's and early 1930's, if then. In that later period it is certainly true that some landlords had reason to be grateful for police power to protect them from physical violence at the height of tenancy disputes, but the general level of violence was not high. Even in 1930, when the largest number of violent incidents was reported, it was only 175, and total arrests involved 1,076 persons in a year when police statistics recorded a total of 1,723 tenancy disputes.[6] Landlords certainly had reason to be grateful to the police for breaking up tenant meetings, arresting the leaders of tenant unions, and protecting their fields when they used "blackleg" labor. They also had reason to be grateful for the strength of their influence over the legislative power—sufficient at prefectural levels in some districts for special by-laws to be passed punishing tenant conspiracy,[7] and sufficient at the national level to quash all attempts in the 1920's to use legislation to extend the rights of tenants at the expense of landlords.

[5] For this interpretation of these early political developments, see R. P. Dore, "The Meiji Landlord: Good or Bad," *Journal of Asian Studies*, XVIII:3 (May 1959).

[6] Naimushō, Keihokyoku [Home Ministry, Police Bureau], *Shōwa-7-nenchū ni okeru shakai-undō no jōkyō* [Social Movements in 1932] (n.d.), p. 1125.

[7] Gakujutsu Shinkōkai [Japan Society for the Promotion of Science], *Jikyoku to nōson* [The General Situation and the Farming Villages], 1936, I, 50. By 1926 at least seventeen prefectures had by-laws which provided for twenty to thirty days' imprisonment for such offences as forcing others to enter tenant unions, demanding interviews after midnight, or ostracising "blacklegs."

Even so, the extent of their dependence on state coercion should not be exaggerated. In 1920 typical rural prefectures like Aomori, Kagoshima, and Nagano had respectively 5.6, 5.2, and 5.5 police per 10,000 population, and in the turbulent decade that followed, the increase in police strength only just kept abreast of population growth. In 1930 the comparable figures for these prefectures were 5.5, 5.2, and 5.9.[8] In England the comparable figures for all county districts were 9.7 in 1912 and 10.2 in 1931.[9] A consideration of these later periods brings us to the next part of the thesis.

> *1. The landlords' position came to be threatened by the impact of industry. The commercialization of agriculture and the growing involvement of tenants in wage labor both led to a growth in contractual attitudes which undermined traditional paternalism. 2. The landlords displayed a clear sense of crisis. 3. They had long since been the main propagators of the conservative doctrines of agrarian collectivism—of nōhonshugi. 4. Consequently, they naturally responded to the crisis by propagating a revision of these traditional doctrines—violent, fascist forms of anticapitalist agrarianism. 5. They did so because they saw this as a chance "to make conservatism popular," to find some cause which would appeal to the revolting tenants, heal the rifts in the social structure, and preserve their own power.*

In attributing a consistent rationality to landlords, the argument certainly has plausibility, but each of the five assertions it contains needs to be examined. The first obviously has a good deal of truth. The tenancy disputes and the growing organization of tenant unions under left-wing leadership after 1922 undoubtedly threatened the security of the landlords' income and, in crisis situations, sometimes threatened them phys-

---

[8] Figures from *Dainihon Teikoku tōkei nenkan* [Statistical Yearbook of the Japanese Empire].

[9] U.K., *Report from the Select Committee on Police Forces* (*British Parliamentary Papers, 1931-32,* V), 293. Corresponding figures for urban areas excluding London were 14.2 and 13.9.

ically. The erosion of paternalism under the influence of industrialization was surely a factor contributing to this situation, but it certainly was not the only one. (See the remarks made above concerning the short time-lag between the first tenancy disputes in the most unpaternalistic areas and their spread to the most paternalistic North.) One element in the situation was the enhancement of the tenants' self-confidence and powers of organization resulting from their experience as army conscripts—not in itself an integral part of the industrialization process. Another equally important factor was the concomitant development of an industrial labor movement, which in turn has to be explained not only by the internal logic of the growth of Japanese industry, but also by ideological influences —notably the impact of the Russian Revolution. One cannot ignore the effect of educational developments. By the 1920's there were a good number of tenant farmers with eight years' schooling—schooling which, whatever the conservative bias of its explicit content, at least served to widen horizons and contacts, to enhance receptivity to new ideas, to make it possible to see local issues in national terms. Again, education can hardly be counted simply as a consequence of industrialization.

How far, to turn to the second assertion, were the landlords in fact threatened? It certainly became more difficult for many of them to collect the prescribed rent in years of bad harvest; some of them were cajoled into granting not only hardship reductions but also permanent reductions in rent rates. (Though not many: rents per tan fell by some nine percent between 1919 and 1935.) Some landlords who invested in land improvement and actually hoped to increase rents were thwarted in their ambition; many, doubtless, could not collect their rents without a good deal of unpleasantness or even litigation. It is also true that in the early years of the tenant movement, under the influence of Bukharin's first draft of a program for the Japanese Communist party, there was some evidence of a long-term threat in demands for the ultimate "socialization" of the land. Such demands reappeared among the slogans of other left-wing groups in succeeding years, but they never became a realistic threat, partly because the only slogan with any appeal to the peasants—"Land to the Tiller" —was seen by some left-wing leaders as serving only to stimulate among the rural poor petty bourgeois instincts on which the government's plans to assist the tenants towards land ownership could capitalize.[10] The landlords themselves were not much threatened by these government plans, which were attempts by reformist officials to solve rural class conflict by increasing the proportion of owner-farmers. Such schemes (which started in 1922) always provided for the full market-price compensation of landlords and depended entirely on the landlord's willingness to sell.

In terms of threats to their incomes, therefore, the landlords were not in extreme danger. In fact they suffered a good deal more from the fall in the price of rice from 1926 onwards than they did from a decline in the volume of rice they received in rent. In this respect they were direct, not indirect, victims of industrialization, in so far, at least, as the declining price of rice was actively sought, through colonial development policies, by industrialists concerned with keeping food prices low and wages cheap.

The question of whether or not the landlords were *objectively* threatened is perhaps less important for the present argument than the question of whether or not they subjectively *felt* threatened. What evidence is there that landlords experienced a sense of crisis as a result of the threat posed by tenant unrest? They certainly responded by organizing themselves for self-defence. Local landlord unions were formed to resist tenant demands, and in 1926 a national organization emerged. Still, there is little evidence of anything approaching panic. We have already quoted figures to suggest that the level of violence was not high. One does read of occasional incidents in which land-

[10] Thus, for instance, in the 1932 platform of the left-wing Zenkoku Kaigiha, "land to the tiller" comes fifty-sixth in a list of fifty-seven policy objectives. Naimushō, Keihokyoku, *op.cit.*, p. 1158.

lords and their families were beaten with sticks and improvised spears, but these remained isolated incidents. Tension in the countryside never reached the point, for instance, at which large numbers of landlords started equipping themselves with pistols to defend their families from attack.

If there is no indication that landlords felt themselves gravely threatened physically, what evidence is there that they entertained deep fears for their economic future? If they had such fears, one would have expected them to be reflected in a fall in the price of land. To be sure, the landlord demand schedule for rice land—the prices landlords were willing to pay to acquire land for the sake of the rent income to be derived from it—is only one of the determining factors in the price of land.[11] Nevertheless, the landlord demand for land was a sufficiently important factor in determining average prices for the following figures to be significant:

FLUCTUATIONS IN THE PRICE OF RICE AND RICE LAND[12]

(1915-17 = 100)

	Rice	Rice-Land
1915-17	100	100
1920-22	234	210
1925-27	242	193
1930-32	137	147
1935-37	200	153

[11] Others are: 1) fluctuations in the price of rice, since this determined the monetary value of rents in kind; 2) the varying attractiveness of other forms of investment; 3) fluctuations in the supply of land —chiefly in the number of owner-cultivators being forced to sell out; and 4) fluctuations in the proportion, among would-be buyers, of rent-seeking landlords to owner-cultivators or those seeking land for non-agricultural uses (house-lots, etc.), the latter having quite different demand schedules.

[12] Figures for rice: Nōrinshō, Nōseikyoku [Agriculture and Forestry Ministry, Agricultural Administration Bureau], *Hompō nōgyō yōran* [Survey of Japanese Agriculture] (Tokyo, 1942), pp. 231-33. Figures for land: Nihon Kangyō Ginkō [Japan Hypothec Bank], *Tahata baibai kakaku oyobi kosakuryō* [Sale Prices and Rentals of Rice Land], annual.

There are, indeed, reasons for asserting that land became a less attractive investment after the outbreak of tenant unrest. Until 1922 the secular tendency had been for rice-land prices to rise faster than the price of rice. After that date both indices fell together, though given the wider fluctuations in rice prices, it is hard to say which fell faster. It must be remembered, though, that it was not just the deterrent of tenant rebellion that was responsible; this was a time when industrial shares yielded a higher return on investment than land ownership. Although it is easy to document individual instances of landlords selling their land and putting their money into securities, this could not have been a widespread phenomenon: the change in the price trend is certainly not of such proportions as to indicate a panic flight from land ownership. In short, there is little indication of any very deep sense of crisis stemming from conflicts over tenancy. It is not until the end of the 1920's and the early 1930's that the "agrarian crisis" becomes a catch-phrase of Japanese politics, and then it is not tenant unrest that is referred to but the collapse in prices—first of silk and later of rice and other products—which affected all sections of the rural community, landlords, tenants, and owner-cultivators alike.

The third assertion is that the landlords had been chiefly responsible for upholding the traditional forms of *nōhonshugi*—the romantic idealization of the rural way of life and of the organic harmony of the village community, uniting high and low, young and old, rich and poor in one large family which shares its joys and sorrows, its achievements and its tribulations, etc., etc. This is hard to prove but nevertheless plausible. Some of the most articulate formulators of these ideals at the beginning of the century—men such as Yokoi Jikei—were certainly landlords or the friends of landlords. At a less articulate level, as village mayors, as chairmen of agricultural societies, as school teachers, as honorary patrons of their tenants' thrift societies and self-improvement societies of the Hōtokukai type, landlords doubtless played an important part in reinforcing these ideals in the villages. Nevertheless, by the 1920's, even *before nōhonshugi* agrarianism became associated with right-wing radicalism and militarism, there was already a divorce between it and the defence of the hierarchical order and the tenancy system on which it rested. Gondō Seikyō's ideal "self-governing village communities" were unstratified communities of working farmers.[13] Officials such as Ishiguro Tadaatsu might be called *nōhonshugisha* by virtue of their interest in preserving the traditional virtues of rural life and the importance of agriculture in the economy, but they took the lead in seeking some regulation of tenancy at the landlord's expense.

When we come to the fourth assertion—that the landlords actively promoted the anticapitalist radical versions of *nōhonshugi,* or that they were in some way responsible for them—the case becomes considerably weaker. The rural activists who were involved in assassinations and attempted coups d'état—Tachibana Kōsaburō or Inoue Nisshō—were neither landlords themselves nor dependent on landlord support.[14] There is no evidence that the young officers involved in the 1932 coup were motivated by desire to maintain the landlords' hold on the villages rather than, as they claimed at their trials, by pity for the starving peasants of the famine-stricken north and by anger that the army should be endangered by the poor physique of its rural conscripts and the poor morale which resulted from their constant concern with the plight of their families in the

[13] See M. Maruyama, *Thought and Behaviour in Modern Japanese Politics* (London, 1963), pp. 42-44.

[14] A possible exception is Kanada Kennosuke, the young farmer and ex-marine in Ibaragi who secretly stole his father's pistol from the family ancestral *butsudan* altar and set off in 1933 to murder Fujiwara Ginjirō for his perfidy in making a corner in fertilizer and profiteering out of the tenants' misery. Was his father's pistol a landlord's self-defence pistol? Or was his father a reserve officer (in which case probably also a landlord)? In any case he was probably not a particularly rich landlord since Kanada had had only an elementary education. (Naimushō, Keihokyoku [Home Ministry, Police Bureau], *Shōwa-8-nen-chū ni okeru shakai-undō no jōkyō* [Social Movements in 1933], n.d., p. 912.)

villages.[15] To be sure, explicit attacks on landlords did not form a central part of their manifestoes, although Kita Ikki's plan for the revolutionary reconstruction of Japan involved a land reform and the 1934 pamphlet embodying the ideas of the army radicals gives the "tenancy problem" fourth place in a list of the causes of rural poverty—"the greatest internal problem Japan faces." (It comes after the instability of farm prices, an inefficient distribution system, and excess of labor.)[16] This relative lack of attention to the landlord-tenant problem, however, is not necessarily suspicious evidence that the rightists were being either carefully indulgent of landlord manipulators or patrons or just subconsciously considerate towards landlord fathers or second cousins. By 1930 the fall in agricultural prices, exacerbated in the north by poor harvests in the succeeding years, really had overshadowed the long-standing tenancy problem. Owner-farmers and small landlords were suffering too, and even on the Left the national peasant organizations which began as class organizations, uniting tenants to combat landlords, had become, by 1931, more predominantly peasant unions demanding policies to save the villages as a whole and seeking a broader base of village support in the process. Another reason why the radicals were less concerned with attacking landlords was doubtless the fact that they were less attractive targets. In their impetuous search for quick solutions, the radicals needed enemies who were wealthy, could plausibly be accused of decadence and corruption, were nationally powerful, well known, and assassinable. Capitalists and bourgeois politicians filled the bill admirably, but Japan had no landlords prominent in national politics.

In short, subtle landlord maneuvers in defence of their interests are neither a necessary explanation of the rightist agrarian radicalism of the 1930's, nor even a plausible one, though per-

[15] See Maruyama, *op.cit.*, p. 45.
[16] Rikugunshō, Shimbunhan [Army Ministry, Newspaper Squad], *Kokubō no hongi to sono kyōka no teishō* [On the Principles of National Defense and Its Strengthening] (Tokyo, 1934), p. 32.

haps before going further one ought to consider a secondary, weaker, form of the argument. Granted, it might be said, that the landlords had little direct connection with the violent radical movements of the 1930's, nevertheless these developments had a prelude in the more "respectable" conservative nationalist movements of the 1920's. Without the climate of opinion created by such bodies as the Kokuhonsha—patronised by generals and civil servants, national politicians and business leaders—the more violent movements of the 1930's might never have emerged. And it might well be that these semiofficially-patronised bodies owed some of their strength to landlord support.

A police list of the chairmen of district branches of two of these "respectable" conservative bodies—the Kokuhonsha and the Meijikai—provides a means of checking on this hypothesis.[17] It is not hard to imagine the kind of man one would expect to find in such a position in provincial towns—a landowner and local notable, probably a director of a rice-marketing or fertilizer company and the director of a local savings bank, a prominent local politician, and perhaps the mayor.

Of the sixty-five men listed, the authors have obtained details on the careers and positions of thirty-two. Of these, eight more or less fit such a landlord–local notable stereotype, though with some variations. (One was professor at a local medical school, one was just a landlord with no other public position except that of leader of the local Reservists' Association, one had spent most of his career as a stationmaster in Manchuria.) Three others had some clear connection with land ownership, though in a way that makes it hard to imagine that their property status played much part in the total sum of their activities. (They were: a young school teacher with a couple of hectares of land, a retired general in Kyoto with a small inherited portion of land in Nagano prefecture, and a Hokkaido businessman who acquired a temporary concession of government land

[17] Naimushō, Keihokyoku, *Shōwa-7-nen*, pp. 879-81.

which he may or may not have rented to tenants.) Another three or four in the sample were local businessmen in country districts, doubtless heavily dependent on the industries of their rural hinterland.

The majority were "modern" men with no discernible connection with the rural tradition—military men (nine of them), businessmen, local government officials, teachers, lawyers, doctors. Probably a majority were of samurai origins (eleven were certainly so, as compared with eight certainly not and thirteen uncertain) which is likely to preclude connection with the landlord class. It could well be argued that the sample is small, that the composition of the nominal local leadership is not certain indication of the composition of the membership, or that a rural lawyer with no land who serves landlord clients, chats with landlords, and wines and dines with landlords can be as much a spokesman for landlord interests as a landowner. Nevertheless, even granted these reservations, neither this survey of local conservative leaders, nor what one knows of the actual activity of such bodies as the Kokuhonsha, lead one to believe that they can be seriously considered as primarily spokesmen for landlord interests. This being granted, the last of this set of our Aunt Sally assertions—that agrarian fascism was a means of making conservatism popular with the peasant masses—does not have to be considered. The rejection of this part of the argument, however, does not invalidate the next part of the Barrington Moore thesis.

The situation in the villages (if not the subtle efforts of landlords) ensured that agrarian rightist radicalism gained support—not widespread support, perhaps, but sufficient support for the radicals to make their mark on Japanese politics and to set Japan on a new course which, although not what they intended in domestic matters (the capitalists inevitably survived attack as firmly entrenched as ever), ensured the victory of the twin policies of repression at home and aggression abroad.

What *did* the agrarian radicals do? First of all they killed prime ministers, shook governments, and induced an atmosphere of fear among the political and business leaders of the day. Was any degree of popular support a necessary condition for their actions? Almost certainly not. The young officers, at least, seem to have had an élitist contempt for the masses. Not even the Tachibanas and Inoues sought to widen their select conspiratorial circles greatly. Reflecting in prison on the failure of the February 1936 incident, one of the army conspirators wrote: "The lower classes of the nation—the most healthy core of the nation's citizens—remain an unploughed field. It is necsary to arouse them, to mobilize them in unity."[18]

On the other hand, the actions of the young officers had a lasting effect. The governments which followed their coups were more firmly under the influence of the army and more sympathetic to its policies than the governments they destroyed. The extremists failed to gain power, but the exponents of more moderate versions of their views gained influence. It can reasonably be argued that this would not have been the case if the actions of the radical extremists had not received *post hoc* a wide measure of public approval. The case for the thesis outlined above would be stronger if it could be shown that it was rural areas in particular which offered this approval and support.

The public trial of the May 1932 conspirators, the way in which the judges allowed them to issue political manifestoes from the dock, the sympathetic reporting of the trial in the national newspapers, and the lightness of their sentences—reduced to take account of the purity of their motives—are indications of the atmosphere of public sympathy in which the army's influence grew. Despite the fact that it was the "plight of the peasants" (rather than the industrial workers) which was a constant theme in the defendants' expositions of their motives, there is no evidence that they gained more support

[18] Yasuda Yū, *Gokuchū shuki* [Notes in Prison], ms.

in rurai than in urban areas. From the beginning of their trial until December 1933 the court is reported to have received 682 petitions for leniency from various right-wing groups containing 1,148,000 signatures (some of them in blood). Of these, 176, containing over half a million or forty-three percent of the signatures, came from the urban prefectures of Tokyo, Kyoto, Kanagawa, Osaka, and Hyōgo which between them contained only twenty-three percent of the population.[19]

There is certainly evidence, however, that the army sought to win rural support in the few years that followed. The army medical services organized surveys of village health standards and diets and publicized the results.[20] The war minister toured famine areas.[21] The army started its own public works schemes to provide rural employment.[22] The speeches of army generals showed a keen sense that "the villages are the army's electoral constituency," as Tokutomi Sohō wrote on one occasion. At the same time it remains arguable that these army policies were not so much designed to gain support from the farmers as inspired by a very real military concern to improve the health

[19] Naimushō, Keihokyoku, Shōwa-8-nen, pp. 886-89. It is possible, of course, that a number of these signatures were collected in rural areas by bodies with headquarters in the cities. One possible damper on rural activity on this occasion was a warning by the army headquarters of the Reservists' Association that branches were not to undertake petition movements under the association's banner—though 131 of the petitions were in fact by groups identified by the police as being groups of Reservists' Association members.

As for the general weight of rural areas in the right-wing movement, a police count of nationalist organizations and their branches at the end of 1932 showed 54% of all known branches with 63% of total membership to be in the urban prefectures listed above. If Aichi (Nagoya) and Fukuoka are included, the proportion rises to 64% and 72% respectively. Groups counted as agrarian nationalists (nōhonshugi-dantai) amounted to only 5% of the organizations and less than 1% of the members—over half of them concentrated in Ibaragi prefecture.

[20] Tokyo Asahi, November 12, 1934.

[21] Tokyo Nichinichi, October 4, 1934.

[22] Tokyo Asahi, December 19, 1934.

of its rural recruits—and the records of conscript rejections and average heights and weights showed that there was a plausible need for such measures.

Whatever the intention behind these policies, there is some evidence that they gained rural support—or at least strengthened the popularity of the army in the villages. Generalizations about the mass of the peasantry are difficult to substantiate but, for example, there seems to have been not only top level manipulation but also a strong ground swell of popular support when the chiefly rural-based[23] Reservists' Association led the Minobe witch hunt in 1935. Also, the leaders of the peasant movement were not slow to succumb to the army's embraces and to declare themselves for Japanism and against imported ideologies. It would be hard to prove that the peasant movement succumbed more quickly than the labor movement—the top leaders, after all, were active in both—but it can be said that the conversion of the peasant movement was more complete. By 1934 all the important farmers' organizations were seeking an understanding with the army; they were reported to have offered to support military expenditure if the army would support a measure to protect from distraint for debt the basic food supply of hopelessly indebted farmers.[24]

All this having been said, it remains an open question how far the army's popularity in rural areas—or anywhere else, for that matter—was a necessary condition for its success in securing a commanding position in Japanese politics and dragging the nation into war. Doubtless it was a facilitating condition. The army would not have sought to make itself popular otherwise, and the evidence is that it increasingly sought popularity as its ambitions grew—*vide* the propaganda pamphlets of 1934 and the contrast between the central restraint of the reservists

[23] Among the 131 unauthorized Reservists' Association petitions on behalf of the May 1932 defendants only 15 were from the urban prefectures, though they contained about a sixth of the signatures. See note 19 above.

[24] *Tokyo Nichinichi*, October 3, 1934.

in the petition movement of 1933 and the central encouragement of the Minobe incident of 1935. Nevertheless, rural support was *only* a facilitating factor. One must never forget that
Japanese politics were still an élitist affair of maneuvers between relatively small groups, and one must be particularly
careful to remember this when tempted by generalizations that
subsume Japanese and German fascism into the same category
as products of the same processes. It is possible that if the army
had had as bad a press between 1931 and 1936 as it had between
1921 and 1926 it would never have succeeded, but the thesis
is hard to prove. There is no question, at any rate, of popular
enthusiasm propelling the army anywhere. It moved towards
its own goals impelled by the logic of its own ambitions and
ideology. Rural support, at the most, smoothed its path.

There is another, familiar part to the Barrington Moore
thesis. It accepts the élitist nature of Japanese politics and seeks
to explain why, among the various groups in the ruling strata,
the army should have met with less resistance than it might
have.

*The traditional social structure—particularly the labor-re-
pressive form of agriculture—prevented a more egalitarian
distribution of income, which alone could have created
enough demand to allow economic growth without military expansion. It was the lack of domestic purchasing
power—particularly rural purchasing power—that led Japan to seek markets abroad. And it was economic stagnation at home that led to the unrest which made first of all
repression, and then a patriotic appeal to national solidarity
in the face of external enemies, congenial to a wide variety
of élite groups.*

Several of the assertions contained in this argument can be
accepted, though with qualification. Some industrialists were
undoubtedly attracted by the prospect of securing political control over the China market, and the policy became more attractive as the world became more tightly divided into autarchic

blocs. But still, in the early 1930's, the softer foreign policy line of Hamaguchi and Wakatsuki received a good deal of support from the zaibatsu, who saw more trading opportunities to be gained by securing British cooperation in the peaceful penetration of the Chinese market than were to be gained by force of arms. In any case, can the drive for foreign markets be directly linked to rural poverty? Japan did have a resource problem which required exports to obtain necessary imports, and one continuous concern of the army was to secure access to the natural resources necessary for a powerful military machine. Moreover, the period during which economic stagnation could reasonably be attributed to lack of domestic demand was shorter in the case of Japan than in the other industrial countries. Japan, after all, was one of the first countries to regain a buoyant economy by means of the Keynesian reflation policies launched by Takahashi in 1932.

As for the other half of the argument, there is certainly plenty of evidence that the "social problem," the problem of the spread of bad and dangerous thoughts, was a serious preoccupation of industrialists and landlords alike. We have already dealt with and dismissed the argument that landlords were responsible for the counter-growth of agrarian fascist ideas. It remains arguable that the landlords—those in the Seiyūkai, for example—were reluctant to challenge the army's pretensions to power, and happily willing to join, for example, in the demand for Minobe's blood in 1935, because the army seemed to offer a possible answer to their fears. When, as in the 1934 pamphlets, the army laid stress on the dangers of communism (which seemed a menace to the army radicals not only because of its un-Japaneseness but also because Russia seemed the most likely enemy and they feared a fifth column), it surely struck sympathetic cords.[25] Nevertheless, if it was merely the left-

[25] See, for example, *Shisōsen* [The Ideological Struggle] published by the army July 25, 1934, in which the army declared that Japan was suffering a Communist offensive and that the Russian embassy was secretly giving funds to striking trade unions and sending daily propaganda

wing threat which prompted sympathy for the army, those who felt threatened had little cause to see the situation in the 1930's as desperate enough to justify handing the reins of power over to the army. Ever since the late 1920's the police had had the situation pretty well in hand. It seems, indeed, that there was not a widespread sense of the need for an ideological counter-weight to communism until the "rot" got into the middle classes and the "Marx-boy" became a frequent phenomenon among high school and university students. It was then that the bureaucratic establishment became alarmed and that the ideologies of Japanism were given a freer hand.

The Collectivist Ethic

To move away now from the Barrington Moore thesis, if it be assumed that the crucial puzzle of the period lies neither in finding the origins of agrarian radicalism or militarist Japan-ism, nor in explaining the army's drive to internal power and external expansion, but rather in explaining why the resistance to the army was not stronger than it turned out to be, the answer must surely lie in something more complicated than the immediate fear of subversion among those who held power and privilege. We have to explain not only why some people were sympathetic or half-sympathetic to the army's policies, but also why those who were undoubtedly antipathetic towards them managed to put up only such a weak resistance.

The explanation must be sought in the ideological frame-work within which Japanese politics were conducted. The col-lectivist ideology (to which Japan doubtless owed a good deal of her military and economic strength) had a transcendent

---

broadcasts to Japan. The answer to such problems, according to this pamphlet, could "be summed up in one word—*kōka*, the spread of the imperial influence. In its great mission to bring true racial equality, true brotherhood of man, peace and human happiness, and in its effective-ness to these ends, the world-wide spread of the imperial influence prom-ises infinitely more than the world-wide spread of communism, and the struggle between them is the essence of the ideological war."

moral authority in Japan which was not matched in any other contemporary industrial nation. The family, united and transcendent, demanding the subordination of individual interests to the interests of "the house," was a paradigm for all social groups. The state was likened to the family, with the emperor as *pater familias*; the enterprise was a pseudo-family; family-like unity was the ideal state of the harmonious village; even army officers were spoken of as "mothers" to the other ranks, who were called their "children." So all-pervasive was this ideal that, even though Japan had acquired many of the political and economic forms of an individualistic democracy, individualism remained a sin—*kojinshugi*, the usual translation of "individualism," had just as pejorative overtones as *rikoshugi*, the usual translation of "selfishness." As a consequence, the defenders of individualistic democracy had one hand tied behind their backs. They were charged with selfishness, with arrogant contempt of society and of Japanese traditions, with espousing ideals that held no place for the emperor as father of his people. They were vulnerable to such charges not only because of their gravity, given the prevailing atmosphere, but also because they themselves had absorbed so many of the assumptions underlying the collectivist ideology that they lacked the confidence successfully to resist the army and its civilian supporters.

To return to the main theme of this chapter, it can be argued that the rural segment of Japanese society had a lot to do with the prevalence of this ideology.

One might expand on the thesis of the importance of the collectivist ethic by comparing Japan with England. In England the Left was as powerful a threat to the interests of those who held power and property as it was in Japan. Realistically, in England it was even more so: Japan never saw anything like the general strike as a manifestation of the Left's strength. Yet there was no totalitarian repression in England. One reason was the lack of an ethic to justify absolute and total condemnation of the "selfish" assertion of individual rights. The workers were demanding rights, and in the British tradition the demanding of rights in itself was not a wicked thing. Nobles once demanded, and secured, recognition of their rights *vis-à-vis* the king. The middle classes won recognition of their rights *vis-à-vis* the aristocracy. Now the workers were pushing the process through a third round. Those who had power and property to lose resisted as hard as they could, but—although they may have used arguments involving "national interests" and the inherent unfitness of the workers to share in power— their consciousness that they were resisting in their own self-interest was never far below the surface. The situation was seen as a clash between one group's self-interest and another's, neither side having any claim to exclusive moral rectitude.

In Japan, on the other hand, the emphasis on harmony precluded the view of society as a balancing of conflicting self-interests. The demand for recognition of one's rights was in itself unworthy. All should have the interests of the collectivity at heart, and it was only in terms of Japan's interests that demands for a change in the status quo could properly be framed. Of course, as is usual in such situations, those who held power could claim a monopoly right to interpret what the interests of the nation were. Thus the workers did not threaten the interests of the capitalists so much as the harmony of the Japanese state. The tenants did not simply threaten landlords, they jeopardized the traditional peaceful unity of the village. The only legislation to deal with "social problems" which succeeded in passing the Diet in the 1920's was designed, not to define clearly the legitimate rights of trade unions and tenant unions (as some of the more forward-looking bureaucrats and even politicians wanted), but to provide for "conciliation" and the restoration of harmony.

The same assumptions underlay the criticism—from the Center as well as from the radical Right—of the army's stalking horse, the decadent capitalist. One quotation will serve to illustrate the point to be made. In the short period in 1930 when Japan returned to the gold standard, certain Japanese business-

men (notably Mitsui) exported a good deal of gold to buy
dollars—to their own considerable profit, as it turned out,
though to the detriment of the nation's finances. This "dollar-
buying incident" aroused great public comment, and Mitsui
was roundly attacked by everyone from Inoue, the finance minister, downwards. The economist Takahashi Kamekichi later
had this to say about the incident.[26]

> It was illogical for Inoue, having sought to put Japan on the
> gold standard, to say that it was wrong to buy dollars. It was
> freely permitted. It was up to him to arrange matters so that
> nobody wanted to. It was no good just trying to use compul-
> sion. As a matter of fact if he had only tried to use compul-
> sion it would not have mattered so much. But he branded
> them as traitors, as un-Japanese. . . . There's a connection
> between that and the way the rightists later on branded
> everything they disagreed with as un-Japanese. That was the
> most dangerous thing about it all.

England too had its "bankers' conspiracy" supposedly responsible for the collapse of the Labour government in 1931. "The
bankers" were objects of hate, both on the Left and on the
fascist Right, but they were hated on Takahashi's premises,
not on those of the young officers or Inoue. Their defence of
their own interests was considered inevitable and not in itself a sign of personal moral turpitude. What was wrong was
the structure of British society, which made them so powerful
and allowed them to get away with it? It was that which had
to be changed. In Japan, on the other hand, the behavior of
Mitsui in hedging against a fall in yen values was wicked and
traitorous. Consequently it was possible in Japan, but not in
England, to argue that a few assassinations and the moral re-
generation of a few bankers were what was chiefly required to

[26] *Shōwa keizaishi e no shōgen* [Evidence for an Economic History
of the Shōwa Era]; quoted in Ōuchi Tsutomu, *Fascism e no michi*
[The Road to Fascism], Chūō Kōronsha, *Nihon no rekishi* [History of
Japan], no. 24 (1967), p. 178.

mend matters. So, when Baron Dan of Mitsui was assassinated, his assassin gained a good deal of sympathy, and it was Mitsui which had to apologize. Within a year it was trying to improve its public image by large contributions to patriotic charities. The pass had already been sold.

In this respect the 1930's were already different from the 1920's: the collectivist ethic was a good deal stronger. After all, a decade earlier it had been easier to make overt, if tentative, demands for the extension of rights—the right of all men to vote, the right of trade unions to legal protection, the right of political parties to form governments. One reason for the change was that the conservative reaction to such demands, and the social unrest from which they sprang, took the form of a reassertion of the traditional collectivism, reinterpreted, infused with a more deadening sacredness by continuous reference to the emperor and the national polity, and diffused with greater insistence in the schools and through the organs of public opinion. "Respectable" organizations like the Meijikai or the Kokuhonsha had a lot to do with these developments. The founding declaration of the Kokuhonsha is clear enough. "Although," it says, "since the Meiji Restoration, civilization has much advanced and learning and the arts have flourished, ways of wilful and selfish frivolity threaten to overwhelm the spirit of sturdy honesty; strange and extreme ideas sweep aside traditional habits of gentleness and humility, daily society falls into disorder and men's hearts grow violent." Consequently the future of the nation and the race could only be assured if every effort was maintained to "nurture and revive our national spirit, make firm the foundations of the nation, promote intellectual knowledge and moral virtue with equal emphasis, and so make shiningly manifest to the world the quintessential glory of our national polity."[27]

Alone, these respectable rightist associations might not have changed the atmosphere, but many of their members, and many who were not their members, also financed, paid protection

[27] Naimushō, Keihokyoku, *Shōwa-7-nen*, p. 874.

money to, or employed, the less respectable, more violent right-wing groups which specialized in terrorizing the Left and blackmailing the Right. If conservative property-holders had instead relied on the police, or if they had employed ordinary unideological thugs to break up picket lines and demonstrations, the effect might have been different. As it was, Japanese thugs felt impelled to claim a moral respectability by doing their thuggery for the emperor and class harmony, and their financial backers allowed and encouraged them to do so. (Was it because Japanese thugs were different from other thugs, or because only Japan had available, in the tradition of the *rōnin* activists of the 1860's, a legitimating ethic for violence?)

The winds sown by the Kokuhonsha and the financial backers of the right-wing terrorists were reaped as a whirlwind in the 1930's when the violence of the latter and the rhetoric of the former were married to real ideological convictions and genuine hatred for the rich and powerful. Pairs of these three elements—violence, rhetoric, and ideological conviction—had appeared in combination before: the conservative Kokuhonsha rhetoric and establishment-serving violence in the terrorist thugs; reformist ideological convictions and anti-establishment violence in such men as Asahi Heigo, the assassin of the head of the Yasuda zaibatsu in 1921. Ideological conviction, anti-establishment violence, *and* Kokuhonsha-type rhetoric were the hallmark of the planners of a Shōwa Restoration in the 1930's. The difference between Asahi Heigo and the members of the Blood Brotherhood who killed the Mitsui manager ten years later was that the former's call for a Taishō Restoration used little of the conservative rhetoric,[28] whilst the latter's pro-

[28] It was not entirely free of such rhetoric. Asahi does, in his testament, speak of the inrush of foreign ideology and the danger to the "national polity," but neither the emperor nor the national polity figure in his nine-point plan for a Taishō restoration. It is concerned with rooting out class inequality, nationalizing land and big business, and inaugurating universal suffrage. (R. Tsunoda, et al., eds., *Sources of the Japanese Tradition* [1958], p. 768.)

nouncements were deeply imbued with it (*and* they had their pistols supplied by members of the emperor's armed forces).

Some of the very men who had helped to promote Kokuhonsha ideology were nearly gobbled up by the tiger they failed to ride—Ikeda Seihin, for instance, a councilor of the Kokuhonsha, figured on the Blood Brotherhood's assassination list.[29] The point here is that as terror was conjoined with the moral authority of the collectivist ethic, as the new sanction of physical violence was added to the older social sanction implied by charges of un-Japaneseness, traitorous self-seeking, disloyalty, and failure to understand the national polity, it became harder and harder for the liberal opposition to assert itself against the army.

To return to our concern with the villages—if one can find

[29] A disconcerted alarm at a movement got out of hand is well reflected in the preface to the long section on rightist movements in the Home Office Police Bureau's report on social movements in 1933 (Naimushō, Keihokyoku, *Shōwa-8-nen*, p. 922):

In truly sincere nationalist movements, those which are firmly rooted in the great ideals on which our nation was founded, which are based on a central loyalty to the Emperor and seek, at home to promote the nation's welfare, abroad to diffuse the spiritual essence of our Empire throughout the world—in such movements there is, of course, nothing which requires the control of the police authority. To be sure, from time to time, in the development of these movements there have been some who have sheltered behind the admirable slogans of loyalty and patriotism to become professional blackmailers, or who have sometimes resorted to violence or in other ways broken the law, but it has been rare for any special preventive police measures to be required.

Since about 1931, the situation has changed. We have seen the rapid emergence of the so-called modern nationalist movements stressing a need for the total reformation of Japan, a growing number of whose exponents have planned a resort to illegal means in order to carry through a radical social revolution, while accompanying this trend there has been a rapid increase in the circulation of inflammatory literature of an extreme kind, printed in secret and designed to incite to direct action or otherwise to unsettle the public mind.

a reasonably satisfactory explanation for the reinforcement of collectivist Japanism in the events of the 1920's and the reaction to growing class conflict, one is left with the further question why the latent strength of this collectivistic ethic remained sufficiently strong in the 1920's for it to be thus reinforced. Here the rural social structure has importance. It is plausible to argue that it was above all the villages that preserved the ethic—partly because of the inertia of tradition, partly because landlords had an interest in preserving it. Itō Hakubun, writing in Ōkuma's *Fifty Years of New Japan*, had some shrewd things to say about the holistic ethic of Japanese political life. During the Tokugawa period of seclusion, he (or his ghost writer?) wrote:

We had . . . unconsciously become a vast village community where cold intellect and calculation of public events was always restrained and even often hindered by warm emotions between man and man. . . . It is this moral and emotional factor which will, in the future, form a healthy barrier against the threatening advance of socialistic ideas. It must, of course, be admitted that this social peculiarity is not without beneficial influences. It mitigates the conflict, serves as the lubricator of social organisms, and tends generally to act as a powerful lever for the practical application of the moral principle of mutual assistance between fellow citizens. But unless curbed and held in restraint, it too may exercise baneful influences on society, for in any village community, where feelings and emotions hold a higher place than intellect, free discussion is apt to be smothered, attainment and transference of power liable to become a family question of a powerful oligarchy, and the realization of such a regime as constitutional monarchy to become an impossibility, simply because in any representative regime free discussion is a matter of prime necessity. . . .[30]

Itō's use of the village metaphor is instructive. It was the villages that preserved these values and patterns of behavior,

[30] Tsunoda, *op.cit.*, pp. 674-75.

the villages that embodied these values in the established institutions of farming cooperation and in the formal social sanctions of ostracism; it was the village poor who knew that the only means of security lay in the assiduous maintenance of harmonious social relations with neighbors and kin, village families that might divorce a son's bride for her ineptness at maintaining conventional relations with neighbors, and village families that bred into the personalities of their children a deference to all authoritarian demands to conform to the needs of the community as a whole. The fact that three quarters of the politically participant adults in 1930 were born in villages[31] has a lot to do with what happened in the following decade.

[31] In 1903, 79 percent of the population was recorded as living in communities of fewer than 10,000 inhabitants.

CHAPTER VII

The Economic Muddle of the 1920's*

HUGH T. PATRICK

Introduction

IN ANALYZING the dilemmas of Japan's growth in the interwar period, I regard the basic economic question to be: To what extent did economic factors, and precisely what factors, cause Japan to choose, or stumble onto, the path which led to militarism and war? Posing the issue so broadly inevitably raises the problem of complete explanation, since the relative importance of economic factors can be determined only if we know the relative importance of all other causes—political, social, cultural, external, etc. Clearly economic and noneconomic factors are interrelated in complex ways—by feedbacks and interdependence—the facts much less the implications of which are only dimly perceived. Moreover, our understanding of the interwar economy is at a lower level than for either the Meiji or post–World War II periods. All of which has led me to feel that we—or at least I—cannot yet evaluate with complete adequacy even the relevance of economic factors.

The focus of this chapter, then, is on essentially economic questions. What was the actual economic performance? What was the growth of output, in aggregate and by major sector? What was the importance of foreign trade, the balance of payments, and foreign economic relations generally? How about employment, the price level, the institutional framework?

* I am indebted to Yoshiko Kido for research assistance. In addition I benefitted from comments by participants in this Conference, and from participant comments on a revised version presented at the Yale Economic Growth Center Conference on the Role of Government in Economic Development (April 1968) and at the Japan Economic Seminar (May 1968).

What were the relevant government economic policy objectives and actions? These all are considered, not simply as economic history, but to amplify and support my basic argument.

A host of other important economic questions are not directly considered (Alas, one cannot do everything!): To what degree did industrialization bring about, and depend on, an industrial structure which promoted the increasing concentration of economic power? To what degree were the zaibatsu able to, and anxious to, translate economic into political power? Was inequality of income and wealth distribution really widening? What was happening to the level of living of various groups—landlords, farmers, tenants, owners of large firms, of small farms, their employees, etc? Was relative inequality the problem, or was that subordinate to absolute improvement (or deterioration) in levels of living?

As Lockwood points out, there is a great difference between using the power of the economy "as a *means* to securing national and imperial power," and "economic development as the creator, i.e., as a propelling force."[1] In the former case, the economy may be a constraint upon the political decision to pursue certain policies, or a constraint upon the success of those policies (as was ultimately true in World War II). In viewing the economy as a propelling force, important links in the analysis of the causal sequence are weak or nonexistent. It is obvious that Japan had economic problems in the 1920's and early 1930's; they were epitomized in the increasing distress of both the agrarian and urban poor and the increasing concentration of economic power in the hands of the zaibatsu. What is not clear is how these difficulties actually led (or whether they necessarily led) to militarism.

[1] See his thoughtful essay about the influence of economic development on political institutions in Japan: William W. Lockwood, "Economic and Political Modernization—Japan," in Robert E. Ward and Dankwart A. Rustow, eds., *Political Modernization in Japan and Turkey* (Princeton, 1964), p. 128.

The Japanese case is often cited as an example of active and effective government stimulation of economic growth, by fostering a market environment conducive to the sustained expansion of output by private enterprise. The interwar experience weakens this generalization. Stated baldly it is my thesis that the Japanese government's muddled objective to return to the gold standard at pre–World War I par, and the attendant deflationary fiscal and monetary policies taken in the 1920's, were responsible for much of the retardation of growth in that decade. At fault was not the gold standard itself, but the decision to compete internationally by pushing down the domestic price level and returning to gold at the old par, rather than depreciating the yen and establishing a new, lower yen parity with gold. Deflation slowed growth. Slower growth caused, or at least exacerbated, the stresses of industrialization and the social and political conditions which put the militarists in power. It is precisely here that the causal relationship becomes acute, and my essay frankly exploratory.

While a major change in objectives, and concomitant changes in fiscal and monetary policy, resulted in rapid growth from 1932 to 1936 and thereafter for a few more years, by then it was too late; the military was increasingly entrenched in the government and was on the path toward the devastation of World War II. I thus focus on government macro-policies in the fiscal, monetary, and exchange-rate arenas (excluding other areas of government policy) and rather more on the period of the 1920's than the 1930's. I presume that the main economic forces that contributed to the military's ascension to power emerged in the 1920's, and that the later period involved, to a substantial degree, the working out of these forces.

I proceed first by describing briefly the interwar economy, next by discussing the government's macro-policies, and finally by raising some of the broader issues of the relationship of economic policy to the course on which Japan found itself in the 1930's.

Domestic Economic Performance in the Interwar Period

The literature on the Japanese economy refers to the 1920's as a period of lagging or faltering growth. Relative to both the long-run trend (since 1885) and the World War I boom this certainly is correct, as demonstrated in Table 1. The facts[2]

TABLE 1

GROWTH RATE OF REAL NET DOMESTIC PRODUCT PER DECADE
(PER CENT)

1880-1890	29.5	1910-1920	61.5
1890-1900	67.6	1920-1930	33.4
1900-1910	42.7	1930-1940	72.1

NOTE: Based on midpoint of five-year averages.

SOURCE: Derived from Yujiro Hayami and Saburo Yamada, "Agricultural Productivity at the Beginning of Industrialization," in Kazushi Ohkawa, Bruce F. Johnston, and Hiromitsu Kaneda, eds., *Agriculture and Economic Growth: Japan's Experience* (Princeton and Tokyo, 1970), Appendix C, p. 135.

of the growth of net domestic product (NDP) and of agriculture and manufacturing—the two major components for which

[2] The aggregate "facts" are fairly rough. The basic estimates of Japan's interwar GNP, *in toto* and by sector of production and type of use, in current prices and adjusted for price changes, in absolute amount and growth rates, secularly and cyclically, are in a jumble. The standard Ohkawa estimates prepared in the early 1950's are being revised by Professor Ohkawa and others at the Economic Research Institute, Hitotsubashi University, based upon new estimates of agricultural and industrial production and other important data. The new estimates will appear, as have already appeared some of the underlying data, in the thirteen-volume series *Estimates of Long-Term Economic Statistics of Japan Since 1868* (Tokyo, 1965 and later), hereafter referred to as *LTES*. For this paper I use interim aggregate output and related estimates which are better than the older published data, but which no doubt will be superseded by the new *LTES* estimates once they are completed. My estimates are based on the method used by Hayami and Yamada (see Table 1). The tertiary sector output, almost half the total, is estimated by applying ratios to primary and secondary production. Manufacturing output is based on the Shionoya industrial production index. Price deflation of the various output series in order to exclude the effects of changes in the price level is imperfect and, to some extent, hazardous.

relatively good data are available—suggest the following. First, the growth of NDP throughout the 1920's was indeed moderate but on the whole respectable, at a peak-to-peak (1919-1928) annual rate of 3.2 percent, and trough-to-trough (1920-1930) rate also of 3.2 percent. During the 1930's, however, growth was considerably more rapid: 5.5 percent annually between 1928 and 1938. (The 5.9 percent rate between 1930 and 1938 is somewhat misleading since 1930 was the bottom of a recession while 1938 represented continued high growth.)

Secondly, the increase in NDP during the 1920's was entirely in manufacturing and services; as a trend, value added in agriculture did not rise at all. Not only was the stagnation of agriculture the dominant contributor to the retardation of the overall growth rate, but also it had important implications for intersectoral relationships and for the growing agrarian distress. This very poor agrarian performance was true of both the 1920's and the 1930's.

Thirdly, the year-to-year growth rate of NDP fluctuated considerably. The absolute decline of 1920 was followed by a short-lived boom, and the Tokyo-Yokohama earthquake of 1923 by another short-lived boom, while 1929-1930 saw another absolute decline (though the statistics indicate a substantially less drastic decline than my conventional impression). Thereafter, the growth rate was rapid, except for a brief slowdown in 1934. Probably the methods for estimating NDP (especially manufacturing value added) understate the actual degree of cyclical instability. For example, Professor Yasuba's index of industrial production, while not substantially different from that of Professor Shionoya, for the period 1919-1935 as a whole, measures absolute declines of 1.4 percent in manufacturing value added in 1930 and a further 5.5 percent in 1931. Moreover, the NDP figures mask what happened in the major goods-producing sectors. Agricultural production fluctuated rather widely, and real value added in agriculture swung back and forth even further (reflecting changes in the real prices of output and current inputs—fertilizers, etc.).

These aggregate results carry over directly into per worker and per capita terms. NDP per worker increased by ninety-three percent and relative to total population by seventy-eight percent between 1919 and 1938, with most of the growth occurring in the 1930's. Agricultural output per worker increased very slowly, and then really only after 1934 (when some decline in the agricultural labor force began).

Average personal consumption per worker and per capita also rose moderately, though less rapidly than NDP since a higher proportion of output was devoted to government expenditures and private investment. Per capita average consumption grew only five percent between the 1922 and 1928 peaks, but subsequently declined almost as much to the low in 1932; the real increase came only thereafter. Moreover, this average level of living disguises what was probably an increasing inequality of living standards. The benefits of growth apparently accrued mainly to owners and employees of large-scale enterprise, skilled workers, government officials, landlords, and professionals, while workers in small-scale manufacturing and service establishments and most farmers had no improvement, and even declines. For them productivity was virtually constant, and real wages (deflated for changes in the cost of living), which remained high in the 1920's, declined in the Great Depression and were slow to rise thereafter. It was this problem of income distribution, rather than substantial overall declines in output, that would seem to account for the distress and tensions of the period.

RETARDATION IN AGRICULTURE

Why did this occur? One answer lies in the nature of economic performance in agriculture and manufacturing respectively. The striking change was the slowdown in agricultural output (in both total production and value added). This was due almost entirely to a slowdown in the growth of total productivity, since there was only a small decrease in the growth rate of total inputs (a weighted average of land, labor, capital, and current inputs such as seeds and fertilizers). Current inputs actually increased, and capital inputs grew at about the same rate as earlier (though notably not in trees, as the silk boom finally ground to a halt). The growth of arable land area slowed down considerably, and the agrarian labor force actually decreased somewhat—but not in substantial numbers until the mid-1930's.[3]

Why then did the rate of growth of agricultural output per unit of land, and per worker, slow down so much? The issue is complex, and we do not have definitive answers. Clearly, agrarian price declines and the deflationary policy were important factors.[4]

On net balance, price incentives for farmers to produce declined substantially between 1925 and the 1931 low for relevant price indices.[5] Prices farmers received dropped by 53.4 percent, although, of course, nonagricultural prices also decreased sharply (the manufacturers' price index by 46.0 percent and wholesale price index by 42.7 percent). The impact on real farm incomes was twofold: in terms of the absolute decline and relative to the decrease in prices of goods purchased by farmers.

The absolute decline in prices increased the burden of agricultural debt proportionately. Farm debt, as surveyed in 1929, was high; at 4.59 billion yen it was 86.6 percent greater than

[3] For supporting data see Mataji Umemura et al., *Agriculture, LTES*, IX.

[4] Ohkawa and Johnston cite these, together with a reduced potential for technological advance in the agricultural structure of small farms and substantial tenantry, as the major causes of the slowdown. See Kazushi Ohkawa and Bruce F. Johnston, "The Transferability of the Japanese Pattern of Modernizing Traditional Agriculture," in Erik Thorbecke, ed., *The Role of Agriculture in Economic Development*, Universities–National Bureau Conference Series No. 21 (New York, 1969).

[5] For price data see Kazushi Ohkawa et al., *Prices, LTES*, VIII; Mataji Umemura et al., *op.cit.*

value added in agriculture that year. Most (56.5 percent) was owed to moneylenders and other individuals.[6] Moreover, the price of land declined substantially, so that the value of debts relative to assets rose substantially. Rents, however, adjusted. In kind (*koku* of rice per *tan* of paddy) they actually decreased slightly, and in money terms (for upland fields) they dropped commensurately. Moneylenders, but not rentiers, benefitted from the deflation so long as their borrowers did not go bankrupt.

To a considerable extent the adverse impact on real farm income of the absolute decline in prices received for agricultural goods sold was offset by the decrease in prices paid by farmers for goods they used in production and consumption. Prices for fertilizer and other current inputs actually decreased slightly more than prices of agricultural output. However, the rural consumption price index did not decline as much (32.9 percent). The terms of trade did turn somewhat against agriculture, however measured.[7]

This decline in farm prices occurred for a variety of reasons. One was the government policy to increase imports of cheap rice from Taiwan and Korea, which bid the price down in Japan. Liu and Suits have estimated that "the inclusion of Korea and Formosa in the Japanese rice market resulted in the suppression of the rice price in Japan by 18 per cent," and that "a 1 per cent increase in the total rice imports from the colonies would result in a 1.75 per cent reduction in the price of rice," and hence that the incentives in the rice market operated so as to restrict rice output in Japan and encourage it in the colonies.[8] The second reason was the general deflationary policy of

[6] Asakura Kōkichi, *Nōgyō kinyūron* [Treatise on Agricultural Finance] (Tokyo, 1949), p. 54.

[7] Between 1925 and the 1931 trough the ratio of rural to urban consumer prices dropped by 5.6 percent; the ratio of prices farmers received to rural consumer prices, by 30.7 percent; and the ratio of prices farmers received to the manufactured goods price index, by 13.7 percent.

[8] Jung-Chao Liu and Daniel B. Suits, "An Econometric Model of a Rice Market," *Tunghai Journal* (Taiwan, July 1962).

the government until 1931; probably prices were less elastic for agricultural than for manufactured goods. The third, the slide-off of world prices for agricultural goods beginning in the mid-1920's, and particularly (for Japan) the decline in the price of raw silk, put downward pressure on Japanese agricultural prices.

The decrease of silk prices by thirty-two percent between 1925 and 1929, and by another third by 1931, had a widespread agrarian impact, since two farm families out of five relied to some extent upon sericulture as a source of cash income. However, the average extent of this adversity may have been exaggerated. Sericulture at its maximum (in 1925 and again in 1929) constituted nineteen percent of total farm production at current prices; the minimum was eight percent in 1934 (when the price was unusually low). Suppose we take 1925 as the "right" base[9] for the price of silk relative to all agricultural goods (and this is favorable to silk since its price was at a peak) and assume that the price of silk had declined no more than the prices of all agricultural goods (excluding silk). The increase in the value of agricultural output in 1931 would have been about ninety million yen (in 1934-36 constant prices), or approximately three percent; in 1934 it would have been about 275 million yen (eight percent).[10]

Presumably the decreases in prices reduced incentives for farmers to produce. The labor inputs are measured in man-years, so we do not know whether or not farmers worked fewer man-hours per year. It appears that they did,[11] since the proportion

[9] Prices of silk tended to fluctuate more than agricultural commodities *in toto*, rising more during the World War I boom, falling more between 1925 and 1931, and rising more thereafter. This makes it particularly difficult to determine a "normal" base year.

[10] This is computed by applying the percentage decline in agricultural prices (excluding silk weighted at 10 percent) to the 1925 silk price and multiplying it by the quantity produced. This figure is compared with the value when the actual price decline is used.

[11] Takekazu Ogura, ed., *Agricultural Development in Modern Japan* (Tokyo, 1963), p. 38.

of land double-cropped actually decreased slightly. Furthermore, the deflationary conditions in the 1920's and early 1930's slowed the rate of growth in nonfarm employment opportunities—especially in highly productive, large-scale manufacturing —as well as reducing the rate of growth of demand for agricultural products.

MANUFACTURING: OUTPUT, EMPLOYMENT, WAGES

The interwar performance of the manufacturing sector, in terms of output, was considerably better than that of the agricultural sector. Between 1919 and 1940, value added in manufacturing grew at a 6.0 percent average annual rate. Following a slowdown in the early 1920's, the growth rate accelerated from an average annual rate of 7.0 percent for 1925-30, to 8.2 percent for 1930-35, and 11.0 percent for 1935-40. While the cotton textile industry came into full bloom, as a result of the World War I boom, there was continued diversification of production, particularly in iron and steel, chemicals, and machinery. Large firms probably grew in relative importance. Nonetheless, as late as 1929, of gross output in factories of five or more employees, as recorded in the census of manufactures, slightly less than one-third was produced by firms of 500 or more employees, and about forty percent came from firms of from five to ninety-nine employees. Firms with four or fewer employees produced from a fourth to a fifth of total manufacturing output.

As an absorber of labor, the manufacturing sector's performance was not as good. The population censuses of 1920, 1930, and 1940 provide us the most complete information on the ways in which the economically active population (labor force) was used. Manufacturing absorbed only eleven percent of the increase in the labor force in the 1920's, but seventy-four percent in the 1930's.[12] The 1920's and early 1930's were a period of workers looking anywhere for jobs; not until the mid-1930's

---

[12] Irene B. Taeuber, *The Population of Japan* (Princeton, 1958), p. 87.

did productive jobs became available. The result was a large swelling of the labor force in low-productivity service activities, notably retail trade and personal services, with correspondingly low incomes. Industrialization and population growth resulted in "surplus labor" spilling over from agriculture into the cities.

Even those absorbed into manufacturing between 1920 and 1930 were hired mainly by small, low-productivity establishments.[13] Employment in firms of 500 or more workers decreased by 90,000 (15.8 percent of the 1920 base) over the decade, a decline from 1927 on more than offsetting earlier increases. Not until 1933 did employment in such large firms begin to grow significantly. Corresponding to this distribution of labor was a large and widening difference in output per worker and wages per worker relative to firm size.[14] Overall, output per worker in manufacturing rose both absolutely and relative to agriculture. However, the productivity and wages of small manufacturing firms were probably fairly closely related to those in agriculture. The large firms were able to increase capital per worker substantially and to take advantage of the most modern technology, thereby enhancing output per worker. This gave them the ability to pay higher wages, which they did for reasons which are not entirely clear. Some partial explanations are that large firms probably used more skilled labor, they wanted to reduce labor turnover, they used relatively more males than females, they set higher educational standards for

[13] If we assume the same industrial definitions for the population census and the census of factory manufacturing, then of the 264,000 increase in employment in manufacturing between 1920 and 1930, 147,000 were in establishments of four workers or less, 95,000 in firms of from five to ninety-nine employees, 112,000 in firms of 100-499 employees, and minus 90,000 in firms of 500 or more employees.

[14] See Miyohei Shinohara, *Growth and Cycles in the Japanese Economy* (Tokyo, 1962), pp. 14-16; Koji Taira, "The Dynamics of Japanese Wage Differentials, 1881-1959," Ph.D. dissertation, Stanford University, 1961, pp. 74-84; and Konosuke Odaka, "A History of Money Wages in the Northern Kyūshū Industrial Area, 1898-1939," *Hitotsubashi Journal of Economics*, VIII:2 (February 1968).

hiring employees, they wanted first pick of employees. The interwar period was characterized by what Ohkawa and Rosovsky have termed the "differential structure"—a widening productivity and wage gap between the modern sector, comprising large-scale industrial enterprises (using modern technology and relatively large amounts of capital per worker), and the traditional sector of small-scale, labor-intensive units of production (using traditional, or less modern, techniques). The traditional sector was typified by agriculture, many small manufacturing enterprises, and certain components of the service sectors.[15]

During the World War I boom, money wages in manufacturing and agriculture rose rapidly, but the cost of living went up at an equal rate, so that real wages remained constant. In 1919, and again in 1921 when the cost of living increase had halted, money and real wages increased sharply for both skilled and unskilled labor. The remainder of the 1920's and the early 1930's were a time of erratic but persistent and heightening deflation. The cost of living decreased at first slightly and then, between 1928 and 1932, sharply. Money wages also declined slightly during the 1920's, so that real wages were relatively constant until 1930, and at considerably higher levels than those prior to 1919.

With the onslaught of the Great Depression, the pattern of money and real wages diverged for skilled and for unskilled labor.[16] For unskilled labor (typified by female workers in agriculture and textiles—whose relative wage rates remained very stable—and by male workers in agriculture) money wages were reduced even more than the sharp decline in prices, so that real wages dropped by twenty percent or more before beginning to rise again in the mid-1930's. For skilled labor (typified by male workers in iron and steel and in machinery), money wages

[15] Kazushi Ohkawa and Henry Rosovsky, "A Century of Japanese Economic Growth," in W. W. Lockwood, ed., *The State and Economic Enterprise in Japan* (Princeton, 1965).

[16] See Kazushi Ohkawa et al., *op.cit.*; Mataji Umemura et al., *op.cit.*; and Odaka, *op.cit.*

declined only slightly and real wages actually increased between 1929 and 1933. Hence, the skilled-worker wages rose relative to the unskilled. This, together with the real wage patterns during the 1920's, suggests the existence of two distinct labor markets in interwar Japan: skilled and unskilled. The supply of skilled workers was neither highly elastic nor increasing more rapidly than increases in demand. Demand for skilled workers grew owing to the overall growth of industry; its changing composition, particularly the rise of such industries as machinery, iron and steel, and chemicals, which required a higher proportion of skilled workers; and a rising capital/labor ratio, embodying more skill-using technologies. In contrast, the supply of unskilled workers was highly elastic; indeed, there was an overflow into services. Yet demand for unskilled workers increased only slowly.

How do we explain these wage-employment-output relationships? The World War I boom culminated in a temporary labor shortage, even for unskilled labor. As indicated above, the continuing real wage increases for skilled workers is consonant with demand-supply relationships for their services. For unskilled workers the answers are less clear. During the 1920's unskilled workers were not being absorbed into manufacturing in sufficient numbers, relative to supply, to suggest continuing shortage.

It appears that an important component of the explanation lies in the downward stickiness of money wages. For unskilled workers there was some actual decline during the 1920's in money wage rates, but it was resisted, as the rising number of labor disputes, and their causes, testify. Not until the 1930-32 depression were firms able to push unskilled-worker money wages down substantially.[17] The downward stickiness of

[17] For example, money wages for female and cotton textile workers were 0.92 yen/day in 1922, 0.82 in 1928, and thereafter fell sharply to 0.55 in 1932. In part, mills substituted younger for older girls. There was substantial turnover of workers; new workers could be and were hired at lower wage rates.

money wage rates appears to be a common characteristic of industrial countries, rather than a characteristic that was specific to Japan. Indeed, in the face of real adversity, the Japanese wage and price structure was considerably more flexible than that in the United Kingdom, Germany, or the United States.[18]

My interpretation is that all this was produced by a combination of a disequilibria induced by the World War I boom, the subsequent deflationary expectations of businessmen about price movements, and a downward stickiness of money wages. The World War I boom was tremendous; it engendered the most rapid industrial and overall growth Japan had ever had and, in the process, resulted in a shortage of industrial labor, high prices (a doubling of the price level), and high money wages. It is likely that temporarily the price of labor relative to capital was higher than relative stocks of labor and capital would dictate in equilibrium. If these relative prices tended to continue, it would pay firms to substitute capital for labor. Businessmen realized that their prices for goods were high and that the pressures of foreign competition would push prices down. They could anticipate deflationary fiscal and monetary policies. This made it imperative that ways be found to reduce the costs of production. Moreover, they probably felt that it would not be easy to push money wages down much unless there was a serious recession, whereas they could (correctly) expect some decrease in the price of investment goods, especially imported (or import-competitive) machinery. Hence, firms felt it economical to obtain a more stable labor force, to train it more as skill requirements increased, and to use more capital-intensive techniques of production.

Institutional factors were not unimportant. It was known that legislation restricting night shift work by women and children would go into effect in the late 1920's. This struck particularly hard at the textile industry, which alone accounted for more than half of all factory employment. Firms responded

[18] See the comparisons for 1929-31 in W. Arthur Lewis, *Economic Survey, 1919-1939* (London, 1949), p. 118.

by "rationalization"; for example, in cotton spinning the number of operative spindles per worker increased from twenty-three in 1922 (not much different from the pre–World War I average) to forty-two in 1930 and fifty-three in 1935.

The substitution of capital for labor was probably reinforced by an imperfect capital market in which large firms, and firms affiliated with large banks, obtained access to funds to finance investment fairly easily and at relatively low cost, whereas smaller firms had difficulty borrowing and issuing bonds and had to do so at higher cost. Moreover, the same gap probably existed in the ability to borrow and absorb foreign technology. All of this ties in with economies of scale. To the extent that the differential structure resulted from skill differentials and market imperfections, it is probably a characteristic common to all industrializing countries.

Restoration of International Equilibrium: The Dilemmas of Economic Policy

A continuing motif of the previous section is the impact of deflationary pressures culminating in 1931: their impact on agricultural productivity; on the capital/labor ratio in manufacturing (especially in large firms); on output per worker in manufacturing and on the ability (inability really) of the manufacturing sector to absorb the growing labor force; on the persistently high level of real wages due to the downward stickiness of money wages; and on the distribution of income. The deflationary pressures were essentially a policy response by the government to the difficulties, emanating from World War I, in restoring the equilibrium between Japan's domestic economy and its economic activity with the rest of the world.[19] The

[19] In this section I have relied on a variety of materials but especially on Ministry of Finance, *Kinyū Shōwa zaisei shi* [A Financial History of the Shōwa Era], X (Tokyo, 1955); Ōshima Kiyoshi, *Nihon kyōkō shi ron* [A History of Economic Crises in Japan] (Tokyo, 1955); Mitani Katsumi, *Kokusai shūshi to Nihon no seichō* [The Balance of Payments and the Growth of Japan] (Tokyo, 1957); Kajinishi Mitsu-

basic problem was that prices in Japan had risen more than they had abroad; once the war ended, Japan was not able to compete sufficiently in international markets despite the war-induced growth and diversification of her industry. These difficulties manifested themselves both in Japan's balance of payments and in the exchange rates between yen and foreign currencies. Restoration of the international equilibrium was the most important economic issue of the 1920's. The government saw the essence of the issue in the question: When, and under what conditions, should Japan return to the gold standard?

The emphasis on the return to the gold standard was not something uniquely Japanese. Indeed, it underlay the policy objectives of all the major industrial countries.[20] The restoration of a nation's currency to convertibility and to a stable international value was generally regarded as fundamental to an international system of multilateral, relatively free trade. This was the only way European recovery could be achieved and international prosperity assured. Given the experience prior to World War I, it was quite natural that countries conceived of such a fixed exchange standard: convertibility of one's currency was to gold, rather than simply to another country's currency. Throughout the 1920's the major nations struggled to return to gold, but on a piecemeal basis without much coordination. Some—the United Kingdom was archetypical—returned at a seriously overvalued exchange rate; others—notably France—at a seriously undervalued exchange rate.

For Japan, World War I was a great boon—an external, exogenous demand stimulus for Japanese exports and a depressant of imports which had out-competed domestic producers.

---

haya et al., *Nihon shihonshugi no botsuraku* [The Collapse of Japanese Capitalism] (Tokyo, 1960), esp. vol. I; and Moon H. Kang, "The Monetary Aspect of the Economic Development in Japan with Special Reference to Monetary Policies: 1868-1935," Ph.D. dissertation, University of Nebraska, 1960.

[20] See Lewis, *op.cit.*, p. 156; Ragnar Nurkse, *International Currency Experience* (League of Nations, 1944), pp. 116f.

The result was a surge of domestic growth, inflation, and a large current account surplus in the balance of payments, which by 1919 had resulted in a cumulation of foreign assets in excess of the heavy indebtedness position of 1913. Most of the war-related increase in foreign assets was held by the government and the central bank (the Bank of Japan). Accordingly, the money supply had virtually tripled, enabling prices to rise sharply despite government budget surpluses between 1914 and 1919. We do not have solid data for all types of capital flows; the information on nongovernmental short-term capital flows is particularly weak. Nonetheless, the rough estimates in Table 2 provide an adequate indication of the major shifts in the total

TABLE 2

JAPANESE BALANCE OF INTERNATIONAL INDEBTEDNESS
EXCLUSIVE OF SHORT-TERM CAPITAL[a]
(rough estimates in million yen)

	1913	1919	1929
Japanese Long-Term Liabilities	2,070	1,822	2,549
Borrowing from Abroad	1,970	1,722	2,304
Foreign Direct Investment in Japan	100	100	245
Japanese Long-Term Assets	529	1,850	1,676
Loans to Abroad	61	975	245
China	55	417	244[b]
Allies	....	557	........[b]
Japanese Direct Investment	468	875	1,431
China	278	(600)	(750)
South Manchuria Railway	100	100	391
Net Long-Term Position	−1,541	28	−873
Foreign Exchange Reserves	376	2,045	1,343
Net Position Excluding Short-Term Balances	−1,165	2,073	470

SOURCE: Derived from Harold G. Moulton, Japan, *An Economic and Financial Appraisal* (Washington, D.C., 1931), pp. 390-403; Bank of Japan, *Hundred-Year Statistics of Japanese Economy* (Tokyo, 1966).

[a] Japan's investment in its empire are also excluded.

[b] Excluded are defaulted loans of 271 million yen to the Chinese government and 240 million yen to Czarist Russia. The direct investment estimates are crude, particularly Japanese investment in China, which for 1919 and 1929 are no more than orders of magnitude. For China the distinction between loans and direct investment is somewhat arbitrary.

227

long-term indebtedness, in foreign exchange reserves, and in certain of the specific items. Japan used its current account surplus (see Table 3)[21] to increase its own loans and investments in China, to help Britain, France, and Russia,[22] and to build up its foreign exchange reserves while not paying off its own foreign borrowings in advance to any substantial extent.

Japan ended the war in the strongest foreign exchange reserve position in her history. Reserves were equivalent to about ten-months' imports. Most were held abroad,[23] but Japan had also imported substantial gold for reserve purposes, until September 1917, when the United States embargoed gold exports. (England had gone off the gold standard earlier.) Thereupon Japan also went off the gold standard, which meant that the government and the Bank of Japan refused to sell gold or allow it to leave the country. The government and the Bank of Japan, however, bought up the foreign exchange balances accruing to Japanese banks financing exports, in effect pegging the exchange rate at close to the gold standard par (100 yen equal to $49.85).[24]

What did Japan need to return to the gold standard at a particular par rate? The most important requisite was competitive export strength sufficient, in terms of domestic prices converted into international prices at the target exchange rate, to be able to pay for imports (given capital flows) commensurate with a desired or expected rate of growth of GNP. More-

[21] The balance of payments is for the empire; while the main reason is pragmatic (this is all that is available), for my purpose it is a reasonable substitute for a proper balance of Japanese payments because it contains all transactions which involve foreign exchange; since the colonies used yen as currency, current and capital flows between them and Japan had no direct foreign exchange implications.

[22] Britain and France repaid by the mid-1920's, but Japan had to write off 240 million yen in loans to Czarist Russia.

[23] Japan had in effect been on a gold exchange standard since its inception in 1897, investing much of its foreign exchange reserves in safe, short-term assets in London and New York.

[24] The rate did appreciate somewhat, to a maximum of $51.50 (a 3.3 percent increase), in 1919.

over, Japan needed sufficient foreign exchange reserves to be able to combat any immediate or eventual temporary excess of demand for foreign exchange over supply. Related to this, the government had to inspire confidence that the exchange rate and the timing were correct in order not to provoke adverse speculation. An additional concern was to have adequate gold backing, held in Japan, for the Bank of Japan paper currency in circulation.[25]

The Japanese government was astounded at the bold United States move to return (in June 1919) to the gold standard, at the prewar par, rather soon after the war ended. It moved much more cautiously, and for good reasons. The immediate reason was the speculative bubble of late 1919 and early 1920 which burst in March 1920. Businessmen had expected the prices of goods to continue to rise: since anything could be sold at a profit, it was delivery, not price, that became important. This spread from the commodities market into the stock market, where a speculative mania erupted. It also spilled over into foreign trade, with a big upsurge of imports leading to a current account deficit. This in turn produced an automatic contraction of the domestic money supply. The bubble burst from the combined impact of cheap imports and tighter money. The downturn was sharp. Wholesale prices, which had gone from 200.3 (1913 = 100) in May 1919 to 321.5 by March 1920, declined precipitously to 247.7 by June, and continued to slide off to a low of 189.8 in April 1921, when the government's counter-recession policies took hold. For there was indeed a recession, in Japan and throughout the world—the downturn in England and the United States did not begin until the summer of 1920 and continued longer than in Japan.

[25] See S. Y. Furuya, *Japan's Foreign Exchange and Her Balance of International Payments* (New York, 1928). The holding of gold relative to the domestic currency supply rather than balance of payments needs was one of the "rules of the game" of the gold standard system. It was a very expensive anachronism of the system carrying over from the days of mistrust in banknotes. Japan was not alone in its concern; *vide* United States policy in the fall of 1931.

TABLE 3

SUMMARY BALANCE OF PAYMENTS OF THE JAPANESE EMPIRE[a]
(million yen)

	1908-1913	1914-1919	1920	1921	1922	1923	1920-1923
I. Balance on							
Current Account[b]	−1142.4	3035.0	− 79.3	−246.2	−181.5	−447.9	− 95
1. Trade Balance	− 706.5	1197.5	−500.1	−442.0	−336.1	−617.7	−189
2. Invisible Balance	− 435.9	1837.5	420.8	195.8	154.6	169.8	94
II. Changes in Foreign Exchange[c]	167.7	1700.7	126.7	− 74.7	−238.5	−171.1	− 35
3. Gold Flows	− 59.7	603.8	407.5	132.5	1.1	− 0.1	54
4. Balances Held Abroad	227.4	1096.9	−280.8	−207.2	−239.6	−171.0	− 89
III. Other Capital Flows[d]	−1310.1	1334.3	−206.0	−171.5	57.0	−276.8	− 59
5. Long-Term	− 524.6	1409.7	226.3	72.3	128.2	−214.7	21
6. Short-Term	− 785.5	−75.4	−432.3	−243.8	− 71.2	− 62.1	− 80
IV. Errors and Omissions (I-II-III)[e]	....	....	....	....	....	....	....

TABLE 3 (continued)

	1924	1925	1926	1927	1928	1929	1924-1929
I. Balance on							
Current Account[b]	−565.6	−202.1	−302.5	−141.1	−172.7	19.0	−1365
1. Trade Balance	−729.8	−357.0	−442.5	−289.0	−333.9	−168.3	−232
2. Invisible Balance	164.2	154.9	140.0	147.9	161.2	187.3	955
II. Changes in Foreign Exchange[c]	−118.5	− 90.0	− 59.8	− 80.0	− 71.6	144.0	− 27
3. Gold Flows	0	− 22.0	− 31.8	− 36.0	0.4	0.5	− 88
4. Balances Held Abroad	−118.5	− 68.0	− 28.0	− 44.0	− 72.0	143.5	− 18
III. Other Capital Flows[d]	−447.1	−112.1	−242.7	− 2.4	− 44.6	− 86.5	−1088
5. Long-Term	−238.0	− 63.9	− 36.9	+126.2	− 53.4	52.8	21
6. Short-Term	−209.1	− 48.2	−205.8	−128.6	8.8	−139.3	− 87
IV. Errors and Omissions (I-II-III)[e]	....	....	....	− 58.7	− 56.5	− 38.5	....

TABLE 3 (continued)

	1930	1931	1930-1931	1932	1933	1934
I. Balance on Current Account[b]	− 27.3	− 57.5	− 84.8	43.3	31.9	62.9
1. Trade Balance	−160.3	−141.1	−301.4	− 58.8	− 77.9	−129.3
2. Invisible Balance	133.0	83.6	216.6	102.1	109.8	192.2
II. Changes in Foreign Exchange[c]	−383.0	−403.0	−786.0	− 3.0	− 59.0	0
3. Gold Flows	−286.8	−388.2	−675.0	−112.1	− 20.9	0
4. Balances Held Abroad	− 96.2	− 14.8	−111.0	109.1	− 38.1	0
III. Other Capital Flows[d]	319.7	328.7	720.4	127.8	152.5	− 2.9
5. Long-Term	92.0	233.9	325.9	167.8	41.0	233.2
6. Short-Term	227.7	94.8	494.5	− 40.0	111.5	−226.1
IV. Errors and Omissions[e] (I-II-III)	− 36.0	16.8	− 19.2	−174.1	−179.6	− 65.8

TABLE 3 (concluded)

	1935	1936	1937[f]	1932-1937
I. Balance on Current Account[b]	310.1	−131.0	− 653.0	− 73.8
1. Trade Balance	131.8	−101.9	− 635.0	− 871.1
2. Invisible Balance	178.3	232.9	− 18.0	797.3
II. Changes in Foreign Exchange[c]	36.0	46.0	−1220.1	−1200.1
3. Gold Flows	0.1	0	− 866.9	− 999.8
4. Balances Held Abroad	35.9	46.0	− 353.2	− 200.3
III. Other Capital Flows[d]	245.8	130.7	567.1	1221.0
5. Long-Term	454.6	226.6	567.1	1123.2
6. Short-Term	−208.8	− 95.9	....	97.8
IV. Errors and Omissions[e] (I-II-III)	28.3	− 45.7	....	....

SOURCE: E. B. Schumpeter, ed. *The Industrialization of Japan and Manchukuo 1930-1940*, appendix table III; Ministry of Finance, *Zaisei kinyū tōkei geppō*, no. 5 (May 1950).
a Japan proper, Taiwan, Korea, South Sea mandated islands.
b Minus indicates net inflow.
c Minus indicates net decrease of reserves and outflow of gold.
d Minus indicates net inflow of capital.
e Where information not available, assumed to be fully in (short-term) capital account.
f 1937 capital and foreign exchange data are not fully comparable with previous years; "balances held abroad" might equally well be classified under short-term capital flows.

Another immediate, and pervasive, reason for the Japanese government's caution was highly political. Although in 1919 government bureaucrats favored an early return to the gold standard, Finance Minister Takahashi Korekiyo rejected it on the grounds that it would probably result in an outflow of gold from Japan and Japan needed the gold for expansion into China. China needed investment in railroads and industry, and if Japan did not lend her the funds, England and the United States would. Whoever did so would be able to dominate China. Inouye, then president of the Bank of Japan, supported Takahashi's position.[26]

The government was too caught up in its immediate problems, and the uncertainties which they engendered, to move toward a quick re-establishment of the gold standard at the prewar par. The underlying problem was more serious: during World War I, Japan's prices had risen more than, and in the 1920-21 recession did not decline nearly as much as, those of her major competitors in world markets. This was particularly true of the United States (see Table 4), which constituted about one-third of Japan's trade. While prices in the United Kingdom went up further, they also rapidly declined more. At the prewar par exchange rate, at about which the actual rate continued due to government pegging, Japanese exports were too expensive and foreign imports too cheap. The consequence was inevitable: the current account of the balance of payments moved from surplus to deficit.

POLICY ALTERNATIVES

What policy alternatives were available to Japan to restore equilibrium to its balance of payments? The fundamental problem under such circumstances is to obtain and maintain a balance between domestic and world price levels. One method is to let domestic prices go their own way (to achieve domestic goals) and to achieve international equilibrium by a fluctuating

[26] Ministry of Finance, *op.cit.*, p. 157.

TABLE 4

WHOLESALE PRICES, TERMS OF TRADE, AND THE FOREIGN EXCHANGE RATE

Whole Price Index

United Kingdom	United States	Japan	Adjusted for Changes in the Exchange Rate (Japan)	Terms of Trade	Average Foreign Exchange Rate 100 yen/$	yen/shilling
100.0	100.0	100.0	100.0	100.0	49.375	2/-1/2
100.0	97.9	95.5	95.3	94.3	49.500	2/-1/4
127.0	100.0	96.6	95.6	90.5	48.875	2/-9/16
160.0	122.9	116.8	118.3	98.5	50.000	2/10 1/4
206.0	167.2	147.0	150.3	94.5	50.500	2/10 9/16
226.0	187.9	192.5	200.3	82.3	51.375	2/10 15/16
242.0	198.9	235.9	241.9	99.9	50.625	2/3-
307.0	220.8	259.3	260.6	98.1	49.625	2/7 1/2
197.0	139.9	200.3	194.7	142.0	48.000	2/5 7/8
159.0	138.9	195.8	189.9	134.2	47.875	2/1 3/4
159.0	143.9	199.2	197.2	136.6	48.875	2/1 9/16
166.0	140.8	206.5	175.7	117.7	42.000	1/10 13/16
159.0	147.9	201.7	166.5	108.2	40.750	1/8 1/4
147.9	142.9	178.7	169.7	109.3	46.875	1/11 1/8
141.9	137.0	169.8	162.9	117.5	47.375	1/11 7/16
140.0	139.9	170.9	160.9	105.5	46.500	1/10 7/8
137.0	137.9	166.1	155.0	106.6	46.070	1/10.755
119.9	125.1	136.7	136.7	98.6	49.367	2/0.342
105.2	105.7	115.6	114.4	100.6	48.871	2/1.947
102.6	93.8	128.2	73.0	84.6	28.120	1/7.157
102.7	95.4	147.0	75.1	77.6	25.227	1/2.409
105.6	108.4	149.8	89.5	67.4	29.511	1/2.069
106.7	115.7	153.7	88.9	62.7	28.570	1/2-
113.3	117.0	160.1	93.9	65.6	28.951	1/2-
130.4	150.5	194.4	113.4	64.1	28.813	1/2-
121.6	137.0	205.0	118.3	68.4	28.496	1/2-
123.3	111.6	226.6	119.3	81.9	25.984	1/2.054

SOURCES: Bank of Japan, *Hundred-Year Statistics*; Kazushi Ohkawa et al., *Prices, LTES*,
.

NOTE: To adjust the Japanese wholesale price index for changes in the exchange rate it
been multiplied by the average exchange rate in dollars.

233

exchange rate. In addition to having some adverse effects on foreign traders by increasing uncertainty, this approach was the antithesis of the objective to return to the gold standard (fixed exchange rate) system. Under the fixed-exchange-rate system the only way to adjust to world prices is to change the domestic price level. Japan had two choices: to return at the prewar gold value of yen, or to establish a new value. For Japan, the former meant a deflationary policy sufficient to get domestic prices in line with (declining) world prices; the latter meant devaluation—setting a new parity, less yen to the dollar and pound—sufficient to avoid the need for domestic deflation.[27]

Devaluation, however, was not considered a really suitable alternative for major, advanced countries—in the 1920's even more than today. A country had to bear its burden, swallow its medicine, and do the right thing. After all, look how England fought stubbornly and valiantly to get back to the gold standard at the ordained par—even if domestic deflation did mean

[27] A simple application of the purchasing power theory, using a 1922 price index of 140 for the United States and 200 for Japan, would suggest a new par of 100 yen = $34.90. This perhaps would have been too low, because of the increase in industrial capacity in Japan during World War I and the immense increase in the American demand for Japanese silk during the 1920's. On the other hand, in the 1913 base year the yen was probably overvalued; Japan had run a current account deficit for more than a decade and was reaching the limit of its international borrowing ability. Moreover, much of the industrial capacity created during World War I was in new industries which arose because they temporarily had little foreign competition in either domestic or foreign markets, so they could sell high-cost goods at high prices. In terms of long-run growth as well as short-term (war) gains, it probably was desirable to have these industries develop at this time even though they faced considerable difficulties once the war ended. The time period for a new industry to become competitive was too long for these industries to contribute much to exports until the mid-1930's (and then mainly for Japanese investment in its empire) or, in some cases, until the mid-1950's. See William V. Rapp, "A Theory of Changing Trade Patterns under Economic Growth: Tested for Japan," *Yale Economic Essays*, VII:2 (Fall 1967), 69-135.

234

ten percent unemployment and took until 1925. Apparently devaluation—returning to the gold standard at a new, lower par—was never considered seriously by Japanese policymakers in the 1920's. The only choice was to push prices down at home. (We must remember that in the 1920's it was not well understood that an important part of this adjustment process was not just the lowering of prices but the slowing of economic growth.)

The data in Table 3 make clear that Japan was running a substantial deficit in its current (trade plus invisibles) transactions with the rest of the world. While the net figures convey what is essential for the analysis here, they do nothing to explain the rich complexity of Japan's foreign trade patterns of the 1920's and 1930's. That merits special analysis, but it cannot be encompassed in this already overlong chapter. Nevertheless, several points should be made. First, by World War I Japan had developed a shipping industry large enough to constitute an important foreign exchange earner; these services, combined with other invisible transactions, generated a substantial net surplus, offsetting more than half the merchandise deficit. Secondly, Japan's export performance in the 1920's, while not as good as earlier (or later), was not all that bad. Thirdly, it was thus in substantial part the higher level and rate of growth of imports which resulted in the trade and current account deficits of the 1920's. Japan's secular trend of economic growth and her evolving industrial structure had long been generating rising import demand; the implications for the balance of payments had been masked earlier, first by heavy foreign borrowing and then by the foreign trade windfalls of World War I. Given these import requirements, Japan's export earnings simply had to be larger than in fact could be achieved under the exchange rate and degree of international price competitiveness prevailing in the 1920's.

There were other ways in which Japan could at least mitigate the fundamental disequilibrium in her balance of payments. One was to restrict import demand by raising tariffs.[28] Another was to return to a pattern of net foreign borrowing, which after all had successfully shored up the gold standard before World War I. At first this would simply involve the drawing of accumulated foreign exchange reserves, but eventually it would necessitate substantial long-term borrowing. Given her income level and growth potential, there is no reason why Japan should not have been a net borrower.

During the 1920's Japan tried all these methods, in concert and sequentially: fluctuation of the exchange rate resulting in depreciation, deflation, increases in tariffs, exhaustion of foreign exchange reserves and renewed foreign borrowing, and finally, return to the gold standard at the prewar par. But none of these policies were pushed long and hard enough until 1929—they were palliatives reflecting a fundamental indecisiveness at the highest policy level. I believe this was a basic cause of the malaise of the 1920's. Before turning to a discussion of the deflationary approach, I will briefly trace the use of other policy measures.

Japan had a sharply depreciating and then again rising exchange rate between March 1924 and mid-1926 not because of a deliberate government policy but because the government could no longer maintain the pegged rate near parity. The basic reason was a persistent current account deficit which ate up foreign exchange reserves; the pegged rate simply could not be maintained indefinitely. There was also a very important immediate cause: the highly destructive Tokyo-Yokohama earthquake of September 1, 1923. Quick reconstruction required a large amount of imports over and above regular needs, and intended exports were needed at home. Moreover, substantial productive capacity had been destroyed or rendered inoperative. The trade deficit worsened sharply. Successive governments insisted that the exchange rate remain pegged,

[28] Quotas were not in the arsenal of accepted weapons in the 1920's, though of course in the economic warfare of the 1930's any weapon could be, and was, used.

but it began to slip in New York. A divergence between New York and Tokyo rates could not be maintained; finally on March 18, 1924 the government had to abandon pegging and allow the rate to find a market-determined level. The rate dropped sharply, to a low of $38.50 per 100 yen by year-end, a decline of twenty-two percent. The trade balance responded favorably: the demand for imports slowed down and exports increased.

The improvement in the balance of trade, an increased receptivity to Japanese borrowing in foreign capital markets, and a policy decision to ship out government gold all tended to raise the exchange rate in 1925. There was also a speculative element. Those who had previously speculated against the yen now speculated for it because of the more favorable underlying factors plus renewed expectation that the government would support the parity rate.[29] Thereafter the foreign exchange rate meandered between $44-49, rising fairly sharply from this lower level in the second half of 1929 when Japan had finally determined to return to the gold standard at prewar parity.

Tariff policy was also used to restrict imports, but for reasons of protection as much as balance of payments. Certain World War I growth industries, such as chemicals and iron and steel, which were not yet fully competitive against imports, obtained increased tariff protection in 1920. The Great Earthquake was quite naturally an occasion for the imposition of 100 percent *ad valorem* duties on some 120 luxury items (primarily manufactured consumer goods). In 1926 there was a complete revision of tariffs, thereby embodying and formalizing principles which were already in operation. Industrial raw materials were duty free; this increased the effective tariff protection of manufactured goods and made their export more

[29] This speculative demand began first in Shanghai in February 1925, and several months later was joined by demand from New York. Inouye has some amusing comments on the difference between Chinese and American speculators; see Junnosuke Inouye, *Problems of the Japanese Exchange, 1914-1926* (London, 1931), pp. 114-26.

competitive. Some important infant industries—iron and steel, sugar, copper, dyestuffs, woolen textiles—were protected, though engineering was not particularly. High duties continued on the luxuries.[30]

In addition to the apparently rather large amount of short-term capital, at least partially speculative, which flowed into Japan between 1920 and 1929, Japan was a net long-term borrower. The net foreign capital inflow, both short-term and long, was about fifteen percent of gross domestic investment, a ratio half that of the period of heavy borrowing between 1904 and 1913. Unlike the earlier period, the national government was only a sporadic borrower at this time: 229 million yen (£25 million 6.0 percent 35-year bonds issued at 87½ and $150 million 6.5 percent 40-year bonds issued at 92½) in February 1924 to redeem sterling loans falling due and to pay for earthquake reconstruction; and 102.5 million yen (£12.5 million 5.5 percent 35-year bonds issued at 90 and $71 million 5.5 percent 35-year bonds issued at 90) in May 1930 to redeem sterling bonds falling due between July 1930 and January 1931. In addition, outstanding government domestic bonds were purchased by foreigners, especially when the exchange rate was low. Municipalities sold some bonds abroad, but the main long-term issues abroad were of industrial debentures, notably by Japanese electric power firms. Thus, while the prewar borrowing was on public portfolio, borrowing in the 1920's was mainly in the form of private portfolio and direct investment.

The balance of payments data in Table 3 are net estimates, while Japan's gross foreign capital needs were somewhat larger, in order to finance Japanese lending and investment outside the empire much less in Korea and Taiwan. From the rough estimates of Table 2, it appears that the long-term foreign assets of the empire as a whole increased only moderately between 1919 and 1929, from 1,850 million yen to 2,187 million

[30] See G. C. Allen, "Japanese Industry: Its Organization and Development to 1937," in E. B. Schumpeter, ed., *The Industrialization of Japan and Manchukuo 1930-1940* (New York, 1940), 737-38.

yen (including 511 million yen in bad debts). This excludes Japan's increasing investment in Taiwan, Korea, and other parts of the empire.

Overall Japan was not able, or did not try hard enough, to borrow sufficient long-term capital to finance more than a small fraction of her current account deficit.[31] The immediate alternative was to use up foreign exchange reserves. The longer-run solution lay only in restoration of export competitiveness by domestic deflation.

The indecisiveness in deflationary policy during the decade of the 1920's was, to my mind, a fatal weakness. If it had to be done at all—and clearly a preferable policy would have been to devalue and thereby return to the gold standard at a lower par soon after World War I (say in 1921 or 1922), or certainly after the excuse provided by the Great Earthquake—deflation should have been more swift and severe. The twenty percent decline in 1921 from the 1920 average wholesale price level was not enough; perhaps as much as another twenty percent would have been required. Such a policy would have ruined many more firms, caused the collapse of many more banks, and probably led to a really severe disruption of the economy, but at least it would have cleared the slate for a renewed emphasis on growth. On the other hand, erratic doses of deflation, countered by renewed counter-deflationary expansion of demand through fiscal and especially monetary policy, was essentially debilitating. The problem with the former, more drastic approach is like a problem with major surgery: the operation may be a success but the patient may die.

STRUCTURAL DEFECTS OF THE BANKING SYSTEM

Why didn't the government push through a fully effective deflationary policy until 1929? The main reason seems to lie in a series of minor economic crises emanating from a variety

[31] For the 1924-29 period for which we have data it was only 15.6 percent; for 1930-31 there was a net outflow of long-term (as well as short-term) capital, in addition to a current account deficit.

of exogenous and endogenous sources: the Great Earthquake, shifts in foreign demand due to the world business cycle, the domestic speculative mania of 1919-20, the banking system crisis of 1927, and the deflationary policy itself. In all these instances difficulties were exacerbated by the inherent weakness of the domestic financial system. In order to prevent the system from collapsing, at the first (or eventual) signs of trouble the Bank of Japan had to hastily pump in liquidity. This inevitably undercut the deflationary policy.

Why, and in what ways, did the difficulties in the economy show up in the financial sector? First, the financial system in most market economies is the usual intermediary of a tight or easy monetary policy, spreading effects of government policy to producers and distributors by shifts in its willingness and ability to lend. On the whole, the evolving Japanese banking system had demonstrated its ability to assist in the financing of economic growth when things were going well—when funds were available and business wanted to borrow for investment purposes. Indeed, the banking system, as it developed prior to[32] and during World War I, was highly responsive to the types of financing needed for growth, unlike British commercial banking with its inhibiting rules.

However, Japan's banking system was not well constructed to withstand the pressures of recessions, deflation, or sporadic random shocks. The deficiencies of the system can be summed up in three interrelated characteristics: there were a large number of small, unit banks; many banks tended to concentrate the risk of default by lenders, rather than diversifying it, by making large loans (relative to net worth) to a few borrowers; and depositors had no guaranteed means of protection.

While the number of ordinary (commercial) banks had declined from a peak of 1841 in 1901, many remained at the end of World War I (see Table 5). Although there were a number of banks of intermediate size, in essence there were two groups: a

[32] See Hugh T. Patrick, "Japan, 1868-1914," in Rondo Cameron et al., *Banking in the Early Stages of Industrialization* (New York, 1967).

TABLE 5

Growth of Ordinary Banks, 1919-38

	Number of Bank Offices			1,000 People per Bank Office	Net Worth (million yen)	Average Net Worth (1,000 yen)	Deposits (million yen)	Loans and Advances (million yen)
ar	Head Office	Branches	Total					
19	1,340	2,540	3,880	14.27	878	655.2	5,744	5,666
20	1,322	2,772	4,094	13.66	1,211	916.0	5,826	5,902
21	1,327	3,129	4,456	12.71	1,364	1027.9	6,444	6,242
22	1,794	5,122	6,916	8.29	1,918	1069.1	7,801	7,848
23	1,698	5,239	6,937	8.41	2,011	1184.3	7,805	8,059
24	1,626	5,288	6,914	8.51	2,071	1273.7	8,093	8,289
25	1,534	6,320	7,854	7.61	2,114	1378.1	8,726	8,842
26	1,417	5,297	6,714	9.01	2,146	1443.9	9,178	9,219
27	1,280	5,218	6,498	9.44	2,097	1638.3	9,027	8,180
28	1,028	5,044	6,072	10.23	1,963	1909.5	9,330	7,545
29	878	4,917	5,795	10.86	1,976	2250.6	9,292	7,246
30	779	4,763	5,542	11.63	1,878	2410.8	8,738	6,818
31	680	4,542	5,222	12.52	1,776	2611.8	8,269	6,594
32	538	4,311	4,849	13.67	1,747	3247.2	8,319	6,343
33	516	4,021	4,537	14.82	1,701	3296.5	8,815	6,085
34	484	3,893	4,377	15.58	1,702	3516.5	9,438	5,987
35	466	3,708	4,174	16.59	1,698	3643.8	9,950	6,193
36	424	3,654	4,078	17.23	1,685	3974.1	11,007	6,765
37	377	3,621	3,998	17.82	1,644	4360.7	12,434	7,793
38	346	3,600	3,946	18.30	1,646	4757.2	15,191	8,848

Sources: Bank of Japan, *Hundred-Year Statistics*; Kazushi Ohkawa et al., *The Growth te of the Japanese Economy*.

Note: The large increase in ordinary banks in 1922 was due to changes in the Savings nk Law whereby many institutions found it desirable to alter their status.

small number (epitomized by the "Big Five") of very large banks located in the major cities, notably Tokyo and Osaka; and a large number of quite small banks located in the smaller towns as well as the larger cities. The government, in principle, did not allow new banks to be established during the interwar period. It encouraged the reduction in total number by mergers among small, weak banks in the same locality. Mergers often did not help much, being only amalgamations of dubious assets. The decline in total bank net worth attests to the necessary writing down of reserves and capital upon merger. The occasional crises forced many small banks to fail; they were usually absorbed by larger banks. In this way there was some increase in the number of branch offices of the large city banks, though the increase remained moderate until the 1930's. The amalgamation of banks from 1925 on led to a reduction in the total number of bank offices. The apparent decline in service to the population was compensated, in part at least, by increasing urbanization.

Many of the banks—both large and small—were owned and controlled by stockholders who also had industrial interests. Such banks, and others as well, tended to lend a high proportion of their funds to these related business interests—to help their growth in good times and prevent, if necessary, their bankruptcy in bad times. There were no restrictions on the maximum size of a loan in relation to a bank's worth, and bank inspection did not become a significant factor until after the panic of 1927. Many banks had aggressive growth aims. Not only did they expand loans to affiliated borrowers, they borrowed funds in the call market to do so. This made them even more vulnerable to adversity, since other financial institutions making call loans might well refuse to continue their loans to the bank.

Depositors were attracted to a bank by its convenience of location, deposit interest rate, and degree of safety. The larger banks did not have many offices, so it often was not convenient to deposit with them. A wise man would withdraw his deposit in currency if he thought his bank might somehow be in, or on the verge of, trouble. There was no deposit insurance against default by the bank due to its inability to cash in deposits for currency.

The system was made for panic-stricken bank runs. An individual bank was heavily loaned up, holding small reserves. It was subject to insolvency (having to close its doors, refusing to provide currency for deposits) either because of a depositor run or due to the difficulties of one of its major borrowers. A major borrower could be either in temporary straits (fundamentally sound but in a liquidity crisis because, for example, a buyer might delay in paying his bill) or bankrupt (assets less than liabilities). Either way, the bank would have to lend to such a borrower or else face the likelihood of its loan being defaulted. News of the business' difficulty might get out; people, knowing of its close relationship with the bank, would fear for the safety of their deposits and hurry to withdraw them. Or the bank and its borrowers might be in perfectly sound condition, but a run might have started on another small bank in town and depositors, becoming generally apprehensive, would decide to withdraw. These shifts in liquidity preference happened rapidly, and spread rapidly and cumulatively, in the manner of a self-fulfilling prophecy. No single bank could afford to hold currency in its vaults sufficient to meet a sudden, large-scale demand to pay off its depositors. It had to receive currency from other banks—from larger banks with which it had a correspondent or other relationship, and ultimately from the Bank of Japan as the central bank.

Several problems existed. One was simply the technical difficulty of timing: of having a delivery of currency made before the bank subject to a run ran out. The bank might close its doors for a few hours or days, but at the price of reducing its future creditability. The more serious problem was to obtain a loan of currency. The financial institution doing the lending wanted sound collateral, not the bad or risky debts of affiliated, small enterprises. Moreover, the large banks were perhaps not so sorry to see runs occur, so long as the runs were of minor proportions and did not affect them. After all, depositors at the small banks under pressure didn't simply hold the cash they had withdrawn; they deposited in the large bank. Moreover, the small banks would be forced into amalgamation with the large banks on terms favorable to the latter.

Hence the system was intrinsically subject to failures of individual banks and to depositor runs on the banks. Public loss of confidence in banks disrupts the economy, making it difficult to finance economic activity. The Bank of Japan and the government were well aware of this, and whenever a panic got underway, they stepped in quickly to avert its spread.

MONETARY POLICY AND FINANCIAL CRISIS

The monetary authorities were impaled on the horns of a dilemma. The basic policy was to restrict central bank credit and money supply enough to reduce prices sufficiently to restore equilibrium to the balance of payments. But equally basic was a determination to prevent widespread financial panics. The relief measures inevitably involved central bank loans, by direct or indirect routes, to affected banks and business enterprises. Money supply, particularly currency, inevitably increased. This directly undercut the deflationary policy and made it necessary, once the crisis was over, to have an even stiffer deflationary policy.

Data on the net change in Bank of Japan credit during the 1920's are presented in Table 6. Credit did not significantly contract until 1929-31; since the economy was growing, the net impact was deflationary (as evidenced by the decline in wholesale prices in Table 4). Money supply had a very slightly declining trend during the 1920's before dropping off sharply in 1930 and 1931; to some extent this was offset, by an increase in income velocity.[33] The persisting deficit in the current account of the balance of payments, together with the continued loss of foreign exchange reserves, indicates that the deflation was not sufficient until 1929-30—at which point the Great Depression completely changed the game and its rules.

A serious problem of a deflation is that it creates large amounts of bad debts. A financial crisis does so, too. The pur-

[33] The best money supply estimates have been made by Professor Shōzaburō Fujino; they are not yet published. I rely here on the net domestic product estimates underlying Table 1 and Fujino's money supply as adjusted in W. C. Hoekendorf, "The Secular Trend of Income Velocity in Japan, 1879-1940," Ph.D. dissertation, University of Washington, 1961.

TABLE 6

INCREASES IN BANK OF JAPAN CREDIT (million yen)

r	To Government	To Private Sector			To Finance Gold and Other Reserves[a]	Total[b]
		Total	Loans	Other		
9-1913	28	—139	— 1	—138	168	57
4-1919	—2123	1,551	559	992	1,701	1,129
0	431	—678	—481	—197	127	—116
1	91	91	139	— 48	— 75	107
2	478	—227	176	—403	—239	12
3	27	289	303	— 14	—171	145
4	246	—168	—130	— 38	—119	— 41
5	279	—220	— 26	—194	— 90	— 31
6	154	—156	—110	— 46	— 60	— 62
7	— 15	208	306	— 98	— 80	113
8	236	—107	— 44	— 63	— 72	57
9	— 148	— 94	—169	75	144	— 98
0	159	19	74	— 55	—383	—205
1	212	85	210	—125	—403	—106
2	75	—168	—192	24	— 3	96
3	165	12	84	— 72	— 59	118
4	66	17	21	— 4	0	83
5	85	18	— 35	53	36	139
6	229	—176	— 97	— 79	46	99

SOURCES: Bank of Japan, *Hundred-Year Statistics of the Japanese Economy*; Table 3 above.
Foreign exchange reserves are here consolidated to the Bank of Japan so that credit to government was for domestic purposes. The changes in credit for foreign exchange reserves (the mirror image of changes in reserves themselves) had their impact directly on private sector.
Equivalent to changes in Bank of Japan currency issue outstanding.

pose is to encourage greater efficiency in given uses of resources, to reallocate resources to more efficient uses, and to squeeze out inefficient users. However, it is not clear that deflation does not penalize firms which may simply be illiquid (because of rapid growth, or discrimination in credit markets, or small size) rather than basically inefficient. Certainly there is no clear evidence that the incidence of financial crisis is higher among the inefficient and the uncompetitive than among others who are unlucky in location, in financing connections, or in liquidity position. It is a tricky operation to estimate what is really bad debt in the sense that underlying assets have a lower value than liabilities, both immediately and even if the economy were growing. Neither severe deflation nor inflation are good allocators of resources; moreover, both have undesirable income distribution effects.

The Bank of Japan's greatest success in the 1920's was in overcoming the potential financial chaos which the Great Earthquake engendered not only by destroying housing and businesses but also by putting the Tokyo financial system out of operation. The Bank of Japan immediately agreed to provide virtually unlimited loans to affected banks, and thus to businesses, by discounting commercial paper which came to be known as "earthquake bills."[34] The government guaranteed the Bank of Japan against loss to 100 million yen, in effect absorbing part of any eventual net loss from inability of business borrowers to repay.

There was a feeling during the 1920's that somehow the bad debts from the excesses of the World War I boom had never been written off, and that to them had been added bad debts in the form of the remaining earthquake bills, for which there were no underlying assets, as well as a cumulation of bad debts from each successive financial crisis. Somehow all this had to be cleaned up. One proposal in early 1927 was that the government go ahead and provide financial aid to buy up and write off the outstanding earthquake bills rather than extend their life by another year. In the course of public discussion it became known that certain large banks, notably the Bank of Taiwan and the Fifteenth (Peers) Bank, which held earthquake bills, appeared in unsound condition due to large loans outstanding to borrowers who appeared unable to pay.

[34] The Bank of Japan rediscounted 431 million yen of earthquake bills, and large banks held considerably more, confident of the bank's guarantee; the total amount issued is estimated at 2,100 million yen. All but 276 million yen had been paid off by November 1924; this remainder proved difficult to liquidate (reflecting underlying bad debts); in early 1927, 207 million yen remained outstanding, almost half held by the Bank of Japan.

A monetary panic ensued in the spring of 1927. It was of much larger proportions than had ever occurred before. Not just small banks were involved, but large banks of impeccable credentials. At the core of the scandal was the Bank of Taiwan, a semiofficial bank of the government with the power of banknote issue for Taiwan.

The Bank of Taiwan was an extreme case of a highly growth-oriented financial institution, willing to incur high risks in gambling on the continued prosperity of the Japanese economy and especially its major borrowers. Earlier in the 1920's it had decided to expand aggressively by lending in Japan rather than restricting its operations to Taiwan. It made especially large loans to the rapidly growing Suzuki conglomerate, which was based on extensive commercial interests in and with Taiwan, but which sought further growth in undertaking various manufacturing activities in Japan. While deposits at the bank had been at the level of its loans during World War I, from 1919 on deposits declined sharply to only twenty-three percent of the 1918 peak in 1926, and less in 1927. In contrast, loans expanded by sixty-six percent over the same period. This loan expansion was financed primarily by call loans to the Bank of Taiwan from large banks in Japan.

In early 1927 it appeared possible that Suzuki was overextended. Not only could it not repay loans, but some of its operations had liabilities greater than assets—the collateral for a portion of its loans was worthless, even though termed "earthquake bills." The banks lending call funds to the Bank of Taiwan recalled them. The Bank of Japan was unwilling to extend emergency loans without a government guarantee against losses due to accepting worthless collateral. This took time, and political machinations in the Diet were disruptive. The Bank of Taiwan, the Fifteenth Bank, and other banks, large and small, had to close their doors. The run was on.

This time public fear was not restricted to a particular locality, or to small banks. Everyone wanted cash. The Bank of Japan responded valiantly, increasing its loans from 539 million to 1484 million yen in a few weeks; correspondingly, Bank of Japan currency in circulation rose by fifty percent. But even this was not enough. A three-week bank moratorium was declared on April 22, 1927. Many banks failed. Others, including the Fifteenth, had to be merged.

The extent of the financial crisis of 1927 severely frightened the monetary authorities; they haven't gotten over it yet. They determined to press ahead with the elimination of as many of the small banks as possible by merger with each other or with larger banks. A new banking act, raising the minimum capital requirement and making possible greater supervision, was passed in 1927. As Table 5 indicates, the number of banks dropped sharply after 1927, and average net worth per bank increased as sharply. It had been decided that the way to strengthen the system was to centralize it, to eliminate the presumably weakest elements.[35] In this way the Bank of Japan could more readily step in and help individual banks in times of crisis, and thereby prevent the development of panics. Nothing was done, however, to insure deposits for the benefit of depositors, or to restrict the proportion of loans (relative, say, to net worth) of a single bank going to a single firm or group of interrelated firms.

The Bank of Japan was not alone in trying to stem the chronic financial instability of the 1920's. The government took a vigorous role, not just in guaranteeing at times the financial system against losses due to default on discounted paper, but also in its own lending activities. It used the government-dominated special long-term credit banks, notably the Industrial Bank and the Hypothec Bank, to extend relief loans in emer-

[35] This also resulted in a considerable increase in concentration in the financial sector. The "Big Five" banks (Yasuda, Mitsubishi, Mitsui, Sumitomo, Daiichi) as a group had only 19.5 percent of loans and 24.3 percent of deposits of all ordinary banks in 1926; the shares increased thereafter, to 27.8 percent and 34.5 percent respectively in 1929, to 30.5 percent and 40.1 percent in 1931, and to 39.3 percent and 42.1 percent in 1937. See Ōshima Kiyoshi, op.cit., p. 284; and Fuji Bank, *Banking in Modern Japan* (Tokyo, 1961), p. 96.

gencies. These loans came essentially from funds amassed by the Ministry of Finance's Deposit Bureau through postal savings, government bond issue, and government budgetary surpluses. Such loans constituted an important component of the relief packages put together when panics occurred. For example, in the 1920 crisis as much as forty percent of the Industrial Bank's loans were for the relief of large enterprises.[36] While there undoubtedly was a bias in the government's relief programs in favor of big business, some loans were made to smaller firms, particularly in the 1927 debacle.

OSCILLATING FISCAL POLICY

In part because monetary policy was preoccupied with the instability of the financial system, fiscal measures were heavily relied upon to implement the deflationary policy. This was also consistent with the legacy of budgetary orthodoxy that prevailed in Japan, as elsewhere, in the 1920's. The basic estimates of government expenditures and revenues[37] are presented in Table 7, and pertinent ratios in Table 8. The decrease in government expenditures relative to net domestic product between 1921 and 1925 is impressive, as is the even sharper rise during the next three years, the abrupt decline in 1929-30 (especially at the central level), and the rapid rise in 1931-32. Thereafter the growth of government expenditures was outstripped by the growth of net domestic product. Interestingly, the total government sector ran deficits continuously from 1926 on, while the central government deficit between 1927 and 1929 turned to surplus in 1930-31, before turning again to deficits. This suggests that fiscal policy had a deflationary impact until the mid-1920's, but was more or less expansive thereafter except for 1929-31.

[36] Kajinishi Mitsuhaya et al., *op.cit.*, p. 154.

[37] The data are consolidated for central plus local governments; the latter were dominated by the central government. While the local governments ran budgetary deficits between 1920 and 1940, central government expenditures and revenues (and central government general account expenditures) moved closely with the total in Table 7.

TABLE 7

CONSOLIDATED CENTRAL PLUS LOCAL GOVERNMENT EXPENDITURES AND REVENUES
(million yen)

Year	Government Expenditures[a]			Government Revenues		Government Surplus or Deficit[e]	Central Government Surplus
	Total (1)	Military[b] (2)	Investment[c] (3)	Total (4)	Savings[d] (5)	(6)	(7)
1910	680	186	167	697	184	17	78
1911	828	206	214	803	189	− 25	17
1912	696	201	185	803	292	107	138
1913	682	192	186	813	317	131	149
1914	698	222	165	782	248	84	94
1915	657	240	143	768	254	111	97
1916	661	273	139	894	372	233	204
1917	897	391	207	1,118	428	221	190
1918	1,250	641	270	1,358	377	108	65
1919	1,817	981	432	1,864	479	47	31
1920	2,350	940	685	1,902	237	−448	−383
1921	2,404	842	681	2,163	440	−241	−160
1922	2,487	693	756	2,489	758	2	36
1923	2,331	530	747	2,256	672	− 75	− 14
1924	2,425	487	778	2,465	818	40	47
1925	2,351	448	753	2,535	937	184	202
1926	2,503	437	872	2,445	814	− 58	78
1927	2,837	494	878	2,456	497	−381	− 93
1928	3,148	519	865	2,574	291	−574	−173
1929	2,912	497	871	2,518	477	−394	−156
1930	2,438	444	608	2,121	291	−317	265
1931	2,690	462	545	2,045	−100	−645	50
1932	3,076	705	631	2,077	−368	−999	−473
1933	3,384	886	679	2,209	−496	−1,175	−470
1934	3,309	953	632	2,543	−134	− 766	−547
1935	3,550	1,043	647	2,715	−188	− 835	−561
1936	3,684	1,089	687	2,978	− 19	− 706	−385
1937	5,788	3,299	755	4,286	−747	−1,502	−2,047
1938	8,007	5,984	901	4,107	−2,999	−3,900	−3,799
1939	8,778	6,495	1,167	4,785	−2,826	−3,993	−3,992
1940	11,711	7,967	1,472	6,510	−3,729	−5,201	−4,588

SOURCE: Koichi Emi and Yuichi Shionoya, *Government Expenditures*, Vol. 7, LTES. Data in Col. 7 for 1930-40 are based on general account revenues in Prime Minister's office, *Japan Statistical Yearbook 1950* (Tokyo, 1951).

[a] Expenditures consist of purchases of goods and services plus current subsidies and transfers to the private sector.

[b] Narrowly defined to exclude military pensions and interest on the government debt.

[c] Excludes all military investment; all military expenditures are regarded as current.

[d] Government revenues minus the sum of government current purchases of goods and services, subsidies and transfers.

[e] Government revenues minus expenditures (Col. 4 − Col. 1); by definition it also government savings minus investment (Col. 5 − Col. 3).

TABLE 8

	Military Expenditures to				Central Plus Local to Net Domestic Product
	Central Government Expenditures	Central plus Local Government Expenditures	Net Domestic Product	Central to Net Domestic Product	
Year					
1910	43.5	27.4	5.8	13.2	21.0
1911	42.5	24.9	5.3	12.5	21.3
1912	49.9	28.9	4.6	9.1	15.8
1913	46.6	28.2	4.2	9.1	15.0
1914	50.9	31.8	5.4	10.5	16.8
1915	57.7	36.5	5.6	9.7	15.4
1916	65.2	41.3	5.1	7.8	12.4
1917	64.7	43.6	5.3	8.2	12.2
1918	73.0	51.3	6.1	8.4	12.0
1919	76.2	54.0	7.7	10.1	14.3
1920	60.5	40.0	7.1	11.7	17.8
1921	56.2	35.0	6.7	11.9	19.0
1922	48.4	27.9	5.4	11.2	19.4
1923	39.7	22.7	4.0	10.1	17.7
1924	33.9	20.1	3.4	10.0	16.9
1925	34.2	19.1	3.0	8.8	15.8
1926	31.6	17.5	3.0	9.6	17.3
1927	30.3	12.4	3.4	11.2	19.4
1928	29.4	16.5	3.6	12.1	21.6
1929	29.5	17.1	3.5	11.8	20.4
1930	41.7	18.2	3.6	8.7	18.9
1931	34.9	17.2	4.1	11.6	21.9
1932	39.1	22.9	5.5	14.2	22.9
1933	46.0	26.2	6.1	13.3	21.5
1934	48.3	28.8	6.3	13.0	21.3
1935	50.7	29.4	6.3	12.5	20.7
1936	52.0	29.6	5.9	11.4	19.3
1937	77.3	57.0	15.4	19.9	26.9
1938	92.0	74.7	23.0	25.0	30.8
1939	88.3	74.0	19.3	21.9	26.1
1940	85.9	68.0	21.2	24.7	31.1

Sources: Table 7 and NDP data underlying Table 1 above.

The change in the composition of expenditures in the 1920's is striking. Military expenditures dropped sharply on an absolute basis, and even more sharply relative to total government expenditures and to net domestic product. This was possible because of the Washington Conference of 1922, which not only forestalled an imminent arms race but also provided the basis for a Japanese security policy of "armament reduction and cooperation with the Western powers."[38] Government investment expenditures, for public works, etc., rose, as did current expenditures for nonmilitary purposes.

THE DISASTROUS RETURN TO THE GOLD STANDARD
AT PREWAR PARITY

The government's spasmodic use of fiscal and monetary measures during the 1920's not only was insufficient in deflationary effect to restore equilibrium to the balance of payments and prewar parity to the exchange rate, but also resulted in a general malaise in the economy. The 1927 financial crisis at home, and the return of all the major Western powers to the gold standard by 1928 was too much. The pressures in Japan to resolve the gold standard problem once and for all finally came to a boil. The drift had continued too long. The chronic instability of the domestic financial system and of domestic economic performance seemed somehow tied up with the government's prolonged failure to take care of the matter.

Businessmen producing for foreign trade and foreign traders felt that exchange rate fluctuation, which had become much more erratic in the spring of 1928 due to the troubles in China, was detrimental to business since it increased the risk of the profitability of foreign trade.[39] Large banks had come out of

[38] James B. Crowley, *Japan's Quest for Autonomy—National Security and Foreign Policy 1930-1938* (Princeton, 1966), p. 30.

[39] The Yokohama Specie Bank had to change its stated rate for dollars ninety times during 1928. In addition, silk spinners were hurt by the seasonality of trade, since they tended to export in the fall (following the spring cocoon crop) when the trade balance tended toward sur-

the 1927 crisis with large amounts of surplus funds; deposits had accrued to them and they became somewhat conservative in lending to Japanese business. They wanted to make liquid investments in the United States as interest rates there rose during 1928 and most of 1929. The banks were anxious to see Japan return to the gold standard at the old parity to be protected from possible losses on anticipated foreign loans due to exchange rate fluctuation.

Ministry of Finance officials were worried about the 230 million yen sterling debt falling due between July 1930 and January 1931. They wanted to refund it by new debt issue, but apparently financial houses in London and New York were unwilling to underwrite a new government bond issue unless Japan displayed its creditworthiness by following sensible economic policies—including return to a gold standard fixed exchange rate.[40] Japan still had fairly large foreign exchange reserves (1,199 million yen at the end of 1928), and most (1,084 million yen) were held at home in the form of gold.

It is difficult to disentangle this concatenation of forces to determine which were the most important. It was probably quite natural that the Hamaguchi Cabinet, coming into power in July 1929, announced a decision to return to the gold standard, at the prewar par, at the earliest possible date. The decision was based on an expectation that some domestic adjustment would be necessary, but that it would not be great because of the continued prosperity of the world economy. Prior to the decision several economic commentators urged a return to gold at a lower parity, around $40/100 yen. Their views were brushed off by those making the decision. Apparently the feeling prevailed that devaluation would be a shameful affront to

---

plus, the exchange rate rose, and the yen proceeds of given dollars sales declined.

[40] A Ministry of Finance official who took a trip abroad between February and May 1929 to survey foreign opinion was advised that Japan should return to the gold standard, but at a new, lower parity. Ministry of Finance, *op.cit.*, p. 211.

national honor.[41] Japan's exchange rate was then pegged at $45/100 yen, and its wholesale price level was at about 165 (1913 = 100) still substantially above wholesale price levels in England and the United States. A precondition for returning to the gold standard was to push down Japan's price level sufficiently, and thereby force the market-determined exchange rate to move up normally to the desired parity level.

An orthodox approach was implemented: an austere fiscal and somewhat restrictive monetary policy, with main reliance, symbolically and in terms of its economic impact, on the former. Government expenditures were cut, while tax rates were maintained. The Bank of Japan did not raise its discount rate, but reduced its loans. A serious difficulty for monetary policy was the liquidity of the banking system resulting from the liberal steps taken by the Bank of Japan in the 1927 crisis; this reduced subsequent Bank of Japan control. Interest rates reversed a tendency to drift downwards. The government also aided industries in the process of cost-cutting, already underway.

The policy was successful in terms of its objectives. The wholesale price index declined by six percent in six months, and continued to drop sharply in 1930 (though in part as a result of the transmission of the world depression to Japan). The foreign exchange rate quickly moved up to par. Moreover, foreign exchange reserves increased significantly. This was a result not only of the actions taken by the government but also of the expectations thus generated. Speculators saw the opportunity and bought yen (for foreign currency); the inflow of short-term capital was substantial. Foreign traders postponed the purchase of imports and rushed exports. Both of these helped to push up the yen exchange rate. However, both these forces were temporary and inevitably to be reversed once the gold standard was reattained; to the extent that they were significant, they resulted in an overestimation of the true restoration of Japan's competitive position. As it turned out, this prob-

[41] Mitani Katsumi, *op.cit.*, pp. 228-30.

ably did not matter too much, because Japan's competitive position was due to be severely eroded and her gold standard status attacked by the rapid deterioration of the international economy and thus by the institutional environment for world trade and capital flows in 1930-31.

I have argued that it was a fundamental mistake to return to the gold standard at the prewar parity anytime in the 1920's. The deflationary burden, the costs in terms of economic growth, the social and political effects in terms of income redistribution, distress, and tensions, were all too great. Moreover, by coincidence, the timing of Japan's return to the gold standard (on January 11, 1930) could not have been worse: the world economy had just begun to toboggan down into the most serious and extended adversity it has ever had to suffer. Unfortunately, the Japanese did not realize that; New York's stock market crash appeared to be only a temporary set-back.

World prices declined sharply (see Table 4); accelerated deflation in Japan could not keep pace. The bottom fell out of the United States silk market, Japan's single most important export commodity.[42] The current account of the balance of payments was in deficit. On a net basis long-term capital flowed out rather than in. Even worse was the tremendous outflow of short-term capital. Speculators, who had previously felt confident that Japan could go onto the gold standard, now felt equally sure that, because of the changed world environment, Japan could not remain on the gold standard. Many large banks and trust companies, and eventually wealthy individual investors, participated in these short-term capital outflows, for reasons of both interest rate differential and speculation. Speculation against the yen was enhanced when England went off the gold standard in September 1931. Gold poured out of the country—some 675 millions worth. Overall, Japan lost 786

[42] Silk exports in 1929 were valued at 781 million yen, 36.3 percent of total exports of 2,149 million yen; in 1930 they were 417 million yen, 28.4 percent of much smaller total exports of 1,470 million yen. The decline in the value of cotton textiles was also substantial.

million yen (58.5 percent) of its foreign exchange reserves in the brief period it was on the gold standard. At the same time the Japanese economy was sinking into the slough of depression, due both to the deflationary policies and to the impact of the collapsing world economy.

"DAMN THE EXCHANGE RATE, FULL SPEED AHEAD!"

It was inevitable that Japan should go off the gold standard, as it did in December 1931. What followed probably could not have been anticipated: one of the most successful combinations of fiscal, monetary, and foreign exchange rate policies, in an adverse international environment, that the world has ever seen. The basic decision was to generate income and demand at home by large-scale deficit financing and easy money, and to let the balance of payments take care of itself by allowing the exchange rate to depreciate as much as necessary. This would encourage exports and discourage imports, both desirable for domestic expansion. The crucial decision was to forsake the interrelated objectives of being on the gold standard and having the yen exchange at its prewar parity. Adherence to these objectives was the ultimate cause of the difficulties of the 1920's. Their repudiation removed the major obstacle to expansionary fiscal and monetary policies to get out of the depression and once again start on rapid growth.[43]

The only effective way for an industrial country to come out of a (excess capacity) depression is to spend its way out. In this the government has to take the lead, since business expectations are usually quite pessimistic about the future. The Japanese government pursued this approach with great vigor and success. From 1931 to 1933, government expenditures increased

[43] Professor William Lockwood has suggested that the "efficacy" of macro policy between 1932 and 1936 may have been little more than a political response to pressures to expand expenditures (by the military, business, etc.) without raising taxes, rather than a reasoned analysis and understanding of aggregate demand. The point is well taken, though clearly talk of "reflation" had imbedded in it a vague appreciation of what subsequently has been termed Keynesian economics.

by twenty-six percent, and net domestic product grew at a comparable rate. Probably equally important, three-quarters of the rise in government expenditures was deficit-financed; tax revenues were held down, providing a multiplicative effect on private demand (Table 7). Throughout the 1930's the government ran large deficits—sufficiently large that revenues did not even cover current purchases of goods and services and transfer payments (that is, government saving was negative).

"Success" may have come at a high long-run political price: almost three-fifths of the increase in government expenditures during the 1930's prior to the outbreak of the war with China in 1937, was for military uses. Much of the increase followed immediately upon the Manchurian incident of 1931. We have fairly detailed functional estimates only for central government expenditures in certain benchmark years. Between 1930 and 1935, of the 946 million yen increase in central government expenditures, sixty-two percent was for military uses, fourteen percent for social welfare, seven percent for transportation, agriculture, and other economic services, and seventeen percent for interest on the expanding national debt.[44]

Monetary policy was an important complement to fiscal policy, though, as is probably inevitable in a depression, it was less important since financial institutions were wary of lending to business. The Bank of Japan probably should have taken positive steps to increase commercial bank reserves rather than standing ready to rediscount upon request. Since requests were limited, as shown in Table 6, it did not expand credit greatly to the private sector. Money supply increased only moderately until 1937. What the Bank of Japan did do was to underwrite the government bond issues from 1932 on. It purchased outright that portion not subscribed to by the Ministry of Finance Deposit Bureau. As government deficit-financed expenditures resulted in an increase in commercial bank deposits, banks were eager to purchase government bonds from the Bank of Japan until the mid-1930's when they began, once again, to engage

[44] Emi and Shionoya, *op.cit.*, pp. 270-73.

in private lending. The Bank of Japan lowered its discount rate far below any previous minimum level, to 3.29 percent in 1936 as compared with 6.57 percent at the end of 1931. The average yield on government bonds decreased from 6.0 to 3.9 percent between 1932 and 1936; the commercial bank average lending rate did not decline so much, from 5.8 to 4.6 percent. Lowered interest rates and easy money abetted the rapid recovery and the new surge of growth that was soon underway.

The foreign exchange rate plummeted as soon as Japan left the gold standard, hitting the pre–World War II low, relative to the dollar, of $20.70/100 yen in December 1932. The pound was also depreciating relative to the dollar. At the end of 1933, the Japanese government decided to peg the yen to the pound, but at a rate some forty-three percent below what it had been when both yen and pound had been on the gold standard (see Table 4). This was a major net depreciation in a world of depreciating currencies.

The effect on Japanese exports of drastically reduced prices in terms of foreign currencies was highly beneficial; exports increased rapidly. The net effect on the world was probably beneficial also because, with the balance-of-payments constraint lifted, Japan grew more rapidly and thereby increased its demand for imports. Exchange rate depreciation was sufficiently large that Japan's trade balance tended to improve; its balance on current account moved to surplus and remained so until 1937. There is some merit in the criticism that Japan pursued a beggar-my-neighbor policy, but in the world economy at that time neighbors had to look out for themselves.

It has been argued[45] that Japan depreciated excessively, that the yen was fundamentally undervalued after 1932. By standard criteria for an equilibrium exchange rate—full use of resources, reasonably rapid growth, no increase in direct controls over foreign economic transactions, and equilibrium in the balance of payments—this does not seem to have been the case. However, the commodity terms of trade deteriorated severely

[45] See, for example, Lewis, *op.cit.*, pp. 121-23.

(see Table 4): Japan had to give up considerably more exports per unit of imports than earlier. Judicious applications of import controls to cut out nonessentials would have required a smaller decline in the terms of trade—but there weren't many nonessentials in Japan's import bill. Perhaps however, Japan's foreign relations would not have gone so badly. Japan antagonized the West by her determined and successful export drive in a declining world market. The feedback from foreign hostility in turn had its impact on Japanese perceptions and reactions.

Viewed entirely by criteria of domestic growth, Japanese economic policy during this period was highly successful, despite the more difficult world environment as compared with the 1920's. This success is indicated by the rapid economic growth once the new policies were undertaken (see Table 1), but it occurred too late. By 1936 the military was entrenched in a strong power position, perhaps impossible to dislodge. As the economy approached capacity operation in 1936, it became desirable to slow down the expansion of government expenditures. This was, of course, in conflict with the desires of the military. The assassination on February 25, 1936, of Finance Minister Takahashi, who had so ably guided Japan through its "reflation" period, marked the end of any possibility of restoring power to the business–political parties group. The expansive fiscal and monetary policies were to continue, and increasingly strict direct controls were to be imposed, as Japan went onto wartime footing first to fight China and eventually the United States.

Some Implications of Economic Policy and Performance

It remains to explore in this section a few of the broader implications of Japan's interwar economic performance, and to raise questions if not provide answers. In so doing I avoid the general problem of historical interpretation: whether Japan's path in the 1930's was an aberration from the basic trend of the democratic modernization process of the 1920's and earlier, renewed after World War II; or a natural, likely, perhaps virtually inevitable, consequence of the social and political stresses and strains emanating from the very process of modernization; or primarily a response to the external, uncontrollable events of world depression and trade restrictiveness, combined with the existing system of colonies.

Can we really say that the 1920's represented a failure in economic policy? Failure relative to what? After all, compared with most European countries and the United States, Japan did reasonably well. Growth of manufacturing output was good; if she had only done well in agriculture Japan's growth would have been fine. And isn't it unfair to use present-day tools of economic theory to judge policy at a time when economic science was rather more backward than now?

The last point first. Of course to understand economic policy in a particular historical context one must know and be sympathetic to the state of the science at that particular time, and more broadly the political, social, and intellectual as well as economic environment in which the policy operated. But there is no reason why one must apply lower standards of evaluation. This, however, is not really the substance of the matter.

I regard Japanese economic policy in the 1920's to have been a failure in that the economy did not achieve anywhere near its own potential for growth—a potential that is evident from rapid previous growth (between 1910 and 1920) and rapid subsequent growth (in the 1930's). One important manifestation of this failure was the very slow—slower than previously or subsequently, slower than necessary—absorption of labor by the manufacturing sector. The basic reason for the failure was the unwillingness, or inability, of the government to come to grips with the issue of return to the gold standard. This was reflected not just in the problem of determining the appropriate exchange rate, but especially in the unfortunate and unsuccessful attempts at deflation through restrictive fiscal and monetary policy. In terms of international comparisons, perhaps the appropriate hypothesis is not that Japan did relatively well but that as a young and fragile democracy Japan could less well afford not to do well economically than more firmly established democracies.

I may be castigating the Japanese government policymakers for failing to achieve objectives—economic growth and productive employment—which they did not actually have. Or these goals may have been subservient to others, such as short-run stability, which on the whole they handled better, until 1930-31. However, given Japan's historical emphasis on economic growth, and my reading of the economic history of the 1920's, I believe I have interpreted their objectives correctly. (And since I have laden this chapter with normative statements, I might as well say that if the dominant government policy objective in the 1920's was short-run stability then it was misguided.)

With the gradual passing away of the Meiji oligarchy, the 1920's presented an opportunity for the nascent parliamentary democracy, based on business-oriented political parties, to display its ability as a system to sustain relatively rapid economic growth, to overcome or at least ameliorate the tensions of growth, and to cope with the country's security objectives. The basic policy stance of the governments of the 1920's was internationalist, a policy of cooperation in the world order of the West. Economically this meant the early postwar restoration of multilateral, relatively free trade and of a gold standard fixed exchange rate system, together with the free movement of short- and long-term capital. National security was also met by cooperation with the West, including general acceptance of the status quo, which implied Japanese hegemony in East Asia. In this international environment, created in large part by the Washington Conference of 1922 and the Kellogg-Briand Pact, it was possible to retrench on armaments and overall military expenditures.

The internationalist policy of the 1920's, with its parliamentary democracy and political parties, failed the test that opportunity presented. I do not mean to imply that this was the only test, or that failure inevitably signalled the effective end of the party system; those judgments are for political historians to make. Nor do I mean that the military immediately and directly took over; its encroachment was less rapid until 1936 or 1937. It appears that the failure was in substantial part attributable to economic causes. Two such factors, one exogenous and the other endogenous, were critical: the breakdown, with the Great Depression, of the world economic order, and the mediocre performance of Japan's economy in the 1920's.

The collapse of the world economy, in addition to sharply lowering total demand for internationally traded goods, brought an end to long-term capital lending and shifted the emphasis away from free trade to increasing trade restrictions, away from multilateralism to increasing bilateralism, and away from fixed exchange rates based on parity with gold to fluctuating, competitively depreciating exchange rates unlinked to gold. In this new, essentially counter-productive and retrograde, international game with new rules Japan played superlatively. The exchange rate and the balance of payments were no longer constraints on domestic economic growth.

It is ironic that at the time when Japan's international economic performance was so successful, the domestic swing in its policy stance was towards autarchy. The very success of Japan's performance in world markets between 1932 and 1936 suggests that we should attribute the dominant economic factor in the failure of parliamentary democracy to the distinct lack of success of economic macro-policy prior to 1932. Japanese policymakers had succeeded only in exacerbating social tensions, not in ameliorating them. Let me put the argument in stark, perhaps extreme, terms.

The off-again-on-again deflationary policy of the 1920's was clearly a calamitous mistake. The acceptance of, say, the 1922 level of prices as reasonable, a correspondingly appropriate exchange rate adjustment, and the return then to the gold standard would, by hindsight, have been much more efficacious. The domestic economy would not have needed to be subjected to the continual buffeting it received and could have gone about its business of growth. The fundamental error of returning to gold at the prewar par was compounded by the cataclysmic timing of the actual re-establishment of the prewar parity in returning to the gold standard at the beginning of 1930. Incidentally, big business, by speculating against the yen in 1930 and 1931, succeeded in undercutting the very basis of its political power. From then on, it increasingly had to make deals directly with the military.

The alternative to internationalism was decreased reliance on the West and, eventually, on autarkic bloc economy. Not surprisingly, the proponent of this option was the military, who saw the issues primarily in security rather than economic terms. The military leaders were apprehensive over the London Naval Treaty of 1930, whereby it appeared that national security was being compromised for the sake of budgetary retrenchment and adherence to the gold standard.[46] These men were not a bunch of wild-eyed, right-wing, young conspirators intent upon a coup by which they could manipulate ministers of state. They, and those from all elements of Japan's broadly defined elite who supported them, were on the whole reasonable, responsible men making relatively conscious, mostly incremental, decisions based on their perceptions of the changing world and the options available. In the perceptions of the militarists and many others the internationalist approach had failed by 1931, for both foreign and domestic reasons. They proposed what they considered to be superior alternatives. This is not to say that the military was wholly altruistic; it too was elitist and presumptuous, contemptuous of parliamentary democracy. The retrenchment of expenditures in the 1920's, predicted on absolute cut-backs of personnel and restrictions of armament aims, disturbed the military leaders greatly. They had been used to a

---

[46] See Crowley, *op.cit.*, chap. 1. Professor Crowley's thinking on national security has strongly influenced mine.

greater share of the central government budget and of GNP, and of the attendant political power, and they wanted "their share" back.

If the problem of the foreign exchange rate and the balance of payments had been solved in the early 1920's and the economy had grown more rapidly and more stably, would the difficulties inherent in the differential structure have been resolved? They would probably have been no more than ameliorated, but perhaps that would have been enough. More rapid growth would have occurred mainly in the industrial sector, and with stable prices there would probably have been less substitution of capital and labor. Together these would have meant a greater absorption of unskilled labor into manufacturing, as indeed occurred during the 1930's, but the unskilled-skilled wage differential would have remained. Would this relative deprivation of the unskilled have led to their discontent? Or was it the inability to find factory jobs and the absolute decline in money wages that were the real issues generating so much friction? I suspect it was the latter.

The real difficulty, even with successful industrial performance, could well have been agriculture. Even though the differential structure would likely have remained there, a lower exchange rate and a stable price, instead of the deflationary policy, would have made for more favorable price incentives for farmers than existed. Silk incomes, in yen, would have been even higher, but still subject to the precipitous decline in world prices after 1926. Rice was imported from the colonies which were on the yen standard, so exchange rate devaluation would not have helped. In principle the policy of importing cheap rice was efficient in the long run, since resources in Japanese agriculture were to be transferred into manufacturing. But the rub was in the long time it would take these resources—particularly labor—to be absorbed in manufacturing. It simply could not have been achieved quickly enough to prevent a long adjustment period of relative agrarian deprivation and, presumably, discontent. The government was on the horns of an income distribution dilemma: relatively high prices for rice and other foodstuffs would maintain, and enhance, incomes in agriculture, but at the expense of the discontent of urban workers and capitalists; while an import program that helped urban workers and their employers hurt farm incomes. However, a better pricing policy would at least have prevented agricultural incomes from declining absolutely.

Even if better price incentives had existed, it is not clear that this alone would have been sufficient to increase agricultural productivity at the rate at which it had been growing between 1885 and 1919. It seems inevitable that a differential structure emerges in that phase of the industrialization process in which the demand for skilled labor outstrips supply and large reservoirs of unskilled labor remain. Until the industrial sector is large enough and growing rapidly enough to absorb large amounts of unskilled workers, their wages will not increase substantially. Perhaps social tensions are bound to increase during this phase of development because of the observable differences in income received by capitalists, by skilled workers, and by farmers and unskilled nonfarm workers.

The problem then for the government of an industrializing nation is how to keep these tensions within bounds, to ameliorate conditions so that military coups, or revolutions, do not occur. At the least, the real incomes of large groups cannot be allowed to fall absolutely. More positively, the real incomes of the surplus labor (notably that in agriculture) may well have to rise somewhat, though less than that of capitalists or of skilled labor. Minimum-wage type legislation will not achieve this. It may even be difficult, and perhaps undesirable for the developmental process of mobilizing savings, to move the agricultural-manufacturing terms of trade in favor of agriculture. Essentially, the only hope seems to lie in raising productivity, output, and hence real income in agriculture.

Objective economic conditions are important not only in themselves but particularly as they affect the perceptions, objectives, and tactics of those in political power and those attempting to achieve power. For Japan this involved on the one hand the political activities of various enonomic interest groups—such as "old" and "new" zaibatsu, workers, landlords, small land-owning farmers, tenants, and whatever organizations they had. On the other hand it involved the concern of the various political actors with economic issues and with economic bases of (economic and political) support—parties, various strata of the army and navy, etc. We should separate the influence of economic difficulties on the objectives of political actors from their capitalizing on these difficulties as a means of attaining power. Objectively, some of the economic issues of the late 1920's and early 1930's were false, though probably not entirely so in the perceptions of the important political actors.

We need much more analysis of the political actors' perceptions of the economic realities of interwar Japan. For example, the military perception that the basic agricultural conflict was the capitalist versus the farmer, rather than the landlord versus the tenant, is highly revealing. So are military and bureaucratic perceptions of the foreign trade environments, particularly the evolving feeling that world prices for many imports necessary for military purposes were rigged by international cartels and that Japan simply could not obtain sufficient foreign exchange for her (expanding) definition of minimum military requirements. Increasingly the military and the bureaucracy came to feel that the only viable alternative was for Japan to develop its own bloc economy in a relatively autarkic manner. The complexities of these issues suggest that we need to explore the varying relationships among big business, the political parties, the bureaucracy, and the military—and the degree to which these relationships were affected by economic causes—before we can assess fully the extent to which economic factors, and which factors, were responsible for Japan's taking the militaristic path of the 1930's.

CHAPTER VIII

Big Business and Politics in Prewar Japan

ARTHUR E. TIEDEMANN

THE aim of this chapter is to examine various aspects of the relation between big business and politics in prewar Japan. By big business I mean primarily the large-scale modernized sector of the economy which began to emerge in the last decades of the nineteenth century and which reached a mature stage in the twentieth century. To a certain extent the term may be taken to be loosely synonymous with what is called the zaibatsu, but as used here it also includes all large-scale modern enterprises whether customarily designated as zaibatsu or not. A knowledge of this relation between big business and politics is indispensable to a full understanding of developments in modern Japan. The subject, however, is still a largely unexplored field, and little more can be done here than scratch the surface of the phenomenon. The first half of this chapter seeks to give a quick sketch of the relation as it developed from early Meiji through the late 1920's. The last half treats in more detail the turbulent decade of the 1930's.

The Tradition of Special Privilege for Special Service

Relations between business and politics do not, of course, suddenly begin with the Meiji Restoration. Ever since the Sengoku period there had been a close symbiotic relation between Japan's political elite and her businessmen. At the side of the Sengoku daimyō was his quartermaster-general, an official charged with the responsibility of mobilizing the economic resources of the domain and securing from beyond its borders any essential materials lacking within the domain itself. The official was usually drawn from the merchant class and in return for his services was accorded special privileges in the private commercial transactions which he carried on along with the business he did for his master. This tradition of the domain achieving economic objectives through the development of special relations between the political authorities and selected merchants continued into the Tokugawa period. After it came to power in 1868, the Meiji government also relied on this traditional technique to meet many of its economic needs. For instance, when, early in its career, the Meiji government sought to organize the export of silk and other products in order to obtain the specie vital to the import program required by its modernization plans, the task in the Kansai region was entrusted to the Mitsui. This old merchant house was obliged to establish a government-financed foreign trade company which exporters were compelled to join and which was given a monopoly on dealings with the foreigners.[1] The pattern was to be repeated many times: special privileges for special services.[2]

This was not, it should be emphasized, a system by which merchants obtained economic advantages through political pressure or corrupt deals with government officials, though there were, of course, instances of the latter. Almost always the initiative lay with the government; and the merchant, although he might make suggestions which on occasion were adopted, was in a strictly subordinate position. Even whatever organization he had was usually made possible only through government support and financing. When the Tokyo Chamber of Commerce was set up in 1878, it came into being at the request

[1] Shibusawa Keizō, ed., *Japanese Society in the Meiji Era* (Tokyo, 1958), p. 481; Takahashi Makoto, *Meiji zaiseishi kenkyū* [A Study of the Financial History of the Meiji Era] (Tokyo, 1964), p. 17.

[2] Perhaps the most well-known example of this is Mitsubishi in maritime transport. For others see Horie Yasuzō, "Foreign Trade Policy in the Early Meiji Era," *Kyoto University Economic Review*, XXII: 2 (October 1952), 1-21; and Kajinishi Mitsuhaya, *Seishō* [Political Businessmen] (Tokyo, 1963).

of the government and with a government subsidy.[3] The government's immediate purpose was to secure an expression of public opinion which could be used to pressure the powers into treaty revision, but it was also interested in employing the organization as a source of information about economic matters.

The Rise of an Independent Business Community

In the late 1880's and the early 1890's the Japanese business community developed more of a sense of independence, largely because of the success of private businessmen in creating the modern yarn industry by their own efforts. The *Bōseki Rengōkai* (Cotton Spinners Association) was probably the first truly significant independent business organization, financed entirely by the spinning companies and oriented exclusively toward the furtherance of its own particular interests. The example of the cotton spinners was widely imitated and by the end of the century almost every important line of production, particularly in the export field, was represented by a national trade organization. This trend was encouraged as the direction of government economic policy moved from very specific *ad hoc* measures relying on arrangements with special agents to broad legislation dealing with general categories of economic activity.[4] In these new circumstances it became meaningful for business-

[3] Yamaguchi Kazuo, *Meiji zenki keizai no bunseki* [An Analysis of the Early Meiji Economy] (Tokyo, 1956), pp. 227-334; Nagata Masaomi, "Meiji seifu no kanshō seisaku to shōhō kaigisho" [The Chamber of Commerce and the Commercial Policy of the Meiji Government] *Kenkyū Ronshū* (Komazawa Daigaku), no. 4 (October 1963), pp. 11-129.

[4] This shift from *ad hoc* aid for specific favored companies to aid extended to any company meeting general qualifications set forth by law is illustrated by the Navigation Subsidy and Shipbuilding Encouragement Laws of 1896. See Tominaga Yūji, *Kōtsū ni okeru shihon shugi no hatten* [Capitalistic Development in the Communications Industry] (Tokyo, 1953), pp. 139-63.

men in the same industry to band together to influence government policymakers and the newly established Diet to act favorably on measures advantageous to their whole field. In the 1890's the particular field of activity for these new economic pressure groups was tariff legislation. Different types of exporters, for example, demanded the abolition of the export duty on their particular product.[5] As Japan began to achieve increasing tariff autonomy from 1896 on, the trade organizations launched themselves on the never-ending struggle to make sure that their domestic market was protected or that the imports needed by their field received favorable treatment.

In the deliberations of the new trade organizations the business community began in the 1890's to develop its own conceptions of what the nation's economic policy should be. The government, which until then had enjoyed a clear field in this matter, soon found that its views were no longer automatically accepted by businessmen. An outstanding example of this is the debates of the Currency System Investigation Committee (1893-95).[6] The government members of the committee argued that the adoption of the gold standard was absolutely essential to the future development of Japan. The business members, however, rejected these arguments and insisted that Japan could not throw away the advantages of silver: its protective tariff effect on foreign goods in Japan, its cheapening of Japanese prices in western markets, and its tie-in with China's monetary system. In the end the government was not able to persuade a majority of the committee to vote in favor of the gold standard.

Recognizing the need to achieve some coordination between its own views and those of the business community, the gov-

[5] See, for instance, the discussion of the movement to abolish the duty on cotton yarn exports in Matsui Kiyoshi, ed., *Kindai Nihon bōekishi* [A History of Japanese Trade], 3 vols. (Tokyo, 1959-63), II, 247-63.

[6] See discussions in Ōuchi Hyōe and Tsuchiya Takao, eds., *Meiji zenki zaisei keizai shiryō shūsei* [Collected Materials on Finance and Economy During the Early Meiji Era], 21 vols. (Tokyo, 1931-36), XII, 379-441.

ernment established in 1896 the Higher Agricultural, Commercial, and Industrial Committee, the first of a long series of mixed government, business, and academic bodies designed to achieve the formulation of commonly accepted economic policies.[7] The first meeting of the committee again revealed sharp divergences of opinion between the government and business. The second meeting, called in the spring of 1897 to secure backing for the government's imminent enforcement of the gold standard, proved so acrimoniously hostile to the government's plan that the minutes of the meeting were suppressed and the membership of the committee revamped.

The docility of the early Meiji era was gone and henceforth the government was going to have to treat business as an independent power. Nothing demonstrated this more dramatically than the new policy instituted by Nakamigawa Hikojirō when he took over in 1890 as the general manager for Mitsui. Nakamigawa was absolutely determined to sever all Mitsui's ties with the government and to conduct its affairs on a strictly business-like basis, neither seeking favors from nor doing favors for political figures. The ultimate symbol of the new attitude was Nakamigawa's refusal to continue Itō Hirobumi's long standing privilege of making loans without collateral.[8]

The growing independence of the modern-style business entrepreneur was somewhat awkward, for by the late 1890's Itō and other Meiji government leaders had come to feel that it was just this group which was most likely to support both the government's plans to expand Japan's role in East Asia and the heavy military budgets this entailed. The agricultural community and the exporters dealing in silk and other agricultural products were oriented entirely toward the Western markets

[7] Tsūshō Sangyōshō [Ministry of International Trade and Industry], ed., *Shōkō seisakushi* [A History of Commercial and Industrial Policy], IV (Tokyo, 1961), 3-51.

[8] Hattori Shisō and Irimajiri Yoshinaga, eds., *Kindai Nihon jimbutsu keizaishi* [Profiles in the Economic History of Modern Japan], 2 vols. (Tokyo, 1955), I, 167.

271

and could see little profit in the high taxes they were being asked to pay to build the military forces necessary to develop Japan's position on the continent. The entrepreneurs involved in the new industries imported from the West were convinced that their products could be competitive primarily in Asian markets and were susceptible to government arguments for expansion there. Much of the new Western industry was also, of course, closely tied in with supplying the needs of the military and profited enormously from the climbing military budgets. To this must be added the special tax and other economic advantages given to the Western-style industries because the government regarded the development of that sector as essential to both its foreign policy and its military policy. The government's program, therefore, brought many gains to the Japanese entrepreneur connected with the Western-style industries while permitting him to escape most of the burden of its costs.

The Development of a Symbiotic Relationship with the Parties

When in 1898 Itō Hirobumi decided to organize his own political party as a means of solving the problem of getting through the Diet the tax increase required to finance the government's military expansion, he tried to rally behind his new party the business community, which up till then had been largely uninvolved in party politics.[9] Operating through Inoue

[9] Masumi Junnosuke, *Nihon seitō shiron* [A History of Japanese Political Parties], 4 vols. (Tokyo, 1965-68), II, 292-93; Sumiya Mikio, *Dai Nihon Teikoku no shiren* [The Ordeal of the Japanese Empire], *Chūō Kōronsha Nihon no rekishi* [History of Japan], XXII (Tokyo, 1966), pp. 147-49. Joyce Lebra notes the small number of businessmen among the 1882 Kaishintō sample she examined. This party has, of course, traditionally been regarded as having close business connections. Joyce Lebra, "The Kaishintō as a Political Elite," in Bernard S. Silberman and H. D. Harootunian, eds., *Modern Japanese Leadership* (Tucson, 1966), pp. 377-78. Byron Marshall cites some early but unfruitful stirrings among the business community in 1888, 1889, and 1892. Byron K. Marshall, *Capitalism and Nationalism in Prewar Japan: The Ideology of the Business Elite, 1868-1941* (Stanford, 1967), pp. 44, 127.

272

Kaoru, Itō secured the support of Shibusawa Eiichi, Ōkura Kihachirō, Magoshi Kyōhei, and other leaders of the business community. A meeting was arranged on June 14, 1898 at the old Imperial Hotel. Itō spoke, asking for the guests' support and holding forth to them the bait of China:

What a splendid thing it would be to develop China's sources of revenue, the Chinese people's pecuniary resources and China's natural resources. . . . Japan occupies the most advantageous position with regard to China's foreign trade. If we really skillfully exploit this position to develop trade with China, how could it be difficult for us to make our country the fountainhead of commodity supplies and to become dominant in the trade of every Chinese port, north and south?[10]

Unfortunately for Itō's plans, Iwasaki Yanosuke opposed the attempt to recruit business support and through his influential position as president of the Bank of Japan was able to kill the movement. Nevertheless some gain was made by the government, for a few months later, in December 1898, business support for the Yamagata tax bill was tangibly manifested in the League for the Increase of the Land Tax, organized by, among others, Shibusawa Eiichi, Yasuda Zenjirō, Asano Sōichirō, Nezu Kaichirō, Masuda Takashi, Ōkura Kihachirō, Toyokawa Ryōhei, Magoshi Kyōhei, and Kataoka Naoharu.[11]

Heartened by this and other evidence of business support, both Itō in his third Cabinet and Yamagata in his second Cabinet introduced Election Law revision bills which would have increased the influence of the business community in elections for the House of Representatives. Itō proposed to set the qualifications for voting at five yen for those paying the new land tax but at three yen for those paying the income or business enterprise taxes or any combination of these two. He also intro-

[10] Quoted by Fujii Shōichi, "Nichiro sensō" [The Russo-Japanese War] in *Iwanami kōza Nihon rekishi* [Iwanami Japanese History Series], XVIII (gendai 1) (Tokyo, 1963), p. 130.

[11] Masumi, *op.cit.*, II, 312-13; Marshall, *op.cit.*, pp. 44-46.

duced the principle of the unsigned ballot in order to reduce the influence of the larger landlords over peasant owners and local businessmen. In addition, each city was established as a separate election district and given representatives on the basis of one for the first 100,000 residents and one additional representative for each additional 50,000 residents, whereas the rural districts (*gun*) were given a straight one representative for each 100,000. The Yamagata bill was very similar to Itō's except that the cities were given one representative for each 80,000 residents, the *gun* one representative for each 120,000 residents. This blatant attempt to give the business community a disproportionately large share of the Diet seats was rejected by a still overwhelmingly rural House of Representatives. The final version of the 1900 Election Law set the tax qualification at any ten-yen combination of national taxes, and pro-rated representation at one for every 130,000 residents in every type of district, but it did establish every city with a population of 30,000 or more as a separate district.[12]

At the same time that the government leaders were trying to draw the businessmen into a more active involvement with politics, a movement developed within the Jiyūtō to improve its power position by seeking closer ties with the business community. The leader of this movement was Hoshi Tōru who in 1898 expressed himself as follows:

Historically our party has had the trust of the agriculturalists, but we have not had either the confidence of the palace or the trust of the businessmen. The reason for this is that our leaders have been punished for political offences and therefore the Satchō clique have been able to use this record falsely to accuse the Jiyūtō of being a revolutionary party. In this way they have turned the feeling of the palace against the Jiyūtō. The Kaishintō have used this charge to make the businessmen feel that the Jiyūtō was a violent, radical party

[12] Takahashi Seigo, *Gendai seiji no shomondai* [Problems of Contemporary Politics] (Tokyo, 1937), pp. 234-71.

274

ARTHUR E. TIEDEMANN

with which they must not associate. In our national polity
no matter how much confidence the people have in you if
you do not have the palace's confidence, you can not obtain
control of the government. Moreover, no matter how much
the agriculturalists trust you, if you do not have the confidence of the businessmen you can not smoothly manage state
affairs. Consequently, henceforth the Jiyūtō must endeavor to
gain the confidence of the palace and to conciliate those engaged in commerce and industry. In order to gain the confidence of the palace the unavoidable expedient is to use the
Satchō clique. To conciliate those engaged in commerce and
industry, the means are the exchange problem, the railroad
problem, and Election Law revision.[18]

Hoshi encouraged his *kobun* to assure themselves of living expenses and campaign funds by making connections with the
business world, particularly with the electric light and transportation industries which were developing very rapidly at the
turn of the century. In 1899 Hoshi became a member of the
Tokyo City Council in order to further his business contacts,
since practically every important Japanese businessman was associated with one or another of the many companies seeking
franchises from that body. Hoshi's own main business connection was with immigration to the United States and Hawaii.
It was for this reason that he chose appointment as Japanese
minister to Washington as his reward for the Jiyūtō's cooperating with the second Itō Cabinet in 1896 and that he tried
to maneuver the annexation of Hawaii in 1898. The bank
which did most of the financing for the immigration traffic,
the *Keihin Ginkō*, was also Hoshi's principal source of political
funds. Though it cost him his life through assassination in
1901, the pattern suggested by Hoshi was followed by many
politicians and, verging as it frequently did on the outright
sale of political favors, added an unsavory air to Japanese politi-

[18] Toshimitsu Tsurumatsu, *Toshimitsu Tsurumatsu ō shuki* [Toshi-
mitsu Tsurumatsu Memoirs] (Tokyo, 1957), pp. 243-44.

275

cal life. It did, however, encourage a penetration of the business world by professional politicians.[14]

The reverse phenomenon, the penetration of the world of politics by professional businessmen, was largely a product of the post–Russo-Japanese War period. The economic expansion which occurred after 1895 had brought to the fore a new, large self-confident group of younger businessmen who were very proud of having made it on their own with no special favors from the government. They spoke of themselves as *shimmin* ("new people") and referred contemptuously to Mitsui and Mitsubishi as *kyūmin* ("old people"). These men were particularly incensed by the heavy tax increases which had been imposed after the Russo-Japanese War and which were moving more and more in the direction of consumer and commercial taxes. In 1907 their irritation with government tax policy was intensified when the depression conditions of that year made them feel the tax bite even more sharply. It was to this group that Nakano Buei, the president of the Tokyo Chamber of Commerce, was directing the appeal he made at the 1908 meeting of the *Shōgyō Kaigisho Rengōkai* [Federation of Chambers of Commerce]:

Today at this meeting I would like to digress from our official business and consult with you about an idea which I have entirely in my simple capacity as an individual businessman. The matter I wish to discuss is the election of representatives to the Diet. . . . To whatever extent is possible, I would like chamber of commerce members to bestir themselves and stand as candidates in the forthcoming Diet election. . . . It may be said that up to now we have been followers or lantern carriers in the battles among the political parties. . . . However, this time the businessman must separate himself from the political parties and set himself up as

[14] For biographical details on Hoshi Tōru see Nakamura Kikuo, *Meijiteki ningenzō Hoshi Tōru to kindai Nihon seiji* [A Meiji Japanese: Hoshi Tōru and Modern Japanese Politics] (Tokyo, 1957), and *Hoshi Tōru* [A Biography of Hoshi Tōru] (Tokyo, 1963).

a candidate in the interest of this business organization. In short, till now we have had no representatives in the Diet. . . . I wish we would set up [within the Diet] a business group . . . which is based on the position of our business organization, a position completely different from that of the present political parties. . . . In so far as this is not done, any matter we discuss will be extremely difficult to carry out.[15]

The short sessions of the Diet made it feasible to combine a business career with legislative service, so in various parts of the country businessmen responded to Nakano's appeal and put themselves into the field. For instance, in Shiga prefecture about three hundred businessmen organized a club to "harmonize business and politics" and in May 1908 were successful in electing Fujii Zennosuke, a bona fide businessman who became an important leader of the Inukai wing of the Kensei Hontō.[16] From this election on businessmen began to play an

[15] Susukida Sadayoshi, *Nakano Buei ō no nanajūnen* [A Biography of Nakano Buei] (Tokyo, 1934), pp. 215-16.

Ishida Takeshi notes the increasing independence of business organizations after the turn of the century. "Business organizations came to recruit their leaders increasingly on their own volition and quite independently of interference by the government. . . . From this time on the leaders of business organizations came to be recruited not from the bureaucracy but from the business community itself, and the functional separation between politicians and businessmen grew wider, while the 'political merchant' or businessman with bureaucratic background or connections was replaced more and more by professional businessmen." Takeshi Ishida, "The Development of Interest Groups and the Pattern of Political Modernization in Japan," in Robert E. Ward, ed., *Political Development in Modern Japan* (Princeton, 1968), p. 304.

[16] Yamamoto Shirō, "Taishō seihen" [The Taishō Political Crisis] in *Iwanami kōza Nihon rekishi*, XVIII (gendai 1) (Tokyo, 1963), 258-59; Kumagawa Chiyoki, ed., *Fujii Zennosuke den* [A Biography of Fujii Zennosuke] (Tokyo, 1932), pp. 114-74. For a general description of business relations with politics in the late Meiji and early Taishō periods, see also Robert A. Scalapino, *Democracy and the Party Movement in Prewar Japan: The Failure of the First Attempt* (Berkeley, 1953), pp. 246-70. It should be noted that the official statistics on the occupations of Diet members compiled by the Shūgiin Jimukyoku can-

increasingly important role in the Diet, although it should be noted that most of those who actually became Diet members were associated with small- and middle-sized enterprises rather than big business.

It was also about this time that Mitsubishi influence was actively brought into Diet politics. Of course, Iwasaki Yanosuke had played a part in bringing the second Matsukata Cabinet into existence in 1896, but his political intervention was sporadic. From 1908 on, however, his cousin, Toyokawa Ryōhei, head of the Mitsubishi Bank and chief director of the Tokyo Clearing House, undertook a role of leadership among Diet representatives. During Katsura's second Cabinet, Toyokawa was the prime minister's main adviser on economic policy and worked very hard to build support for Katsura in the Diet. This tie between the Mitsubishi group and Katsura continued into the Taishō *seihen* period and was an important element in the formation of the Dōshikai, the progenitor of the later Minseitō. It also caused Mitsui men, who had not been very active in party politics till then, to gravitate toward Katsura's opposition, the Seiyūkai.[17]

Out of the Taishō *seihen* emerged the two-party political structure which was to be characteristic of Diet politics until 1932.[18] Each major party had associated with it the three essential ingredients for achieving political power: professional politicians to do the nitty-gritty of day-to-day party management; former bureaucrats who had the administrative talents required to form a viable alternative government acceptable to

---

not be accepted uncritically. The Shūgiin Jimukyoku simply took whatever occupation the Diet member set down for himself and I have found numerous instances where this self-categorization did not reflect the man's actual occupation.

[17] Yamamoto, *op.cit.*, pp. 259-60. For details on Toyokawa's political activities see Uzaki Kumakichi, *Toyokawa Ryōhei* [A Biography of Toyokawa Ryōhei] (Tokyo, 1922).

[18] Tetsuo Najita, *Hara Kei in the Politics of Compromise, 1905-1915* (Cambridge, 1967); Peter Duus, *Party Rivalry and Political Change in Taishō Japan* (Cambridge, 1968), pp. 28-49; Masumi, *op.cit.*, III, 1-124.

the genrō; and businessmen who could supply the funds and influence essential to successful election campaigns. When the role of political parties in the Japanese government grew stronger after 1918, so did the influence of the business community. Of course, the business community did not confine its attempts at gaining a voice in policy to the political parties alone. Businessmen also had extensive connections in the House of Peers. In addition, their custom of employing former bureaucrats and military officers not only gave them useful contacts with the *kōhai* of these men still serving in the government, but also encouraged every hopeful bureaucrat to deal considerately with them.

The business community also represented itself to the government authorities through more formal organizations such as the *Nihon Kōgyō Kurabu* (Japan Industrial Club) founded 1917, the *Nihon Keizai Remmei* (Japan Economic League) founded 1922, the *Shōkō Kaigisho Rengōkai* (Federation of Chambers of Commerce and Industry), and the Tokyo Clearing House Association, as well as a host of more specialized organizations such as the *Nikka Jitsugyō Kyōkai* (Japan-China Businessmen's Association). So far very little has been done to study systematically either the direction in which these organizations sought to move government policy on specific issues or their rate of success.[19] There is a vast quantity of material available, so this should prove a very fruitful field for research. The whole area of business-government relations in the interwar years is almost untouched by researchers and holds great possibilities for the future.

Some quantitative measure of the extent of the interpenetration of the business and political elites can be drawn from an

[19] See, however, Ishida, *op.cit.* See also Horikoshi Teizō, *Keizai Dantai Rengōkai zenshi* [An Early History of the Federation of Economic Organizations] (Tokyo, 1962); Morita Yoshio, *Nihon keieisha dantai hattenshi* [A History of the Development of Employers' Associations in Japan] (Tokyo, 1958); Nagata Masaomi, *Keizai dantai hattenshi* [A History of the Development of Economic Organizations] (Tokyo, 1956).

examination of the members of the fifty-eighth Diet in 1930, a period when the system was at its peak.[20] The largest occupational group in both the House of Representatives and the House of Peers was businessmen: in the lower house, thirty-two percent; in the upper house, thirty-four percent. If one includes those who though primarily in another occupation also held positions in business enterprises, the level rises to fifty-five percent in the lower house and forty-five percent in the upper house. In all, members of the House of Representatives held positions in 492 companies; members of the House of Peers, in 641.

For convenience one may take the number of members associated with zaibatsu concerns as a rough measure of the pres-

[20] This analysis is based on a collation of material derived from the following: *Jinji kōshinroku* [Who's Who] (Tokyo, 1931 edn.); *Nihon shinshiroku* [Japan Who's Who] (Tokyo, 1931 edn.); *Taishū jinjiroku* [Popular Who's Who] (Tokyo, 1927 and 1932 edns.); *Who's Who in Japan* (Tokyo, 1931 edn.); Shūgiin Jimukyoku, *Shūgiin yōran* (*otsu*) [A Concise Guide to the House of Representatives], II (Tokyo, 1930); Kizokuin Jimukyoko, *Kizokuin yōran* (*hei*) [A Concise Guide to the House of Peers], III (Tokyo, 1932); Chūgai Sangyō Chōsakai, *Chūkyō zaibatsu no shinkenkyū* [A New Study of the Zaibatsu in Central Japan] (Tokyo, 1937); Chūgai Sangyō Chōsakai, *Chūken zaibatsu no shinkenkyū: Kantō hen* [A New Study of the Zaibatsu: Kantō District] (Tokyo, 1937); Chūgai Sangyō Chōsakai, *Chūken zaibatsu no shinkenkyū*: Kansai hen [A New Study of the Zaibatsu: Kansai District] (Tokyo, 1938); Chūgai Sangyō Chōsakai, *Kyūshū zaibatsu no shinkenkyū* [A New Study of the Zaibatsu in Kyūshū] (Tokyo, 1938); Iwai Ryōtarō, *Mitsubishi kontserun tokuhon* [The Mitsubishi Concern] (Tokyo, 1937); Katsuda Teiji, *Ōkura Nezu kontserun tokuhon* [The Ōkura and Nezu Concerns] (Tokyo, 1938); Kimura Shigeru and Miyake Seiki, *Kawanishi Ōhara Itō Katakura kontserun tokuhon* [The Kawanishi, Ōhara, Itō, and Katakura Concerns] (Tokyo, 1938); Kuribayashi Seishū, *Shōken zaibatsu tokuhon* [The Securities Zaibatsu] (Tokyo, 1937); Nishino Kiyosaku, *Sumitomo kontserun tokuhon* [The Sumitomo Concern] (Tokyo, 1937); Nishinoiri Aiichi, *Asano Shibusawa Ōkawa Furukawa kontserun tokuhon* [The Asano, Shibusawa, Ōkawa, and Furukawa Concerns] (Tokyo, 1937); Obama Toshie, *Yasuda kontserun tokuhon* [The Yasuda Concern] (Tokyo, 1937); and Wada Hidekichi, *Mitsui kontserun tokuhon* [The Mitsui Concern] (Tokyo, 1937).

ence of big business in the Diet. Some thirty-seven lower house members, eight percent of the membership, held positions with zaibatsu concerns. Another eighteen members had close relatives who were employees of zaibatsu concerns. Thus twelve percent of the lower house was connected with zaibatsu concerns either directly or through relatives. Both the Seiyūkai and the Minseitō lower-house members were equally involved, twelve and eleven percent respectively. In the House of Peers eighty-three members, twenty-two percent of the membership, currently held positions with zaibatsu concerns while another twenty-four members had close relations so employed. Thus twenty-eight percent of the upper house was connected with zaibatsu concerns either directly or through relatives.

The zaibatsu with the most Diet members on its payroll was Mitsubishi: sixteen lower house members and thirty-four upper house members. In addition, it employed close relatives of six lower house members and ten upper house members. Thus a grand total of sixty-six Diet members were connected with Mitsubishi. After Mitsubishi came Mitsui, which employed ten lower house members, seventeen upper house members, seven relatives of lower house members, and fourteen relatives of upper house members for a grand total of forty-eight. In view of the popular belief that the Minseitō was associated with Mitsubishi and the Seiyūkai with Mitsui, it is pertinent to note that just about equal proportions of both parties were employed by each of these zaibatsu.[21] After all, since World

[21] The percentage of each party's delegation in the House of Representatives currently holding positions in Mitsui and Mitsubishi companies was as follows:

	Minseitō	Seiyūkai
Mitsui	1.8%	1.7%
Mitsubishi	3.7%	3.4%

If relatives are added to members the percentages of each party's delegation involved with Mitsui and Mitsubishi are as follows:

	Minseitō	Seiyūkai
Mitsui	3.7%	2.9%
Mitsubishi	5.5%	3.4%

War I the major zaibatsu had become vast economic organizations, and no rational modern business would want to tie the fate of its enterprises exclusively to the fortunes of one party. Political diversification was as much of a zaibatsu principle as economic diversification.

It must be admitted, however, that the popular belief received some support from the makeup of the Hamaguchi Cabinet. The foreign minister, Shidehara Kijūrō, was married into the Iwasaki family; the president of the South Manchurian Railroad, Sengoku Mitsugi, was an Iwasaki relative; the justice minister, Watanabe Chifuyū, was a Mitsubishi company director; the army parliamentary vice-minister, Mizoguchi Nāosuke, was a Mitsubishi company auditor; both the education minister, Tanaka Ryūzō, and the commerce and industry minister, Tawara Magoichi, had sons employed by Mitsubishi. The only exception was the overseas minister, Matsuda Genji, who had a brother employed by Mitsui.

The open question in all this is precisely to what extent these business associations influenced a man's political activity. The usual practice among Japanese historians is merely to assume that it did and not to bother to show precisely how it did. Shidehara is often spoken of as carrying out a Mitsubishi foreign policy, but it may be wondered just how much at any precise moment in the 1920's the foreign policy ideas of the Mitsui top echelon differed from those of the Mitsubishi top echelon. No one has really demonstrated that there was a Mitsubishi foreign policy as opposed to a Mitsui foreign policy. Certainly Shidehara always vehemently denied that having an Iwasaki wife in any way affected his diplomatic decisions. The possibility of his denial being true is supported by the case of the Finance Ministry official Sakatani Yoshirō. Sakatani was the son-in-law of Shibusawa Eiichi, yet when they were both members of the Currency System Investigation Committee, Sakatani as leader of the gold forces vigorously and directly opposed Shibusawa, the chief spokesman for the silver group.[22]

[22] See *Meiji zenki zaisei keizai shiryō shūsei*, XII, 389-91, 429-32.

When we look at the number of Diet members with zai-batsu connections, we can also raise the question of whether, given the prominence of zaibatsu concerns in the Japanese economy, that number really goes beyond what would be expected and whether attempts to influence decisions in favor of zaibatsu interests were actually made. There is probably some significance to the fact that in the fifty-ninth Diet, for example, the lower house committees with the highest concentration of zaibatsu-connected members were those considering the Major Industries Control Law (four out of nine) and the Electrical Enterprises Law (seven out of eighteen),[23] and that in the upper house zaibatsu-connected members were in a majority on the committees considering the Major Industries Control Law, the Electrical Enterprises Law, the Labor Law, the Customs Rates Law, the Mining Law, and the Cooperatives Central Bank Law.[24] However, no conclusion about the importance of the membership can be reached without a study of exactly what went on in these committees.[25] The precise nature of the influence exercised on political parties by big business in this period is as yet a largely unexamined question. Still, it can be said that the parties had policies of their own and were certainly never mere puppets of big business. An outstanding illustration of this is the Labor Law mentioned above. Every important businessman and business organization was opposed to this bill. In spite of this opposition it was passed by the House of Representatives, though not by the House of Peers.

So far we have been dealing with matters which are, so to

[23] For committee membership, see Shūgiin Jimukyoku, *Dai Gojūku Teikoku Gikai Shūgiin iinkai kaigiroku* [Committee Minutes of the House of Representatives, Imperial Diet, 59th Session] (Tokyo, 1931), passim.

[24] For committee membership, see Kizokuin Jimukyoku, *Dai Gojūku Teikoku Gikai Kizokuin iinkai giji sokkiroku* [Committee Minutes of the House of Peers, Imperial Diet, 59th Session] (Tokyo, 1931), passim.

[25] A task presently being undertaken by the author in connection with a wider study of the Hamaguchi Cabinet.

speak, on the public record and can be investigated. When it comes, however, to the dark labyrinth of business contributions to election funds, it must be confessed that it is doubtful we will ever get the story clear. Without a doubt, in the 1920's officials of the great companies gave contributions to party leaders, but these rather proud executives would have considered it demeaning to have tied grants in with requests for specific action. When one examines the numerous bribery cases of the time, it quickly becomes apparent that it was the smaller businessmen, the men on the make who could not rely on their own economic strength, who got involved in purchasing specific favors from politicians. All big business wanted was a friendly environment arranged to facilitate their operations. One zaibatsu executive's picture of election contributions was expressed as follows:

> Since we had rapidly grown big through our own strength alone, we had no need to borrow strength from the government. . . . Military men seeing only that the zaibatsu were giving money thought that the zaibatsu must be doing improper things, but I certainly never did anything improper. . . . Small zaibatsu may have tried to make money in this way, but big zaibatsu such as Mitsui or Mitsubishi or Sumitomo did not use such sordid business methods. I do not know about early Meiji, but when we had expanded there was no need for such petty stuff. . . . Of course it is only human to think that because money is being spent something underhanded is being done. However, there was no reason to have done anything underhanded.

> Since Mitsui had a great many friends among the Seiyūkai men and Mitsubishi among the Minseitō, each used to give help to these friends at the time of a general election. It was not a matter of managing the Diet by making requests of these men. It was simply helping them at the time of a real general election. I think these men felt sympathy for Mitsui or, as the case might be, Mitsubishi. Therefore if there was some blunder committed and Mitsui or Mitsubishi were at-

tacked, these men would probably sympathize and speak up for us behind the scene. But there were no deals. In my time we made no deals with these men. . . .[26]

The Threat to Business in the 1930's

The pleasant symbiosis of the 1920's was shattered, as is well-known, by the political and economic events of 1929-32.

[26] Ikeda statement quoted in Imamura Takeo, *Ikeda Seihin den* [A Biography of Ikeda Seihin] (Tokyo, 1962), pp. 210-11. On two other occasions Ikeda said more or less the same thing. "Because Mitsui had gotten to be as big as it was and the Bank, the Mining Company, and the Trading Company were doing splendid work, there was no necessity of receiving favors from the government. Since all we asked for was good and fair administration, it was not necessary to make special requests of the government." (Ikeda Seihin, *Zaikai kaiko* [Reminiscences of the Financial World], ed. Yanagisawa Ken [Tokyo, 1949], p. 184) "All we wanted was fair government. We did not need to ask special assistance from the political parties. It may have been different in the past . . . but in my time there was no special need for government help. Since we had been able to become big by ourselves and through ordinary business procedures, there was not the slightest need to receive government favors. However, it would have been troublesome to have been interfered with or obstructed. Consequently, after the rise of party cabinets [we desired to] avoid having party governments regard us with a jaundiced eye, and this became the origin of what has been called the improper relation between the zaibatsu and the political parties." ("Ikeda Seihin shi ni kiku" [An Interview with Ikeda Seihin], *Shisō no Kagaku*, IV: 1 [January 1949], 54)

Ikeda claimed the only time he had to go and ask the government for anything was in the matter of the awarding of court rank and decorations, things which the Mitsui family were fond of receiving. ("Ikeda Seihin shi ni kiku," p. 46, and Ikeda Seihin, "Ashiato," *Keizai Ōrai* [Economic World], II′1:4 [April 1950], 38-39) According to Ikeda, before he became the chief executive of Mitsui Gōmei the distribution of funds for general elections had been handled exclusively by Dan Takuma, Ariga Chōbun, and Fukui Kikusaburō, but they never told him anything about these matters and no records were kept in the company's files. Therefore Ikeda had no certain knowledge of the nature and extent of Mitsui contributions when these three men ran the show (Ikeda, *Zaikai kaiko*, p. 182). For his own activities see below.

With the elimination of party Cabinets after May 1932, big business suddenly lost one of its main means of assuring government policies consonant with their interests. Within the bureaucracy a younger group of officials was emerging, officials who were convinced they could do a much better job of running the economy than the businessmen. To radical young army officers and other right-wing groups, the zaibatsu were corrupt and corrupting self-seeking exploiters of the masses, always willing to sacrifice the national interest in the pursuit of private gain. To the small- and middle-sized businessmen going through the throes of the Great Depression, they were unfair competitors mercilessly strangling the little man. To the consumer, especially to the farmer, they were monopolists squeezing the last bit of profit out of every sale.[27]

Japanese big business was, in a sense, reaping a harvest which it had helped to sow. It had pursued policies which had advanced Japan economically, but it had failed to make any contribution to the solution of the social problems created by the changes economic development brought in its wake. Big business had been rather narrowly concerned with furthering its own immediate interests and had short-sightedly neglected the troubles developing in the wider social and political context within which it was operating. Business executives' concern with politics, for instance, was purely practical and limited to serving their own immediate economic ends. They rarely evinced any will to play an active role in "cleaning up" govern-

---

[27] Ikeda explained the inevitability of this as follows: "When you walk on the road, it is not your intention to crush ants. However, although you are not walking so as to especially crush ants, you do end up killing ants and other small insects. Our problem is just like that. Though we are walking straight down the road fairly and squarely, our bodies and our feet have become big and it naturally comes about that we trample down the small fellows. Although we have not the slightest intention that this should be so, it is from this that the difference between the big fellow and the little fellow comes. . . . In foreign trade the small trader who is competing with the big fellow can not make a living. In domestic trade it is the same thing." (*Keizai Ōrai*, II'1:4, 32)

ment and developing a more healthy political life the way, say, that many American businessmen did during the Progressive Era of the late nineteenth and early twentieth centuries. They made little effort to transform Japan's parliamentary government into a system which the Japanese people could respect morally and could believe was endeavoring to deal honestly and equitably with the nation's problems. Quite the contrary. Once big business had been accommodated within the Japanese power structure, it had used its position to develop and maintain its advantages over other groups. Though the reasons for this behavior are many and complex, the root seems to have been a basic fear that any improvement in the conditions of other groups, labor for example, could only come at the cost of weakening the developmental potential and competitive ability of the Japanese economy, thereby undermining the whole basis of the modern Japanese nation. Big business felt that it could assert that the highest of patriotic motives underlay its attitude towards the claims of other groups, but the disadvantaged saw only selfish exploitation and responded enthusiastically to anti-zaibatsu propaganda.[28]

Ikeda Seihin's Efforts to Save Mitsui

By the early 1930's, then, the environment had become decidedly hostile for big business, and the vital question was how the major business combines were going to adapt themselves to survive in these changed conditions. One of the key figures in providing an answer to this question was Ikeda Seihin, the Mitsui executive, and the rest of this chapter will be devoted to an examination of his activities during the 1930's.[29] Of course,

[28] For a description of business-party relations in the 1920's and an analysis of the business failure to make a greater contribution to democratic development, see Scalapino, *op.cit.*, pp. 270-93.

[29] Ikeda Seihin (1867-1950) has left several accounts of his activities and ideas: *Zaikai kaiko*, ed. Yanagisawa Ken (Tokyo, 1949); *Watakushi no jinseikan* [My Views of Life] (Tokyo, 1951); *Watakushi no takenoko tetsugaku* [My Basic Philosophy] (Tokyo, 1952); *Zoku zaikai kaiko-kojin konjin* [Reminiscences of the Financial World Continued], ed.

there were a great variety of responses among big business executives to the new forces which began to emerge on the Japanese scene after 1931. Among the older-style zaibatsu executives the reactions covered the whole spectrum of possibilities. At one end was Fujiwara Ginjirō, who saw a great deal to be admired in the new programs being advocated by the army. At the other was Matsunaga Yasuzaemon, who blasted the arrogant presumption of the new power holders and retired from active business life rather than cooperate with them.[30] In a class by

Yanagisawa Ken (Tokyo, 1953); Hōchi Shimbun Keizaibu, eds., *Zaikai hizakurige* [Financial World] (Tokyo, 1928), pp. 63-67; "Ikeda Seihin shi ni kiku," *Shisō no Kagaku*, IV:1 (January 1949), 34-66; "Ashiato" [My Path], *Keizai Ōrai*, II:1:3 (March 1950), 30-38, and II:1:4 (April 1950), 30-39. There are three prewar biographies: Takakura Shinobu, *Ikeda Seihin* (Tokyo, 1937); Tōgō Yutaka, *Ikeda Seihin* (Tokyo, 1938); and Ōnuma Hiroyoshi, *Ōkura daijin—shōkō daijin Ikeda Seihin* [Ikeda Seihin, Minister of Finance and of Commerce and Industry] (Tokyo, 1938). In the postwar period there have been three book-length biographies: Nishitani Yahei, *Ikeda Seihin den* (Tokyo, 1954); Imamura, *op.cit.*; and Kojima Naoki, *Ikeda Seihin—tomi to jūken* (Tokyo, 1967). In addition there are a number of shorter accounts: Aritake Shūji, *Shōwa zaiseika ron* [On Shōwa Financial Leaders] (Tokyo, 1949), pp. 155-77; Shima Yasuhiko, "Ikeda Seihin," in Inoue Kiyoshi, ed., *Nihon rekishi kōza* [Lectures on Japanese History], VII (Tokyo, 1953), 211-15; Hattori and Irimajiri, *op.cit.*, II, 177-205; Yoshino Toshihiko, *Rekidai Nihon Ginkō sōsai ron* [On Presidents of the Bank of Japan] (Tokyo, 1957), pp. 243-69; Katō Toshihiko, "Mitsui Ginkō to Ikeda Seihin" [The Mitsui Bank and Ikeda Seihin], *Shakai Kagaku Kenkyū*, XII:4 (February 1961), 156-75; Miyake Seiki et al., eds., *Nihon zaikai jimbutsu retsuden* [Profiles of Japanese Financial Leaders], I (Tokyo, 1963), 737-47; Oe Shinobu, *Senryaku keieisha retsuden* [On Business Leaders] (Tokyo, 1963), pp. 141-205; Katō Toshihiko, "Ikeda Seihin," in Endō Shōkichi, Katō Toshihiko, and Takahashi Makoto, *Nihon no ōkura daijin* [Finance Ministers of Japan] (Tokyo, 1964), pp. 199-219; Hayashi Shigeru, ed., *Jimbutsu Nihon no rekishi* [Profiles in Japanese History], XIV (Tokyo, 1966), 212-35.

[30] Fujiwara's attitude is expressed by the following statement: "Money spent on armaments is capital which promotes the advance of us businessmen. From the people's point of view armament is a kind of investment. They invest and develop the nation's power. Using this power producers steadily and confidently advance in the world. If this were

themselves were the "new zaibatsu," a free-wheeling group coming, like Ayukawa Gisuke, largely from a technological background and psychologically in tune with the army economic planners, since they were production rather than finance oriented and had a technologist's interest in the manipulation of raw materials. Considerable research needs to be done before it can be said with any assurance what response was most characteristic of big business executives. Ikeda Seihin has been chosen as the subject of this chapter because the very central and influential position he occupied in the business world makes him, I believe, a rather representative figure.

Ikeda was born in 1867, the son of a Yonezawa han samurai. A graduate of both Keiō and Harvard (class of 1895), he entered the Mitsui Bank on his return from America, later married the daughter of Nakamigawa Hikojirō, and by 1909 had become managing director of the bank, a position which he still held in 1932. He also held numerous posts in various business organizations, including the chief directorship of the Tokyo Clearing House. He had the reputation of being a shrewd but honest businessman and of combining in his personal character all the best traits of the Japanese samurai and the English gentleman.

In the matter of dealing with the adverse conditions of the early 1930's, Ikeda had his task cut out for him, since at that time there was a tendency for anti-zaibatsu feeling to concentrate more on Mitsui than on the other large combines. One reason for this was the fact that the traditional sharp commercial practices of Mitsui Bussan had become legendary and were firmly fixed in the mind of the average Japanese. In addition, the activities of Mitsui were more widespread and impinged upon the daily lives of more people than, say, Mitsubishi. Moreover, in the fall of 1931 the Mitsui Bank's "dollar buying" episode had aroused great antipathy and raised the

not so, the nation would not develop." (Fujiwara Ginjirō, *Kōgyō Nihon seishin* [Industry and Japanese Spirit], rev. ed.; Tokyo, 1935, pp. 201-202.) For Matsunaga, see Usami Shōgo, *Matsunaga Yasuzaemon* [A Biography of Matsunaga Yasuzaemon] (Tokyo, 1959), pp. 170-78.

accusation that Mitsui was callously making a profit out of a national disaster.[31] In November 1931 there were public demonstrations against Mitsui, and in December rumors of Ikeda's assassination were printed. After Baron Dan Takuma, the Mitsui Gōmei (Holding Company) managing director, was actually assassinated on March 5, 1932, Ikeda was closely guarded and took to wearing a bulletproof vest and using an automobile with bulletproof glass.[32]

The assassination of Baron Dan opened the way for Ikeda to take over the management of the Mitsui enterprises. Until his death Dan had run Mitsui in ostensible cooperation with Ariga Chōbun and Fukui Kikusaburō. With Dan removed from the scene, however, Ariga and Fukui proved incapable of making decisions and the affairs of the combine began to drift. Mitsui Hachirōeimon, the head of the house, decided Ikeda was the only man who could deal with the situation and asked him to become managing director of Mitsui Gōmei. Ikeda held back until he was assured of full control and until the Shimpeitai incident of July 1933, one of whose targets was the Japan Industrial Club, convinced him that action to counter the anti-zaibatsu movement was essential. In September 1933, at the age of sixty-seven, he finally became the top Mitsui executive, over the head of his seniors Ariga and Fukui.[33]

[31] For accounts of this incident, see Ikeda, *Zaikai kaiko*, pp. 135-64; Imamura, *op.cit.*, pp. 193-208; Kojima, *op.cit.*, pp. 155-78; Nishitani, *op.cit.*, pp. 192-210; Ōkurashō Shōwa Zaiseishi Henshūshitsu, *Shōwa zaiseishi* [Financial History of the Shōwa Era], X (Tokyo, 1955), 276-99, and XIII (Tokyo, 1963), 95-112. The public outcry raised against the Mitsui Bank was largely unjustified. The bank's dollar purchases in the fall of 1931 represented a reasonable and sensible effort to protect its foreign exchange position against the tie-up of funds and the losses caused by the British decision to abandon the gold standard.

[32] From this time until after the end of World War II Ikeda was under either private or police guard. See his description in Ikeda, *Zaikai kaiko*, pp. 173-75, 179-83 and *Keizai Ōrai*, II'1:4, 35-37.

[33] Ikeda, *Zaibatsu kaiko*, pp. 186-89; Hattori and Irimajiri, *op.cit.*, II, 177-82.

Immediately upon taking office Ikeda launched a campaign to change the public's image of Mitsui that has since come to be called the *zaibatsu no tenkō* ("zaibatsu conversion").[34] The Mitsui name, he said, must cease being associated with money-making and come to be synonymous with money-giving. The pride of the Mitsui families prevented them from accepting his suggestion that the name Mitsui be dropped from the names of their companies, but he did succeed in getting authorization to establish in October 1933 a charitable foundation, with a capital of 30,000,000 yen, to be known as the *Mitsui Hōonkai* (Mitsui Repayment of Kindness Society). A few months previously he had persuaded the Mitsui to donate 3,000,000 yen for the relief of the unemployed, a gesture quickly followed by 3,000,000 yen from Mitsubishi and 1,000,000 from Sumitomo. Altogether between March 1932 and May 1936 Mitsui gave some 60,000,000 yen for charitable works of various kinds.[35]

Ikeda also sought to counter the charge that Mitsui monopolized profits; he put stock owned by Mitsui in various first-class companies on sale to the public. In the fall of 1933 Mitsui sold 105,000 shares of Ōji Seishi; 330,000 shares of Tōyō Rēyon; 75,000 shares of Tōyō Kōatsu; and 25,000 shares of Miike Chisō. In the following February 90,000 shares of Hokkaidō Tankō Kisen were sold to six life insurance companies. Mitsui propaganda heralded these sales as the socialization of Mitsui enterprises (*jigyō no shakaika*), but the public was quick to recognize that the sales did not endanger Mitsui corporate control. Some cynics even pointed out that the capital brought in by these sales released Mitsui funds for investment in the new military supply industries associated with the post-Manchurian incident budgets and permitted Mitsui to begin to enter fields

---

[34] For a skeptical account of the "conversion," see Suzuki Mōsaburō, *Zaikai jimbutsu tokuhon* [Readings on Financial Leaders] (Tokyo, 1937), pp. 43-50.

[35] Ikeda, *Zaikai kaiko*, pp. 126-27, 187-88; Wada, *op.cit.*, pp. 349-55; Nishitani, *op.cit.*, pp. 247-52.

previously dominated by the new zaibatsu, like Ayukawa Gisuke.[36]

A third item on Ikeda's agenda was the problem of removing from the public's mind the image of Mitsui Bussan as an enterprise insatiably greedy for profits and not too finicky about how it made them. For many years the president of Mitsui Bussan had been Yasukawa Yūnosuke, a man with a fast eye for profit and a lightning-like pounce. In the midst of the Manchurian incident he sold salt to Chang Hsueh-liang, and when the Shanghai incident began he sold barbed wire to the Chinese Nineteenth Route Army. He had even skirted the Exchange Control Law by secretly exporting to New York some Taiwan Denryoku bonds. "No matter how much Mitsui reforms its appearance," said Ikeda to the Mitsui family head, "so long as Yasukawa conducts the business of Mitsui Bussan the way he does, the public will always be critical of Mitsui. ... We must quickly get rid of Yasukawa."[37] And by January 1934, despite strong opposition, get rid of him he did. Ikeda replaced him with a gentleman of his own type, Nanjō Kaneo. Under the new management dubious deals were avoided and the competitive pressure on small- and middle-sized businessmen was eased.[38]

Another reform instituted by Ikeda was the removal of

[36] Ikeda, *Zaikai kaiko*, pp. 130-31, 188; Wada, *op.cit.*, pp. 302-304; Hattori and Irimajiri, *op.cit.*, II, 183-84; Nishitani, *op.cit.*, pp. 239-40. Ikeda had taken up this idea as early as 1919 when he arranged for the sale of Mitsui Bank stock to the public. A recent commentator sees the whole *tenkō* process as an effort to modernize the Mitsui organization. *Tenkō*, he says, "must be evaluated not as a mere gesture necessitated to ease the anti-zaibatsu public opinion but as an initial step taken towards rationalization of the zaibatsu themselves to provide for the stage of conversion to heavy and chemical industry—the stage of full-scale monopoly." (Chō Yukio, "From the Shōwa Economic Crisis to the Military Economy," *The Developing Economies*, V:4 [December 1967], 595.)

[37] Ikeda, *Zaikai kaiko*, p. 129.

[38] Nishitani, *op.cit.*, pp. 241-47; Suzuki, *op.cit.*, pp. 48-51; Wada, *op.cit.*, pp. 304-312.

Mitsui family members from all offices in Mitsui companies. This is frequently interpreted as the action of the loyal *bantō* who was trying to provide for the safety of his masters by removing them from the line of fire. That may have been part of the story, but actually Ikeda also had some more practical objectives in view. Soon after going to the Gōmei, Ikeda complained that seventy percent of his time was taken up dealing with the busybodies among the eleven Mitsui families. Most of the family members who held imposing positions as president of this or that company were really figureheads incapable of functioning as true executives. Behind them was always the man who actually did the work. Ikeda felt that it was better for morale if he who did the work had the title. This change removed a great deal of deadwood and provided greater flexibility in management during the crisis produced by the readjustment of Mitsui operations to the demands of the times. It also placed greater emphasis on the open, public character of the Mitsui enterprises. Ikeda's plan aroused a great deal of opposition among the Mitsui, one of whom insisted, "this is the very kind of critical situation in which the Mitsui family ought to work in the front line." Nevertheless, after much expenditure of effort Ikeda succeeded in getting his plan implemented during the course of 1934 and 1935.[39]

On the political front Ikeda's name has been linked to a movement which developed during the fall of 1933 to revive party Cabinets as a defense against military domination. Despite its loudly expressed concern for the rural population, the army had chosen guns over funds for agricultural relief in the budget of 1934, and this had begun to disenchant the farmers. The idea grew that now was the time to force a return to party Cabinets by unifying the Seiyūkai and the Minseitō and launching an all-out attack on the military.[40] A key role in

[39] Ikeda, *Zaikai kaiko*, pp. 128, 186-87; Wada, *op.cit.*, pp. 301-302.

[40] For a full description of this, see Ichihara Ryōhei, "Seitō rengō undō no kiban—'zaibatsu no tenkō' o shōten to shite" [Bases for the Political Party Amalgamation Movement: The Zaibatsu Conversion],

this movement was played by the members of the *Banchō-ƙai*, a group of businessmen who met at Baron Gō Seinosuke's home to discuss business and political problems. Since Baron Gō was commonly regarded as a Mitsui agent, it was thought that Ikeda was behind the movement. One member of the *Banchō-ƙai*, Nakajima Kumakichi, was the Saitō Cabinet minister of commerce and industry, and it was he who took the lead in pushing the union of the parties. In this he was encouraged by the Breakfast Club,[41] in which he was also a participant. On December 25, 1933 he actually reached the point of holding a meeting of leaders from both parties.

Unfortunately, at this juncture the movement to unify the parties became involved with the famous Teijin case.[42] The Teikoku Jinken company was a subsidiary of the old Suzuki combine. The Bank of Taiwan held 225,000 shares of Teikoku Jinken stock as collateral against a loan to the Suzuki company and when the Suzuki company went bankrupt in 1927 the Bank of Taiwan took title to the shares. However, because of the loans that the Bank of Taiwan received from the Bank of Japan in 1927, it in turn was required to deposit these stocks

---

Keizai Ronsō, LXXIII:2 (February 1955), 106-122, and LXXIII:3 (March 1955), 161-82.

[41] This *Asameshiƙai* ("Breakfast Club") is not to be confused with the one associated with the Konoe entourage. (See Chalmers Johnson, *An Instance of Treason—Ozaƙi Hotsumi and the Sorge Spy Ring*, Stanford, 1964, pp. 125-27.) The "Breakfast Club" involved in the incident now under discussion embraced such men as Nagata Tetsuzan, Izawa Takio, Gotō Fumio, Kido Kōichi, Harada Kumao, Okabe Nagakage, Karasawa Toshiki, and Kuroda Nagakazu. (Ichihara, *op.cit.*, pp. 166-67). Ikeda seems actually to have attended a few Breakfast Club meetings. (See Robert M. Spaulding, "Japan's 'New Bureaucrats,' 1932-45," in George M. Wilson, ed., *Crisis Politics in Prewar Japan* [Tokyo, 1970], p. 56.)

[42] Ichihara, *op.cit.*, pp. 171-80; Hattori and Irimajiri, *op.cit.*, II, 188-90; Andō Yoshio, ed., *Shōwa ƙeizaishi e no shōgen* [Evidence for an Economic History of the Shōwa Era], 3 vols. (Tokyo, 1965-66), II, 11-12, 17-35.

with the Bank of Japan. Moreover, since the Bank of Japan had advanced funds guaranteed by the government, it was ruled that no disposition could be made of the stock without the permission of the Finance Ministry. The stocks rose in value as time went on and many speculators tried to buy them, but in order to do so one had to clear the purchase with the Bank of Japan and the Finance Ministry as well as the owner, the Bank of Taiwan. No one succeeded in doing so until the *Banchō-kai* organized a purchasing syndicate and using a member of the club, Shōriki Shōtarō, as a go-between persuaded Hatoyama Ichirō, the education minister, to secure the approval of the Finance Ministry. After gifts of money seemed to have changed hands all along the line, the *Banchō-kai* group bought 100,000 shares of the Teijin stock in May 1933.

A deal of this magnitude could not be kept quiet and the inevitable rumors of corruption spread. These were taken up in January 1934 by a series of articles in the *Jiji Shimpō* exposing the *Banchō-kai*. Shortly thereafter Baron Kikuchi Takeo indicted Nakajima in the House of Peers, and Okamoto Ichiki, a Kuhara group man, denounced both Nakajima and Hatoyama in the House of Representatives. The two ministers resigned and soon the case was in the hands of the procurators. Within a few months the procurators' net had drawn in businessmen, Bank of Taiwan officials, and finally even the finance vice-minister. Eventually a public trial was held which lasted from June 22, 1935, to October 5, 1937, and involved dozens of defendants as well as hundreds of witnesses. The main aim of the procurators seems to have been to demonstrate the utter corruption of the business world and the political parties. In many ways the handling of the case appears to have been designed to play the same role in disciplining the business world that the Minobe case did in silencing the academicians.[48] It completely discredited the parties and stopped in its tracks the

[48] In both instances General Baron Kikuchi Takeo led off the attack in the House of Peers. Both attacks were made by Kikuchi on February 7, 1934.

movement to restore party Cabinets. After this, zaibatsu executives like Ikeda ceased giving funds to the parties, which thus had to rely on smaller businessmen and consequently tended henceforth to protect the interests of small business against the big concerns.[44]

While Ikeda was abandoning the parties, he was reaching out in other directions. It is only natural that the radical young military officers should have intrigued him and that he should have wished to learn more about them. As early as June 1931, during the course of the one and only real talk which he had with Saionji, he told the genrō: "It is worthless to listen only to the talk of the marshals and the generals. You must listen to what the young officers are saying."[45] This remark was inspired by the experience he had had during a dinner at the Peers Club with Hiranuma Kiichirō and Hashimoto Kingorō.

[44] The only general election held while Ikeda was Mitsui Gōmei managing director was that of February 1936. In view of the adverse public opinion which had developed regarding the ties between the zaibatsu and the political parties, Ikeda decided that the connection must be cut if Mitsui were not to be destroyed. He discussed this with the head of the Mitsui family saying, ". . . we must accept the fact that the political parties will be angry [if we do this]. However, since we do not receive favors from the government, it does not matter how angry the political parties get. . . . The public's misunderstanding [of the zaibatsu–political party relationship] will have an effect on our business and will be injurious to Mitsui. Therefore it is my policy to cut the tie between the zaibatsu and the parties. Even if we are hated by the government, we will have to accept that cost. I am absolutely determined not to give any election funds. Undoubtedly people will come to you complaining about this, but I would like you to please put up with that patiently." [The government referred to here is a possible future one formed by a political party.] Ikeda's course of action was approved, and he therefore refused all requests for funds from the Seiyūkai, the Minseitō, and the smaller parties. However, though he did not give aid to any party as such, he did give money to individuals. ". . . I had to extend some amount of help to certain upright individual party members who, irrespective of their party affiliation, had a special relation with Mitsui. . . . I could not suddenly cut them off. . . ." (Ikeda, *Zaikai kaiko,* pp. 183-84. See a slightly different version in "Ikeda Seihin shi ni kiku," p. 54.)

[45] Ikeda, *Zoku zaikai kaiko,* p. 14.

Hashimoto's entire conversation had been an attack on the Japanese capitalists. At one point he said: "I am the emperor's soldier. I don't listen to what the government says. The government may get into trouble and order out the troops, but I won't obey them." When Ikeda was introduced to him, Hashimoto's sole response was to say, "When I shoot, it's not going to be at the masses that I shoot." Ikeda went away quite shocked at the type of officer who occupied a responsible position on the Army General Staff.[46]

In September 1933, shortly after Ikeda had become managing director of the Gōmei, he decided that the time had come to meet some of the young officers in order to find out for himself exactly what they were like. He asked a friend who had contacts with the officers to arrange a meeting with the most rabid one there was. The most rabid one refused to see Ikeda, but the friend was successful in arranging an interview with the man he considered to be the second most rabid young officer. The meeting, which lasted from 4 P.M. until 10 P.M., was held secretly in an unoccupied Japanese-style house on the grounds of Marquess Hachisuka's mansion. By specification of the officers the food served was a simple box supper. A Lieutenant-Colonel Hayabuchi showed up accompanied by three other officers. These three were Captain Yamaguchi, a son-in-law of General Honjō Shigeru and a leader in the February 26th uprising; Katō Tetsuya, a finance officer who later became a close friend of Ikeda's; and Mitsui Sakichi. Mitsui had once appeared in uniform to make an anti-Mitsui speech to the townspeople of Omuta in Kyushu, who were having a dispute with Mitsui Mining Company. At the present meeting his remarks consisted merely of diatribes against Mitsui Mining. Captain Yamaguchi spent his time carefully explaining to Ikeda why Japan must have a revolution in which blood was shed. At the end Ikeda dismissed them saying: "I understand the way you think, so I have achieved my purpose. The differ-

[46] *Ibid.*

ence in our opinions is just one of those things that can't be helped."[47]

Ikeda's next direct contact with young officers occurred in the fall of 1935 when the Italo-Ethiopian War broke out. At that time three officers from the First and Third Regiments came to ask for three ships and 5,000,000 yen in order to finance an expeditionary force to help the Ethiopians. Ikeda put them off, saying it was liable to damage Mitsui Bussan's business. Later the officers came back to say they had given up the expedition to Ethiopia but would like money for their young officers movement. Again Ikeda refused their request. However, there were times when money was given for various projects of the military—such as an inspection trip to Manchuria for students at the War College, the settlement of White Russians or right-wing Japanese on the Manchurian border, and investments in various Manchurian economic enterprises to show that Mitsui was cooperating in national policy.[48]

In early 1936 Ikeda had some additional contacts with two of the officers with whom he had met in 1933. Captain Yamaguchi turned up in January 1936 to ask for 3,000 yen to pay a printing bill for propaganda leaflets. Ikeda turned him down and later refused to see him when he again sought an interview on February 22.[49] At about this same time, Lieutenant-Colonel Mitsui Sakichi, who was acting as a special defense counsel at Lieutenant-Colonel Aizawa Saburō's courtmartial

[47] Ikeda, *Zaikai kaiko*, pp. 166-69. See also Kojima, *op.cit.*, pp. 220-27, which includes a slightly variant version by Ikeda's secretary, Miyahara Takeo. The Mitsui Sakichi mentioned here is no relation to the Mitsui zaibatsu family. In fact, the first character of his name differs from that of the famous Mitsui family.

[48] Hattori and Irimajiri, *op.cit.*, II, 190. From 1932 through 1936 Mitsui contributed 2,680,000 yen to various projects connected with national defense and the military. In addition, another 10,000,000 yen was invested in Manchuria under army pressure shortly after Manchukuo was established. See Wada, *op.cit.*, pp. 329-63, for Mitsui contributions in general. Details of military contributions are given by Wada on pp. 336-39.

[49] Ikeda, *Zaikai kaiko*, p. 169.

for the assassination of General Nagata Tetsuzan, asked that Ikeda be summoned as a witness. Mitsui claimed that Ikeda had developed a very close relation with Nagata Tetsuzan, the two meeting frequently to plot the suppression of the young officers advocating a Shōwa restoration. Mitsui implied that Nagata had received money from Ikeda and that after the general's death Ikeda continued to give economic support to Nagata's family. Mitsui's plan was to show that Ikeda, who controlled the genrō, the bureaucracy, and the political parties, was seeking to use Nagata to corrupt the military, the only group in Japan which was resisting him. Ikeda himself claimed that he had met Nagata only once, that a common friend had brought them together shortly before Nagata's death so the general could pass on the impressions he had garnered on a recent inspection trip to China.[50] That there may have been something in Mitsui's story is indicated by the statement from the friend who brought them together that Nagata planned to set up a Cabinet with Ikeda as prime minister.[51] The court-martial summoned Ikeda to appear before it on February 27, 1936. Of course, the February 26th uprising intervened, and when next the court met the whole atmosphere of the trial had changed and the court was no longer interested in giving Mitsui an opportunity to question Ikeda Seihin.

The February 26th incident caught Ikeda at his Ōiso villa, to which the police telephoned the message that the same assassins who had attacked Makino at Yugawara were on their way to kill him. Twenty policemen were sent to guard him, but since there were only three guns among them the nervous officer-in-charge insisted that Ikeda leave the villa. Ikeda fled through the night by car to the Grand Hotel at Yokohama,

---

[50] *Ibid.*, pp. 175-77; Kosaka Keisuke, *Tokkō* [Special Police] (Tokyo, 1954), pp. 52-65, reproduces Mitsui Sakichi's statement on this to the court trying Lt. Col. Aizawa. The date was February 24, 1936. Ikeda claimed that Mitsui Sakichi had had a close relationship with Ariga Chōbun. See also *Keizai Ōrai*, II′1:4, 37-38.

[51] Imamura, *op.cit.*, p. 240.

where again police guards felt insecure and asked him to go into hiding. In the end Ikeda entered a private Yokohama hospital under an assumed name and stayed out of sight until things had quieted down.[52] Ikeda later attributed the failure of the assassins to seek him out to Kita Ikki, with whom he had become acquainted through the Mitsui Gōmei director, Ariga Chōbun. According to Ikeda, when the question came up of assassinating him, Kita shunted it aside by remarking, "Why bother with him? He's only a clerk."[53]

Though Ikeda had escaped the assassins, it was now the Kempeitai who turned their attention to him.[54] Grave suspi-

[52] Ikeda, *Zaikai kaiko*, pp. 177-79.

[53] *Ibid.*, p. 181. During his interrogation Kita, who was trying to deny any direct contact with the conspirators, attributed this suggestion to Nishida Zei rather than to himself. See his *Chōshusho* in *Gendaishi shiryō* [Source Materials on Modern Japanese History], V, ed. Takahashi Masae (Tokyo, 1964), p. 734.

[54] See the account of the investigating officer, Fukumoto Kameji, in his *Ryūketsu no hanran ni • ni • roku jiken shinsōshi—hei ni tsugu* [The February 26th Incident] (Tokyo, 1954), pp. 210-13. Fukumoto feels that though he could not legally pin anything on Ikeda, Ikeda was not without a moral responsibility for the February 26th incident. He estimates that Mitsui spent about 150,000 yen a month for intelligence gathering and that the payments made to Kita by Ikeda came from this source. In his interrogation Kita admitted receiving 10,000 yen every June and December from Ariga Chōbun and said that Ikeda continued this arrangement. (*Gendaishi shiryō*, V, 733) Ikeda would seem to have had a widespread intelligence net organized to pick up hints of danger. He sometimes got information more quickly or accurately than the Kempeitai or the police. Indeed, he seems to have had informants within the Kempeitai. (Ikeda, *Zaikai kaiko*, p. 175)

In a written statement to the head of the Tokyo Kempeitai, Ikeda admitted that he met Kita through Ariga Chōbun in 1932 and thereafter saw him several times, the last time being in the autumn of 1935. In August 1932 he gave Kita 5,000 yen to go to China and use his friendship with a well-placed Chinese official to improve Sino-Japanese relations, but Kita spent the money for other purposes. Another time he gave him 5,000 yen for rent, the installation of a telephone, and other household expenses. Finally in December 1935 he supplied him with 10,000 yen. He claimed to be unable to resist Kita's persistent importun-

cions were entertained concerning Ikeda's connection with Kita Ikki, Nishida Zei, and the February 26th uprising. In order to avoid repercussions in the financial world, the Kempeitai decided to keep their investigation absolutely quiet and conducted their inquiries at Ikeda's own house under cover of night. The conclusions of the investigating officer were as follows:

> Ikeda Seihin gave Kita Ikki thousands of yen every month for living expenses. In exchange Kita supplied Ikeda with information about the military and the right wing. From this money Kita every month gave Nishida several hundred yen. The money in excess of Kita's living expenses was used as political funds and to gain control of the young officers. At the beginning of February . . . Ikeda gave money to Kita. However, he asserts this was the usual money for information and was not given as funds for the uprising. It is not clear if around the time of the uprising Kita did or did not give a confidential report to Ikeda. Kita keeps his mouth shut and will say nothing, Ikeda himself strenuously denies it, and no material evidence has been obtained.

The Kempeitai eventually decided to drop the matter, but Ikeda was quite shaken by his close call and went into seclusion at his Azabu home. Suffering from an aggravated gallstone condition and depressed by the increased public opposition to Mitsui and to himself personally that flared up anew after the February 26th incident, Ikeda decided to resign from his position as managing director of Mitsui Gōmei. When he discussed his resignation with the Mitsui family head, Ikeda told him that ". . . Mitsui must use the occasion of the February 26th incident to effect a change in policy. One such

---

ing and therefore agreed to make payments to him every June and December. Ikeda's statement is reproduced in Imamura, *op.cit.,* pp. 242-45. For additional details on Ikeda's relation with Kita, see Matsumoto Seichō, *Shōwashi hakkutsu* [Delving into Shōwa History], VIII (Tokyo, 1969), pp. 253-71.

change would be to retire the old men and put forward the young fellows." Ikeda, therefore, recommended the institution of a compulsory retirement age for Mitsui executives, who had previously stayed on until death, contributing to the growth of a top-heavy, slow-moving managerial apparatus. In April 1936 the Mitsui combine formally adopted Ikeda's suggestion and established a general retirement age of fifty, only a few very high positions being allowed to exceed this. At one sweep all the old crowd, of whom the public had such a bad impression, went out and there was a complete change in the managerial personnel. Into power came the "young executives," who were expected to have more rapport with the "young officers" and the "young bureaucrats," and who would bring more imagination and vigor to the task of assuring Mitsui a prominent role in the new economic structure which was arising in Japan.[55]

Cooperation with the Army

At the end of May 1936, Ikeda, aged sixty-nine, retired from Mitsui Gōmei and from every other public and private post he occupied. Meanwhile, after the February 26th incident the Hirota Cabinet had come to power and brought in Baba Eiichi, president of the Hypothec Bank, as its finance minister. Baba completely reversed the assassinated Takahashi Korekiyo's policy of gradually moving toward a reduction of expenditure and a contraction of the national debt. He increased Takahashi's budget by 700,000,000 yen, or about thirty-four percent, and instituted a program of deficit financing and low interest funds. Since by this time excess plant capacity had been reduced to a minimum, the mere news of the budget's figures began to send prices shooting upwards. It was very difficult for the economy to absorb the funds Baba was trying to pour into it, and at the same time it was also very difficult for financial institutions to absorb the bonds he was issuing. Material shortages developed, imports expanded, exchange dif-

[55] Ikeda, *Zoku zaikai kaiko*, pp. 63-64; Wada, *op.cit.*, pp. 318-20.

ficulties arose, and things seemed to be going wrong in just about every possible way. Financial leaders fell into a state of panic, for Baba's policies appeared to be on the verge of bringing the nation's economy down in a resounding crash.[56]

This kind of economic crisis was, of course, the very last thing that the leaders of the army wanted. Men like Hayashi Senjūrō and Ishiwara Kanji whose ideas came to dominate army policy for a time after the February 26th incident, placed their primary emphasis on an orderly expansion of productive capacity. They understood that it would take some time before Japan could be economically independent and that one must therefore be prepared for compromises, such as, for instance, making the provisions necessary to assure the export earnings in Western markets required to pay for machine tool imports. To this end they desired to enlist the skills of Japan's business community and were quite willing to forego social reforms, which by disrupting that community would be detrimental to the achievement of their economic goals. The "cleanup campaign" of Terauchi, Hirota's army minister, suppressed the socialist-oriented elements within the army, and by the winter of 1936-37 the army leadership was ready to effect a compromise with the business community. I sometimes wonder if one important reason for Terauchi's destruction of the Hirota Cabinet in January 1937 was not a desire to get rid of Baba Eiichi and open the way to incorporating into the government men who were more in tune with the thinking of the business world.[57] At any rate, to make plain its friendly attitude, the

[56] For a description of economic conditions in 1936 and 1937, see *Shōwa zaiseishi*, I (Tokyo, 1965), pp. 150-59; Takahashi Kamekichi, *Taishō Shōwa zaikai hendōshi* [A History of the Financial World During the Taishō Shōwa Era], 3 vols. (Tokyo, 1954-56), III, 1663-1895; Andō, *op.cit.*, II, 177-97

[57] Kaya Okinori reports that when Hirota and he were fellow prisoners in Sugamo the former prime minister often said: ". . . my cabinet was destroyed by the economic situation. We had reached an impasse and things were at a standstill. It couldn't be helped. It was entirely due to the economic situation that my cabinet collapsed." (Andō, *op.cit.*, II, 184)

army, at about the time negotiations for the Hayashi Cabinet were being conducted issued the following statement:

> It appears there is the rumor that the army wishes a radical upheaval in the country's economic organization and that this in turn will produce conditions which will throw the financial world into chaos. What the army desires is a reform consonant with the times and we are well aware that a radical upheaval would, contrary to our purpose, create disadvantageous effects and would be ineffectual in attaining our aim.[58]

In a sense the final seal was set on the new policy of compromise by the disposition of the Teijin case. On October 5, 1937, the court at long last handed down its decision: all the defendants were found not guilty. The procurators had good grounds for pursuing the matter further by making an appeal, but no one any longer had any reason for keeping up the affair, so it was allowed to drop.[59]

Looking around for a man who would be respected enough to maintain the confidence of the business community and yet who would be talented enough to secure the expansion of Japan's productive capacity in the directions dictated by military plans, Hayashi and Ishiwara finally decided on Ikeda Seihin as the one most likely to fill their needs, a decision which may already have been foreshadowed by Nagata Tetzuzan.[60] They sent Miyazaki Seigi, an official of the South Manchurian Railway, to ask Ikeda to become both finance minister and president of the Bank of Japan. On the grounds of poor health Ikeda refused both positions, recommending Yūki Toyo-

[58] *Nihon Keizai Nempō* [Japan Economic Yearbook], no. 27 (1937), p. 269.

[59] Ichihara, *op.cit.*, p. 182.

[60] Ikeda, *Zaikai kaiko*, pp. 206-207; Endō Shōkichi, "Gumbu to shihon to no hampatsu to shinwa" [Antagonism and Cooperation between the Military and Capital], *Shisō*, no. 358 (April 1954), p. 444; Harada Kumao, *Saionji kō to seikyoku* [Saionji Memoirs], 8 vols. (Tokyo, 1950-52), V, 248-51.

tarō, the president of the Industrial Bank, for the finance ministership. On being asked to suggest a commerce and industry minister, Ikeda named Tsuda Shingo, the president of Kanegafuchi. Although Hayashi accepted both of Ikeda's suggestions, only Yūki would consent to serve. Tsuda was replaced by Godō Takuo, a former admiral who as president of Japan Iron had worked well with the major industrial combines. Yūki, in turn, managed to persuade Ikeda to take on the presidency of the Bank of Japan. In explaining his decision to Harada Kumao, Ikeda said:

> In the concrete plans which Ishiwara Kanji has advanced, there are difficulties. The perfection of national defense demanded by the Army can only, of course, be carried out in conformity with international conditions. The base of the present economic structure must not be destroyed. Now, if the Bank of Japan, which is the very heart of the financial system, is not handled skillfully, we will be in great danger. In truth, financial and fiscal policy are today of extreme importance to the fate of the nation. The situation has developed in such a way that things must be done in accordance with the wishes of the middle-grade officers, who possess the greatest power among the military. If the present economic structure is spoiled, things will be in a hopeless mess.[61]

Businessmen reacted very favorably to the news of Yūki's appointment. A statement by Mori, the president of the Yasuda Bank, nicely sums up their expectations:

> I am very happy that Yūki Toyotarō, a man with an intimate knowledge of financial conditions, will enter the Cabinet as finance minister. Although financial circles are not responsible for Mr. Yūki's selection, I think he was appointed with the idea that he represented the financial world and there will be adopted financial and economic policies which incorporate the views of the financial world. What financial cir-

[61] Harada, *op.cit.*, V, 254-55.

cles especially expect of Mr. Yūki is that he will stand between them and the military, where hitherto there has been
a tendency towards estrangement, and that he will use his
influence to bring the opinions of both sides into harmony.
Thus the mutual understanding of the military and the
financiers will be deepened and the development of any misunderstanding will be precluded.[62]

Yūki reworked Baba's 1937 budget, managing to cut 300,-
000,000 yen from it. Most of the cuts were in nonmilitary expenses; the military portion was expanded by 300,000,000 yen
and rose to fifty percent of the total expenditure. To meet the
business demand for a better balanced budget, Yūki also increased taxes and postal rates. However, deficit financing still
continued, though at a level below that which Baba had
planned, and Yūki recognized that price rises were inevitable.
This meant a strengthening of economic controls was necessary, but Yūki tried to hold such measures to a minimum and
preferred to rely, in so far as was possible, on an expansion of
productive capacity achieved through the free investment decisions of private capital.

Ikeda, Yūki, and the business community in general raised
no public questions about the necessity of the economic developments which the army was demanding. If handled properly these developments seemed bound to further economic
growth, and the association of patriotism with industrial production unquestionably eased the formerly vexatious problem
of dealing with labor. Their primary concern was that the
process not be rendered disruptive or perhaps even fatal by
haste, ineptitude, or failure to give due consideration to all the
interests involved. It was Yūki's function to guard against
this and his policy was, in a series of steps no one of which
was too alarming in itself, gradually to ease Japan into what
would be called a semi-war economy. Not that Yūki and Ikeda
desired war or thought of their policies as preliminaries that

[62] *Nihon Keizai Nempō*, no. 27 (1937), p. 269.

would inevitably lead to war. Ikeda certainly did not believe that an actual war could bring anything but trouble to Japan's economy. Needless to say, he was filled with dismay when shortly afterwards the country slid into the China conflict and seemed unable to extricate itself.[63]

Yūki's financial policy called for increasing the flow of funds into productive enterprises and into the purchase of government bonds. As long as the commercial banks were expected both to make loans to industry and to purchase bonds, these two uses of funds competed with one another. Money loaned to increase production meant so much less money available for the purchase of bonds and vice versa. It was Ikeda's problem to resolve this dilemma, and he did it in a very simple way.[64] The Bank of Japan, which had traditionally confined its open market operations to selling bonds, now expanded its operations to purchasing as well. In this way the issuance of bonds became, in fact, an indirect way of increasing the Bank of Japan's currency issue. The funds of the commercial banks could now be used primarily for loans to business. The Bank of Japan itself began to supply funds for industrial purposes, sometimes directly, sometimes through the Industrial Bank. It was for this purpose that Ikeda widened the range of things which could be accepted as collateral by the bank. Ikeda also worked out ways of reducing the gold coverage for the currency so that more gold was made available for settling the balance of payments. In his brief tenure as president of the Bank of Japan he made a fundamental contribution to devising the techniques by which Japan financed its military and industrial expansion. He and Yūki demonstrated that the

[63] Endō, "Gumbu to shihon to no hampatsu to shinwa," pp. 444-45.

[64] For Ikeda's activities as president of the Bank of Japan, see Ikeda, *Zaikai kaiko*, pp. 203-206, 208-212; Endō, "Gumbu to shihon to no hampatsu to shinwa," pp. 445-46; Yoshino, *Rekidai Nihon Ginkō sōsai ron*, pp. 253-65, and his *Nihon Ginkō seido kaikakushi* [A History of Reforms of the Bank of Japan] (Tokyo, 1962), pp. 368-92. See also Suzuki, *op.cit.*, pp. 159-80 where he discusses Yūki, Ikeda, and Tsuda under the title "Who Is Japan's Schacht?"

army's objectives could be accommodated within the existing structure of economic relations and thereby earned the right for the business community to share, and share profitably, in the control of the transformation that was occurring in Japanese society.

Shortly after the first Konoe Cabinet came to power, Ikeda's gall stones began acting up and he felt obliged to leave the presidency of the Bank of Japan. His successor was Yūki who had just retired as finance minister. Soon, however, the crisis of the China War led Konoe to ask Ikeda to join a special group of councilors (*sangi*) created in October 1937 to strengthen the government.[65] The other members of this neatly balanced group were Generals Ugaki and Araki, Admirals Suetsugu and Abo, Machida Chūji, Maeda Yonezō, Akita Kiyoshi, and Matsuoka Yōsuke. With the widening of the China War the economic situation in the fall and winter of 1937-38 went from bad to worse. Interest rates climbed; prices went up; exports fell off, particularly to the United States where there was a recession; yet heavy imports were required to feed the war, and the balance of payments worsened dangerously. Kaya Okinori and Yoshino Shinji, career officials who had become respectively the finance minister and the commerce and industry minister, proved incapable of managing the situation with the requisite skill. In the end, the two ministers were even at loggerheads since the Commerce and Industry Ministry would frequently authorize imports for which the Finance Ministry denied the requisite foreign exchange.

Ikeda's Service in the First Konoe Cabinet

As early as November 1937 Konoe invited Ikeda to become finance minister, but Ikeda refused this and several subsequent offers since he was very pessimistic about the Cabinet's ability

[65] Ikeda, *Zaikai kaiko*, pp. 288-89. With a brief interruption, Ikeda remained a Cabinet councilor until the post was abolished by the Tōjō Cabinet.

to extricate itself from the China situation. When he discovered in May 1938 that Ugaki was to become foreign minister, he changed his mind and agreed to become not only finance minister but also commerce and industry minister. The combination of the two jobs was considered necessary in order to coordinate economic policy, though it was denounced by many bureaucrats as a violation of their "sectionalism" principle. With himself directing economic policy and Ugaki unifying diplomatic and military policy, Ikeda believed there was a real chance of settling the China crisis into which the nation had stumbled.[66]

On the economic front Ikeda concentrated on securing military supplies, controlling prices, and expanding exports (especially through the institution of the link system).[67] However, most of his time was spent at the prime minister's residence rather than at either of his two ministries. Konoe made him a kind of deputy prime minister and involved him in seeking solutions to the China War and in devising plans to convert the economy to a war status if the war should be a long one. In June 1938 Konoe instituted his version of the Five-Ministers Conference, which used to meet on one or two afternoons a week. On the mornings of scheduled meeting days Konoe would gather with Ugaki and Ikeda in a "three-ministers conference" to plot strategy for dealing with the military in the full conference. Thus Ikeda played an important role in Konoe's attempts to control army action.[68]

Ikeda's great hopes that Ugaki would be able to end the China War were dashed when Ugaki resigned on September 30, 1938, over the issue of creating a China Board which would supervise Chinese matters in complete independence of the

[66] *Ibid.*, pp. 289-95; Endō, "Gumbu to shihon to no hampatsu to shinwa," pp. 447-49; Imamura, *op.cit.*, pp. 279-83; Yabe Teiji, *Konoe Fumimaro* [A Biography of Konoe Fumimaro], 2 vols. (Tokyo, 1952), I, 507-522; *Keizai Ōrai*, II′1:3, 32.

[67] For Ikeda's activities as finance minister, see Endō, Katō, and Takahashi, *op.cit.*, pp. 214-18.

[68] Ikeda, *Zaikai kaiko*, 290-91.

Foreign Ministry. Ugaki grasped the full significance of this move and adamantly opposed it. Ikeda approved the plan, for he thought that it would at least remove political and economic affairs in China from the military's control. He realized his error when a general became the board's first president. Ugaki's departure nearly brought the Cabinet down, but at the request of both the palace officials and the army Konoe continued in office and Ikeda, angry at Ugaki for resigning without informing him beforehand, decided to stay on also.[69]

After the fall of the Wuhan area, Ikeda realized that there was no hope of ending the war soon and that economic controls were now unavoidable. When Article Six of the Mobilization Law was invoked in November to impose controls on labor, the home minister, Admiral Suetsugu, demanded that Article Eleven, which gave the power to limit dividends and institute forced loans, also be put into force. If this were not done, he would, he asserted, have great difficulty maintaining public peace. At this Ikeda, in full Cabinet meeting, said: "Do you really think a factory worker knows how much stockholders receive as dividends? . . . Why do you say such a damned foolish thing? Is there any connection between a stockholder's dividends and the public peace?"[70]

When he left the meeting, Ikeda immediately held a press conference in which he announced that though limitation of dividends might be politically desirable it was economically unsound. "If you limit stock profits, you will destroy the entrepreneurial spirit and there will be no hope for the very important expansion of production our country now needs."[71] He

[69] Imamura, *op.cit.*, pp. 291-95; Yabe, *op.cit.*, I, 539-53; Harada, *op.cit.*, VII, 147. For Ikeda's discussion of Ugaki, see Ikeda, *Zoku zaikai kaiko*, pp. 192-95, and *Keizai Ōrai*, II'1:3, 33-35.

[70] Ikeda, *Zoku zaikai kaiko*, pp. 183-84. For accounts of the dividend limitation problem, see Ichitani, *op.cit.*, pp. 278-80; Imamura, *op.cit.*, pp. 300-308; Kojima, *op.cit.*, pp. 255-63; Yabe, *op.cit.*, I, 607-609; Harada, *op.cit.*, VII, 199, 207, 211.

[71] Quoted in Imamura, *op.cit.*, pp. 302-303. This public defense of the necessity of profit-making to the entrepreneurial spirit is an interesting

also expressed the fear that forcing banks to make loans would adversely affect the economy through the uneasy feeling it would arouse among depositors. In private Ikeda accused Suetsugu of propagandizing "almost like a Red" and of completely unnerving the financial community.

For his opposition to dividend limitation Ikeda was publicly denounced by Satō Kenryō, the chief of the Army Information Bureau. Suetsugu pressed Konoe to get rid of Ikeda or else face his own resignation. However, the navy minister, Yonai, agreeing that the "most important thing is to create an atmosphere which allows Ikeda to carry on," refused to cooperate in the attempted ouster.[72] It was agreed to establish a limitation on dividends, but at the rate of ten percent a year. It was further agreed that forced loans would be made only by the Industrial Bank. In the future, controls over capital would become tighter, but Ikeda had set the pattern for making the controls on the business community the lightest of all in the war economy.

As a member of the Five-Ministers Conference Ikeda natu-

---

contrast to the heavy emphasis on traditional Japanese values and service to the nation which Byron K. Marshall has found to be typical of the Japanese business elite's ideology. Of course, Marshall's book deals with "the ideas utilized by business spokesmen to justify the private ownership of industry and to legitimatize the authority of the managerial class" (*op.cit.*, p. 4) and is "not . . . concerned with the ultimate *motives* of the entrepreneurs" (p. 18). Marshall himself gives an excellent example of the entire business establishment rallying to the defense of profits in 1940 (pp. 108-109). It may be that when we have more information about the day-to-day decision-making of the Japanese businessman we will find that the range and strength of his motivations are not so different from those of businessmen everywhere.

On the subject of patriotism, it is interesting to note an exchange that occurred when Yamamoto Jōtarō was trying to persuade Ikeda to become the Tanaka Cabinet's president of the Bank of Japan. Yamamoto asked Ikeda point-blank, "Which is more important to you, Mitsui or Japan?" To which Ikeda replied, "Mitsui is more important to me." (Ikeda, *Zoku zaikai kaiko*, p. 93.)

[72] Harada, *op.cit.*, VII, 211.

rally became involved in foreign policy discussions. When in the summer and fall of 1938 Ōshima's negotiations with the Germans presented the Konoe government with the problem of whether or not to expand the coverage of the Anti-Comintern Pact beyond Russia to include England and France, Ikeda joined Ugaki and Yonai in opposing the move.[73] He had no desire to antagonize England and the United States, for he shared the hope that somehow or other these two countries could be used to settle the China question. Moreover, as the Cabinet member primarily responsible for economic policy, he was also convinced that a deterioration in relations with England and America would be disastrous for the Japanese economy. At about this time he said:

> It is basically impossible for Japan's finances and economy to operate in defiance of America and England.[74]

> If just England alone were to deny us access to financing in London, foreign trade would become absolutely impossible. ... It is very disadvantageous to make enemies of England and America. At Cabinet meetings I am always saying that it is absolutely no good to make enemies of England and America.[75]

[73] Imamura, *op.cit.*, pp. 328-30; Yabe, *op.cit.*, I, 593-605. Ikeda was also instrumental in keeping Matsuoka Yōsuke from succeeding as foreign minister when Ugaki resigned. (Yabe, *op.cit.*, pp. 558-59.) When the treaty problem was discussed at the Imperial Conference of November 30, 1938, Hiranuma asked, "If England and America unite and bring economic pressure to bear on Japan, has the government countermeasures for such a situation?" Ikeda flatly answered, "No." (Harada, *op.cit.*, VII, 243.) See also Nihon Kokusai Seiji Gakkai, Taiheiyō sensō genin kenkyūbu, comp., *Taiheiyō sensō e no michi—kaisen gaikōshi* [The Road to the Pacific War], 8 vols. (Tokyo, 1962-63), V, 73, 74, 85, 89 and *Keizai Ōrai*, II'1:3, 36-38.

[74] Harada, *op.cit.*, VII, 238.

[75] *Ibid.*, p. 230. Ikeda went on to say, "There are those in the army who suggest borrowing money from England; there are others who argue for the overthrow of England. It is really very troublesome that

It was inconceivable to Ikeda that the economic expansion planned for Japan could take place without access to Western machinery, Western raw materials, and Western short-term financing for the import of raw materials destined for reexport. Therefore, in policy discussions his weight was always thrown on the side of maintaining friendly relations with England and America.

By December 1938 Ikeda was, however, very pessimistic about the success of his efforts and had become disillusioned with Konoe. "It is very difficult," he complained, "when the prime minister silently looks on while the right wing and part of the army interfere with what I am trying to do and make it impossible for me to do my work and discharge my responsibilities."[76] If stronger support were not forthcoming from the prime minister, Ikeda believed he had little choice but to give up his post as finance minister. For his part Konoe felt overwhelmed by the difficulties arising from the Ikeda-Suetsugu quarrel and the German negotiations. Around December 22 he confided to Ikeda and a few other key persons that he wished to resign because the coming Diet session would be too troublesome. In the face of this weakness Ikeda was quite willing to throw in the towel and readily agreed to the Cabinet's leaving office.[77]

The question of who was to form the next Cabinet was settled in consultation among Konoe, Ikeda, and Kido (the welfare minister). Konoe first suggested Hiranuma. Ikeda had been friendly with Hiranuma since 1927 and had lent his name

---

there is no unity of opinion. . . . Even when American feeling toward Japan is not good as a result of the German-Japanese tie, the [American] Jews still sell goods to Japan. However, if Japan imitates Germany's 'severe control of the Jews, discrimination will develop in connection with our foreign trade."

[76] *Ibid.*, p. 239.

[77] Ikeda, *Zaikai kaiko*, pp. 289-91, and *Zoku zaikai kaiko*, p. 26; Yabe, *op.cit.*, I, 610-18; Imamura, *op.cit.*, pp. 310-11.

to Hiranuma for use in connection with the Kokuhonsha.[78]
When Hiranuma anticipated becoming prime minister in
1932, it was his plan to make Ikeda his finance minister.[79] Yet
when Konoe threw out Hiranuma's name, Ikeda rejected the
suggestion on the ground Hiranuma would not be able to
hold down the army in the vital matter of foreign relations.
Only the navy could do this, he argued, and therefore Yonai
should be the next prime minister. Yonai was asked but declined, so the ultimate choice fell on Hiranuma.[80] Gravely
troubled about the prospects for Japan's relations with England
and America under a Hiranuma cabinet, Ikeda saw the prime
minister-designate several times and sought to impress on him
the absolute necessity of avoiding any action which would
alienate the two Western powers.[81]

Although Ikeda was considered as a candidate for prime
minister on the occasion of the fall of both the Hiranuma Cabinet and its successor, the Abe Cabinet, he was never to hold
Cabinet office again.[82] His candidacy always foundered against
the adamantine opposition of important elements of the army.[83]

[78] Ikeda, *Zoku zaikai kaiko*, pp. 178-79. Ikeda says that Hiranuma
loved to organize societies and was always including him as a member.
He claims that although he was listed as an auditor of the Kokuhonsha,
Hiranuma had never asked his permission for this. According to Ikeda
he never attended any meetings or paid any dues and was merely a
member in name only.

[79] Hayashi, *op.cit.*, p. 229.

[80] Yabe, *op.cit.*, I, 618-26; Imamura, *op.cit.*, pp. 311-12; Harada, *op.cit.*,
VII, 245-55; Ikeda, *Zaikai kaiko*, p. 292; *Keizai Ōrai*, II'1:3, 36-37.

[81] Harada, *op.cit.*, VII, 246-47, 249-50, 283-84.

[82] Ikeda, *Zaikai kaiko*, p. 273; Imamura, *op.cit.*, pp. 334-40; Harada,
op.cit., VIII, 59-61, 155, 158, 164-65, 168, 171.

[83] In discussing this antipathy, Harada reports as follows: ". . . while
in Germany Ambassador Ōshima was told by Goering, 'Since Japan
holds finance capitalists [*kinyū shihonka*] in great respect, it has become pro-English. In Germany we eventually forced out Schacht and
the rest of the pro-English crowd. If Japan does not likewise esteem the
production capitalists [*sangyō shihonka*] rather than the finance capitalists, she will get nowhere.' After he returned to Japan, Ōshima told
this to the army leaders. Adopting these words as their guiding principle

He did, however, become a kind of elder statesman, eventually being elevated to the Privy Council in October 1941.[84] From the time he left office until the end of the Pacific War, Ikeda belonged to that dwindling group which supported whatever moves there were to preserve peace with the West and to moderate the power of the military.[85] After him there were to be other prominent businessmen in Cabinet office—Kobayashi Ichizō (Mitsui), Fujiwara Ginjirō (Ōji Seishi), Murata Shōzō (OSK), Ogura Masatsune (Sumitomo), but none of them ever achieved the degree of influence on general policy which had been Ikeda's. Nevertheless, by their presence in the government they were able to resist bureaucratic and military attempts to take away from big business control of the management of its organizations.

The end result was that the industrial combines came

---

and using them to hotly denounce Ikeda and Yūki, the army is hoping to put production capitalists in everywhere." (Harada, *op.cit.*, VIII, 168.)

The army even refused to accept Ikeda again as finance minister. (*Ibid.*, p. 75.) Some army extremists were so outraged by his pro-Western views that in January 1940 they planned to assassinate him and several others whom they considered to be seeking a rapprochement with England and the United States. (*Ibid.*, p. 154.) The Ikeda family has also felt that army malevolence was behind the drafting of Ikeda's thirty-five-year-old second son and his dispatch to China where he died of malaria. (Imamura, *op.cit.*, pp. 363-64)

[84] Ikeda, *Zaikai kaiko*, pp. 284-86. This appointment was made when the Tōjō Cabinet abolished the position of Cabinet councilor. Ikeda had been approached twice in connection with membership in the Privy Council. An offer by the Hirota Cabinet was blocked by the military and he himself refused one from the Yonai Cabinet.

[85] Harada, *op.cit.*, VIII, 120-21, 130, 142-43, 146-47, 154, 185. In his concern to control the military, Ikeda turned to the navy. For instance, early in 1940 he asked Admiral Yonai, then prime minister, if the navy were not making plans to prevent the emperor falling into the hands of army rebels in the event of another rising like that of February 26, 1936. He suggested that the navy should perhaps take the emperor aboard a battleship. Yonai assured him preparations for the emperor's safety had been made and there was nothing to worry about. (*Ibid.*, p. 210.)

through the destruction of war intact and arose phoenix-like to even greater heights in the postwar period. For them the Occupation reforms proved but a passing phase, except in so far as the efficiency of the combines may actually have been improved by the stripping away of the irrational impedimenta which had lingered from the days of their origin as family businesses. The industrial combines had successfully preserved their organization, built up their technical skills, and were ready to take advantage of the opportunities for growth presented in the 1950's and 1960's. They and the bureaucracy have survived war and defeat to become, for the present at least, the dominating elements on the Japanese scene.[86]

[86] See Kozo Yamamura, *Economic Policy in Postwar Japan: Growth versus Economic Democracy* (Berkeley, 1967); Chitoshi Yanaga, *Big Business in Japanese Politics* (New Haven, 1968); and Arnold J. Heidenheimer and Frank C. Langdon, *Business Associations and the Financing of Political Parties: A Comparative Study of the Evolution of Practices in Germany, Norway and Japan* (The Hague, 1968), pp. 130-205.

PART THREE

Intellectual

CHAPTER IX

Intellectuals as Visionaries of the New Asian Order

JAMES B. CROWLEY

A Reappraisal of the Prewar Intellectuals

AGAINST the blinding implosions at Hiroshima and Nagasaki, Japanese historians understandably came to view the course of Japan's national policy in the 1930's as a "valley of darkness." Henceforth, the story of this decade would be told primarily in terms of a limited number of characters—ultranationalists, fascists, and militarists. The central theme became the pernicious spectre of these groups trampling Taishō democracy underfoot, driving the nation into atavistic aggression and reactionary totalitarianism. And, of course, the main villain became the military establishment, impelling the nation into a war which was, in Churchill's language, incompatible, "with prudence or even with sanity."[1] In essence, Japanese historians have been inclined to portray the 1930's as a process of fascistization which stemmed from the arrogance and ignorance of the military and their extremist civilian cohorts. The role of bona fide intellectuals and responsible government officials has been obscured. Indeed, says Maruyama Masao, during the valley of darkness "intellectuals in the proper sense" were not "positive advocates of the driving forces of the fascist movement. Rather, their mood was generally one of vague antipathy toward it, an antipathy that amounted to passive resistance."[2] Those so-called intellectuals who had obviously championed a sense of Japan's manifest

[1] Winston Churchill, *The War Speeches of Winston S. Churchill, 1939-1945* (London, 1952), II, 150.
[2] Masao Maruyama, *Thought and Behaviour in Modern Japanese Politics* (New York, 1963), p. 58.

319

destiny in Asia, are often explained as the victims of *tenkō* (an apostasy of basic beliefs) because of duress exerted by the police, or of *gisō-tenkō* (a pseudo recantation) in order to placate governmental authorities.[3] And yet, on occasion one does hear these charitable recollections guardedly questioned. The shared experience of a lost war, one critic notes, infuses discussions of *tenkō* with "a sense of fellowship."[4] The intimation is there that many intellectuals had, in fact, advocated some type of national cause—that they had, in fact, enunciated positive convictions and displayed positive behavior on behalf of the policies which ultimately led to Hiroshima and Nagasaki.

Pursuing this approach to prewar Japan, this chapter is concerned with the process by which at least some informed and articulate Japanese did not oppose, look away, or pretend, but actually did participate positively in the formulation of the dream of a New Asian Order. The key questions under consideration are not, therefore, whether or not most intellectuals were "passive resisters" or whether or not, under duress, some intellectuals truly or falsely recanted or apostatized their basic convictions. Rather this chapter presupposes a different cluster of questions—namely,

How did men who, in their own eyes, were neither chauvinists nor fascists but responsible officials and informed critics, view Japanese society?

What options seemed most creditable and most humane to

[3] Tsurumi Shunsuke, et al., *Tenkō* [Apostasy], II (Tokyo, 1960); Maruyama Masao, et al., *Kindai Nihon shisōshi kōza* [Historical Essays on Modern Japanese Thought], I (Tokyo, 1959); and Honda Shūgo, *Tenkō bungakuron* [Essay on Literary Apostasy] (2nd edn.); (Tokyo, 1964). Shunsuke Tsurumi, "Cooperative Research on Ideological Transformation," *Journal of Social and Political Ideas in Japan*, II:1 (April 1964), 54-58; Ryū Shintarō, "Japanese Thought in Post-Meiji Japan," *Japan Quarterly*, XIII:2 (April-June 1966), 157-71; and Chalmers Johnson, *An Instance of Treason: Ozaki Hotsumi and the Sorge Spy Ring* (Stanford, 1964).

[4] Nakajima Kenzō, *Shōwa jidai* [Shōwa Era] (Tokyo, 1957), p. 149.

intellectuals overtly concerned with the existing state of affairs?

What national aspirations beguiled the imagination as just and civilized?

Questions of this sort admit no pat answers or early generalizations. Still, some clues to the thought and behavior of Japanese intellectuals in the 1930's can be gained by a discussion of the sentiments and ideas voiced by members of the Shōwa Kenkyūkai (Shōwa Research Association).

This association has eluded systematic study and analysis. Even so, it is generally regarded as one of the most significant facets of prewar Japan. Some have branded the Shōwa Kenkyūkai "communist," mainly because Ozaki Hotsumi was one of its members; others have termed it "fascist" because of its deep involvement in the Imperial Rule Assistance movement.[5] Despite the divergent characterizations, few deny that its membership included the cream of Japanese intellectuals, or that it was Prince Konoe's main advisory group, his brain trust on domestic and foreign affairs. Thus, by concentrating on this association and its patron, Prince Konoe, one may explicitly relate ideas and politics, and, at this micro-level, gain some insight into the thought and behavior of a significant cluster of intellectuals and officials in prewar Japan. Since that is the central purpose of this chapter, no attempt will be made to probe deeply into the organizational structure or to cover all the research teams and projects of the association. The intent

[5] A convenient review of the historiography on the Shōwa Kenkyū-kai is Murata Katsumi, "Shōwa kenkyūkai ni taisuru hyōka" [Appraisal of the Shōwa Research Association], *Tōyō Kenkyū* [Studies of Asia and Africa], IX (October 1964), 59-72. The best published source on the association is Gotō Ryūnosuke, *Shōwa Kenkyūkai* (Tokyo, 1968). This collection of essays appeared after the writing of this chapter. In addition to reprinting several articles by former members of the association, it includes several key documents and the membership lists of various task forces organized within the association.

here is restricted to etching some of the dominant concerns and proposals articulated within the Shōwa Kenkyūkai between 1936 and 1938—from the traumatic rebellion of February 26, 1936, to Premier Konoe's proclamation in November 1938 of the quest for a New Asian Order as the basic objective of Japan's national policies. Given this framework, the basic theme is the process and manner in which some distinguished intellectuals and important officials formulated and subscribed to the vision of the New Asian Order.

The Establishment of the Shōwa Kenkyūkai

If the historian or social scientist of the 1930's had been endowed with a seismological scale to measure the intensity of social unrest, no doubt Japan in that period would have been regarded as a present-day Matsushiro. The social tremors of the 1930's—dramatized by the May 15th and the February 26th incidents—were not, however, traceable to a constant and irreversible fault of nature, nor could they be gauged by a universally accepted scientific criterion. At best, they signified a profound social malaise, which spawned a multiplicity of diagnoses and proffered cures, ranging from the pastoral idealism of a Gondō Seikyō to the anticipated birth of a classless society that was to emerge phoenix-like out of the revolutionary destruction of the imperial system. Despite the multiplicity of proffered solutions, the dramatic rebellion of February 26 unquestionably generated a pervasive conviction that the intense suspicion and animosity directed at both the "emperor's advisors" and the "conservative leadership" of the government by young officers and the rightist organization could not be ignored any longer. In response, the Hirota Cabinet articulated one type of political solution to these domestic tensions, a commitment to a program predicated on the "national defense requisites." This appeal was superficially compelling. Japan's withdrawal from the League of Nations and the abrogation of the naval limitations treaties rationalized the demand for a doubling of armament expenditures. And, without doubt, the creation of Manchukuo and the North China "autonomy" movement rendered Sino-Japanese relations the most pressing and the potentially most explosive diplomatic-military issue confronting the empire. Few Japanese openly challenged "the expanded requisites of national defense" propounded by the Hirota Cabinet; and few Japanese seriously contended that the Hirota Cabinet was providing the political leadership sufficient for the mastery of the social and political malaise that had characterized Japanese society since the early 1930's. Anomie, as expressed in acts of assassination and rebellion, was too rampant to be denied. Nor could any responsible critic ignore the visible contentions between the parties and the Cabinet, between the soldiers and the sailors, between the diplomats and the army.

Speaking on this theme in July 1936, Prince Konoe declared:

> Although there were all sorts of contentions before the Russo-Japanese war, there was a basic agreement to ally with Great Britain and thrash Russia; and national policy had been unified. Today, however, multiple and divergent courses are being urged according to particular preferences—a situation which resembles that prevalent in imperial Germany before the Great War. . . . Japanese public opinion is deeply divided; and there are many serious confrontations, including those existing between villages and cities, the army and the navy, and soldiers and diplomats. When I think of Germany before the Great War and examine the contemporary situation in Japan, no longer can I contain my profound sense of anxiety.[6]

Despite this concern, Prince Konoe, in harmony with all the political leaders of the nation, was as yet unprepared to offer a cogent sense of national mission which could compel a unity of national purpose. Unlike his political peers, Prince Konoe sought the active assistance of a group of intellectuals and

[6] Baba Tsunego, *Konoe naikaku shiron* [Historical Essay on the Konoe cabinet] (Tokyo, 1946), p. 87.

important government officials in the demanding task of formulating a new statement of Japan's role in Asia. The result, in November 1936, was the formal establishment of the Shōwa Kenkyūkai.

The breadth and quality of its membership may be conveyed by listing a few of the key participants in the various research associations created by the Shōwa Kenkyūkai: namely, Rōyama Masamichi, Yabe Teiji, Sasa Hirō, Ryū Shintarō, Miki Kiyoshi, Gotō Ryūnosuke, Taira Teizō, as well as Yoshida Shigeru, Kazami Akira, Kaya Okinori, Gotō Fumio, and Arita Hachirō. These men were already public personalities by the mid-1930's. Rōyama and Yabe were both professors at Tokyo University as well as advisors to Prince Konoe; Sasa and Ryū were popular political and economic pundits for the *Asahi*; Gotō Ryūnosuke was a classmate and sometime personal secretary to Prince Konoe; Taira, a classmate of Professor Rōyama, was a recognized authority on the economic affairs of China and Manchuria; Miki Kiyoshi, a distinguished philosopher and authority on European intellectual affairs, was considered to be one of the most famous disciples of Nishida Kitarō; Kazami, a flamboyant Seiyūkai politician and confidant of Prince Konoe, would be the chief Cabinet secretary in the First Konoe Cabinet and justice minister in the Second Konoe Cabinet; and Kaya, Gotō Fumio, and Arita Hachirō were senior civil servants—Gotō serving as home minister in the Saitō Cabinet, Kaya as finance minister in the First Konoe Cabinet and again in Tōjō's Cabinet, and Arita as foreign minister in four different Cabinets between 1936 and 1940. These men defined the purpose of their association as follows:

In recent years, Japan's political and economic position in the world has undergone a fundamental transformation. Despite the fact that our diplomatic, security, economic, social and administrative policies should evolve in adaptation to this new situation, many aspects of the old state of affairs persist; and, consequently, in the midst of the existing serious international situation, we are repeating in our national policies and attitudes, the old confusions and contradictions. In order to extricate ourselves from this situation, there must be a general mobilization of the experience and intelligence of the entire nation. Accordingly, since the cornerstone of this mobilization requires a complete agreement on national intentions among all sections of Japan's society—among the military, scholars, essayists, bureaucrats and businessmen— there is a pressing need for the formation of a research organization which will undertake the task of formulating a proper national policy. For this reason, we have organized the Shōwa Kenkyūkai.[7]

The initial meetings of the new association recapitulated the outstanding social-political-economic problems facing the Japanese government. This review was mainly carried out by Sasa Hirō and Rōyama Masamichi, both of whom stressed, in particular, the need to curtail sharply the authority of the House of Peers, to increase governmental control over big business, and to extend major government assistance to the depressed agricultural sector. These opinions mirrored familiar sentiments, but they failed to spark any comprehensive view of Japan, one that embraced foreign and domestic issues in one cogent package.

TAKAHASHI KAMEKICHI'S "WHITHER JAPAN?"

In early March 1937, Takahashi Kamekichi presented two essays on Japan's present and future national course: "One View of the Fundamental Problems of Establishing a National

[7] "Shōwa kenkyūkai taikō" [Prospectus of the Shōwa Research Association], 1939, Daitō Bunka University Collection. Hereafter, this collection of documents is cited DTB. One should note that this association was first organized on an informal basis in 1933. (Gotō Ryūnosuke, *op.cit.*, p. 8.) I am grateful to Mr. Kishi Kōichi for his assistance and for arranging access to this documentary collection. In addition, I am indebted to Ōyama Iwao, Gotō Ryūnosuke, Doi Akira, Taira Teizō, and Sakai Saburō for their thoughtful and candid recollections about the Shōwa Kenkyūkai.

Policy" and "Whither Japan?—A General Prospectus."[8] Directly after his presentation, notes the first prospectus of the association, "we decided to continue this type of comprehensive research and to solicit opinions from all possible circles, not just those of our staff, on the subject of The Formulation of the Basic Principles of National Policy."[9] In short, Takahashi's essays crystallized the subsequent point of departure for the research activities of the association, and for this reason it is reasonable to regard his views as a reliable index to the prevailing climate of opinion among those officials and intellectuals active in the Shōwa Research Association in the spring of 1937.

As Takahashi saw things, the establishment of a viable national policy was contingent on a sense of history, on an awareness of the "direction of world trends." This awareness depended, in turn, on the types of questions one asked about Japan and the world: Did one regard the contemporary world as an age of revolutionary change or as temporary crisis? Did one consider the May 15th incident, the decline of party Cabinets, the abortion of the Ugaki Cabinet, as accidents, or did one seek to diagnose the basic disease causing these "unlucky omens"? Did one evaluate Japan's diplomatic plight as the consequence of "ineptitude" or as the "inevitable" result of changing patterns of international trade and diplomacy? Did one regard foreign policy as a matter of "power politics," or did one see it against the drama of the "conflict among communism, fascism, and liberalism"? Could national policy dis-

[8] "Kokusaku juritsu no kompon mondai to sore no mikata," DTB, 6 pp. "Nippon wa doku e yuku ka?" DTB, 47 pp. Takahashi was a popular free lance commentator, former editor of the *Tōyō Keizai Shimpōsha*, and president of the Takahashi Institute of Economic Research. He was also active in the Institute of Pacific Relations and held various positions in the Finance Ministry and Ministry of Commerce and Industry. In 1967, Takahashi was awarded the Second Order of Merit by the Japanese government.

[9] "Shōwa Kenkyūkai no kenkyū kaiko" [Research Prospectus of the Shōwa Research Association], June 1937, DTB, p. 2.

count the impact of European and American capitalism on international trade? Could Japan, by its existing political system, marshal sufficient economic and military strength to realize its avowed burden, namely, to become the stabilizing influence in East Asia? If this basis was currently lacking, could it be provided without fundamental domestic reforms? If not, what were these reforms? In response to his rhetorical questions, Takahashi offered his analysis of Japan's present position.

As a consequence of the Manchurian incident, Japan became diplomatically isolated, at odds with Nationalist China, Communist Russia, and the Anglo-American nations. This situation, Takahashi stressed, was not a passing phase. In fact, Japan could never restore the old pattern of international relations. Indeed, the creation of Manchukuo and Japan's withdrawal from the League of Nations, Takahashi reasoned, had been the consequence of the inherent weakness of the then existing world peace structure; and Japan, along with the other great powers, was faced with "the anguishing process of creating a new stability in the world." In order to participate effectively in this anguishing process, Japan would have to "radically transform" her domestic and foreign policies; but, lamented Takahashi, "there is presently a vacuum of talent in our highest political and economic circles."[10] Japanese leaders at that time remained emotionally bound to the old status quo, verbally acknowledging but not really grasping the implications of the new world situation. At the "middle level" of government ministries, for example, there were many individuals who understood the "trends" evident in domestic and foreign affairs, but their comprehension was "limited to only those issues which they have personally confronted. Even they lack, as yet, a grasp of the general meaning of this transformation."[11] Consequently, middle-ranking officials proposed piecemeal reforms, which often unnecessarily conflicted with other proposed reforms. The result was unnecessary confusion and tur-

[10] "Nippon wa doko e yuku ka?" *op.cit.*, p. 3.
[11] *Ibid.*

moil: some tried to change policy by "rule from below," as in the February 26th incident, but no one had voiced a basic policy which could bring about the unity of the whole nation. This sad state of affairs would persist, judged Takahashi, until there was a general perception of the complete change in Japan's foreign relations and in the direction of world-wide political and economic trends.

In particular, ventured Takahashi, all Japanese had to realize that throughout the world, not simply in Japan, "the disintegration of the ancien regime" was taking place. The old style of economic liberalism was dead: free trade had given way to economic nationalism; managed currencies had replaced the gold standard; and economic planning had displaced total dependence on the market. The collapse of the old trade patterns would, moreover, heighten the prospect of wars; and the efforts of England and the United States to form regional economic blocks would of necessity compel countries with limited possessions to expand and to augment their military power. Inherently this meant, for the foreseeable future, the end to any international armament limitation program. It also meant that the "have nations" (England, France, and the United States) would decline relative to the advance of the "have-not nations" (Germany, Italy, and Japan). This "have–have not" dialectic, reasoned Takahashi, was enticing an age of profound transformation, a transformation that was being propelled by three fundamental configurations. First, the Soviet Union had emerged as a major military power and as a society which offered viable ideological and economic alternatives to those expressed by the liberal-capitalistic nations. Secondly, the Versailles peace settlement, which had sought to stabilize the position of France by the impoverishment of Germany, had nurtured the Nazi movement and, under Hitler, the disintegration of the Versailles order was inevitable. Thirdly, the Great Depression had forced the capitalistic countries into policies of rampant economic nationalism, thereby accentuating nationalist movements in colonial and semi-colonial regions and destroying the fabric of international cooperation.

Crucial as these three developments were, they were not, Takahashi noted, the only trends influencing Japan's policies. There was, as well, a cluster of considerations peculiar to East Asia and of paramount relevance to Japan. Specifically, the isolationist policies of the United States, when combined with the armament limitations of the 1920's, had, in actuality, transformed Japan into the stabilizing power of East Asia. At the same time, though, the Soviet Union was advancing into the frontier zone of Outer and Inner Mongolia and, via the Comintern, was fomenting Chinese nationalism against Japan. Moreover, once Japan had moved into Manchuria and created Manchukuo, "this changed Japan from an island nation into a continental power. Consequently, our national policy has been transformed by this basic alteration."[12] As a result of the establishment of Manchukuo, plus the rapid growth in the production of manufactured goods and in the development of chemical and heavy industries, there was a "leap" in Japan's overseas investment capability and in her ability to increase the public debt.

Confronted by the world-wide trend toward regional economic blocks, the disintegration of the Washington treaty order and the Versailles peace settlement, the military power and subversive actions of the Soviet Union, the comparative strength of Japan militarily and economically, and the diplomatic isolation of the empire, Japan had no choice except to pursue an "autonomous foreign policy." Of course, Takahashi noted, the Western powers would, in order to preserve their former dominance in Asia, henceforth seek to instigate both China and Russia against Japan. To cope with this new challenge, as well as those presented by the dynamics of Chinese nationalism and Soviet communism, would demand major domestic reforms and new directions in foreign policy. The prelude to these changes was a recognition by all Japanese of

[12] *Ibid.*, p. 13.

the demands and challenges inherent in the nation's "autonomous foreign policy." As Takahashi phrased it: "Historically speaking, Japan's coming to the forefront as a great world power is a momentous development. It has muffled the beat of wardrums, first heard some one hundred years ago, the beat which sounded the hegemony of the Caucasian."[13]

To muffle permanently the drum of Occidental hegemony in Asia would, in Takahashi's estimate, require prompt and radical changes in domestic and foreign policy. These changes were interrelated, embracing the dual tenets of a planned economy and a moderate China policy. Japan should, Takahashi affirmed, endeavor to cast aside the prevailing colonial and semi-colonial order in Asia, and she should set aside the principles of laissez-faire economics in Japan. In the realm of foreign policy, Japan should, in short, champion nationalistic movements throughout Southeast Asia and the Philippines and promote the stability of the Nanking government. Above all, Japan should avoid the use of overt force in China. "Reliance on military strength," warned Takahashi, "cannot avert a catastrophe in Sino-Japanese relations and basic to this issue is the precarious situation imposed by Japan's current international isolation."[14] Domestically, he insisted, first priority should be given to the development of chemical and heavy industries. These would be needed for armament expansion, and it was self-evident that a potential military-industrial complex would enable Japan to pursue its foreign policies in Asia against "a silent military background." In turn, this economic program would require extensive capital investment and here the problem would be "how to devise a policy which finances national defense expenditures without repressing either general industrial development or the livelihood of the people."[15] Each of these latter dangers could be avoided, in Takahashi's opinion, by a government program which encouraged the regional dispersal of industries, by fractionalizing the great industrial cartels into autonomous industrial units, and by promoting agri-

[13] *Ibid.*, p. 25.   [14] *Ibid.*, p. 24.   [15] *Ibid.*, p. 29.

cultural cooperatives. The envisioned economic planning, however, was not without its dangers. In particular, cautioned Takahashi, "the new structure must include capable intelligentsia who are not [now] government officials and it must prevent bureaucratic absolutism."[16] In addition, educational reform was required, especially the development of a technological education which would be appropriate to the demands of modern society. More crucially, he said, "we must establish a new political system which will smash the self-complacency of the military and the bureaucracy."[17]

Takahashi's prospectus was, in the opinion of his peers, a persuasive and appealing assessment of Japan's present situation. Japan, in this view, was strong enough to become the dominant power in Asia; she had military and naval superiority over the Western powers; and she was capable of "sailing forth" as a great industrial power and of sustaining this superiority in the years ahead. Nonetheless, this hegemony could not be stabilized by adhering to existing foreign and domestic policies. Domestically, unrest was too pronounced to go unheeded, and an efficient mobilization program required greater government control over the zaibatsu and the political parties. In particular, Takahashi insisted, Japan's political and economic leaders would have to shed the doctrine of economic liberalism and accept the proposition that armaments were not incompatible with economic development and social reform. On the contrary, since a strong national defense posture was the basis for continued economic growth, this posture could and should be adopted as part of a progressive social and economic program. This government policy, however, should not simply serve to sustain "monopoly capitalism" in Japan or to promote "imperialism" throughout Asia. Only by eschewing aggression and imperialism, by espousing the dismantling of the existing colonial and semi-colonial arrangements in Asia, by avoiding a China war and by seeking an accommodation with Nationalist China could Japan, in this vision, formulate

[16] *Ibid.*, p. 35.   [17] *Ibid.*, p. 41.

331

a national policy worthy of her imperial traditions. A worthy policy would confirm Japan's leadership in Asia, bring about an Asian block economy which would be free from the monopoly rights and interests of the wealthy nations, and create a domestic order which would avoid "the putrefication of bourgeois liberalism," "the degeneration of capitalism," "the impracticality of Marxist socialism," and "the crudeness of fascist totalitarianism."[18]

"Whither Japan?", if nothing else, terminated the hitherto introspective, insular orientation of the discussions and research units of the Shōwa Kenkyūkai. Domestic reform would henceforth be seen in a "global" context in which the "trends of the times" seemed, not surprisingly, to enhance and sustain the style of domestic reform preferred within the association. Given this perspective, the first task confronting Gotō Ryūnosuke and Rōyama Masamichi was naturally the recruitment of "bright young men" intimately familiar with European and British history and thought. The talents of Inukai Ken, Saionji Kinkazu, Miki Kiyoshi, Ryū Shintarō, and Ozaki Hotsumi, among others, were soon solicited by Gotō and Rōyama, especially in the realm of "foreign economic policy" and "philosophic principles." Of these bright young men, Ozaki Hotsumi is probably the most widely known outside Japan, a distinction earned by his role in the Japanese espionage network woven by the master spy, Richard Sorge. His compatriots, however, were no less distinguished: Ryū Shintarō subsequently became the senior editor of the *Asahi*; Miki Kiyoshi, by common concurrence, is revered as one of Japan's most imaginative and original thinkers, second only in prestige to Nishida Kitarō; Inukai Ken and Saionji Kinkazu, themselves tangentially entangled in the Sorge incident, carry the prestige of their families (Inukai's father was premier of Japan, assassinated in the famous May 15th incident, and Prince Saionji, the last of the genrō, was Kinkazu's grandfather); and, today, Saionji Kinkazu commonly acts as Peking's official greeter for important

[18] *Ibid.*, p. 22.

visiting Japanese dignitaries. Subsequently, the views of these men, and their associates, will engage our attention in greater detail. Here, the relevant point is that, in the spring of 1937, the Shōwa Research Association was paying serious attention to the international scene, and its focus was filtered through the looking glass of Japan's domestic politics and the demand for reform unleashed in the whiplash of the February 26th incident.

TANAKA KANAE'S ANALYSIS OF THE CHINA PROBLEM

Although Takahashi's "Whither Japan?" called for a world policy, the standpoint or axiomatic basis of this global perspective was Sino-Japanese relations. Since the China problem seemed the cardinal foreign policy issue, the prism through which Japan should evaluate and formulate all other diplomatic policies, a China Problem Research Group quickly formed under the direction of Kazami Akira and Gotō Ryūnosuke. The opening session of the group not unexpectedly explored the general configuration of Sino-Japanese relations, and the views expressed there afford a convenient clue to the prevailing ideas and sentiments in vogue on the eve of the outbreak of the China incident. Tanaka Kanae's paper, "Concerning the Unification of China," launched this research group, structuring the conversation around the most significant and turbulent development in contemporary China: the drive towards national unification.[19] The basic thrust of this unification movement, Tanaka judged, was provided by the Kuomintang. Originally, in the 1920's, the central objectives of the Kuomintang had been "the suppression of imperialism" and "the suppression of warlordism," a dual motif that, in Tanaka's opinion, invested the Kuomintang with a coherent revolution-

[19] "Shina no tōitsu ni tsuite," April 6, 1937, DTB, *Shina mondai kenkyūkai* [China Problem Research Group] folio, item 9. Tanaka Kanae, in the 1930's, was one of the bright stars of the *Mainichi* staff, specializing in Chinese affairs. Subsequently he became chief editor of this newspaper and is currently managing director of the *Mainichi*.

ary program which enabled it to create a sense of national consciousness among the Chinese masses. This feature of China's domestic scene, Tanaka stressed, could be neither ignored nor discounted. No doubt Chiang Kai-shek, in the late 1920's and early 1930's had forged alliances with the northern warlords and the Shanghai financial crowd. Nonetheless, Tanaka contended, his program remained focused on the destruction of regional military and financial cabals. Nationalism, not regionalism, was the overriding characteristic of the Nanking government and, most crucially, this indissolvable link between anti-imperialism and Chinese nationalism had, in turn radically transformed Sino-Japanese relations. Following the Manchurian incident, Tanaka observed, the European powers, in order to protect their own interests, had rejected their earlier stance of promoting disunity and had lent financial aid to the Nanking government, thereby permitting Chiang to forge another temporary alliance in his battle against warlordism and imperialism. Unfortunately, Tanaka lamented, this also meant that Chinese nationalism was now channeled against Japan, a portentous development engineered by the wily statecraft of Great Britain and the Soviet Union.

As yet, Tanaka allowed, unification was an ideal, not a reality in China. Militarily, the authority of the Nationalist army did not extend beyond central China, and its officer corps remained riddled with feudalistic cliques; economically, the Nanking government was dependent on the resources of the Shanghai and Canton financial interests. Even so, through the Whampoa academy Chiang was molding a professional officer corps, and through his anti-Communist program he was extending both his political and his financial authority over regional dominions. By invoking the requirements of the anti-Communist campaign, Tanaka observed, Chiang had shrewdly promoted a central banking system; and by making Japan the butt of anti-imperialist thought, he had muffled the competing interests of Western and Chinese capitalists. Moreover, Chiang realized that he could produce national unity behind the campaign of strengthening preparations for war against Japan. Even the Chinese Communists, Tanaka noted, accepted the centrality of Japanese imperialism under the argument that the powers would assist China's unification in order to preserve their own financial interests. The ominous implications of this syndrome, Tanaka remarked, became apparent with the Sian incident, when a popular front of warlords, Communists, comprador-capitalists, and Nationalists materialized. Sian, in effect, created a "modern nation-state structure," which under Chiang Kai-shek, the "most illustrious and influential national personality," was no longer simply the Nanking regime. This, Tanaka ventured, had moved the unification movement one step further along, allowing the exertion of "viable leadership" and a spirit of "nationalist support for Chinese unification." Consequently, Japan should anticipate greater political and economic unification and a more potent anti-Japanese environment throughout China.[20]

Tanaka's analysis sharply defined the dilemma underlying Sino-Japanese relations. Chiang Kai-shek was, in his estimate, building a modern nation-state and adroitly manipulating the warlords, capitalists, and Communists with his anti-Japanese ideology. Professor Horie Muraichi, however, wondered if the Sian incident had, in fact, buttressed Chiang's position. Admittedly, Tanaka responded, the short-term objective of the fifth anti-Communist campaign had been shattered at Sian, but "this does not alter Chiang's preeminent position."[21] Ozaki Hotsumi challenged Tanaka with a different (Communist) line of inquiry. Chiang's alliance with the Shanghai financial circles, Ozaki claimed, was as much "a source of weakness" as a source of strength. Moreover, by cooperation with the Western powers, China could not attain "true" nationalistic unification under the Kuomintang. In the long run, Tanaka conceded, this might well be true, but, as he saw it, for the present Chiang's policy meant that Japan could not use force against Nanking without being able to deal with the Western

[20] *Ibid.*, p. 9.   [21] *Ibid.*, p. 12.

powers. On this point, Ozaki readily concurred; he then asked about the "united-front" against Japan. "In the battle for the masses," Ozaki wondered, "which will prevail, the Chinese Communist party or the Kuomintang?"[22] Tanaka thought the odds were with Chiang's group. The Kuomintang, he observed, has a morbid fear of the Communists, and while professing a policy of cooperation "it will probably endeavor to destroy the power of the Chinese Communist party."[23]

In the light of this discussion and Tanaka's formal presentation, Professor Horie Muraichi suggested that the research group consider "the unification movement" as the most important factor in the China problem. Tanaka, of course, responded affirmatively, adding that in the future Chinese nationalism would augment the political, economic, and military strength of the Nanking authorities. Granting this fact, Tanaka still believed a basic contradiction or paradox would plague the Kuomintang's unification movement: since Chiang Kai-shek could not perfect China's national strength with Chinese capital, he would be dependent on the assistance of the capitalist powers. Professor Horie read this to mean that, temporarily, the Chinese bourgeoisie, the Chinese Communists, the Western capitalists, and the Soviet Union would utilize the unification movement for the "coercion of Japan" but that, after unification, the rights of the powers would be fated for dissolution. Exactly, Tanaka commented, and for this reason the Chinese Communists were cooperating with the Nanking unification movement. Ozaki then developed this consensus by observing that the Soviets were therefore correct in their contention that the driving power behind China's unification was mainly the strength of the capitalist countries. Specifically, Ozaki commented, England was the main source of aid to Nanking, and her assistance was contingent on Chiang's resistance to Japan. "This policy, in my opinion, is not in the true interest of China."[24] England's aim, Ozaki affirmed, was simply to augment her position in China at Japan's expense.

[22] *Ibid.*, p. 15. [23] *Ibid.* [24] *Ibid.*, p. 17.

He allowed that this policy would be successful because for the moment the contradictions between foreign capital and national capital had been contained, but he felt that ultimately, with China's "true unification," the issue of foreign capital would have to be resolved.

By the end of this opening discussion, the China Problem Research Group had reached a first-level order of agreement: China was at the stage of semi-colonialism; unification under the Nanking government would proceed by an alliance between Western capitalism and a united front movement against Japan; and the dominant force in contemporary China was the "militaristic ideology" of the Chinese Nationalist movement. Within this frame of reference, the group decided to scrutinize Chinese economic development and the policies of the Western powers, commissioning Professor Horie to study the former topic, and Ozaki Hotsumi, the latter.

HORIE MURAICHI'S DISCUSSION OF CHINA'S ECONOMY

On April 22 and May 4, the China Problem Research Group considered Professor Horie's "The Economic Development of China."[25] Horie developed the thesis that the China problem had to be seen in terms of the contradictions of the postwar capitalism that had caused the Great Depression. As a consequence of the depression, Horie observed, Japan had "plunged into the Manchurian incident," a deed which had "weakened American and European influence," "extended Japan's influence," and of necessity compelled Japan to assume the role of "being the stabilizing influence of Asia."[26] Two adverse con-

[25] "Shina ni okeru keizai kensetsu ni tsuite," DTB, *Shina mondai kenkyūkai* folio, item 16, 54 pp. Horie Muraichi was a protégé of Kawakami Hajime and a close associate of Ozaki Hotsumi. In the 1930's, he was a professor at Takamatsu Higher School of Commerce, a popular commentator on current events, and a special advisor to the Research Bureau of the South Manchurian Railway. Presently, he is regarded as one of the most prominent Marxist commentators on international and Soviet affairs.

[26] *Ibid.*, p. 2.

sequences, Horie judged, were occasioned by this transformation. Japan had expended huge sums of capital in Manchuria without resolving the nation's internal political crisis; and secondly, Japan's continental advance had provoked countermeasures by the Western powers. The result was a new "balance of power" between Japan and the powers in which the Western countries had several advantages. In particular, the Chinese Communists had adopted a "united front" against Japanese imperialism; the Soviet Union was cooperating with the Nanking government; the warlords, no longer financed by world capitalism, bowed to Chiang's authority; and, most decisively, England had decided to render positive assistance for the economic development of the Nanking regime.

Disturbing as these developments were, Horie discerned additional complications confronting Japan. Manchukuo, he reasoned, had humiliated Chiang; and it had weakened popular support for his anti-Communist campaigns. Yet, "the criticism levelled against Japan made the unification of the country possible," and "the suppression campaigns actually promoted unification by the Nanking government."[27] Chiang's anti-Communist orientation, Horie noted, had brought him the financial support "of indigenous capitalism and the capitalist powers," and the failure of his campaigns had not "weakened the military strength of the Communist army."[28] On the contrary, the Communists built a huge Soviet district in Yenan, and at Sian they had compelled Chiang to forge a common front against Japan. Militarily, this united front posed added burdens for the imperial army, and it would also enable Chiang to build stronger "economic and political unity." But, wondered Horie: "Is this true nationalism? In actuality, it will be bourgeois nationalism."[29] Equally relevant, Horie reasoned, was the fact that the united front would promote the long-term interests of the Chinese Reds. "If the Nationalist regime does not possess an anti-capitalist spirit, this would strengthen the popular front," but, given "the reality of capitalism in China," the

[27] *Ibid.*, pp. 3 and 6.   [28] *Ibid.*, pp. 6-7.   [29] *Ibid.*, p. 9.

338

Nanking government could not become anti-capitalist.[30] Herein, as Professor Horie diagnosed the China problem, lay the crux of Sino-Japanese relations. China could not, by virtue of her dependence on foreign capital, become a "monopoly-capitalist state." The country was still at the economic stage of building railways, communications, and light industry; and it was not politically unified, being subdivided into warlord regimes and a vast Soviet zone. Confronted by these realities, Horie reasoned, China's economic development hinged on balancing the opposing interests of the Western powers and the popular front movement. Given the present Communist line that the national liberation movement should stress the war against Japan over the battle against Chinese capitalism, this harmony of interests among Western capitalists, the Chinese Reds, and the Chinese Communists rested on a fragile reed—on the ability of Nanking to promote Chinese capitalism and to capitalize on the current balance of power in East Asia. If either of these contingencies were compromised, Horie judged, China would face a grave crisis.

In view of the confrontations and disputes among the powers, Horie observed, there was a heated debate in Chinese and Japanese intellectual circles over whether or not China could develop economically into a strong nation state under the leadership of the Kuomintang. Chiang, Horie confessed, was harassed by several contradictions. Closely bound to the bourgeoisie, he had to promote Chinese capitalism, but the anti-imperialist basis of Chinese nationalism could not be flaunted by subservience to Western capitalists, as this policy would lose "the confidence of the masses." Moreover, the Kuomintang itself was riddled by the contradictory aspirations of the "warlords," "landlords," and "bourgeois nationalists." If the Nanking authorities, Horie reasoned, were to tone down their "anti-imperialist spirit, this would weaken the popular front"; and if they failed to adopt an anti-capitalist spirit and at the same time to develop Chinese capitalism, "the Soviet district will

[30] *Ibid.*, p. 53.

become stronger in its opposition to imperialist influence."[31]
It was self-evident that the success of the united front and of
the Kuomintang's political and economic policies, ultimately
resided with Great Britain. Would England provide sufficient
aid to promote China's capitalism and opposition to Japan?
Without assistance on this scale, Horie asserted, Chiang would
be compelled to yield power to the Communists or to cooperate with Japan for help with his economic program and his
political-military struggle against the Chinese Communists.
The logical corollary was equally self-evident: Sino-Japanese
cooperation—based on the promotion of bourgeois nationalism
and anti-communism—was contingent on Japan's ability to
sever or compromise the link between British capitalism and
the Nanking government. Was it England, after all, and not
militant Chinese nationalism, that was the main obstacle to
resolving the China problem? This question was entrusted to
Ozaki Hotsumi, and, not unexpectedly, his answer was af-
firmative.

OZAKI HOTSUMI'S FOCUS ON BRITAIN

Since Ozaki's "instance of treason" intrigues and baffles
those concerned with the elusive motives prompting his behavior, one may discern some clues to his *weltanschauung*, as
well as to that of the association's research group, in his initial
presentation. Addressing himself to the subject "British Influence on China,"[32] Ozaki employed a sweeping perspective,
conceptualizing the major "transitions" in Britain's role in
Asia in terms of her evolution from commercial capitalism to
industrial capitalism, her evolution from industrial capitalism
to imperialism, and her behavior since the Great Depression.
After these broad strokes, Ozaki filled in the details of British
policy a trifle more precisely. In the early 1920's, he contended,

[31] *Ibid.*, pp. 52-53.
[32] "Shina ni okeru Eikoku no seiryoku ni tsuite," DTB, *Shina mondai
kenkyūkai kaigō yōkō* [Summary of the Third Session of the China
Problem Research Group] folio, May 24 and 31, 1937, 24 pp.

Britain had reacted negatively to the growing power of the Chinese bourgeoisie and working class because she was obsessed with safeguarding her commercial and financial interests. In 1927, however, she perceived Chiang Kai-shek's susceptibility to monopoly-capitalism, that is, his willingness to underwrite the comprador-system of the treaty ports in return for assistance against the Communists and working class. This switch in British policy was comprehensible: Britain had undergone the Industrial Revolution first; her capitalism and imperialism were the strongest of all nations; and once the market for British goods had been saturated in China, she could turn to financial imperialism there. The unification of China and a stabilized market for British capital investment, Ozaki contended, were now the overriding British objectives. Consequently, Britain opposed Japan's commercial activities in China, and throughout the commonwealth. Moreover, unaware of the Communist danger in China, England did not contest Soviet maneuvers in Outer Mongolia. "England opposes communism, but only as it affects the Chinese labor movement. In contrast to Japan, she is not directly concerned with the [Soviet] Red Army."[33] Accordingly, Ozaki reasoned, Britain would not cooperate with Japan against the Soviet Union because she feared Japan's commercial penetration in China more than the dangers of bolshevism. Consequently, Britain, not the Soviet Union, constituted Japan's and China's deadliest enemy, because working in tandem with France and the comprador-landlord cabal of Shanghai and Canton, she was encouraging Chinese and Soviet resistance to Japan's Manchurian and China policies. This configuration, Ozaki insisted, heralded the end of the illusions spawned in the heyday of the Anglo-Japanese alliance: cooperation with the Anglo-French sea powers was an impossibility, given British financial interests in the reactionary Nanking government.

In the spring of 1937, Ozaki, like many members of the Shōwa Kenkyūkai, obviously regarded the Nanking regime

[33] *Ibid.*, p. 22.

contemptuously, branding it "that comprador-landlord-merchant cabal." In this context, they viewed English policy as the regime's basic prop, as well as Japan's most serious threat in Asia. In the coming two years, Ozaki, along with most members of the association, gradually proceeded from this general frame of reference to the vision of a comprehensive program of political, economic, and diplomatic reform—the New Asian Order. Ozaki's subtle mind, plus his stress on the Chinese peasants, inspired confidence in his views of the world, and through the Shōwa Research Association he became a member of Konoe's inner circle of advisors. His later involvement in the Sorge ring pinned the label of "Communist" on the Shōwa Research Association and embarrassed Konoe. Since this facet of Japanese politics is beyond our purview, one may note here that Ozaki's views were fully consistent with his covert and treasonous ties with Sorge. Indeed, the core of Marxist thought about Asia—the "reactionary" nature of the Nanking government, the fated clash of Japanese and Western capitalism, and the foul alliance of British capital and Chinese compradors—was internalized by many Japanese intellectuals. It led Ozaki to the path of treason; it led many others along the road of building a new order, in Japan, in East Asia, and eventually in Greater East Asia. These sentiments flowed spontaneously from a disenchantment with European capitalism and liberalism, and from the conviction that Japan must "transcend" the pitfalls of imperialism and capitalism by eradicating European patterns of thought in Japan.

ON THE EVE OF THE CHINA INCIDENT

Throughout the spring of 1937, the Shōwa Research Association filtered its vision of the China problem through the themes of "monopoly capitalism" and the "contradictions" of Chinese nationalism, especially as they bore on the desire for national independence and reliance on Britain's financial aid. Implicit, but not yet openly articulated in these discussions, were the "contradictions" of Japan's continental policies, including the search for one domestic and foreign policy which would eliminate Japanese internal unrest and diplomatic tension with China. Although such concerns were somewhat less evident in the association's Foreign Policy Deliberative Committee, these experts on diplomacy still arrived at the same terminal point as Ozaki Hotsumi, although by a different path. In sum, Anglo-Japanese relations were the key to Japan's Asian policy.

The formation of the committee on diplomatic affairs consumed several weeks, and its organization was different from that of existing research groups. Composed of prominent and busy personalities, the deliberative committee was designed to formulate general guidelines, "a fixed standpoint," for the other research groups, and specifically for the permanent research staff. Accordingly, the committee included the power-structure of the association, namely, Gotō Fumio, Kazami Akira, Aoki Kazuo, Rōyama Masamichi, Sasa Hirō, Gotō Ryūnosuke, and Takahashi Kamekichi.[34] This membership list, if nothing else, signified that foreign policy had become the dominant concern within the association. Moreover, since this committee crystallized shortly after Konoe's appointment as premier, it is reasonable to assume that Kazami Akira, the chief secretary of the Konoe Cabinet, was able to attract such luminaries on the proper supposition that this committee would help assist and advise the new premier in his search for a foreign policy appropriate to the demands of the time.

Meeting on June 29, under the chairmanship of former foreign minister Arita Hachirō, the Foreign Policy Deliberative Committee received an amorphous assignment. Noting that the association had created separate research groups, "composed of bright young men," which were already exploring "The China Problem" and "Economic Diplomacy," Kazami

[34] Original members of this committee included Arita Hachirō, Nagai Matsuzō, Yamakawa Hashio, Satō Yasunosuke, Hayashi Hisajirō, Kawashima Shintarō, Ishida Reisuke, Ashida Hitoshi, Itō Masanori, and Furugaki Tetsurō.

Akira invited this committee to formulate "a consensus on foreign affairs" which would bring about "a unified public opinion."[35] This charge, an immodest task under any circumstances, was to prove intractable. Even when the problem came into focus easily enough, unanimity on solutions eluded this committee, as it did governmental authorities. The prime issue, Arita declared, in his opening comment, was the need for a "fixed national policy." Japan's diplomacy, he thought, was floundering on the antithetical thrusts of the desire for an Anglo-Japanese détente and the German-Japanese anti-comintern alliance. From this perspective, Arita fixed the prime target of the Shōwa Research Association as the formulation "of a particular standpoint from which it could assay and understand Japan's diplomacy."[36] In response to an inquiry as to whether the group should seek "an idealistic" policy or one "that can actually deal with existing domestic and foreign issues," Arita allowed that "these may be two different standpoints, but they need not be mutually exclusive."[37] The first step, in Arita's opinion, was the delineation of "the fundamental issues affecting our diplomacy."

On this note, the discussion turned to economic issues. Basically, the committee judged the nation's economic diplomacy was bound to the tenets of "economic liberalism and free trade," even though these principles were being subjected to strong currents of criticism and change on the domestic and international scenes. In this context, uncertainty and disunity would persist. A particular source of controversy, noted one participant, was "the problem of the utilization of world-wide colonies." Each power, he observed, was pursuing a "bloc economy" approach to its possessions; but Japan, without world-wide colonies, was preoccupied with China. Could Japan subscribe to "free trade" in China, if the powers retained "exclu-

---

[35] "Ippan gaikō iinkai dai ikkai kaigō yōroku" [Summary of the First Session of the Foreign Policy Deliberative Committee], June 29, 1937, DTB, *Ippan gaikō iinkai* folio, p. 1.

[36] *Ibid.*, p. 2.   [37] *Ibid.*, p. 3.

sive" rights in their colonies? In the judgment of another member:

> We cannot adopt a bamboo attitude. We must move in the direction of India and Africa. Today, however, in these parts of the world the "Open Door" has been shut tightly. Hence, again we have returned to China and this time, if China does not listen, we can open the "Open Door" by military strength. We must, therefore, first consider our trade policy *vis-à-vis* China.[38]

On this theme the committee easily attained a basic agreement: since Japan could not promote her trade with China "in terms of free trade," she had two diplomatic options in her approach to China. On the one hand, she could seek a détente with England based upon a British *de facto* recognition of Manchukuo and Japanese cooperation against Germany. On the other hand, she could seek to strengthen the anti-comintern pact with Germany and apply pressure on Britain in China. No one questioned the validity of this Hobbesian choice, and all concurred that the decisive factor would be Japan's strength, her ability to use force on behalf of her continental policy. The nation aspired to create a "bloc economy" of Japan, China, and Manchukuo, but unfortunately neither the Western powers nor China had accepted this goal as a legitimate policy. Perhaps, ventured one committee member, this nettle could be handled if Japan's economic policy "does not see China solely in terms of the economic development of Japan."[39] Arita, realizing the futility of this tack, promptly called for fewer generalities and solicited some thoughts on "other practical problems."

This beginning unleashed a spate of criticism of Japan's political and military behavior. One observer suggested that in the light of Soviet power and Chiang's unification program, the time had come "to change our previous militaristic continental policy." Pursuing this thought, another member complained about the preponderance of military leadership: "Since the

[38] *Ibid.*, p. 7.   [39] *Ibid.*, p. 11.

Manchurian incident, our diplomacy has been solely a diplomacy of the military. . . . We need strong politicians, not military officers; and we must prevent a diplomacy spearheaded by the military."[40] The military was not the only quarter chastised. One participant insisted that views on international affairs should not be limited to the standpoint of the Foreign Ministry. In his judgment, the nation needed something "comparable to the English Chatham House," and he hoped that the Shōwa Kenkyūkai would perform this role. The professional diplomats, Arita included, quickly turned this thought aside, calling for an organization which would "guide public opinion" and "support the views of the Foreign Ministry."[41] As they saw it, free-wheeling discussions of diplomacy had many disadvantages *vis-à-vis* foreign countries—including the assumption that expressions of disunity over foreign policy at home might be interpreted as weakness abroad. The champion of the Royal Institute of International Affairs persisted, however, citing the "opposition" views of the British Labour party as a hallmark of British strength. At the same time, he confirmed, "Japan lacks these counterparts, and she also has the autocracy of the military."[42] Despite its emotional appeal, the idea that Shōwa Kenkyūkai should become a Chatham House, was torpedoed by the argument that "England is a fine democratic country; but England and the United States are different from Japan. . . . We must consider the internal and external situation of contemporary Japan."[43] After this thought, Arita reminded everyone that the task at hand was the formulation of policy guide lines, "including what course Japan should follow today." In his eyes, the Chatham House model was not a realistic basis for a discussion or appraisal of Japan's present situation. Instead, Arita suggested that the committee come to terms with a tangible and pressing problem, the North China issue.

This issue seemed a Gordian knot. "Neither Japan nor

[40] *Ibid.*, p. 12. [41] *Ibid.*, p. 13. [42] *Ibid.*, p. 15.
[43] *Ibid.*, p. 16.

China," observed one discussant, "has a specific plan to settle the North China controversy."[44] Still, the basis for a tangible compromise existed because, as an authority on military affairs had affirmed earlier in the discussion, the army "no longer considers the resources of North China to be absolutely essential."[45] North China was still of prime importance for the security of Manchukuo, but he believed that the War and Foreign Ministries no longer had to confront one another over North China. If they were able to form some common view on this issue, the government could then reach an agreement with Chiang Kai-shek. On this note, the issue of Anglo-Japanese relations surfaced again, as everyone concurred that Chiang Kai-shek would cooperate in North China on the basis of an anti-comintern policy, only if he were deprived of British assistance. The discussion had made a full circle of Arita's opening observation—namely, that an Anglo-Japanese détente over China and the anti-comintern pact with Nazi Germany were antithetical. Summarizing this dilemma, one discussant noted that "from the British standpoint, there is no possibility of an Anglo-Japanese alliance if a German-Japanese pact exists."[46] On this last note, after bitterly remarking that the anti-comintern pact had been followed by a "German penetration into the China market," Arita wondered if the pact had not merely "ended in the [Soviet] reinforcement of Siberia?"[47]

The conference ended as it began. Japan needed a global policy, yet cooperation with the European powers was stymied by Anglo-German tensions rooted in Italy's Ethiopian ambitions and by Anglo-German interests in the China market. Sino-Japanese cooperation continued in abeyance, subject to a rapprochement over North China. However, no one challenged the observation of one discussant that "in terms of Anglo-Japanese relations, the status quo is impossible."[48] Under existing circumstances, Japan could not strike to the north, nor build a China-Manchukuo bloc, nor expand into the colo-

[44] *Ibid.*, p. 13. [45] *Ibid.*, p. 14. [46] *Ibid.*, p. 21.
[47] *Ibid.*, p. 22. [48] *Ibid.*, p. 24.

nial blocks of the powers via the free trade passport. "What course should Japan pursue? What standpoint should she take?" These questions Arita posed repeatedly, but their constant articulation produced no magic answer. The Foreign Policy Deliberative Committee was unable, as yet, to provide a "fixed standpoint" for Prince Konoe, a deficiency they shared with the ministries of state and the two general staffs. Ten days later, on July 7, a skirmish at the Marco Polo Bridge reopened the North China question. In coping with this crisis, the Konoe Cabinet rashly decided to rectify the intolerable status quo by finding a fundamental resolution of Sino-Japanese relations, a decision which willy-nilly provided the "fixed basis" for Japan's national policy.

The Problem of Purpose Posed by the China Incident

The search for a fundamental resolution of the China incident led first to a "war of chastisement" against Chiang Kai-shek, and later, after January 1938, to the pledge of the "rejuvenation of China" and the "annihilation of the Nationalist government." This escalation of operations and objectives was not viewed with equanimity within the Shōwa Research Association. By early spring, however, two facts seemed manifest: the Konoe Cabinet had thrust imperial Japan forward in two complementary directions. First, the general mobilization legislation, originally desired by many reform-oriented intellectuals and by the proponents of the "total war" philosophy within the various ministries of state, had been passed, in modified form, by the Diet in April 1938. Secondly, the resolution to smash the political viability of the Nationalist government, as the essential prelude to the construction of a "new" China and an "indissoluable bloc" composed of Japan, Manchukuo, and China, manifestly augured additional operations which would link the North and Central field armies, as well as extend operations as far as Hankow and Canton. In actuality, neither of these objectives—major economic reform or the dissolution of the Kuomintang—appeared to be within imme-

348

diate realization. Even though the major parties, along with the zaibatsu, had endorsed the mobilization bill recommended by the Cabinet, this legislation was, at best, reluctantly regarded as a necessity dictated by the new scale of the China incident. In place of a commitment to any program avowedly designed to resolve the "grave social and economic inequalities" within Japan, the parties and big business remained primarily concerned with safeguarding their political and economic authority against the administrative controls sought by the government ministries, in the name of general mobilization. If the smashing of Chiang's regime was tactically progressing in a satisfactory fashion, in what Prince Konoe termed "one victory after another," nonetheless ominous strategic implications persisted.[49] Contrary to the euphoric predictions of the preceding November, the "rape" or "seizure" of Nanking had instilled neither an overwhelming awe of Japanese military prowess nor a bitter rejection of Chiang's political leadership. Chinese animosity, not a pervasive demand for capitulation, was the main consequence of the assault on Nanking; and, when faced with the stark alternative of complete surrender or the dismaying pursuit of a long-term war against a "superior" military force, the Nationalist government understandably vowed its adherence to maintain the "steady course" of opposition to imperial Japan.

The lack of a viable reform orientation to the drafting and implementation of the General Mobilization Law, the mercurial quality of the army's "victories" on the mainland, and the notion of subduing Chinese nationalism by a reliance on force, understandably disturbed many intellectuals and governmental officials active in the Shōwa Kenkyūkai. Their uneasiness about the existing state of affairs was, moreover, heightened by the sharp realizations that the dynamics of the China incident were inexorably leading to extended operations, that the intensification of the program of political pacification would pro-

[49] Harada Kumao, *Saionjikō to seikyoku* [Saionji Memoirs], vol. 6 (Tokyo, 1951), entry of January 19, 1938.

ceed by enlarging the "military" or "puppet" governments already created in Peking and Shanghai, and that the government would inevitably, as part of the projected Japan-Man-chukuo-China bloc, compromise the existing treaty rights and economic interests of England and the United States. In turn, this policy configuration would strengthen Chiang's conviction that negotiations with Japan were futile; it would channel Chinese nationalism exclusively against Japan and those provisional governments underwritten by its field armies; and, eventually, it would induce the maritime countries to extend additional political and economic assistance to the Nationalist government. Manifestly, Japan's China venture was grievously flawed.

"After reflecting on the circumstances underlying this incident," the East Asian Political Group of the Shōwa Research Association drafted, in early May 1938, a set of observations "for the purpose of providing a basic classification of the problem."[50] Here, the obvious was not denied, namely, that Japan had been gradually pulled into a great conflict which had grown like Topsy. "Because of a lack of preparation, today we are burdened with a difficult task."[51] Plagued by uncertainty over objectives, the government had first projected a "nonenlargement" policy in July 1937; and, within five months, it had affirmed a "nonrecognition" declaration *vis-à-vis* Chiang's government. In the judgment of this research group, it was self-evident that the nation would, first of all, have to formulate and adopt a comprehensive China policy, a task which in turn meant facing facts and acknowledging past errors of judgment. In particular, the government would have to admit that it had grievously underestimated the strength of Chinese nationalism, "overlooking the possibility of total Chinese resist-

---

[50] "Shina jihen kentō (yōyaku)" [A Discussion of the China Incident: Summary], May 27, 1938, DTB, *Tōa seiji kenkyūkai* [East Asia Politics Research Group] folio, item 5, p. 1.

[51] *Ibid.*

ance and miscalculating that the war would readily produce the internal political disintegration of China."[52] These observations, however, served as no prelude to either a denial of the nonrecognition stance or a search for an armistice. Excessive attention to the nationalist movement headed by the Kuomintang, reasoned this presentation, had in fact blunted an awareness of "the newly awakened opportunity for building a modern nation state in China." No one, not the army nor the government nor the business community, in this analysis, sufficiently appreciated the "clash of generations" in China, nor had they grasped the fact that China's youth would not embrace the "jeweled nature" of Japanese policies in the midst of a war which offered no constructive vision of China's destiny.

The consequences of these deficiencies in national policy, in the opinion of this group, were regrettable indeed. Japan had formed separate governments in North and Central China, each lacking political and economic viability; the military campaign against Chiang's forces remained, as yet, unsupported by cooperative economic and political enterprises directed at the Chinese youth; and Chiang Kai-shek had transformed the support of the powers into "his great fortress for the resolution of the incident." In effect, Japan faced three distinct problems —that is, a military campaign against the Nationalist forces, a politico-economic campaign for the allegiance of the Chinese youth, and a diplomatic campaign to sever Chiang's dependence on the powers. As things stood, none of these battles could be won quickly. Japan was confronted with the challenge of a long-term conflict, one which could not be resolved solely on the field of battle or in the chancellories of foreign ministries. It was evident that the nation needed a constructive program to guide its China policy along the twin paths of promoting domestic unity and fostering the birth of a new China. The China incident was a test of fortitude between Chiang's forces and the Japanese nation:

[52] *Ibid.*, p. 2.

By the so-called method of war, the incident will probably be resolved by a growing sense of weariness with the existing confrontation. There is no mistaken belief that the total defeat of China is at hand; but, since China lacks the strength to retaliate, in order for Japan to continue the present state of affairs of both sides glaring at one another, it will probably be necessary to intensify our domestic strength.[53]

On this point, the East Asian Political Group voiced the concern that, under the present "stop-gap" China policy, the Japanese people might "grow weary of the present confrontation. . . . There is already among the people a call for withdrawal from this conflict."[54] Such negativism had to be checked, not simply because of its deleterious repercussions in Japan, but also because it symbolized the basic flaw in Japan's handling of the China incident. According to the research group, the inclination to favor withdrawal "was most strongly evident among business groups returning from China. These groups lack the necessary mentality for the construction of China by working with the Chinese for the mutual economic development of China and Japan."[55] Disillusioned by the cost of the military operations and by the occupational governments, and void of any cooperative spirit, these groups both endangered public unanimity and hampered the growth of viable programs in China.

This type of investigation of the China incident, in effect, saddled the capitalistic spirit and business interests with prime responsibility for Japan's present difficulties. As the East Asian Political Group defined the issues, the promotion of Japanese business was not the purpose of the incident, and reservations about the conflict based on this tabulation had hindered the articulation of a comprehensive China policy. "The basic purpose of the China incident," ventured this task force, was the "creation of an indivisible cooperative system among China,

[53] *Ibid.*, p. 4.   [54] *Ibid.*, p. 3.   [55] *Ibid.*

Japan, and Manchukuo, based on the independence of each nation."

> This cooperative system, however, is not a league or federation predicated on the principles of freedom and equality for all nations in their reciprocal relations, nor is it based on an imperialistic economic bloc relationship. Rather, from the standpoint of a new national economy which does not even esteem national selfishness, this cooperative system will form an integrated unity which emphasizes the interests of each nation as the basis of cooperative relations.[56]

Thus, if the nation would abandon the ideas of private profit and parochial national self-interests, Japan could foster "a new Chinese political entity" that would simultaneously promote "special and indivisible ties" among China, Japan, and Manchukuo, and assist "in the development of a new nation state that will unify China." As envisioned by this group, Japan's China policy should henceforth proceed in three phases. First, "without recognizing a new national government," Japan should effect a series of agreements with the provisional government of North China that would "necessarily create the pattern of a special anti-Communist base in China composed of the Shanghai Delta, North China, and Inner Mongolia."[57] Secondly, Japan should create a new national government and "season the occasion of the birth of a new China by reorganizing Japan-Manchukuo relations and forming a tripartite cooperative relationship among China, Japan, and Manchukuo."[58] Finally, once this cooperative relationship had been organized, Japan "should honestly strive to join hands" in fomenting cooperative economic, security, and political programs in China.[59]

[56] "Nichi Man Shi seiji renkei hōsaku" [Policy for Political Liaison among Japan, Manchukuo, and China], May 1938, DTB, *Tōa seiji kenkyūkai* folio, item 7, p. 1.

[57] *Ibid.*, pp. 1-2.   [58] *Ibid.*, p. 2.   [59] *Ibid.*

Foregoing any precise delineation of how Japan would "clasp hands" with China, the East Asian Political Group focused on the need for a new sense of national purpose. "We must, above all, resolutely pursue revolutionary economic and political changes in Japan, create a new national economy, enhance the nation's strength, and strive for the building of a new political and economic order in Japan, Manchukuo, and China."[60] Ideology—the principle of cooperativism—now became the key to resolving the China incident and, within this frame of reference, the China incident had come full circle: causes became effects and limitations became stimulants. Chinese nationalism was no longer discounted, but Chiang Kai-shek became the symbol of the older generation, not of China's youth. Existing provisional governments no longer seemed credible vehicles for China's rebirth, but, by infusing these entities with cooperativism, they would become midwives for the new China. No longer were Chiang's forces to be destroyed on the field of battle, but this new war of attrition became the basis for revolutionary domestic changes. Japan should no longer stumble into the Chinese wilderness, lacking the compass of a clear national purpose; she should plunge deeper into the depths of China as part of the blueprint for the construction of a new order in China and in Japan. The tragic paradoxes of the "investigation" of the China incident need no elaboration. By June 1938, it was clear that Japan could not settle the incident by existing diplomatic, military, and political policies. This reality, however, had spawned the conviction that existing limitations were to be transcended by a new order in East Asia. As of this date, "cooperativism" had not yet permeated Japan's economic system, nor had it been manifested in the provisional governments of China. The China embroglio nonetheless became the hope, not the bane, of Sino-Japanese relations.

[60] *Ibid.*, p. 4.

THE SEARCH FOR A COMPREHENSIVE CHINA POLICY

Once convinced of the necessity for a new program, a new definition of the China incident, the Shōwa Research Association created a special task force composed of Yabe Teiji, Saionji Kinkazu, Doi Akira, Ozaki Hotsumi, Taira Teizō, Wada Hirō, Rōyama Masamichi, and Hosokawa Ryōzen. Its charge was to devise "practical answers" to the "various problems of Japan's continental policy." Meeting weekly, these men, along with the permanent staff of the association, canvassed many subjects, for example: "The Economic Strength Required for our Continental Policy," "What to do about the Existing Nationalist Government," "What Type of Agency is Needed for Executing Our China Policy?" "The Problem of the Economic Development of China," and "What to do about an Asian Economic Bloc System."[61] All these issues quickly reduced themselves to the need for a "Basic Policy to Cope with the China Incident," and from late May to early July the Shōwa Kenkyūkai prepared several draft policies on this issue for the guidance of Prince Konoe.

During these weeks, as the China problem specialists approached this issue, their prime concern became the search for a coherent grasp of "our entire continental policy." Lacking this, Japan could never, in their opinion, formulate her priorities and pursue a balanced and integrated set of foreign, military, economic, and domestic policies. In late May, "the immediate objectives of Japan's continental policy" appeared clear: the first priority centered on the issue of "war with the Soviet Union," the second was "the resolution of the China problem," and the third was the "program of southern advancement."[62]

[61] "Shina mondai kenkyū tēma" [Research Themes of the China Problem], May 1938, DTB, *Shina mondai kenkyūkai* [China Problem Research Group] folio, item 21.

[62] "Shina jihen ni taisho subeki kompon hōsaku ni tsuite" [Concerning the Basic Policy to Cope with the China Incident], May 1938, DTB, *Shina mondai kenkyūkai* folio, item 19, p. 4.

In view of the recent Changkufeng clash, this stress on the Soviet issue was comprehensible, and since it was judged that Japan would have to prepare for an eventual confrontation with the Soviet Union, these specialists ventured that the success of Japan's China policy was the prerequisite for this conflict. Japan's China policy also constituted the crux both of her relations with the European nations and of the development of her economic strength. In view of centrality of this policy, the nation would have to establish a "liaison agency" (China Affairs Board) to coordinate its "long-range" China policy, and it would have to "advance beyond the policy of preserving the Nationalist government."[63] Under the circumstances, only one line of action seemed immediately feasible: Japan should pursue both a vigorous military program that would "shake and shatter" the Nationalist government and a political program that would build new "political authorities in Central and North China." The long-term political strategy seemed equally clear, namely, the establishment of a Japan-China-Manchukuo politico-economic bloc. By organizing a new political government in China, by devising an economic (yen) bloc, and by destroying Chiang's forces, Japan would be able "to build a unified China," "to gain the cooperation of the powers," and to free herself "to cope with the Soviet Union."[64]

If the long-term objectives were transparent, the China problem specialists stressed the ticklish and complex nature of short-term practical steps. The cooperation of the powers and of the Chinese people had to be gained and, admittedly, this type of cooperation would require prudent and bold action. In the diplomatic realm, England remained the decisive factor. Scrutinizing the subject of relations among the Western powers, China, and Japan, on the assumption that "British rights in North China are on the verge of expiring," the China specialists reasoned as follows:

[63] *Ibid.*, p. 5.   [64] *Ibid.*, pp. 6-7.

On the one hand, by a systematic prosecution of our policy of self-sufficiency and self-support, we should [be able to] eliminate the trend toward isolation by utilizing the apprehension about the rights and interests of the powers in China and the confrontations among the powers. And, by the policy of fostering some safeguards for these rights in China, we should [be able to] anticipate á compromise policy which does not violate our continental policy and which positively promotes new relationships *vis-à-vis* the rights and interests of the powers in China.[65]

In short, in return for a guarantee of British interests in South and Central China, England would write off North China; and once this was attained, Japan could emphasize a strong anti-Communist policy, in East Asia and throughout the world. "By cooperation with England" and by forging "a world-wide anti-Communist policy" with Italy and Germany, Japan would then "dampen any Anglo-Soviet rapprochement and, in the process, prevent the Soviet Union from directing its attention away from Europe."[66] This would, in turn, compel the diversion of Soviet forces to their European borders and curtail Soviet assistance to the Eighth Route Army of the Chinese Communists. Japan, fortified by the economy of North China, would then be able to increase her armament preparations against the Soviet Union. The advantages of this diplomacy appeared undeniable, assuming Britain would "cooperate" over China and against the Soviet Union.

Vital as England was, the China specialists affirmed, a new Anglo-Japanese relationship would not be forged by diplomacy alone. Japan would have to demonstrate the viability of her China policy to the Chinese people and to the British government. Without a smashing military victory, predicted these specialists, Japan could not anticipate the surrender of the Nationalist government or the end of anti-Japanese feeling

[65] *Ibid.*, p. 11.   [66] *Ibid.*, p. 14.

among the Chinese. This presumed truism dictated Japan's military strategy: Japan must occupy the coastal urban centers of South and Central China and seize the Hankow industrial complex. "This would compel the powers to abandon their aid to the Nationalist government and to withdraw from China's internal political and economic affairs."[67] Temporarily, this strategy would worsen Japan's international relations, but, if Japan were to succeed in constructing a new Chinese government, the powers would ultimately cooperate. Everything depended on Japan's political program in China, on a national awareness that Japan was totally committed to the fixed policy of China's reconstruction. The nation, in effect, would have to wage total war with total mobilization of its resources.

> Our objectives must be publicly and clearly clarified. . . . By means of the basic policy of annihilating the Nationalist government, we will clarify our policy for resolving the incident to the outside world; and this would create a consciousness among our people of the vital significance of this resolution. We must formulate and pursue this objective as our immediate policy, a resolution which will attain national unity.[68]

In conjunction with this public resolution, Japan would have to complement her military operations with a political program appropriate to the task of winning the confidence of the Chinese people; she would have to establish a new order in China and capitalize on Chinese resentment of the semi-colonialism of European and American imperialism. At the same time, of course, the Japanese government should sincerely conduct the incident as a war for the destruction of the colonialist system. This could not be done, warned the Shōwa Kenkyūkai staff, unless the Japanese people possessed a "profound self-

[67] "Shina jihen ni taisho subeki kompon hōshin ni tsuite" [Concerning the Basic Policy Which Should Cope with the China Incident], June 1938, DTB, *Shina mondai kenkyūkai* folio, item 20, p. 1.
[68] *Ibid.*, pp. 1-2.

consciousness that this is not a war for the enhancement of Japanese capitalism."[69]

Pursuing the theme of building a new China, the permanent staff of the Shōwa Research Association, under the close direction of Professors Yabe and Rōyama, Saionji Kinkazu, and Doi Akira, prepared in mid-June "A General Policy for Mastering the China Incident, Together with our Basic Objectives."[70] Since a fundamental transformation of Sino-Japanese relations was obviously the only way to master the incident, Japan's China policy had to be based on "a proper understanding of the fact that the building of a modern economic and political structure and national unification have been the main developmental trends of modern China."[71] In order to channel these trends into a new central government, Japan would have to isolate China and "prevent any diplomatic crisis that would transform this incident into a world war." This necessity was revealed by the Changkufeng clash and, as these China experts admonished, "not a single soldier should be derelict in his duty in the Soviet-Manchukuo border area." At the same time, they proposed that Japan first seek a nonagression pact with the Soviet Union; secondly "promote the neutrality" of the Western powers; thirdly, restrain England and the Soviet Union by "strengthening an anti-comintern agreement" with Italy and Germany. Finally, "although the basic objective of Japan's world policy is the withdrawal of Great Britain from East Asia," Japan should, for the time being, "positively respect her rights and interests in Central and South China and isolate England from the Nationalist government."[72] Towards China herself, they saw two options for mastering the incident. Under Plan A, Japan would not formally adhere to the "nonrecognition" policy but would confirm the Nationalist government as the *de jure* authority for all of China. Japan would then nego-

[69] *Ibid.*, p. 6.
[70] "Shina jihen shūshū no ippanteki hōshin narabini mokuhyō (sōan)," June 1938, DTB, uncatalogued.
[71] *Ibid.*, p. 1.   [72] *Ibid.*, p. 2.

tiate a settlement along the following lines: a) an enlarged demilitarized zone in North China; b) a fixed region of international settlement in Shanghai; c) cessation of anti-Japanese actions and ideology; d) stationing of Japanese troops at strategic points in North and Central China; and e) a peace treaty including a recognition of Manchukuo, participation in an anti-comintern pact, and an indemnity. Plan B was the converse. Japan would smash the Nationalist government by force and develop the provisional and restoration governments in Peking and Nanking. In this case, however, they cautioned that the government should recognize that the existing occupational regimes could not cope with all the dimensions of contemporary China, nor could they win the allegiance of the Chinese masses.

Recognizing the limitations of these pseudo-governments, the Foreign Policy Investigation Committee spelled out the obvious implications. The desire for national unity "was the most striking trend of modern China," and sensitivity to this trend was the only way to promote Japan's "world policy, the formation of an East Asian bloc."[73] The committee preferred to follow Plan A, with certain amendments—namely, the Nationalist government would a) form a new government "which includes the provisional government of North China and the restoration government of Central China"; and b) promote "a mutual Sino-Japanese development" of the resources and industries of North China; and c) grant Japan "preferential treatment" in tariffs and customs. This policy "would serve as an adequate basis for a resolution of the incident," and Japan need not require a "recognition of Manchukuo, the offi-

[73] "Shina jihen shūshū no ippanteki hōshin narabini sono taishō oyobi wakyō jōken" (Kokumin seifu o aite ni wakyō kanō naru baai dai-an) [A General Policy for Settling the China Incident, Along with the Means and Objectives of General Concord Terms (First Draft of Possible Terms for a Concord with the Nationalist Government)], July, 1938, DTB, p. 1.

cial withdrawal of Chiang Kai-shek, participation in an anti-comintern pact, or the payment of an indemnity."[74]

The ambiguities and paradoxes of these policy guides attest to the lack of a credible "comprehensive" China policy. If the problems were clearly defined, solutions seemed elusive. Could Japan construct a viable government in China? Who would organize it? What principles would guide it? As of July 1938, neither Prince Konoe nor his "brain trusters" had yet conceptualized a coherent policy worthy of the tasks posed by "building a modern Chinese nation-state." The best they could offer was that, failing Chiang's willingness to cooperate on Japanese terms, "there is no alternative, save the military destruction of the Nationalist government and the development of the provisional and restoration governments."[75] Plagued by the tone of this alternative, the secretariat of the association fell back on a host of platitudes. Any new government should possess "a maximum degree of independence"; Chinese should participate equally with Japanese in all mutual enterprises; "no monopolization by Japanese capitalists" should be permitted; China's culture "must be revered"; and no efforts should be made "to change the customs, languages or religion of the Chinese people." On the first anniversary of the Marco Polo Bridge incident, the position papers of the foreign affairs group and of the China problem group wallowed in an intellectual quagmire. They knew what Japan desired—"the withdrawal of Great Britain from East Asia" and "a reconstruction of Sino-Japanese relations." They believed the former goal was attainable by an Anglo-Japanese *quid pro quo*—that is, by a Japanese confirmation of British interests in Central and South China, and a British recognition of North China as a Japanese sphere. The latter goal remained a Gordian knot.

[74] *Ibid.*, p. 5.
[75] "Shina jihen shūshū no ippanteki hōshin narabini mokuhyō (sō-an)," *op.cit.*, p. 3.

The major problem is to promote Japan's future in East Asia. The various problems connected with this task will be influenced by the means utilized in the reconstruction of Sino-Japanese relations. From this standpoint, it is imperative that this incident be handled in some kind of form.[76]

But what form?

Only one year earlier, most members of the association had called for an accommodation with Nationalist China, for the championing of national independence movements in the colonies of Southeast Asia, and for the execution of major domestic reforms as the proper and essential program for the Shōwa restoration. Now these individuals were faced with the painful present: Japan was not in the process of witnessing encouraging political and economic reforms; a posture of friendship with Nationalist China was becoming ostentatiously ludicrous; and, to many, Japan seemed on the verge of succumbing to parochial nationalism and crude imperialism. Were the desires of the past spring to be consigned to the wastebasket by Japan's "monopoly-capitalists" and the atavistic impulses of its "militarists"? Could Japan reform herself and China by a program of force and violence directed against the Kuomintang and by a program of economic planning confined to promoting the armaments required for a spiraling conflict? Could domestic "unity" be forthcoming from a relatively negative stance, namely, "crush" the nationalists and "rejuvenate" China with obscure Chinese officials dependent on Japanese bayonets? These apprehensions justifiably signaled the need for a new statement of national policy, for a new sense of national mission. By July 1938, the allaying of these fears and the renewal of earlier hopes constituted the most pressing issue within the Shōwa Research Association; and, on the first anniversary of the Marco Polo Bridge incident, one heard for

[76] "Jihen shūshū ni tomonau ippanteki gaikō seisaku" [A General Foreign Policy to Accompany the Handling of the Incident], July 7, 1938, DTB, p. 3.

the first time a new view of the China incident, a vision which would be elaborated on but not basically altered during the next few years.

MIKI KIYOSHI'S HISTORICAL VIEW

The anniversary of the Marco Polo Bridge incident provided a convenient moment for members of the Shōwa Research Association to reflect on Japan's China policy and to reconsider her present and future course. To this end one of Japan's most supple intellectuals, Miki Kiyoshi, delivered the major address of the evening, "The World Historical Significance of the China Incident."[77] Here, the general membership of the association was given its first glimpse of the new direction of thinking which would soon permeate its numerous study groups. As might be anticipated, Miki's assessment was somewhat abstract, reflecting his long-term academic studies of European philosophies of history. Miki first invited his audience to approach the China incident in terms of world history, to regard the incident as a "world war" that, in reference to Oriental history, marked "the beginning of the twentieth century." The historical and sociological implications of this "world war," however, could not be grasped until the Japanese and other Asian peoples cast aside the prevailing Europe-centric view of history. "The world is not synonymous with Europe," affirmed Miki, and one should not regard the China incident "within the historical frame of reference that accepts a belief in the dominance of the European."[78] Quite the contrary. In order to acquire a coherent understanding of world history, one must escape the limitation of Europeanism.

Of course, Miki allowed, many Europeans were aware of the existence of mature civilizations beyond Europe. Still, these conceptions had not mirrored a profound comprehension of the "distinctive spirit" of other cultures, nor had they signified a deep awareness of the "bankruptcy of Western culture." In

[77] "Shina jihen no sekaishitekiigi," July 7, 1938, DTB.
[78] *Ibid.*, p. 1.

Miki's judgment even Oswald Spengler's *The Decline of the West* failed to express accurately the distinctive qualities of Oriental culture and, most disconcertingly, most Western writers had reverted to traditional patterns of thinking following World War I, thereby marking "a tragic historical consciousness which has not extended beyond Europe and the Great War."

Against the landscape of world history, confessed Miki, modern Europe had nurtured a remarkable civilization derived from a synthesis of the Greco-Roman culture and Christianity. Undeniably, Europe constituted one cultural entity; but Europe was not the world, and Asia was not Europe. In the past century, liberalism and nationalism had acted as the dynamic movements of European civilization, and it had seemed that these principles would serve as universal principles which would subsequently permeate and dominate the globe. With the Great War and the Great Depression, however, liberalism was "reduced to its final extremity," and henceforth it no longer provided a unifying or viable influence throughout the world. In this context, another ideology, communism, claimed worldwide applicability. Accordingly, throughout the globe, one was witnessing an ideological confrontation between democracy and communism. Yet the combination of liberalism, nationalism, and democracy was unable to cope with the major economic, political, and cultural problems of the contemporary world; and, judging by the history of the Weimar Republic, communism was not able to prevail in an industrialized state. Consequently, the claim that communism provided a cogent view of world history also became spurious. Moreover, the European cauldron of nationalism, liberalism, democracy, and communism had brewed the reactionary phenomenon of fascism. In essence, judged Miki, the dominant European ideologies were causing increasing strife, a context which would generate another great holocaust. In such a conflict, all these ideologies—fascism, communism, nationalism, liberalism— would degenerate. Mankind itself would be put in jeopardy, and men would be baffled in their attempt to locate a unifying principle of world history.

In order to transcend this imminent peril, advised Miki, the Japanese and all Asians must devise an alternative to the ideologies conceived within European civilization. This alternative must, he added, emerge from the ongoing China incident. It must also view the China incident in terms more encompassing than Sino-Japanese relations or a Japan-Manchukuo-China bloc. "To speak of Sino-Japanese cooperation or of the unity of Japan-Manchukuo-China will not invest the China incident with any world-wide historical significance. To this end, we must do something which will link this incident with the unification of Asia."[79] For this purpose, two considerations had to be taken into account. First, it was dangerous to conceive of the incident as a Sino-Japanese conflict. In the past, Japan had absorbed a great deal of Chinese culture and, if the incident were to remain exclusively a Sino-Japanese matter, possibly the culture of Japan would eventually be absorbed by that of China. Secondly, neither Japan nor China could resolve their problems independently. Taking this interdependence into account, it was clear, to Miki, that "the general principles required for the reconstruction of China must, simultaneously, be the same principles governing the internal reform of Japan; and the principles of the domestic reform of the nation must, at the same time, be principles possessing universal substance."[80] Once these principles had been perceived, avowed Miki, they would infuse the China incident with world-wide meaning and would constitute the world historical mission of Japan as well.

Having directed his audience to the need for a new vision, Miki then revealed the requisite axiomatic bases of Japan's new course. First, the world was inhabited by several cultures, and these were not to be judged solely by European standards; secondly, in the contemporary world, European civilization was no longer the driving force of Asian history; and, thirdly,

[79] *Ibid.*, p. 7.   [80] *Ibid.*, pp. 9-10.

given the bankruptcy of European ideological-political-economic systems, Japan was compelled to effect a unification of the Asian nations, based on mutual cooperation under Japanese leadership. The key to this unification was the China incident. Unfortunately, Miki noted, the present China policy offered bleak prospects: it would lead to a militaristic occupation of China, and he feared that the end result of this would be a situation in which Japan could not advance beyond "the conscription of Chinese mercenaries and the performance of an endless sentry duty throughout China." This martial role would, moreover, prevent Japan from assuming leadership in the "unification" of the Asian nations.

An alternative policy, insisted Miki, was possible and necessary. Japan had to win the friendship and cooperation of China, and this was feasible only if Japan advocated a set of social and political principles that envisioned not colonialist or imperialist exploitation, but the mutual advancement of all the Asian nations and the expulsion of Western imperialism from Asia. This task, in turn, entrusted the Japanese nation with the duty to "cope with the most fundamental problem in the contemporary world—namely, how to resolve the various contradictions of capitalism." Indeed, pressed Miki, unless this problem were handled, Japan could never realize the unification of Asia. If Japan emulated Western capitalism and imperialism, it could not offer any policy possessing general historical significance. On this note, Miki concluded his talk with this reflection: "If we consider Japan's historic mission in spatial terms, it means the unification of Asia; if we consider it temporally, this mission means the resolution of the contradictions of capitalist societies. Each of these tasks must be realized by the China incident. This, it would seem, is the world historical meaning of the China incident."[81]

THE NEW ASIAN ORDER AS NATIONAL POLICY

With this historical view of the China incident, the Shōwa Research Association would formulate, under the guidance of

[81] *Ibid.*, p. 11.

Miki Kiyoshi, Hasegawa Nyozekan, and Maeda Tamon, "The Philosophical Principles of the New Japan."[82] This, and other important themes, are beyond the scope of this chapter. As of the fall of 1938, one may note that neither Konoe nor his advisors deemed the China conflict as a war of aggression and imperialism. It now symbolized a positive historical force. The burdens and dangers confronting the nation were not ignored; but somehow, despite the demands of the China war and the economic and diplomatic restraints harassing the nation, Japan had to nurture in China, Manchukuo, and Japan a spirit of Asian renaissance free from the egoistic and selfish tracts of bourgeois nationalism, economic liberalism, and racial superiority. The first step in the process, as Saionji Kinkazu advised Konoe on September 30, should be a bold statement of national policy, one which "will inform the world, Japan, and the Chinese" what constitutes our national purpose.[83] The contents of this declaration, as Saionji enumerated them, contained few surprises. Japan should profess her lack of territorial ambition, her desire for peace throughout East Asia, her determination to destroy the anti-Japanese policy of Chiang Kai-shek, and her ambition to eradicate communism from China. In addition to these principles, which were part of existing policy, Saionji called for a proclamation indicating that the ultimate goal was China's cooperation in the realization of the ideal of an Asian renaissance.

With this recommendation, the Shōwa Research Association had abandoned its earlier reservations about China's reconstruction. This notion of a New Asian Order meant, as Saionji indicated, an intensification of the nonrecognition policy *vis-à-vis* Chiang Kai-shek. The key problems, however, remained

[82] *Shin Nihon no shisō genri* (Tokyo, 1939).

[83] "Shina jihen taisaku sō-an" [Draft Plan of Policy for the China Incident], DTB, *Shina jihen tai seisaku iinkai* [Policy Investigation Committee for the China Incident] folio, September 30, 1938, p. 1. Also reprinted in *Gendaishi shiryō* (9): *Ni-Chū sensō* [Source Materials on Modern Japanese History: The Sino-Japanese War] (Tokyo, 1965), II, 543-46.

as before, that is, how to win the loyalty of the Chinese masses and the cooperation of the Western powers. "The prime [diplomatic] objective is to have England lend firm support to Japan and to sever her assistance to Chiang Kai-shek."[84] This was to be done in part by military operations against the Nationalists, in part by diplomatic and economic pressure against British interest in occupied territory, but mainly by a successful China program which would win the cooperation of the Chinese intelligentsia and masses. Such a program, Saionji reasoned, should promote revolutionary Chinese political organizations and viable Chinese economic enterprises. Ideologically speaking, Japan should stress her attacks on "semi-feudalism" and the reactionary Kuomintang and promote the vision of "the autonomous nature of Asia." "Our general principle is the abrogation of the existing rights of the powers in China."[85] Despite this call for a New Asian Order and the banishment of Chiang Kai-shek from its benefits, Saionji's vision, like that of most Japanese, did not yet extend beyond a *Tōa renmei* (East Asian League) embracing China, Manchukuo, and Japan. Moreover, although ready to embark on the program of building a new Chinese government, Saionji appreciated only too well that Japan's ideology was not yet up to the task of capturing Chinese loyalty. The ideals of "Japanism," "Asian cooperativism" and "a world cooperative spirit" were, he confessed, still riddled with internal contradiction.

Should Japan seek a *Shin Tōyō* (New Greater Asia) or a *Tōa* (New East Asia)? What principles should guide Sino-Japanese cooperation, politically and economically? How to avoid the impression that Japan harbored territorial and imperial ambitions in China? These, Saionji advised Konoe, were the crucial questions underlying Sino-Japanese cooperation; and although answers were not yet visible, neither Saionji nor Konoe urged postponement of the quest for a New Asian Order. On November 11, Prince Konoe publicly affirmed Japan's compassion for China's plight. "China," he sighed, had been "the

[84] *Ibid.*, p. 545.   [85] *Ibid.*

368

victim of the imperialist ambitions and rivalries of the Occidental powers," and Japan was "eager to see a new order established in East Asia—a new structure based on true justice."[86] In this mood, the Konoe government declared the quest for a New Asian Order was now the "immutable" policy of imperial Japan; and this scion of the Fujiwara clan, his advisors, and the Japanese nation looked with anticipation to the new age, to the new order. Belatedly, all would discover the obvious. The military, diplomatic, and economic burdens of the China incident, and the quest for a New Asian Order, allowed slight margin for social and political reforms in either China or Japan. This crusade would only accelerate the thrust towards greater bureaucratic absolutism and greater reliance on force as the arbitrator of the new order.

Ideology and Intellectuals in Prewar Japan

The prefatory remarks indicated this chapter would be concerned with ideas, with the political thought and behavior of a cluster of prominent intellectuals and officials—namely, those active in the Shōwa Kenkyūkai. Now that we have glanced briefly at a few groups and individuals, some impressions and observations seem warranted. The popular assertion that the Shōwa Kenkyūkai was an important advisory body to Prince Konoe certainly seems valid, as does the notion that the association was composed of talented and influential individuals. How crucial or decisive an impact this association had on national policy formulation must, for the moment, remain conjectural. Of the task forces considered, two types seem to prevail, those guided by officials and politicians and those directed by academics and journalists. These members were influential in their own right, either as wielders of administrative power or as makers of public opinion, and the views and recommendations voiced within the association were channelled to the highest levels of government, including the premier. To

[86] Royal Institute of International Affairs, *Documents 1938* (London, 1940), pp. 348-49.

this extent, the association constitutes a valuable index to the concerns and ideas being articulated in discussions of national policy. In other respects, the Shōwa Kenkyūkai acted as a communications network and a political forum in which intellectuals sought to impress their notions on government authorities and, conversely, officials tried to marshal intellectuals behind their sentiments and recommendations. Regardless of the effect this had on policy-making and on public opinion, one plain fact seems incontrovertible—namely, that the ideals of a Shōwa Restoration and a New Asian Order were not fantasies conjured solely by militarists, fascists, and ultra-nationalists. They flowed, as well, from a passionate concern with and an informed understanding of the domestic and foreign nettles confronting the empire.

Without reviewing these ideals, as they were perceived and utilized within the Shōwa Kenkyūkai, it is proper to note a few significant patterns of thought. There is, for example, a visible thread of continuity between Prince Konoe's profession of deep anxiety about the lack of a coherent sense of national goals and policies in the wake of the February 26th incident and his proclamation of the quest for a New Asian Order in 1938, a continuity which is equally apparent in Takahashi's exegesis on "Whither Japan?" just before the outbreak of the China conflict and Miki's reflections on "The Historical Significance of the China Incident" in 1938. Common to all members of the association was an acute dissatisfaction with existing affairs and a desire to chart a national course which would be feasible and ethical. They were critics, as well as political and ideological activists, and they were prone to seek answers in abstract, almost utopian, schemes. The socio-political context which sustained this proclivity towards utopianism is not reducible to a neat or clear paradigm. Even so, one does detect a set of common assumptions operative in the association's discussions and papers. Most participants, for example, were not prepared to discuss limits to the strategic capabilities of the empire. On the contrary, they were inclined to accept the premise that Japan was the dominant power in East Asia, and they assumed the preservation and enhancement of this superiority constituted the basic goal of national policy. To some extent, this goal—"to be the stabilizing power in Asia"—became synonomous with gaining "equality" with the Anglo-Saxon nations. With this orientation, it became all too easy to distort and misconstrue Chinese nationalism and to envelop Japanese aggression in the mantle of anti-imperialism. The "open door" policy was seen as a mechanism for the protection of Anglo-American monopoly capitalism, and Japan, by building a New Asian Order, was identified as the architect of an Asian community of nations which would both expel the Western imperialists and repel the evils of Soviet communism.

Several motes in this vision of a New Asian Order were self-evident. One need not linger on the more obvious inconsistencies and paradoxes of the mental gymnastics required for the flights of imagination displayed in the discussions and assessments of Japanese policy. Perhaps the most transparent ideological legerdemain was the rationalization of Japanese hostilities in China in terms of China's "true" national interests. Equally decisive was the casual, almost indifferent, assessment of American power and influence. England, not the United States, was persistently deemed the main diplomatic antagonist. Equally striking were the inclinations to discount the viability of Nationalist China and to blame "outside influences"—Soviet and English—as the basic obstacles to a resolution of the China conflict. With the advantage of hindsight, one might assess these traits as common to most countries mired in a major conflict. In this instance, however, one also senses a volatile racism, compounded by a sense of outrage inspired by Western moral condemnations of Japan's continental policies. In as much as Japanese aggression in China was, at the least, overbearing, this sense of outrage was, to some degree, defensive. Indeed, the compulsion to depict the China conflict as part of the demise of imperialism in Asia attests to a haunting sensitivity to the pitfalls inherent in any explicitly military crusade. Nonetheless, the idea of an Asian confederation of nations, led by Japan, became a potent amulet, allowing and condoning the illusion that China would prefer the closed door syndrome of the New Asian Order to the open door syndrome of the Anglo-American nations.

It would be easy, too easy, to merely pass off the dream of this New Asian Order as part of a tragic nightmare, as part of Japan's valley of darkness. It would be easy to harp on the flaws, however grievous they were, in the rationale for the New Asian Order. It would also be easy to condemn or dismiss the ideas and behavior of the individuals discussed in this brief glimpse at the Shōwa Kenkyūkai. Speaking on the dilemma of morality, man, and the nation state, Reinhold Neibuhr has noted that men do strive to create "structures of culture and civilization wider than the parochial community of the nation. These supernational cultures and systems of value are obviously real. Men would like their nations to be loyal to these higher values. The nations may be loyal, but only to the point where the interests of the nation are not in conflict with the higher values."[87] The dilemmas, political, intellectual, and moral, inherent in the nation-state system which sanctions force as a legitimate instrument of policy were not unique to prewar Japan. Without questioning the ethical tone of the discussions and proposals of the Shōwa Kenkyūkai, one can affirm that the organization was striving to form "a structure of civilization" transcending the "parochial community" of imperial Japan. One gut issue, of course, is the degree to which this association was actually able to articulate "higher values," values that could provide a basis for dissent from national policies. If their motives were humane, the policies they endorsed, as well as the complaints they voiced, eventually ran afoul of the "interests of the nation." Perhaps, the most bitter irony of the Shōwa Kenkyūkai is the fact that its vision of a New Asian Order was also flawed by a limited sense of na-

[87] *Man's Nature and His Communities* (New York, 1965), p. 74.

tional community. However lofty and noble their vision, the reality was a program of foreign aggression and domestic authoritarianism. Their articulation of the Shōwa restoration and the new order becomes all too reminiscent of the Sorcerer's Apprentice: their desire to play magician and transform the nation by ideology helped create a sacred crusade, a crusade which vindicated parochial interests with supranational rhetoric.

CHAPTER X

Nakano Seigō and the Spirit of the Meiji Restoration in Twentieth-Century Japan

TETSUO NAJITA

ONE can read the literature of extreme nationalism in virtually any period in the history of modern Japan before the Pacific War and find recurring, in regular fashion, the frustrated cry for a new *ishin* ("restoration"). Despite a general familiarity with this theme among students of Japanese history, it has not been adequately understood in the West. There has been a tendency, for example, to place its radical manifestations in the 1930's in the context of a definitional model of European fascism. More generally, it has been looked at outside this comparative frame as an obscurantist Japanese phenomenon defying clear explanation. That it was obscurantist cannot be denied, but this, certainly, neither reduces its importance as a historical problem nor places it outside the sphere of rational inquiry. Although it might be perfectly valid to view extreme nationalism as generic to the 1930's, I have decided in this study to put it in broader historical perspective and aim generally at providing a set of meaningful historical guidelines (and hopefully stimulate the search for more) to understand key aspects of the vague yet important problem of extreme nationalism. More concretely, I will examine the political career of Nakano Seigō in an attempt to explain the widely felt psychological need among Japanese nationalists to revive the "spirit" of the Meiji Restoration in the twentieth century.

Although not well known in the West—partly because he was not a violent putschist—Nakano is an important figure in the development of twentieth-century Japanese nationalism. As a widely read journalist and vigorous politician between 1911 and 1943, he provides the historian with evidences for a meaningful thread of logical continuity (an aspect usually not stressed) that was significant in nationalist thinking. Moreover, he serves to emphasize the fact that this thread was spun out of a historical understanding of what the Meiji Restoration meant to twentieth-century Japan.

Nationalists like Nakano looked back to the Meiji Restoration to search for the spiritual source of modern Japan. They sought to incorporate their conception of that spirit into the political life of twentieth-century Japan, hoping thereby to perpetuate a sense of national unity and distinctiveness. The Meiji Restoration, however, like other complex turning points in history, was subject to a variety of highly emotional interpretations. In Nakano's case, he read into that event what it "ought" to have meant (not an uncommon historical phenomenon) and gave this reading projective connotations for the twentieth century. Most certainly this tendency to make myths out of the Meiji Restoration was especially pronounced among those Japanese intellectuals of the twentieth century who had not directly experienced the events of the Restoration. For them, there was at best the vicarious experience provided by the "historian." Nakano Seigō was one of these.

The Spirit of the Meiji Restoration

Nakano Seigō was born in the city of Fukuoka in Kyūshū in 1886. His father came from a poor samurai family, his mother, from a small merchant house. As a youth, he identified with an idealized personality specific to Satsuma, but revered by all in Kyūshū, the "Satsuma hayato"[1] of which the greatest historical manifestation was the famed Saigō Takamori.

---

[1] The term *hayato* literally means "falcon." Nakano's romantic treatment can be found in Nakano Seigō, *Tamashii o haku* [Living Spirit] (Tokyo, 1938), pp. 26-32; and his "Nanshū ō gojūnen saiten ni nozomite" [In Commemoration of Saigō Takamori], *Nakano Seigō shi daienzetsushū* [Collected Speeches of Nakano Seigō] (Tokyo, 1936), pp. 327-30.

This romantic hero was a *bushi* (or samurai) of a unique type. He was loyal and full of love for the common folk, but he was also a rebel. Nourished in the rustic environs of Kyūshū, remote from the main rationalized authority structure in Edo, the *hayato* loathed bureaucratic authority and cherished his distance from it. "From my childhood" Nakano wrote in 1932, "I harbored a great hatred of the government."[2] Indeed, like the *hayato* of Satsuma, he never managed to make peace for very long with the national political order.

Four years as a university student in Tokyo (Waseda, 1909) reinforced rather than diminished his attachment to this youthful heritage. Although he relinquished his special commitment to Kyūshū, accepted industrialism as necessary for modern life, and conceded on occasion the influence of certain aspects of Western political thought, he retained a fierce identification with the image of the Satsuma *hayato*. Indeed, this image took on new historical significance as he came increasingly under the influence of a type of nationalism often referred to by political critics and scholars in Japan as the school of "popular nationalism" or "national peopleism."[3] In this brand of nationalism, primary emphasis was placed on the maintenance of a distinctive spiritual legacy that gave a particular society its unity and strength. Although this historicist argument had roots planted well back in the Tokugawa period, it gained fresh impetus and a new developmental connotation in the 1890's and early 1900's under the influence of German idealism. Through the persuasive and often eloquent writings of such political critics as Kuga Katsunan (1857-1907) and the more famous Miyake Setsurei (1860-1945), the idea that a strong and prosperous nation must be held together internally by a unique and dynamic popular *geist* became one of the major intellectual forces in twentieth-century Japan. Nakano personally deemphasized the "German" influence, which he

[2] *Ibid.*, p. 215.

[3] The Japanese terms often used are *kokuminshugi* and *minzokushugi*.

thought of primarily in the opprobrious sense of "bureaucratic legalism," but he nonetheless accepted the major premises of the school of popular nationalism that owed much to that German influence. In fact, he came to be recognized as one of the principal spokesmen on the political scene of that line of thought.[4]

In 1907, two years before graduating from Waseda, he had already begun to contribute regularly to Miyake Setsurei's *Nihon oyobi Nihonjin* (Japan and the Japanese), one of the most widely read and respected journals of the time, which, as the title explicitly indicates, was founded on the ideas of popular nationalism. Later, in 1912, he forged a lasting personal tie with Miyake by marrying his eldest daughter; and in 1923, he joined with Miyake in establishing a new journal, *Gakan* (Our Views). Quite aside from these personal data, the essays he wrote from his "Waseda home" most certainly reflect an early acceptance of the major assumptions of Miyake and his journal. Expressing his views in a vocabulary he would repeat throughout his career, he challenged the concept of comparabilities between the political experiences of different countries. Like Miyake, he attacked the "Europe-centric" view of the modern world and defended Japan's unique historical development within the Asian cultural community. He pleaded therefore that Japan revive and retain, as the spiritual legacy that gave the Japanese people their distinctive unity and strength, the selfless commitment of the samurai to serve the cause of national development even if this involved individually resisting society and refusing to conform to forces of history. In these writings we see clearly that Nakano had begun to integrate the youthful image of the heroic Satsuma *hayato* into a broad concept of history that had an essential relationship with Japan's modern transformation itself. He now hammered this

[4] Yoshimoto Takaaki, ed., *Nashionarizumu, Gendai Nihon shisōtaikei* [Nationalism: Modern Japanese Thought Series], IV (Tokyo, 1964). See in particular pp. 34-36 for the close relationship between the ideas of Kuga Katsunan and Nakano.

boyhood image into tools of political criticism against conservative "bureaucratic government" and incorporated it, above all, into his interpretation of the Meiji Restoration.[5]

Nakano viewed the Meiji Restoration as the major source of spiritual inspiration for modern Japan. He believed, however, that that great event had faded from social memory, causing a serious decline in the nation's sense of direction. Thus, in his first major set of essays for the newspaper *Asahi*, which he published as a book in 1913,[6] Nakano set out to recapture the "spirit" of the Meiji Restoration and transform it into a total "vicarious" historical experience for his generation.

In Nakano's account, two interrelated polarities emerge as the essential spirit of the Restoration. The first of these was his view of that event as a popular upheaval. The other was his seemingly contradictory view of the Restoration as resulting from the decisive acts of unique individuals. Actually, he saw the mutual interaction of both factors as the dynamic nexus in Japan's transformation into a modern nation. Quite naturally, he saw the harmonious juxtaposition of these polarities as vital to national stability in the twentieth century. In the twilight of his career (in 1942), for example, he expressed his thoughts on those polar categories. Discussing the "revolutionary" implications of the scholarship of Rai Sanyō (1780-1830; an influential historian who described the rise of the samurai as historically contrary to the principle of loyalty to emperor and nation), Nakano wrote: "I am extremely fas-

[5] Nakano Yasuo, *Chichi Nakano Seigō den* [My Father, Nakano Seigō] (Tokyo, 1958), pp. 81-136. Many of Nakano's essays were written for a Fukuoka student journal, *Dōsōkai zasshi*, in a series he titled *"Waseda no sato yori"* (From My Waseda Home). The theme of opposition and resistance found in Miyake Setsurei and others is treated by Maruyama Masao in his stimulating essay on loyalty and treason, "Chūsei to hangyaku" [Loyalty and Treason], *Kindai Nihon shisōshi kōza* [Lectures on the History of Modern Japanese Thought], VI (Tokyo, 1960), 379-470.

[6] Nakano Seigō, *Meiji minkenshi ron* [On the Popular Rights Movement in the Meiji Era] (Tokyo, 1913).

cinated with the power of the individual. His spirit [*tamashii*]
stirs feelings latent in the multitude . . . and gives a unique
stamp to 'an age.' "[7]

Although couched in traditionalistic vocabulary (such as
tamashii), Nakano's nationalism was not in the tradition of
irrational historicism. He did not seek racial purity in time
immemorial, in the "10,000 years" prior to the Chinese impact.[8] He sought an explanation for national distinctiveness in
the intellectual background of the Meiji Restoration, hence his
fascination with Rai Sanyō and other more important persons,
as we shall see, in whose writings he saw the roots of modern
Japan. The point that needs to be underscored, however, is
that he selected from that background what he thought to be
tendencies leading to the coalescence of popular power and
decisive individual action.

The claim of popular upheaval in the Meiji Restoration is,
of course, highly dubious. Nakano did not distinguish between
popular response to institutional changes (legal, social, educational) and popular activity as a positive cause of political
change. In fact Nakano musters little evidence to document
his view. The relative inactivity of the commercial class, the
peasants, and samurai in the overwhelming majority of the
han remains unexplained. His claim, actually amounting to
retrospective conjecture, was, however, a generally accepted
assumption in his day.

It was generally assumed that there must have been seething
popular discontent against the Tokugawa Bakufu for little
other reason than that the system was "despotic." In this general assumption, feudalism represented privileged government[9]

[7] Inomata Keitarō, *Nakano Seigō no shōgai* [The Life of Nakano
Seigō] (Tokyo, 1964), p. 582.

[8] Hayashi Fusao, the well-known nationalist has suggested this. See
for example, Hayashi Fusao and Mishima Yukio, *Taiwa, Nihonjinron*
[Conversation on the Japanese] (Tokyo, 1966), p. 154 and passim.
For Nakano's views, his *Meiji minken*, pp. 1-7.

[9] Nakano's often repeated phrase for government by a privileged elite
was *tokken seiji*. See, e.g., his *Meiji minken*, p. 1.

380

in which semi-private concentrations of power were legally protected. Throughout the country, microcosms of the Bakufu —han governments—held despotic rein over the populace. Thus, the governmental arrangement in the Tokugawa era was at once nonnational and nonpopular. It followed that in destroying privileged and despotic feudal bureaucracies throughout the land, the Meiji Restoration stood *ipso facto* for national and hence popular government. Within this definitional framework, the Restoration reflected the effusion, from the oppressed lower levels of society, of discontented "popular energy,"[10] as Nakano put it. Despite the dubious historicity of this interpretation, it was widely accepted in the twentieth century by most intellectuals regardless of their position on the political spectrum.

Nakano most certainly accepted this interpretation. To him, the Meiji Restoration was a destructive event aimed at feudal despotism. At the same time, it was a constructive process to achieve a truly national and popular arrangement of government. This conception of the Restoration embodied the antifeudal ideals of legal equality, mobility, and political justice for all. Nakano termed it "imperial justice." Thus, the Restoration *liberated* the people from historical obscurity[11] and gave them, for the first time, the right to realize freely their cultural aspirations and, as part of this right, to share in the processes of government. For Nakano, as for many who had come under the influence of the ideas of the Popular Rights movement of the 1880's, the Restoration reaffirmed his unshakable faith that the essence of modernization was the unrestricted right of the individual to self development and of the people to realize their distinctiveness in history. Nakano concluded that because the Restoration affirmed the natural trend toward "popular nationalism" it was a "radical" and "revolutionary" event.[12]

[10] *Ibid.*, p. 1.
[11] The emotional phrase Nakano used was *bammin no tōjō*, literally "the emergence of the masses." *Ibid.*, p. 498.
[12] *Ibid.*, pp. 7-15.

Nakano's belief that the Restoration was radical and popular remained fixed throughout his career. His nationalism never became conservative. He detested the genrō and the persistence of "special advisers" to the throne. He rejected the idea of the emperor as the ultimate source of *de facto* power. He viewed with great distrust those "German" constitutional theorists who sought to freeze power in the emperor's hands. For him, the emperor represented a constant historical ideal symbolizing the capacity of the masses to transform themselves into a dignified "people"—an unchanging ideal of man's power to transcend himself and become "godlike," as Hayashi Fusao has recently suggested.[13] The emperor, then, stood for popular transformation which was realized in "restoration." The emperor and the people were integral aspects of a single historical concept—hence, "the union of the emperor and the people"[14] representing continual dynamic innovation in the face of foreign and domestic challenges.

Having defined the Restoration as transformational and popular, he applied these criteria to assess the early leadership in the Meiji government and then to explain the course of political developments that followed. At the outset, he argued, all the leaders were united in their "heroic" destruction of privileged feudal government.[15] This unity was undermined, however, when some of the leaders were deluded into using bureaucratic techniques to stem the tide of rapid change. Thus, men such as Iwakura Tomomi, whose emotional attachments to aristocratic politics made them prone to bureaucratism, and others such as Okubo Toshimichi, due to a pernicious love of

[13] Hayashi and Mishima, *op.cit.*, pp. 162, 172-76. The complex content of the imperial symbol as a historical force in Japan is discussed at length by John W. Hall, "A Monarch for Modern Japan," in Robert E. Ward, ed., *Political Development in Modern Japan* (Princeton, 1968), pp. 11-64.

[14] This was also referred to often as *ikkun bammin* or *kokuminteki ōsei*. Nakano Seigō, *Meiji minken*, pp. 9-11.

[15] *Ibid.*, p. 27.

power, joined forces and set out to reconstruct in new form another conservative Bakufu. By using despotic techniques, they aborted the natural trend toward popular nationalism. They became reactionary (*zokuron*) and utterly failed to understand the popular ideal for which the imperial institution stood. Nakano condemned them for betraying the spirit of the Meiji Restoration and for being directly responsible for causing, in the long run, political misery among the people.[16]

Who then remained true to the spirit of the Restoration? Nakano's answer was unequivocally Saigō, the great Satsuma *hayato*. He remained true to the radical popular ideal of that event. Here again, however, it was not so much Saigō's actual democratic beliefs (which do not seem to have been strong) that mattered. Rather, it was his opposition to conservative bureaucratism that made him a democrat. Perhaps more important, it was the absolute quality of his opposition that made him the patron saint of popular nationalism and the major inspiration behind the movement for popular rights.[17]

Nakano overlooked the fact that Saigō urged a premature military expedition to Korea. It was not better judgment over a specific policy that mattered—an attitude that recurred in the 1930's. What mattered was Saigō's broader and more fundamental attack on arbitrary bureaucratic government. From this perspective (shared by many of widely differing intellectual persuasions, including, for example, Fukuzawa Yukichi and Uchimura Kanzō) Saigō was not a "militarist" pure and simple. Saigō epitomized the distinctively Japanese spirit of radical protest that made the Restoration possible. Hence he was a defender of popular nationalism. To Nakano, Saigō's band of rebels in Satsuma constituted a "pure revolutionary

[16] *Ibid.*, pp. 29-36.

[17] The term "compromise" is an utterly opprobrious term in Japanese politics, devoid of any redeeming features. The characterization of Saigō as absolutely opposed to compromise (*zettaiteki hidakyō*) made him *ipso facto* an ideal political figure. *Ibid.*, pp. 32-46, 499.

party," and the uprising of that group (the Satsuma Rebellion of 1877) a "revolutionary war."[18]

The historical scheme that Nakano had developed is now clear. Both the Meiji Restoration and the movements for popular rights and party government were part of one consistent sequence of events held together by an identical spirit. In this spirit, the uncompromising commitment on the part of men like Saigō to oppose bureaucratic government reaffirmed the ideal of popular nationalism emerging from the indigenous soil. Those who sought to constitutionalize and freeze the elitist distribution of power had betrayed that spirit, and because Saigō rebelled against these men, his actions took on historical significance for Nakano far beyond what the actual data warranted.

The inaccuracies of this scheme, however, need not concern us here. What needs stressing is its potency as historical myth among twentieth-century Japanese nationalists. It constituted a fundamental premise of theirs in assessing political realities and in placing the outer stakes for future developments. To Nakano, as well as his father-in-law, Miyake Setsurei, the ideal of popular justice imbedded in the Meiji Restoration had not yet been achieved in the twentieth century.[19] Japan's political goal was still, as it had been in early Meiji, the destruction of privileged bureaucratic government and the establishment of popular nationalism. This goal remained the fundamental content of their often uttered phrases, "union of people's parties" and "protect constitutional government."[20]

The pivotal position held down by Saigō in the above scheme had another important implication. As the embodiment of the "spirit" of the Meiji Restoration, Saigō, as the great defeated

[18] His terms are *junzentaru kakumeitō* and *Seinan kakumei. Ibid.*, pp. 47-48.

[19] For example, Miyake Setsurei, *Meiji shisō shōshi* [A Short History of Meiji Thought] (Tokyo, 1913), pp. 4-21, 89-94.

[20] The Japanese terms are *mintō gōdō* and *kensei yōgo.* Both had considerable appeal and are key phrases in the party movement. Nakano Seigō, *Meiji minken*, pp. 7-11, 249, 289-303.

one, symbolized a decisive "opportunity" that had been lost. The romantic connotations of this view are readily apparent. "How long it has been," Nakano wrote, "that the banner of political morality has not waved in the land. Having described the political developments over the first ten years of Meiji, I cannot help but lament and feel dejected."[21] Through this emotion-tinted lens, Nakano tended to view Japan's subsequent political events as a steady decline, straying from the natural course because of the dominance of reactionary bureaucrats. In short, he believed the Meiji Restoration had been abortive, "incomplete," perhaps, more accurately, unfulfilled.[22]

The romanticization of Saigō, then, was part of a futuristic appeal for another "popular" restoration. This is a point worth dwelling on. Despite the fact that his scheme was not held together by the certainties of social theory, it bears remarkable similarities with that of some Marxist scholars. In both cases, the Meiji Restoration was incomplete. For Nakano, popular nationalism had not been fully realized; for Marxist scholars, it was the bourgeois democratic revolution. Both attributed the incompleteness to bureaucratic despotism or the persistence of feudal patterns of exercising power. The difference between "national historicism" and "social theory" as intellectual frameworks is, of course, important. Unlike those relying on social theory, Nakano, and nationalists in general, relied on an interpretation of the historical significance of Saigō. Thus, he did not see the fulfillment of the aims of the Meiji Restoration in terms of social determinism, but in terms of the will of the extraordinary individual, like Saigō, "the greatest hero of the Restoration."[23]

Ōyōmei Intuitionism

The image of Saigō was omnipresent in Nakano's ideas on the individual in Japanese history. Although he did not write

[21] *Ibid.*, p. 52.   [22] *Ibid.*, pp. 189, 208-209.
[23] The phrase reads *Ishin daiichi no eiyū*, in Nakano Seigō, "Nanshū ō," *Nakano daienzetsu*, p. 327.

a systematic treatise on this subject, he developed, in speeches and essays from 1906 (when he asked "who will be the next Saigō")[24] on into the 1930's, a clear theme of what he meant by the extraordinary individual. What is perhaps most striking about this theme is the fact that he placed Saigō squarely in the Ōyōmei tradition of the Tokugawa era. In Japan the Ōyōmei tradition had its roots in the seventeenth century. It combined the intuitionism of Neo-Confucianism (associated with Wang Yang-ming, rendered in Japanese as Ōyōmei) with the particularism of the samurai ethic of loyal service. In this tradition, the individual was defined as a completely autonomous spiritual entity committed to selfless acts of loyalty.

The development of Ōyōmei in Tokugawa history is not easy to trace. It never formed a "school" like the Shūshigaku (Metaphysical School) or the Kogaku (Ancient Studies School). We do not, therefore, find it engaged in active intellectual discourse with the Metaphysical School, as we most certainly do in the case of the Ancient Studies School, and, as Maruyama Masao has argued in his brilliant work on political thought in Tokugawa society, some of the major impulses behind Japan's modernization have their roots in the dialectical engagements of the Metaphysical School.[25] In particular, Ogyū Sorai of the Ancient Studies School takes on crucial significance in the development of rational historicism and functional definitions of government and society. For this reason, scholarly attention has tended to emphasize the intellectual debates between identifiable schools that were conducive to the development of rationalizing themes. The Ōyōmei tradition, however, tended to have a life apart from the main arena of intellectual debates. Hence, its relationship with modern Japan has not been adequately traced. It seems that the Ōyōmei tradition had an important "counter-rationalist" impact on modern Japan, the principal aspect of this impact being a pronounced

[24] Inomata, *Nakano shōgai*, p. 710.
[25] Maruyama Masao, *Nihon seiji shisōshi kenkyū* [A Study of the History of Japanese Political Thought] (Tokyo, 1952).

distrust, based on a particular conception of the individual, of rational authority and bureaucratic specialization. Despite the fact that Ōyōmei was not a school, it became a living tradition among the samurai, perhaps mostly among those samurai living in outlying areas such as Kyūshū. The image of the "Satsuma *hayato*" mentioned earlier would seem to indicate this. And, if modern scholars such as Maruyama have identified (understandably) with Tokugawa rationalism, modern nationalists more often than not have tended to identify closely with the intuitionist tradition of Ōyōmei. This was certainly the case with Nakano.

Nowhere in his writings do we find a discussion of Ogyū and the Ancient Studies School. He pointed instead to the intuitionism of Ōyōmei as the central characteristic of the Japanese spirit and wove this theme into the fabric of the Meiji Restoration. His uncritical division of the early Meiji leaders in terms of conservative bureaucrats and great individuals is clear indication of this. He did not see in the former group ideas that might link them to Tokugawa history. The latter, however, were in the intellectual mainstream (as he understood it) of Tokugawa society and hence "Japanese."

There was another dimension to his emphasis on the tradition of Ōyōmei intuitionism. Nakano believed there were generic resemblances between this tradition and the modernizing concepts of late eighteenth-century French political thought. Although not explicit as to what French thinkers he had in mind, he argued that the concept of individual "natural right" was virtually identical with the unequivocal recognition of individual autonomy in Ōyōmei. In the intuitionist context, absolute moral autonomy was understood as a natural "liberty." To Nakano, therefore, liberty, as suggested in Itagaki's famous phrase of 1883—"Itagaki may die but liberty will not die"— indicated the indestructibility of the natural principle of moral autonomy.[26] And might it not have been in this sense too that

[26] Inomata, *Nakano shōgai*, pp. 492-99. Nakano Seigō, *Meiji minken*, pp. 67, 157-61.

samurai in late Tokugawa shouted *jiyū banzai* ("Long live liberty!")? Nakano seems to have been utterly oblivious to the fact that the position of idealistic historicism to which he subscribed was based on a set of premises which rejected "natural right" theory as logically untenable. It was, after all, precisely because political experiences could not be compared on a universal plane that emphasis was placed on the unfolding of a unique *geist* from a particular historical sequence. In his curiously naïve and journalistic fashion, however, Nakano looked to "complex" France and the idea of natural right to buttress his defense of Ōyōmei tradition as the essential spirit of modern Japan.

The deceptive ease with which Nakano manipulated these complex intellectual forces is actually not as bizarre as one might suppose at first glance. In translating the Western political vocabulary into Japanese in early Meiji, the term "natural right" was rendered in Chinese characters as "heaven given principle" or "reason." In the intuitionist frame of reference, therefore, the term meant the right to realize the natural principle that gave men their moral essence, their individuality. Moreover, the "reason" of nature as understood in Ōyōmei tradition was not simply a timeless metaphysical principle having abstract reality; it was imbedded in the concrete autonomous self.[27] Although principle in man was identical with that of heaven, it was discoverable and understood internally, by the individual, irrespective of institutional arrangements and structured bodies of knowledge. The notion of "natural right" merely buttressed this conception of individualism in the Ōyōmei tradition. When Nakano spoke of the emergence of the masses from obscurity, he meant the possibility at last for *all* Japanese to realize their "right" to spiritual independence and self development. Thus, "natural" or "heaven-given" right as understood in this mode of intuitionism was inextricably related to the particularistic "national spiritual essence."

[27] Nakano's words were: *ri wa ningen no meitokū no naka ni sonawari.* . . . Nakano Seigō, "Nanshū ō," *Nakano daienzetsu,* p. 335.

Perhaps more important for Nakano, who like most intui-
tionists was not a systematic historian of political thought, was
the extreme activism implicit in the Ōyōmei tradition. The
famous phrases in that tradition, *ri-ki ichigen* ("union of reason and matter") and *chigyō gōitsu* ("union of knowledge
and action"), words Nakano frequently uttered, had rebellious implications in Japan that were not readily apparent on
Chinese soil. "Reason" discovered in the depths of the self constituted an absolute imperative to act—a "supreme" or "sovereign command."[28] This took on the meaning of the "right" to
defy authority in the name of internalized moral truth. Nakano therefore observed quite succinctly that Ōyōmei was "the
school of rebellion,"[29] and he also noted that it was akin to the
"right of rebellion" found in late eighteenth-century French
political thought.

In Nakano's eyes the history of Ōyōmei intuitionism revealed
a steady development towards a radical mode of political protest. In the seventeenth and early eighteenth centuries, this mode
was still passive. Drawing evidence from the early figures, however, he noted that even in the early phases, there was already
a decided emphasis on autonomy from formal bureaucracy
along highly individualistic lines. Thus, both Nakae Tōju
(1608-48) and his disciple Kumazawa Banzan (1619-91) severed ties with the Bakufu and directed their actions to other
fields. Nakae returned to the countryside to care for his mother
and to help poor farmers. Kumazawa directed his talents to
improving agricultural techniques to rescue farmers from their
poverty. Both were governed by the Ōyōmei spirit of individualism. Hence both rejected status and power, and committed
their lives to their "inner command" to help the people. This
seemingly apolitical tradition, however, developed *logically*, as
Nakano saw it, into active ("heroic") defiance of political authority.

[28] *Ibid.*, pp. 335-38.
[29] Nakano's phrase is: *Muhon no gaku*. Nakano Seigō, *Tamashii*, pp.
92, 110-11.

The key figure in this development was Ōshio Heihachirō (1794-1837). A samurai serving in the lower bureaucracy of the Bakafu, Ōshio resigned his post and openly rebelled against that order (Tempō Uprising of 1837) for its failure to provide famine relief in the Osaka area. Like Nakae and Kumazawa, Ōshio refused to be a tool of despotic government. Like them, he took a course of action consonant with his inner moral dictate. Unlike his predecessors, however, Ōshio transformed commitment to inner principle into political rebellion on behalf of the common people—hence he had in him elements of modern socialism, Nakano noted.[30]

What Nakano saw in Ōshio was more than a rebellious attitude. He detected a logical sequence of thought which, in his mind, was tantamount to a principle for political change. Laws were necessary and, in general, men should obey them. But laws were creations of men and hence should reflect the principle of justice that was part of the "reason" in men. Laws that were contrary to the welfare of the people, therefore, *ought* to be changed. And if reform (*kaikaku*) were attempted and found impossible because of bureaucratic inertia, then the only recourse consistent with one's moral conviction was revolution (*kakumei*). In this sense, Ōshio's legacy, as Nakano viewed it, was the right of the moral person to defy national laws, to "transcend" them, as he put it.[31] Ōshio was the first to conceptualize explicitly moral individuality[32] as a mode of direct political protest—unto death—against the legal structure. To Nakano, therefore, Ōshio was "revolutionary." He was, moreover, utterly responsible to himself and to the masses; he embodied the fundamental principle of Japanese individualism; he was in every sense "truly free" (*jitsu ni jiyū no kojin nari*).[33]

It is evident that Nakano, like some of his Marxist contem-

[30] Nakano Seigō, "Ōshio Heihachirō o omou," *Nakano daienzetsu*, p. 343.

[31] *Ibid.*, pp. 91-92.

[32] Nakano referred to this as *dokusō jihatsu no kosei*. *Ibid.*, p. 352.

[33] *Ibid.*, pp. 94, 92-105, 343-46.

poraries, viewed the Tempō uprising as the forerunner of the
Meiji Restoration, but, unlike the Marxists, he did not see that
event in terms of class dynamics. He saw it, as he did the
Meiji Restoration, as the convergence of "popular energy" and
the great individual. His central thread, therefore, connected
Ōshio with the rebellious loyalists, Yoshida Shōin, Takasugi
Shinsaku, and above all Saigō. For him, the Meiji Restoration
led by these men was the "heroic" culmination of the "ideol-
ogy of rebellion." As the chief bearer of that Ōyōmei tradition,
Saigō, like Ōshio, was a "revolutionary son" of modern Japan.[34]

Saigō was a dedicated student of Ōyōmei. He had read in-
tensively the major writings in that tradition beginning with
those of Nakae Tōjū in the seventeenth century. Like Nakae
and Kumazawa Banzan, Saigō felt intimately attached to the
rustic countryside and parted company with bureaucracy to
return to it. Like them, he gave up power, official status, and
wealth because he was convinced his position was right. Unlike them, however, he transformed "union of thought and
action" into a principle of political protest. Thus, like Ōshio, he
embodied the Tokugawa legacy of uncompromising dissent as
a supreme moral dictate against arbitrary government. Like
Ōshio, moreover, this internalized imperative transcended formal political structures. It was related only to the "reason of
heaven" in him and to the suffering masses. Being detached
from formal human constructs, Saigō was "free" and, hence,
"revolutionary."[35]

The idea of "liberty" then, unquestionably meant the right
to moral autonomy as expressed in the classic intuitionist
phrase (of Zen origin) "throughout heaven and earth, there is
only you." Yet, by infusing French political thought into the
traditional concept of intuition, Nakano gave Saigō an unmistakably liberal and progressive coloring. If this coloring had
little historical authenticity, it was nonetheless a myth having
broad appeal in Japan. Saigō's "liberal" intuitionism was linked

---

[34] The term is *kakumeiji.* Nakano, "Nanshū ō," *ibid.,* p. 348.
[35] *Ibid.,* p. 348.

to his paternalistic "love of people" and generalized beyond the samurai class to the entire populace. In this way, Saigō became the major connection between the Ōyōmei inspired attack on the Bakufu and the subsequent movements for popular rights and party government. Saigō's uncompromising protest against tyranny symbolized the innovational and liberating thrust of the Meiji Restoration. It was the distinctive ingredient in Japan's quest for modern popular government.

By combining Ōyōmei intuitionism and natural right, Nakano was able to launch a comprehensive critique of conservative bureaucratism as a detrimental force in modern Japan. He made no attempt to see the possible roots of bureaucratic government in Tokugawa rationalism, and instead labeled it as "Western," utterly foreign to the Japanese spirit. To drive home this point, Nakano manipulated a highly seductive historical analogy. He identified the Meiji Restoration with the French Revolution, since both had similar motivating ideas. He then identified Meiji bureaucratism with German reactionary legalism. Using this historical analogy, he condemned the men in power for their usage of bureaucratic tools inspired by the German counterrevolution to the progressivism of the French. The Meiji Constitution, therefore, was "German," legalistic and reactionary, and inimical to the ideas of enlightenment and progress.[36] While attacking the "Germanism" of the bureaucratic elite in power, he reaffirmed in the same breath the radical Japanese nature of the Meiji spirit, which, as already indicated, was the conviction of the individual in his right to moral autonomy against bureaucratic tyranny.

The above account suffices to indicate the qualitative import of the Meiji Restoration for Nakano. His writings do not call for the "restoration" of ultimate *de facto* power to the emperor. They call for the "restoration" of transformational politics consistent with the unchanging idealistic norm imbedded in the imperial institution. The mechanism for realizing this idea was the combination of popular energy and individual will. With-

[36] Nakano Seigō, *Meiji minken*, pp. 129-54, 192-207, 245-50.

out any awareness of the contradiction implicit in these two as causal forces in history, Nakano linked intuitionism of the autonomous person with distinctiveness of the Japanese as a whole. Both were intertwined as the "spirit" of the Meiji Restoration which had been the dynamic force behind Japan's modernization.

Nakano, and many others, believed that this spirit had lost its vitality in the twentieth century. It followed that their principal aim ought to be the revival of that spirit so that the government could be made truly popular. Yet, the expectations for the convergence of the morally autonomous person and collective feelings were doomed to romantic frustration. Somehow these poles had to be brought together within a clearly defined framework. By temperament, however, the emotional attachment to the defiant, rebellious individual always turned out to be far greater than concern for rational organization. The contempt for bureaucracy persisted. Hence the "individual" remained the autonomous rebel; the collective a vague, unstructured, concept of "pure peopleism" and "popular nationalism." Regardless, it was the drive to establish a political relationship between the individual and the people, consistent with the "spirit" of the Meiji Restoration, that threaded the thought and actions of Nakano through the "liberal" and "fascist" phases of his career.

Popular Nationalism as "Liberalism"

At first glance, Nakano's career seems to follow a psychological pattern, common in modern Japan, of a sudden and dramatic shift in intellectual allegiance. While this psychological scheme (frequently referred to as *tenkō*) is often useful in explaining radical shifts from "liberalism" to "fascism" and the like (as Tsurumi Shunsuke and his group have shown),[37] it is not particularly useful as a framework for understanding the continuity that is being considered in this chapter. Certainly

[37] Shisō no Kagaku Kenkyūkai, eds., *Tenkō* [Apostasy], 3 vols. (Tokyo, 1960).

in the case of Nakano, continuity tells us as much and perhaps more about the dynamics of his brand of nationalism than discontinuity. Without adequate tools of analysis, however, his biographers have stressed the theme of abrupt discontinuity in the 1930's, thus clouding the significance of Nakano's political career.[38] To them, the "true" Nakano was the liberal between 1911 and 1931; in his "fascist" phase in the 1930's, he unwittingly strayed from his normal course of development. The cause for this departure is reputed to have been the situational shock of major surgery on his leg and deaths in the family. This is a deceptive and unconvincing explanation indeed, for it distorts the picture of Nakano the liberal as much as it does Nakano the fascist. In fact, beneath superficial changes (for which rational explanation can be attempted) Nakano maintained a remarkable consistency between 1911 and 1943. His techniques may have changed, but his insistence on the need for Japan to maintain her spiritual uniqueness remained a central theme in his career.

Nakano gained his "liberal" image as a prolific journalist commenting on domestic politics and on foreign policy, especially as it related to China. He began his career in 1911 as a writer for the prestigious newspaper *Asahi*. Then, later in the decade, he organized his own journal *Tōhōjiron*, which he combined in 1923 with Miyake Setsurei's famous journal, *Nihon oyobi Nihonjin*. In that same year, as noted earlier, he founded a new journal, *Gakan*, with Miyake. It was as a writer for *Asahi* and editor of his own journals that he wrote essays that were bound into best-selling books.

Of particular interest in his years as a liberal journalist is

[38] The most complete biography is Inomata Keitarō, *Nakano Seigō no Shōgai*, previously cited. He has also written a shorter work, *Nakano Seigō no higeki* [The Tragedy of Nakano Seigō] (Tokyo, 1959). Nakano's long-time friend at *Asahi*, Ogata Taketora, has written *Ningen, Nakano Seigō* [Nakano Seigō, the Man] (Tokyo, 1951). Others include Nakano Yasuo, *Chichi, Nakano Seigō den*, previously cited; and Satō Morio, *Nakano Seigō* [A Biography of Nakano Seigō] (Tokyo, 1951).

Nakano's active involvement in promoting a popular "restoration" and in seeking out and supporting the political figure who would bring this about. This is readily evident in his vigorous participation in the Taishō political crisis in the winter of 1912-13. Only three years out of Waseda and busily writing his account of the Meiji Restoration and subsequent political developments, Nakano saw in the sudden eruption of demonstrations against Prime Minister Katsura Tarō the opportunity to realize "popular government"—in short, a "Taishō Restoration."[39] As a writer for *Asahi*, he launched a vigorous campaign within the political section of that newspaper to support the protest against clique government. This campaign went far in establishing his stature as a liberal; and it also ended his career at *Asahi*. Nakano's actions bring to mind the rebellious individualism he prized in the Ōyōmei tradition. The picture we get of him, therefore, is not so much the liberal as the impatient rebel unwilling to commit himself unequivocably to rational organization. At the height of the crisis he wrote vicious attacks on Katsura ignoring serious reservations about his choice of words by his colleagues and the editorial staff. As a result, he antagonized practically everyone of consequence at *Asahi*. The management of that liberal paper considered him *persona non grata* and had him exiled to Korea as a "special correspondent," a fact which no doubt forced him to establish a journal of his own.[40]

Nakano's extreme impatience was tied to his belief in the recurrence of crises—that is opportunities—in history. The Meiji Restoration had not been fulfilled, but another crisis had presented itself and the time for restoration was at hand. He was convinced of this (as were many other journalists) because the most prominent party politician on the scene had responded to the popular demonstrations and had taken a completely uncompromising stand against bureaucratic elitism. This figure was Inukai Tsuyoshi, with whom Nakano had come to iden-

[39] Nakano Seigō, *Meiji minken*, pp. 495-502.
[40] Inomata, *Nakano shōgai*, pp. 92-122.

tify most closely, although his reasons for doing so were not fundamentally liberal. Inukai was a leading exponent of popular government and his political vocabulary was highly Confucian. Moreover, like Nakano, Inukai was an admirer of Saigō. In a passionate public letter to Inukai in 1913, therefore, Nakano pledged his support to him and to the cause of popular constitutional government. Not surprisingly, he praised Inukai for his commitment to inner virtue, which made him the most independent, consistent, and uncompromising politician, hence the one best suited to lead the country.[41]

For ten years Nakano continued to support Inukai and the movement for pure party government based on a popular union. As a Diet member (elected 1920), he even joined Inukai's *Kakushin Kurabu* (Reform Club) in 1922. The following year, however, Nakano concluded that Inukai was a failure. Inukai had not properly understood the significance of popular organization and had remained content with a small ineffective minority party. The alternatives, Nakano said, were either to organize labor (as the socialists were doing) or transform one of the existing major parties into a popular organization, and he had opted for the latter. He then joined the Kenseikai, partly because he had many friends from Waseda in it, but more importantly because he felt that this party had greater potential for becoming "popular," whereas the Seiyūkai (to which Inukai had drifted) was less desirable because it was more corrupt, more deeply immersed in partisan pork-barrel politics. The Kenseikai, therefore, was the best possible alternative for him in his search for a rational framework within which to organize the people. "Even Saigō," he noted, "needed the backing of Satsuma han."[42] While his joining the Kenseikai seemed

[41] "Inukai Bokudō ni ataeru sho" [A Letter to Inukai Bokudō], *Nihon oyobi Nihonjin* [Japan and the Japanese] (April 1913). From April 1913 to January 1914, Nakano wrote numerous articles in *Nihon oyobi Nihonjin* directed to various politicians and presenting his views on "the fundamental thesis of protecting constitutional government."

[42] Inomata, *Nakano shōgai*, pp. 193, 225.

to indicate his acceptance of parliamentary government, Nakano did not see the party in the context of competition between partisan alignments in which it was deeply involved. The Kenseikai was merely less corrupt.

His other "liberal" acts as a party politician also conform to this pattern. For example, as a member of the Lower House in the 1920's he denounced the Privy Council and the House of Peers in highly publicized interpellations. He criticized these aristocratic institutions because they obstructed the path to popular party government. Reminiscent of his denunciation of Iwakura and Ōkubo for suppressing the spirit of the Meiji Restoration with German bureaucratic techniques, his attacks on these "privileged" institutions charged them with being anachronistic and utterly irrelevant to twentieth-century politics. Still another example that reinforced Nakano's liberal image was his active support of male suffrage as a step toward the fulfillment of the spirit of the Meiji Restoration. Unlike a liberal, however, he did not promote male suffrage out of a recognition of the right of the individual to exercise political choice in the context of party rivalry. Instead, he understood it as a "logical" culmination of the Ōyōmei humanitarian ideal of welfare for the people. He noted, therefore, that the "fundamental spirit" of male suffrage was identical with the ethical precepts of the Ōyōmei tradition.[43]

Despite the liberal image he acquired, Nakano in fact continued to see parliamentary government in the framework of what he thought to be the guiding spirit of the Meiji Restoration. Continuing to think in this manner pre-empted the possibility of his seeing, in either a liberal or a socialist frame of reference, the relationships between "individualism" and "bourgeois" politics and economics. While accepting the industrial power resulting from private capitalism, he did not surrender his intuitionist conception of the individual. The notion of individualism as a legal, class, or economic phenomenon was not of utmost importance to him. Yet he took part in the proc-

[43] Nakano Seigō, "Nanshū ō," *Nakano daienzetsu*, p. 342.

esses of Diet politics, supported private industry, and defended "liberty," even though his concept of "liberty" had little intrinsic relationship with the processes of parliamentary government or capitalism. One need not stretch the imagination to foresee the inevitable disillusionment that would accompany his recognition of that fact.

Perhaps the most deceptive feature of Nakano's liberal image was, however, his view of foreign relations. In 1911, he attacked Tokutomi Sohō (in the 1930's, one of Nakano's most distinguished supporters) for his irrational fear of Chinese republicanism. Rejecting Tokutomi's interventionism, Nakano argued that republicanism was neither dangerous to Japan nor seductive to the rest of Asia. He expressed hope that the revolution in China would succeed. In fact, he journeyed to Canton (November 1911) to give moral support to that revolution. As he recalled later, "Because I loved liberty, I hated the Manchu Court and welcomed the liberating ideas of the revolutionaries."[44] In 1915, he accused Governor General Terauchi of failing to permit the development of popular consciousness in Korea by running a police state, the worst kind of "bureaucratic absolutism."[45] Two years later, he reported, after a brief trip to Europe via Asia, that from China to India, Asia was a string of "broken countries."[46] Again, bureaucratism, this time that of the Western powers, had stifled the natural development of popular consciousness, thereby jeopardizing the cultural existence of these countries. With liberals and socialists from the Shinjinkai, moreover, Nakano denounced the Siberian intervention. He chided the conservatives for their fear of

[44] Inomata, *Nakano shōgai,* p. 508; Nakano Yasuo, *op.cit.,* pp. 186-88. In this regard, Nakano was close to those idealistic nationalists discussed by Marius Jansen in *The Japanese and Sun Yat-sen* (Cambridge, 1954). He was a friend of Tōyama Mitsuru and in 1928 took over as managing editor of Tōyama's newspaper, *Kyūshū Nippō.*

[45] Nakano Seigō, *Waga mitaru Man-Sen* [Manchuria and Korea as I Have Seen Them] (Tokyo, 1915), pp. 4-7.

[46] Nakano Seigō, *Sekai seisaku to kyokutō seisaku* [World Policy and Far Eastern Policy] (Tokyo, 1917).

bolshevism, just as he had attacked Tokutomi earlier.[47] Finally, in a spectacular series of interpellations of Prime Minister Tanaka Giichi in 1928, over the assassination of Chang Tso-lin, he again insisted on nonintervention in light of the inevitability of China's unification along popular lines.[48]

Two opinions in particular reinforced this view of Nakano's. First, the "revolutionary" course in Japan had been set by the Meiji Restoration. Liberation from feudalism and the realization of popular government were part of an overall historical process which could not be altered by revolutions in China or Russia. Second, republicanism should be accepted in the case of China and communism recognized in the case of Russia, because they constituted popular revolts against "privileged government." China especially shared a "spirit" of opposition similar to Japan's struggle against the Bakufu; and, equally important, both countries were involved in the promotion of the general welfare of the people. Both China and Russia should be permitted to realize their own forms of popular government,[49] despite differences in formal structure. All these highly publicized writings and utterances seemed to follow a pattern of noninterventionism argued by leading liberal critics and politicians.

Ostensive liberalism in these matters, however, had another dimension of meaning that often eluded Nakano's audiences and subsequent biographers. Although recognizing popular na-

---

[47] Nakano Seigō, *Man-Sen no kagami ni utsushite* [In Light of the Situation in Manchuria and Korea] (Tokyo, 1921), pp. 49-51, 183-200.

[48] Inomata, *Nakano shōgai*, pp. 266-91. Interestingly, he repeated this theme to Chiang Kai-shek in 1936. Although it was unfortunate that China's nationalism had been stimulated by anti-Japanese feeling, he felt China's unification was inevitable and that Japan should therefore avoid direct confrontation with this drive in North China. Nakano Seigō, *Nihon wa Shina o dō suru* [What is Japan Going to do About China?] (Tokyo, 1937), pp. 201-209; and "Tōyō no shichū, Nihon" [Japan, the Pillar of East Asia], *Nakano daienzetsu*, pp. 389-98.

[49] Nakano Seigō, *Man-Sen no kagami*, pp. 183-200; also, Nakano Yasuo, *op.cit.*, pp. 186-89.

tionalism elsewhere, Nakano's gaze was fixed on domestic politics. The two main elements in the formula used by Nakano, Miyake Setsurei, and others—"popular government at home, popular nationalism abroad"—were not equal halves. One can detect in this formula the psychology of aggression that meshed with the expansionism of the militarists.[50]

Despite having observed to his Chinese friends that popular nationalism was part and parcel of the historical process beginning with the Meiji Restoration,[51] Nakano was not at all personally convinced that Japan was moving towards it. In fact, as noted earlier, it had been stifled by a conservative bureaucratic government. Yet, he firmly believed that popular nationalism had been a critical dimension of the spirit of the Meiji Restoration. It had been decisive in Japan's resistance to Western penetration, as circumstantial evidence in the "broken countries" of Asia indicated. Hence, each country in Asia must also firmly establish its own "unique cultural personality" (*minzokusei*) as a defensive mechanism against Western bureaucratism. After observing the actions of the great powers at Versailles, Nakano was convinced that the success of these efforts in Asia would depend heavily on Japan's ability, as the major Asian power, to maintain her cultural solidarity.[52] This prescription, however, simply did not match his historical as-

[50] His defense of military expansion is best expressed in his *Nankyoku dakai no taiatari* [Resolute Action to Cope With the Crisis] (Tokyo, 1941), pp. 1-40.

[51] See for example his talk in 1925 to friends preparing a new constitution for the Kuomintang: "Kokumin kanjō no hakushu" [Popular Sentiment], *Nakano daienzetsu*, pp. 284-300.

[52] He stressed this need especially after observing the Versailles Conference as a reporter. Upon returning to Japan, he wrote a scathing denunciation of the Western powers for using the conference to maintain their international interests. This pamphlet, *Kōwa kaigi o mokugekishite* [The Peace Conference; An Eyewitness Account] (1919), went through ten printings its first year and influenced a wide variety of people, including the writer Ozaki Shirō and the ultra-nationalist Kita Ikki. See Inomata, *Nakano shōgai*, pp. 148-51.

sessment of Meiji history after the "reactionaries" had taken over.

In Nakano's view, Japan's modernization had not led to popular nationalism. In fact, after the early "heroic" years of Meiji, it deteriorated into a nondescript process, punctuated here and there by lost opportunities. When Nakano opposed intervention and debunked conservative fear of communism, therefore, he was making a point extrinsic to the seeming flow of his logic. He was not denying that communism was "dangerous"; nor was he saying that isolation was good. He was saying simply that blind fear or active intervention would not combat divisive ideas and stabilize Asia. The ability to do this depended on one crucial strength—Japan's ability to recover and maintain her unique spiritual unity and thereby promote the consciousness of national cultural identity throughout Asia.[53]

The foremost task, as Nakano saw it, was to give new life to the distinctive national spirit that had warded off the Western threat in early Meiji. No nation, no culture, Nakano pleaded, could rest on an indistinguishable mass of faded individuals. Japan must recover the basic belief in the moral power of the individual (*jinkaku no zettai ken'i*) and the conviction of becoming "great individuals."[54] Japan would then, as in early Meiji, regain social solidarity and consensuality in all spheres. In short, national defense and the defense of Asia were inextricably intertwined with the intuitionist conception of the individual. It was the revival of this distinctive quality about the Japanese that remained paramount in Nakano's mind, superseding all other considerations. Thus, problems of foreign relations, whether with China, Korea, or Russia, were, in the last analysis, pinned to the prerequisite of "the renovation of popular spirit in Japan."[55] It followed with relative ease from the priorities of this intuitionism, that decisive and uncompromising acts would be seen as manifestations of Japan's

[53] Nakano Seigō, *Man-Sen no kagami*, pp. 220-21.
[54] *Ibid.*, pp. 19, 222; see also Nakano Seigō, *Tamashii*, pp. 94, 340.
[55] Nakano Seigō, *Man-Sen no kagami*, pp. 17-18.

individuality, acts that could help transform dramatically the stagnant spirit in society.

This self-deception emerged with glaring clarity in the early 1930's. Although opposed to direct military intervention, Nakano was trapped by the intuitional framework of his view of politics. Since political leadership had failed to organize properly the feelings of the people, individual Japanese had taken decisive military action. These acts, he said, were "manifestations of our fundamental character" (*honzen no sugata o arawashita mono*) and were therefore indicators of "the road Japan ought to follow" (*Nihon no yukubeki michi*).[56] Nakano, however, felt no sense of contradiction in his support of acts of this kind and his advocacy of national independence for all of Asia. In fact, he did not think of these military actions in terms of acts of aggression against the cultural autonomy of another country. He saw them instead as the kind of acts that would "totally transform popular spirit" within Japan.[57] In short, he saw them in the same light in which he had seen Saigō's demand for a declaration of war against Korea. They were rebellious acts based on internalized truth and selfless commitment to the nation. They were acts aimed primarily at the renovation of ineffective, nondescript, "bureaucratic" leadership that had failed to build a distinctive nation.

Despite Nakano's idealization of militarist actions, he was not a putschist. In this respect, he was quite unlike Kita Ikki, Ōkawa Shūmei, and some of the radical young officers. He remained true to the goal of the Meiji Popular Rights movement to establish a great popular union (*daimintō*). Moreover, like the liberals Maruyama Kanji and Yoshino Sakuzō, he had received his political baptism at a time when large crowds took to the streets protesting or demanding one thing or another. As already mentioned, he took part directly in some of these demonstrations, such as the Taishō political crisis in 1912-13

[56] Nakano Seigō, *Tamashii*, p. 29; "Tōyō no shichū, Nihon," *Nakano daienzetsu*, p. 384.

[57] Nakano Seigō, *Tamashii*, pp. 36-37.

and the suffrage movement of the early 1920's. He had witnessed and reported the explosiveness of these crowds in the Portsmouth Treaty riots of 1905, the Siemens incident of 1914, and the rice riots of 1918. It was entirely consistent with this experience that he should emphasize the possibilities for a popular movement. His idealization of decisive action by the militarists served the purpose of underscoring his argument that government leadership had failed. What was needed, as he saw it, was not more sporadic putsches and coups d'etat, but, what he had urged since 1911, a "rational popular movement." This was what he set out to accomplish in the 1930's, and what earned him the inappropriate epithet, the "Hitler of Japan."

Popular Nationalism as "Fascism"

Reared in the era when crowds had readily taken to the streets, Nakano was convinced—erroneously as it turned out—that the country would rally to the cry for a new popular movement. The people, he said, "demanded a movement"[58] because they realized that, like the economy, the spiritual life of the country had been stagnant in the twentieth century. They believed, moreover, that the fundamental cause for this situation was the continued grip that the privileged political elite had on power. The people knew that modern national politics was not a matter of special political elite or of classes but of the entire people. Without a movement, Nakano concluded, the country would remain depressed and violent upheaval would be inevitable.[59]

Nakano thought that a revolutionary social upheaval was imminent. In the late 1920's, he had read Arthur Young's description of the French countryside on the eve of the revolution. On the basis of his numerous speech tours throughout the regions, he had concluded that conditions in Japan were strik-

[58] Nakano Seigō, "Kokka kaizō no shihyō" [The Direction of National Reform], *Nakano daienzetsu*, p. 17.

[59] Nakano Seigō, *Chintai Nihon no kōsei* [The Revival of Japan] (Tokyo, 1931), p. 1.

ingly similar to those under the *ancien regime* in France. He
felt, moreover, that the roots of poverty and stagnation were
deeply planted in the Meiji era. This was a belief that was
strongly reinforced by the famous novel *Tsuchi* (The Land,
1910), by Nagatsuka Takashi, which he had read at about the
same time that he read Young. The emotional attraction of this
novel was no doubt the author's ringing plea for the farmers
to rely on their individualistic strength to overcome unremit-
ting poverty and degradation. In the context of the 1930's,
Nakano noted, the degradation of the people documented by
Nagatsuka had deepened and had become, in fact, a seething
social malaise requiring immediate attention.[60]

Nakano prescribed a popular movement that would prevent
widespread destruction on the domestic scene. He abhorred
the systematic terrorism of Stalin in the 1920's, and he also
rejected the strategy of sporadic assassinations by young officers, anachronistic agrarian purists (referring to Gondō
Seikyō), and simple-minded "jingoists."[61] To avoid these extreme measures Nakano advocated a comprehensive movement aimed at transforming the existing bureaucracy into a
system responsive to the needs and aspirations of the people.
Critics in his day pointed out that he was advocating a fascist
movement. His wish to organize a movement transcending
class divisions and representing the overriding consensus of
the country indeed strikes a chord of comparability with fascism. However, Nakano's paramount aim in organizing such
a national movement was to re-establish throughout the country the sense of moral cohesion (what Kuga had called "moral
community") that had prevailed in early Meiji; this sense of
cohesion would act as the popular basis for achieving a redefinition of the aims of government. In short, he envisioned, as
he had all along, a movement for "restoration" or a popular
spiritual renovation, which would upend status quo bureauc-

[60] *Ibid.*, pp. 36-48; Inomata, *Nakano shōgai*, pp. 208-209.
[61] Nakano Seigō, *Chintai Nihon*, pp. 115-16.

ratism and return a sense of purpose to national politics.[62] Seen in this light, Nakano's interest in imminent social upheaval indicated a belief that the situation in the early 1930's was identical to that which preceded the Meiji Restoration. In this sense, the "emergency situation" caused by the depression was a great political opportunity, perhaps the greatest since Saigō's time, for the decisive individual (his favorite Western writer was Carlyle)[63] to capture the aspirations of the people and turn the course of history into the natural flow from which it had been diverted.

Nakano's expectations for another popular restoration, however, proved to be unfounded. For reasons that remain obscure, the 1930's were not a period of popular movements in Japan. In dramatic contrast to the period between 1905 and 1925, the people did not riot and take to the streets. In 1905 there had been massive demonstrations against the "unfavorable" Portsmouth Treaty with Russia. In 1931, there were no such riots following the London Conference, although, in a real strategic sense, it was less favorable than the treaty of 1905. Despite Nakano's imputation that the people "demanded" a movement, there does not seem to have been a pervasive feeling of this kind. One possible explanation, in the context of the 1930's, is the absence of a substantial dialectical reaction from the Left that might have moved centrist groups toward Nakano's point of view. By and large, the mainstream of political parties and labor groups tended to hold their positions despite Nakano's appeals. Thousands of enthusiasts attended his rallies; but their numbers were not comparable to those of explosive earlier demonstrations. The putschists sensed this shift in the behavior of the general public and turned to the violent tactic of shock. Nakano did not capitulate to this method. He remained committed to the early Meiji ideal of a popular national union. Nonetheless, he seems to have sensed

[62] Nakano Seigō, "Kokka kaizō no shihyō," *Nakano daienzetsu*, pp. 3, 15-42, 92-94.
[63] Inomata, *Nakano shōgai*, pp. 308-309.

the shift also, and this helps to explain why he later donned the black shirt to make his appeal spectacular.

It would be incorrect, however, to assume that Nakano used irrational techniques alone. He had a platform which he called "A General Plan for National Reorganization."[64] In this plan he described his rational scheme as "social nationalism" (*shakai kokkashugi*), a scheme whose political assumptions closely resembled those of Kuga Katsunan's general plan for "national socialism," formulated in the 1890's. Like Kuga's plan, Nakano's program rejected the laissez-faire definition of government as a thin veil for protecting special economic and political privilege. Instead it defended interventionism: government must intervene in the economic and social life of the country to break the existing structure of privilege and guarantee economic security and equal opportunity for all, regardless of social origin or geographical location. In his plan, therefore, Nakano called for vigorous governmental regulation of the major components of the economy to guarantee economic security for the masses and to prevent the recurrence of economic crisis. He did, however, make a clear distinction between his plan and both "state socialism," meaning the "bureaucratic capitalism" of the Russian model, and direct imperial rule based on German legal theory. The economic and political life of the country would not be directed by a single dictator; nor would the government own or directly manage agrarian, industrial, and financial units. He scrupulously distinguished between bureaucratic regulation and ownership.[65]

Nakano derived some of the specific economic ideas for his plan from the writings of the Fabian socialist G.D.H. Cole.

[64] Nakano Seigō, *Kokka kaizō kaikaku kōryō* [Programs for National Reconstruction] (Tokyo, 1933), especially pp. 1-91. This has been republished recently in Yoshimoto, *op.cit.*, pp. 309-341.

[65] A clear statement of this is his "Tōsei keizai to hijōji kokusaku" [A Controlled Economy and Plan for the National Emergency], *Nakano daienzetsu*, pp. 301-316. Kuga's basic ideas are documented in Yoshimoto, *op.cit.*, pp. 257-309.

In the late 1920's he had perused the arguments then being used in the West to explain and solve the Depression and found Cole's the most relevant to Japan's situation. He found in Cole a convenient set of tools to attack the conservative economic policies of the two major parties, the Minseitō, to which he belonged, and the Seiyūkai. The implications, however, went beyond that. He saw in Cole's critique of the free enterprise system of classical economics two ramifications appropriate to Japan. First, the government must be responsible for regulating the economy and providing absolute economic security for the masses, a point which buttressed Nakano's interventionist definition of government. Secondly, the liberal assumptions behind multilateral trade based on comparative advantage were faulty because, in fact, international trade could not be regulated rationally on that basis. In short, Nakano used Cole to demand a redefinition of the purposes of government and to provide an explanation for the widespread feeling in Japan at that time that a self-sufficient economic bloc was necessary for national economic security. It followed from this manipulation of Cole's ideas that Japan must protect (and control) Manchuria at all costs, an aim that buttressed the expansionism of the militarists.[66]

While he supported the acts of the militarists, which was not his main intention, Nakano was not able to infuse his "socialism" into a national movement, which was his primary aim. The nation, he said, needed a movement stronger than the military—a movement stronger than mere guns.[67] It needed a movement that would persuade the government to provide social welfare out of humanitarian concern—"love of people." From the outset, however, the pattern of frustration is evident. Although he had a "rational" platform premised on interventionism, he did not actually understand rational

[66] Nakano Seigō, "Kokka kaizō no shihyō," *Nakano daienzetsu*, p. 95; "Manshūkoku sokuji shōnin o kochō su" [Demands for the Immediate Recognition of Manchukuo], *ibid.*, pp. 317-26.
[67] Nakano Seigō, "Kokka kaizō no shihyō," *ibid.*, pp. 25-41.

political organization, mostly because such considerations were not central to the intuitionist mode of thought. Without this understanding, he could not cope with the absence of the widespread popular response he had expected; hence, his actions proceeded in fits and starts.

Nakano's first attempt (1931-32) at "national reorganization" was the most conventional of his efforts. He intrigued with men of like minds from the Seiyūkai and the Minseitō to bring about a "union of people's parties" as a framework for the new popular movement. Attempts of this kind had been made all through party history, and Nakano had documented some of them and participated in others. None had succeeded in the past, and once again, the attempt proved abortive. Wakatsuki Reijirō of the Minseitō was not enthused with the idea, and Inukai Tsuyoshi, once Nakano's "hero" and leading exponent of such popular unions, now opposed it as a vicious scheme by opposition groups to undermine his Seiyūkai.[68]

After this approach had failed, Nakano severed ties with the conservative parties. Along with Adachi Kenzō, whom Nakano called *oyabun*, Nakano and some twenty others organized a separate party called Kokumin Dōmei (December 22, 1932). To stir popular enthusiasm and to establish a clear and striking distinction between this new group and the old parties, Nakano and his friends donned black shirts, thus prompting the press to call their group: "the first fascist party" in Japan. Although it had elements that smacked of fascism, it was certainly not a political party in any real sense. Adachi, who had been elevated as president because of his age and prestige, scoffed at the idea of a uniform and refused to put it on. Almost from the outset, the group was divided, disorganized, and ineffective.[69]

[68] Nakano Seigō, "Manshū jiken chokugo no seihenkan" [The Political Crisis Following the Manchurian Incident], *ibid.*, pp. 210-83; also, *Adachi Kenzō jijoden* [The Autobiography of Adachi Kenzō] (Tokyo, 1960), pp. 263-75.

[69] Inomata, *Nakano shōgai*, pp. 344-46.

In the first of two bizarre flirtations with socialist groups Nakano then turned to lead a labor movement. In October 1933, he took over the directorship of the "left wing" of a telephone and telegraph union (Teiyū Dōshikai). Founded in 1925 by the labor leader Suzuki Bunji, this union split into two wings following the Manchurian incident. The nationalistic group (hence, "right wing") formed around Akamatsu Katsumaro (a former member of the Shinjinkai). The left wing turned to Nakano for leadership. "I have joined the labor movement," he told the union members, "because labor is a crucial part of a popular reform movement. . . . The true labor movement in Japan begins today."[70] Ten months later he resigned his directorship. The reason was simple. He could not agree that the aim of a labor union was to strike for economic gain since this was irrelevant to his conception of a popular movement. Later in the decade (1939) he attempted another merger with socialists. He set out to combine his group— called Tōhōkai since 1935—with the Social Masses party (Shakai Taishūtō of Abe Isoo). The result he hoped would be a "social national party," and he came close to achieving it.

Both groups were represented by distinguished men: Tokutomi Sohō and Miyake Setsurei supporting Nakano; Asō Hisashi, Katayama Tetsu, and Miwa Jusō, backing the socialist contingent. An agreement for a union was reached, and in a highly dramatic and widely publicized meeting, Nakano publicly shook hands with Abe Isoo presumably sealing the agreement. In a joint declaration, moreover, both groups pledged to organize a popular union to rebuild Japan. Despite some theoretical differences, read the declaration, both groups were alike in their concern for popular welfare and their union was consistent with this humanitarian concern.[71]

Observers at the time had good reason to believe the union to be a *fait accompli*. John Gunther, for example, believed that Nakano's "fascist party" had "absorbed" the "labor party"; he

[70] *Ibid.*, pp. 351, 350-54.   [71] *Ibid.*, pp. 401-417.

noted that "almost anything can happen in Japan."[72] The highly publicized union between "fascism" and "socialism," however, proved abortive. The plans broke down at the very last stage because neither side could be convinced as to which would "absorb" the other. This was reflected in the debate over distributing the top posts of the new party. Neither side conceded the presidency to the other group. Nakano's Tōhō-kai obviously sought to use the Social Masses party to give the group a more substantial socialist flavor and thereby extend its popular base. The Social Masses party aimed to use Nakano to strengthen it by giving it a greater "nationalist" coloring. When the political motivations for a union became evident, the talks broke down.

To Nakano this failure was the last in a series of "lost opportunities" that began with Saigō's death. He referred to it as the "last delusion" regarding the possibility of a popular "union" in the context of the parliamentary structure. He resigned his Diet seat, noting that while someday the Diet might once again become useful, it was utterly ineffective in a crisis situation.[73] The "delusion," however, was not the failure of popular unions in the context of parliamentary government. The real delusion was his uncompromising belief that Ōyōmei intuitionism could be politicized into a modern national movement. The intuitionist mode of moral autonomy and protest in its pure form simply could not be brought into a rational scheme of organization. By philosophic definition it was an impossibility. Yet, in recognizing the need for social solidarity in modern Japan, Nakano felt driven to use this mode in particular because he believed it most precious to the personality of Japanese individualism. The resulting frustrations made his voice increasingly shrill and drove him to use extreme techniques, which, in the end, proved bankrupt.

At the scores of rallies that Nakano and his group sponsored to organize a popular movement, the black shirt was worn.

[72] John Gunther, *Inside Asia* (New York, 1939), pp. 77, 79.
[73] Nakano Seigō, *Nankyoku dakai*, p. 13; Inomata, *Nakano shōgai*, pp. 413-19.

On the armband was the Japanese character for "East," which some Western observers mistook to be a swastika. This image was a misleading one. Although the external trappings Nakano used to stir the public were fascistic and his program for the movement was based on Fabian ideas, the basis for his beliefs remained riveted to the spiritual ideal of the Meiji Restoration. He was fascinated with European fascism because it seemed to fit his conception of what Japan should be in the twentieth century. In both Italy and Germany, he observed, fascism was "revolutionary." Yet it rejected class warfare, stressing the cultural distinction of the entire people—regardless of class, age-group, or region—and the individual's selfless commitment to that distinctiveness. Hence, when Mussolini told him (in an interview in February 1938) that the essence of the Italian personality was willingness to confront death for the greater good, he understood this in precisely the same way he had understood Ōshio and Saigō. Moreover, Nakano noted with complete naïveté that Mussolini drew his "morality" from knowledge in history and that this was analogous to his own dependence on the history of Ōyōmei "as expounded by the master Nakae Tōjū and exemplified in action by Ōshio Hiehachirō and Saigō Nanshū."[74]

Like Ōyōmei intuitionism, fascism was radical, rebellious, and individualistic. Nakano could not resist the temptation of equating Mussolini's "action" with the Ōyōmei concept of "union of thought and action" (*iwayuru chigyō gōitsu*, as he put it). Thus he called the Duce Italy's "Saigō and overall paternal leader," *sō-oyabun*, a term used exclusively for Japanese relationships. He concluded, "I spoke with Mussolini and read his speeches and realized that the spirit [of fascism] was virtually identical with Ōyōmei. . . ."[75]

Similarly, in assessing Hitler, Nakano could not resist the temptation to refer to the historical analogy he had used in

[74] Nakano Seigō, "Itarī no oyabun (dyuchi) Musorini" [Italy's Boss, Mussolini], *Tamashii*, p. 9.
[75] *Ibid.*, pp. 10-11.

his early writings on Meiji politics. In that analogy he had established as parallels the French Revolution and the Meiji Restoration, the German counterrevolution and the Meiji bureaucratic conservatism. The instruments that were used in Japan to suppress the radical spirit of early Meiji had been forged out of reactionary German legal theory. In this context, he saw Hitler as liberator of the German people from the stifling legalism of the nineteenth century. And Nazism seemed akin to the upsurge of popular energy against Bakufu despotism. Thus, despite his serious doubts about the "bureaucratic absolutism" of the Gestapo, Nakano characterized Hitler as a rebellious, highly individualistic person.[76]

It would be too simple, despite his obvious fascination with fascism, to conclude that Nakano thought himself a fascist. He still viewed himself as a proud inheritor of a particular philosophic tradition whose roots were in the seventeenth century and which was identified with real men. If he romanticized these men in his characterization of them, which he did, they were nonetheless concrete historical figures revered by large segments of the Japanese public. They were not mere fictive types in an immemorial yet heroic past. Moreover, Nakano readily admitted that these heroes, Saigō in particular, were greater than himself—indeed, greater than anyone in Europe. It is entirely dubious whether either Hitler or Mussolini would have admitted greater historical figures than they, for this would have tarnished their image of political infallibility. In these respects Nakano could not have been a "Hittorā." It seems quite certain that he did not see himself as a fascist, but that he thought fascism was strikingly Japanese.

Because he saw a relation between European fascism and his concept of a popular movement, Nakano felt no discomfort in the black shirt. His aim, however, was not to spread fascism in Japan. He was clearly using the argument of similarity

[76] Nakano Seigō, "Shinkō Doitsu no shidōsha Hittorā" [Hitler and the Rise of Germany], *ibid.*, pp. 14-23.

between fascism and the Japanese spirit to underscore the contemporary relevance of Ōyōmei intuitionism in a situation of national crisis. The black shirt was but a superficial device to that end.

This intimate attachment to Ōyōmei individualism is clearly evident during the last years of Nakano's career. Realizing the failure of his techniques and strategies to mount a popular movement, he launched a suicidal verbal attack against "reactionary bureaucratism." He first assailed the Imperial Rule Assistance Association (Taiseiyokusankai, established in October 1940), which acted as the national union of all parties. Nakano had been on its planning committee, but within a year he resigned from it and, contrary to the demands of the authorities, re-established his Tōhōkai as an independent political group. He criticized the association for not being "popular" and for becoming instead (under the direction of the "new bureaucrats") an instrument of the Home Ministry to establish totalitarian control over the country. Joining hands with a few industrialists and ex-party men, he accused it of being part of a broad plan to exercise systematic terror of the Russian type over the people. Nakano carried this attack to Tōjō, labeling him a despot and enemy of the people.[77]

What concerns us is the vocabulary in which he couched his denunciation. The press referred to Nakano's attack as an indication of a return to his "true self," meaning a return to the liberal image of the 1920's, but Nakano had never changed in any fundamental sense. These words are indicative of his constancy: "I will fight [Tōjō's regime] even if I remain all alone."[78] While the press thought statements such as this indicated a reaffirmation of liberal individualism, they were, in fact, a reaffirmation of the rebellious moral individualism of the Ōyōmei tradition. Thus, in much the same way he had understood that "Itagaki may die but liberty will not die," he

[77] Inomata, *Nakano shōgai*, pp. 430-37.
[78] His words, "Boku wa hitori ni natte mo . . . tatakau," may be found in Inomata, *Nakano shōgai*, p. 492.

now claimed that no formal political instrument could kill his concept of "spiritual autonomy."

In a three-hour speech at Waseda's Ōkuma Hall (November 10, 1942), Nakano drove this theme home to the students of his alma mater. Japan should avoid looking to England and America with blind hate denouncing their "Jewish capitalism" (an attack pointed at the propaganda of Tōjō and Kishi Nobusuke). Instead, Japan should refocus on the strength of the Japanese individual. The nation should refocus on the "spirit of freedom," which is "sacred" and "precious" because it means the right to be truly autonomous (*jiritsuteki*, in the philosophic sense) and to generate the power to control one's life and defy oppressive bureaucracy. Quoting from no less an authority than the rebel Patrick Henry, Nakano went on to say that against tyranny the Japanese should cry out "give me liberty or give me death" (*ware ni jiyū o ataeyo, shikarazumba shi o ataeyo*). Harking back to themes he had developed in his work on Meiji political developments, he told his young audience that the individualism of Rousseau and Voltaire was not contrary to the Japanese concept of liberty as understood by Itagaki. In both cases it meant the right to individual autonomy. In Japan, this meant the internalized moral conviction, as exemplified by the great Saigō, to resist the crushing weight of formalized authority. This conviction, he again affirmed, was the essence of the spirit of the Meiji Restoration, the essence of modern Japan. And he summed up this spirit in the explosive phrase "*tenka hitori o motte okoru*," which defies precise translation but which might be rendered roughly as "the power to rise up alone in the world." He was clearly referring to the Ōyōmei concept of moral autonomy as the basis for individual action.[79] This phrase is of particular interest. It captures the theme that threaded Nakano's career together. It is a theme that can be found in his first major attempt to explain the Meiji Restoration and the Popular Rights movement. In that

[79] The speech is quoted at length in *ibid.*, pp. 497-511; and Satō, *op.cit.*, pp. 282-338.

attempt, which we cited earlier, he quoted these words (attributed to one Tsuda Seiichi):

> To manage the great affairs of state, one must be prepared
> to become an enemy of the entire country [tenka o teki ni
> suru no kakugo]. I am not afraid of belonging to a small
> minority—even a minority of one. If I cannot move the
> country [hitori nishite motte kuni o okosu bekarazumba] I
> shall simply fight to the end.[80]

The vocabulary Nakano used to stir the students of Waseda
in November 1942, and for which he is still remembered, was
entirely consistent with the same early Meiji spirit of rebellious individualism that had influenced him well before his
political career began. Despite the fact that he used different
techniques—journalism, party politics, black shirts—this theme
was constant. The individualism that Nakano urged, therefore, was not pacifistic. He was not apologizing for the actions
he took in the 1930's that had struck some as being odd. He
was saying the same thing he had said earlier in praising the
actions of Kwantung Army officers as reflections of the pure
character of the Japanese. He had been saying for twenty years
that self development based on intuitionism must be the basis
of social unity because it made the Japanese a "people"—*minzoku*.

Due to his repeated criticism of Tōjō's despotism[81]—the ma-

[80] Nakano Seigō, *Meiji minken*, p. 143.

[81] Nakano worked with Hatoyama Ichirō, a former Seiyūkai leader,
and Miki Takeyoshi, formerly of the Minseitō. (Both became major
party leaders in the postwar period.) One of their plans was to replace
Tōjō with General Ugaki who allegedly supported a quick settlement
with Chiang and a negotiated peace in the Pacific even if disadvan-
tageous to Japan. Hatoyama Ichirō, *Hatoyama Ichirō kaikoroku*
[Hatoyama Ichirō Memoirs] (Tokyo, 1957), pp. 13-20; Miki Kai, ed.,
Miki Takeyoshi [A Biography of Miki Takeyoshi] (Tokyo, 1958), pp.
240-53; Inomata, *Nakano no higeki*, pp. 79-97, 142-43. A colorful account of Nakano during these months is in Robert Guillain, *Le
Peuple Japonais et La Guerre: Chosen Vues 1939-1946* (Juilliard,
1946), p. 135 and passim.

nipulation of the election of April 1942 and censorship of the press—Nakano was forbidden to make public speeches, then forbidden to write for the press, and finally, placed under house arrest on October 26, 1943. The following night, he took his own life, in classic fashion. Conspicuously placed nearby were the five volumes of the biography of Saigō.

Conclusion

In his stimulating essays on thought and behavior in modern Japan, Maruyama Masao has observed the ironical fact that opposition to Tōjō came from right-wing nationalists such as Nakano Seigō.[82] If we examine a career such as Nakano's outside the immediate context of the 1930's and view it in a historical flow of the engagement between Ōyōmei intuitionism and the processes of Japan's modernization, this is not as ironical as it might seem. Viewed in this broader perspective, it is not ironic at all that the most vociferous protest would come from the Right and be articulated as a defense of individual liberty. The Right was the only politically active segment that preached autonomy of the individual as a basis for open defiance if need be (as it frequently was) *vis-à-vis* the legal structure. It is not surprising, therefore, that Nakano, a conscious inheritor of the "ideology of rebellion," would take the lead in the denunciation of Tōjō's despotism.

It is also not particularly startling that Nakano's protest against Tōjō should only be a verbal one, although he knew full well that this would lead to his self-destruction. The violent implications of intuitionism were muted in Nakano because he had blended them into the notion of political movement. It appears that the Ōyōmei mode of protest developed in two distinguishable patterns in modern Japan. One pattern, a theme I have not treated in this chapter, went in the direction of violent acts of aggression—an egregious example of

[82] Masao Maruyama, *Thought and Behaviour in Modern Japanese Politics* (New York, 1963), pp. 74-75.

this type of Ōyōmei protest is implied in Inoue Nisshō's dictum, "One man, one killing." The other pattern merged with the Popular Rights movement and with popular movements in general. Nakano's extreme nationalism came out of this latter trend. Throughout his career he saw himself in the mainstream of the popular movements of early Meiji.

As we have seen, Nakano made the transition from individual "rebellion" to popular "movement" in two ways and still retained intact the intuitionist tradition. First, he manipulated the image of Saigō into that of the founding father of popular nationalism and the movement for popular rights. By placing Saigō in the main flow of that movement, Nakano could then direct his activities to methods of appealing to public opinion rather than to the tactics of violent uprising. Secondly, he used the French concept of natural right to buttress the intuitionist conception of moral autonomy. As late as 1942, we find Nakano saying that Ōyōmei intuitionism was virtually identical with the individualism of Voltaire and Rousseau (I doubt he knew the difference between these thinkers) and hence politically relevant to organized movements. Both these factors, in any case, seem to have placed Nakano outside the psychological frame of the assassin. The emotional link is there, as indicated in his favorable view of decisive military action in the 1930's, but the distinction is more important if we are to understand his consistent performance as a journalist and propagandist as well as his attempts to gain popular visibility in the 1930's and early 1940's.

The manipulation of history, however, could not overcome the fundamental contradiction between intuitionism and rational political movements. Nakano's career serves to heighten the fact that "Japanese individualism" (and individualism it was) in its uncompromising and extreme form could not be intrinsically related to the modern political framework within which movements were to be launched and sustained. Nakano's propensity for thinking in the mode of radical spiritual autonomy made it virtually impossible for him to relate this autonomy with legal and organizational concepts, such as definitions of property or concrete mechanisms of parliamentary politics. This is not to say that Nakano was unaware of the role of organization in modern society. His joining the Kenseikai in the early 1920's and using Cole's arguments for rational economic regulation would indicate that he was. But he was outmaneuvered in the party movement, and in the 1930's his stirring "fusion of anger and grief," as one admirer put it,[83] did not produce the "rational" organization for a movement. He could not function in terms of the prerequisites of rational organization because his main concern was elsewhere —with the preservation of "Japanese individualism" whose precepts contradicted the need for rational organization. Ōyōmei intuitionism, after all, did not develop out of but in spite of bureaucracies. More often than not, therefore, attempts to revive the spirit of Ōyōmei individualism bypassed rational organization and proceeded directly to the imperial institution as the constant, idealistic, historical norm symbolizing popular "restoration" and the individual's capacity for self development. Yet there persisted in Nakano the nagging feeling that without an organized popular movement, social solidarity would decline and the Japanese would cease to be a "people," thus sacrificing the cultural defense mechanism of Japan (and Asia) against the West. Nakano's extremism in tone of voice, choice of words, and strategy stemmed in large measure from his inability to solve this dilemma of establishing a meaningful relationship between the indigenous tradition of individualism and modern organization. Indeed, might this not be one of the key dilemmas of Japanese development in the twentieth century?

Seen in this perspective, Nakano's importance was not his ability or inability to seize real power. It was his untiring insistence that the process of modernization had steadily eroded Japan's spirit of individualism, the very spirit of the Meiji

[83] The words are those of the writer Ozaki Shirō, quoted in Inomata, *Nakano shōgai*, pp. 150-51.

Restoration that had launched that process. In this respect, Nakano was part of a broader intellectual development emphasizing the pessimistic view of the individual in post-Meiji Japan that we find in Natsume Sōseki, Tokutomi Sohō, Miyake Setsurei, and a host of lesser known intellectuals. Tokutomi and Miyake in particular repeatedly emphasized in their writings the decline of Japanese individuality and the consequent loss of social solidarity and national purpose. Unlike these men, however, Nakano actively involved himself in politics, attempting in a variety of ways to politicize the spirit of Japanese individualism in the context of rapid changes in the international and domestic scenes.

It would be easy to sweep Nakano under the convenient rug of history as a "prewar fascist phenomenon." Although the themes he stressed have been muted by the disasters of the Pacific War, they are still alive today as important intellectual issues. The celebrated novelist Mishima Yukio and Hayashi Fusao, a former member of the Shinjinkai who has written a phenomenally popular account of the Pacific War as "The Hundred Years War in Asia,"[84] have both grappled with them. Like Nakano, both these men have sought to define the determining spirit in Japan's modern development. Both have turned to the events surrounding the Meiji Restoration to do this. They insist on the need for the Japanese to understand their individuality (*koa pa-sonariti*) without which society will remain an indistinct "crowd" and not a "people."[85] Of particular interest is the fact that Mishima has described the "toughness" of the Japanese individual as the uncompromising commitment to resist authority in the face of certain defeat. Nakano identified this "precious thing" as the internalized idealism of

[84] Hayashi Fusao, *Diatōa sensō kōteiron* [In Defense of the Greater East Asia War] (Tokyo, 1964); and, of course, the sequel, *Zoku* (Tokyo, 1965); and also his *Midori no Nihon rettō* [The Green Isles of Japan] (Tokyo, 1966).

[85] The term "crowd" is rendered *taishū*, "a people" as *minzoku*. Hayashi and Mishima, *op.cit.*, pp. 45-48.

NAKANO SEIGŌ

the Ōyōmei tradition, and he pointed to Ōshio and Saigō as outstanding historical manifestations. Mishima looks at the Shimpūren.[86] The concern of these men is neither accurate historical reconstruction nor precise tracing of the individuality of which they speak in the formal structures of government, industry, and education. Their concern is to find its purest expression, hence the tendency to romanticize heroes and minimize the ways it might have influenced the personalities of men who worked effectively within formal organizations. The point is that these heroes epitomize the intuitional mode of total autonomy and total resistance. The purest expression of Japanese individuality, therefore, is rebellious opposition to rational authority.

It is in this light that Nakano himself lingers on as an object of fascination in Japan.[87] For it is clear, as suggested above, that the themes he dealt with touch a sensitive nerve in Japan's seemingly dispassionate quest for modernity. The political manifestations may not be the same—indeed, this aspect may no longer be as centrally relevant as it was to Nakano—but the psychological drive to relate a distinctive conception of the individual to the industrial world persists. Perhaps Hayashi Fusao and Mishima Yukio have a point in criticizing some of us American Japanologists for failing to come to grips with the complex elements in the psychology of Japanese nationalism. They claim we continue to write "horse operas" about

[86] The Shimpūren was a group of rebellious samurai from Kumamoto that started a suicidal uprising in October 1876 against the Meiji government for opening the country to the West. For Mishima's views, see *ibid.*, pp. 132-62, passim.

[87] Documented in Inomata, *Nakano shōgai*, pp. 150-51, 420-21, 460, 610-12. The well-known novelist Hino Ashihei developed the theme of Nakano as defender of liberty in a serial in *Sundé mainichi* (1951). Another writer, Ozaki Shirō (who had been a faithful reader of Nakano) wrote in *Bungei Shunjū* (October 1963) about "Nakano Seigō, The Rebel" (*hankotsu*). Kimura Ki has written *Aru Shishi, Nakano Seigō no saiki* [Nakano Seigō, the Loyalist]. And lesser known people have written of his "tragedy" and of his "futility."

420

Japan, hence, "Thanks but no thanks" (*arigata meiwaku*).[88]
A look at the nationalism of Nakano through the perspective
of the tradition of Ōyōmei individualism hardly begins to
get the job done. But it seems to me that until we isolate and
examine more of these themes in broad historical perspective
we will have left out important dimensions that will frustrate
our attempts at this end of the world to relate the psychology
of nationalism in Japan to comparative definitional models of
personality, culture, and political movement.

[88] Hayashi and Mishima, *op.cit.*, pp. 167-68.

CHAPTER XI

Ōyama Ikuo and the Search for Democracy

PETER DUUS

IN THE fall of 1930, shortly before he was shot by a would-be assassin, Hamaguchi Osachi waxed pessimistic about the state of the political world. "No sooner have the people of our country realized that party government has been established than they have been disappointed at the enormity of its defects," he wrote. "Without taking time to consider deeply whether these defects of party government are the fault of the system or the fault of the party politicians, they have lost hope in the present state of politics and take a gloomy view of the future."[1] His comment, written as economic hard times were settling over the country, echoed what many politicians had been saying and thinking for the past decade. Although the Diet had become a key part of the political process and although the political parties had succeeded in dominating the other political elites, party government still lacked moral persuasiveness among much of the population. There was a considerable disparity between the effectiveness of the political parties and the legitimacy of parliamentary politics.

Disenchantment with the political parties and with representative government sprang from several sources. At one level, there was considerable disgust with the quality of political leadership the Diet produced. The exposure of petty scandal by party members, the close ties between the parties and the zaibatsu, the relatively staid and colorless character of the party leaders, and the disorderly conduct of debate in the Diet cast a poor light on the men in the parties, if not the parliamentary system. At another level, the style of parliamentary politics

---

[1] Hamaguchi Osachi, *Zuikanroku* [Reminiscences] (Tokyo, 1931), p. 141.

itself was at odds with the political values of many Japanese. Public competition for power, overt conflict between competing interests, naked partisanship, and decision-making by the majority ran counter to the collectivist ethic deeply embedded in Japanese culture. It was only natural that those raised in rural communities and nurtured by a primary school education stressing the values of selflessness, loyalty, harmony, and patriotism should often regard Diet politics with a jaundiced eye.

But quite apart from the low state of the Diet's public prestige, there was another dimension to the moral vulnerability of parliamentary politics. This was the defection of much of the intellectual community from the support of party rule during the 1920's. By the end of the decade many intellectuals were convinced that the ideals of parliamentary democracy were hypocritical cant propagated by the entrenched ruling class to rationalize its power. In part, these feelings prompted the spread of Marxism and other forms of left-wing radicalism in the student community, producing a generation of young intellectuals who were *ipso facto* opponents of the political status quo. But even more significantly these feelings led to the rejection of parliamentary politics by men who originally embraced the liberal democratic faith and held that representative government was desirable and appropriate for Japan. At precisely the moment when the liberal intellegentsia might have applauded the growing power of the Diet, they were plunged into a period of disillusionment with the parliamentary process as it operated in Japan.

The most prominent liberal defector of the 1920's was Ōyama Ikuo, an erstwhile champion of "Taishō democracy" who in 1926 became the chairman of the pro-Communist Labor-Farmer party.[2] During the early years of the Taishō period

[2] Details on Ōyama's life may be found in Kitazawa Shinjirō, Suekawa Hiroshi, and Hirano Yoshitarō, comps., *Ōyama Ikuo den* [A Biography of Ōyama Ikuo] (Tokyo, 1956); a briefer account of his personality and his activities as chairman of the Labor-Farmer party may be found in Tabei Kenji, *Ōyama Ikuo* [A Biography of Ōyama Ikuo] (Tokyo, 1947).

he fit the portrait of the genteel liberal democratic intellectual in almost every respect. As professor at Waseda University, as writer for the liberal *Ōsaka Asahi Shimbun*, and as member of the Reimeikai, he fought for the chief liberal causes of the day—parliamentary supremacy, freedom of the press, universal suffrage, academic freedom, and all the rest. One of his students recalled that with his neatly groomed hair and his pince-nez, he even looked a bit like Woodrow Wilson. By the late 1920's, however, he cut quite a different figure. The diffident professor, who once wore white gloves to the theater every Sunday, became the eloquent and rousing leader of the Labor-Farmer party. In place of the pince-nez appeared a set of less "bourgeois" horn rim glasses, and beneath his coat he wore a bullet-proof vest sewn into cloth for him by his wife to protect him from rightist attack.[3] On the public platform, he traded his advocacy of democratic liberalism for a strident attack on party rule, on the society which supported it, and on the democratic theory he himself had once championed.

In many ways, Ōyama's transformation from Taishō democrat to Shōwa radical was exceptional, but in its general outline his spiritual odyssey reflects the experience of many in his generation. It also tells much about the chronic crisis of legitimacy that party government faced by the late 1920's. If those most committed to parliamentary democracy found it difficult to sustain their faith once the parties achieved hegemony, it must have been all the more so for the uncommitted to find this faith persuasive.

The Frustration of Ōyama's Early Liberalism

Ōyama's political career can be understood only if one realizes that he was moved by a profound sense of frustration. Like most of the intellectuals of his day, Ōyama found himself in a political world which he felt wanting in many respects, but which he had little power to change. During the earliest phase of modern Japanese political history, the relation be-

[3] Kitazawa et al., *op.cit.*, appendix entitled, "Ōyama Sensei no omoide" [Ōyama the Teacher], pp. 3-4, 34.

tween political ideas and political involvement had been intimate. To borrow Richard Hofstader's characterization of Revolutionary America, early Meiji Japan was "an unspecialized
and versatile age" in which men of ideas were frequently men
of action.[4] The intellectual fired by a new vision of politics
could become a political activist either as a reform-minded
official in the new government or as a participant in the *jiyū-
minken* movement. It was only the rare intellectual like Fukuzawa who tried to stay aloof from practical politics. By the
early twentieth century, however, it was no longer easy to
move from a life of political reflection or criticism to a life
of political action. The bureaucrat was recruited through the
civil service system, and the party politician through wealth
or personal patronage. With few exceptions, the touter of political ideas, particularly if he were an academic, had to settle for
the role of outsider.

The sense of frustration at being a political outsider was
heightened by profound disappointment at the way the country had developed since the Meiji Restoration. For Ōyama, the
slogans of Meiji politics had lost their appeal, and politics
seemed to have lost a clear sense of direction. The pursuit of
"national wealth and strength," the implicit goal of most Japanese, including the intelligentsia, during the Meiji period no
longer struck a responsive chord. Tokutomi Sohō mournfully
commented on the mood of Ōyama's generation when he
noted in 1916 that the "one great root of the present troubles
of the empire is the lack of national ideals and the lack of
popular ideals."[5] A generation which had seen Japan achieve
diplomatic equality with the West and enter the ranks of the
great powers could no longer be animated by a sense of foreign threat. Rather, it feared that despite Japan's entry into the
ranks of the powers, the country was once again in danger of

[4] Richard Hofstader, *Anti-Intellectualism in American Life* (New
York, 1963), p. 145.
[5] Quoted in Sumiya Mikio, "Kokuminteki vijion no tōgō to bunkai"
[Unity and Diversity in the National Vision] in *Kindai Nihon
shisōshi kōza* [Lectures on Modern Japanese Thought], V, 14.

lagging behind. The pace of change had slowed down, and the forces of conservatism had begun to reassert themselves. No matter how much foreigners might praise Japan for her "miraculous progress," Ōyama once pointed out, they were comparing her with other non-Western countries and not with themselves. The Japanese, who by contrast measured themselves by Western standards, were "vexed and impatient at the slowness and lameness of [Japan's] progress."[6]

The most obvious area of lag was in the functioning of constitutional politics. The rapid changes of the Meiji period had failed to liberate the Japanese people from the "spirit of passivity and submissiveness" nurtured by centuries of authoritarian rule. The Restoration had made a break with the past, but it had not been the work of an aroused people. The overthrow of the Bakufu, the restoration of sovereignty to the emperor, the abolition of feudalism, and the granting of social equality to all classes "were not the result of demands of the people" but of the "xenophile spirit of those in power." The same was true of the establishment of liberal institutions. "The movement for constitutional government was spawned by those who had lost out in the struggle for power, and not by the irresistible beliefs of the people as a whole; consequently, even though the constitution was promulgated and the representative system put into effect, the people were taught to respect it with no reason, and they had no real motive to respect it. . . ."[7] The Japanese constitution, unlike those of the West, was not "dyed with the blood of revolutionary martyrs, but rather was born without difficulty from the fusion of those above with those below."[8] There had been no 1789 in Japan, nor even a 1688.

[6] Ōyama, "Gendai Nihon ni okeru seijiteki shinka to sono shakaiteki haikei" [Political Progress and Its Social Background in Contemporary Japan], Chūō Kōron (hereafter referred to as CK), XXXIII:1, 17-18.

[7] Ōyama, "Seitōkai no kinjō to wagakuni kensei no zento" [Recent Trends in Political Parties and the Future of Constitutional Government], CK, XXXII:2, 5-6.

[8] Ōyama, "Seiji to seikatsu" [Politics and Livelihood], Ōyama Ikuo zenshū [The Complete Works of Ōyama Ikuo] (hereafter referred to as Zenshū; Tokyo, 1948), IV, 119-20.

Lacking the experience of a popular revolution, habits of popular submissiveness and authoritarian elitism persisted beneath the facade of modern politics.

When he looked about him, Ōyama saw much in the world of politics that flowed from this fundamental failure of Meiji modernization. The most striking aspect was the continued influence of an authoritarian elite—the oligarchs, the hanbatsu, and the bureaucracy—who arrogated to themselves the right to control the government, and who shaped national policy with a high-handed disregard for public opinion. Bureaucratic machinations, rather than public debate, still dominated the government despite the promulgation of the constitution and the establishment of the Diet. Like the rest of the Taishō liberals, Ōyama deplored what Yoshino Sakuzō once called "the politics of the secret chamber" (*anshitsu seiji*).[9]

Had Ōyama lived in the 1880's and 1890's, he might have held out hope that power over the government would be wrested from this privileged elite by forces outside it. By the beginning of the Taishō period, however, it was clear that the political parties and the people themselves were neither powerful enough nor interested enough to do so. In contrast to the first generation of Japanese liberals, men like Ōyama found it hard to regard the political parties as the representatives of an aroused public opinion. "While the parties say they represent the will of the people, their actions usually betray the people's demands," he wrote in 1917. "The parties insist they always subordinate their own partisan interests to the public interest of the state, but what they do does not always accord with what they say."[10]

What roused Ōyama's suspicion of the parties was the "politics of compromise" that had characterized them since the

[9] For a sample of this liberal hostility toward the genro and the bureaucracy, see the symposium entitled "Minshū no seiryoku ni yotte jikyoku o kaisen to suru fūchō o ronzu" [The Masses and the Current Political Situation], *CK*, XXIX:4.

[10] Ōyama, "Wagakuni kensei no zento" [The Future of Constitutional Government in Japan], *CK*, XXXII:2, 19-20.

1890's. Though forever crying out for the "destruction of han-batsu politics," the parties were always ready to dally with the hanbatsu when an occasion presented itself. Particularly dis-appointing was the failure of the "Movement for Constitu-tional Government" in 1912-13. In Ōyama's view, though the movement had been buoyed up by long suppressed indigna-tion at hanbatsu interference in politics, the political parties (and the Seiyūkai in particular) had cynically betrayed this protest by striking yet another bargain with a member of the hanbatsu. Aside from creating "two gods of constitutional gov-ernment," he commented bitterly, the movement had little effect.[11]

Equally discouraging was the indifference of the mass of the people toward their government. Unlike the student radicals of the early 1920's, Ōyama did not romanticize the role of the people in Japanese politics. He was too well aware of the real-ities of Japanese society. "The majority of the people of Japan," he wrote in 1916, "probably don't even think they are entrust-ing responsibility for domestic politics and foreign policy to those in office. The idea of a 'public trust' in politics has not become an issue for them. . . . They do not think politics has anything to do with them . . . politics does not shape the content of their lives."[12] Save for idle curiosity or occasional outbursts of indignation (such as the "Movement for Consti-tutional Government"), the people remained detached from political involvement. When they did become involved their tactics were not always desirable. The violence and frenzy of popular demonstrations was for Ōyama, as it was for liberals like Yoshino Sakuzō and Nagai Ryūtarō, not a hopeful sign that the democratic impulse was at work, but rather a symp-tom of the unhealthy state of Japanese politics.[13] Riots were

[11] Ōyama, "Seijiteki shinka to sono shakaiteki haikei," *CK*, XXXIII:1, 12-13.
[12] Ōyama, "Seiji to seikatsu," *Zenshū*, IV, 113.
[13] "Minshū no seiryoku ni yotte jikyoku o kaisen to suru fūchō o ronzu," *CK*, XXIX:4.

dangerous, and no substitute for the involvement of the people as citizens in the government of their country.

Ōyama's appraisal of the political condition of Japan did not lead him to despair, however. His early writings were infused with a strong sense that change and improvement were possible. He was not willing to ascribe the "low level" of constitutional government in Japan to "national character," as some conservative political commentators did. Nor was he willing to accept the determinist, or what he called the materialist, position that the Japanese could not transcend their cultural environment. Rather, he constantly affirmed the power of the creative human impulse as a motor force in the development of society. Unless men could reconstruct or recreate their environment, there would be no such thing as progress. "Contemporary man, because he knows that environment dominates the life of mankind, attempts to reconstruct the old environment or build a new one. The wellsprings of his spirit lie in his attempt to make society better and more beautiful than the society of the past and to make the society of the future even better than the society of the present. . . ."[14] As long as one held that men could change their society, there was no need to lose hope.

Ōyama's formula for constructive change was a program of democratic reform. Like Yoshino Sakuzō, with whom he shared laurels as a representative of the "new political thought," Ōyama held that the best remedy for Japan's political ills was to bring the people into politics and to bring politics closer to the people. His message was a simple one. The "spirit of constitutional government," he said, was government by consent. At times he described this in traditional terms as the "ideal of joint rule by the people and the sovereign" (*kunmin dōchi*) or "the joint operation of the state by the people." But, more frequently, borrowing the language of Anglo-American liberal thought, he spoke of it as the "principle of political equality of opportunity" or simply "political liberty."

[14] Ōyama, "Wagakuni kensei no zento," *CK*, XXXII:2, 7.

Translated into institutional terms, this meant for Ōyama, as
it did for Yoshino, the election of public officials by a broad
electorate, the establishment of legislative control over the
machinery of administration, and the formation of Cabinets
responsible to popularly elected representatives. All of these
ideals he repeatedly pointed out, were compatible with efficient government, strong and able national leadership, and a
sense of national unity.[15]

To bring constitutional politics in Japan closer to democratic
practice, Ōyama insisted on the need for gradualism rather
than revolution. He took the constitutional structure as a given,
and sought to hasten changes through the mechanisms it provided. As he frequently pointed out, constitutional government
gave Japan the means for making political progress without
recourse to a "disgraceful baptism of blood." Revolution was
"a most abhorrent thing," perhaps appropriate for countries
like Russia, but inappropriate for Japan where "respect and
veneration for the imperial house was an unshakeable belief
of the people."[16] To achieve democracy in Japan it was not
necessary to dismantle the whole political system, but only to
remove certain obstacles to the proper functioning of the constitution.

His commitment to the tactics of moderation, however,
meant that the political parties, which he so frequently dis-
paraged, were to be the main vehicle for reform. This posed
no obstacle for he felt that the parties could act "as a kind of
broker to transmit the feelings and the will of the people to
the government." The problem was to promote the "healthy
development" of the political parties. "The people should use
the parties, not be used by them. The people should make the

[15] Ōyama, "Seiji to seikatsu," *Zenshū*, IV, 122-27; "Demokurashii no
seijitetsugakuteki igi" [Democracy as a Political Philosophy], *ibid.*,
pp. 48-63.
[16] Ōyama, "Sekai no minshukateki keikō to Rokoku no kakumei"
[Democratic Trends in the World and the Russian Revolution], *CK*,
XXXII:4, 102ff.

parties the servants of the public. . . ."[17] Ōyama was confident that this could be done because, unlike the genrō, the hanbatsu, and the bureaucracy, the parties could be checked by "the great weapon called the right to vote."[18] The extension of the franchise was therefore the first and most important step toward reform. It would not only make the parties more responsive to the people, but it would also make possible the "education of the people in citizenship."[19] By the end of World War I, Ōyama, like the rest of the liberal intelligentsia, felt that universal suffrage held the key to the eventual democratization of Japan.

Despite his pessimism about the immediate situation in Japan, Ōyama's early essays were suffused with a long-run optimism that democracy would someday triumph in Japan. "The spirit of the age," he wrote, "is the democratization of politics. . . . Just as an individual cannot safely go counter to the opinions of society, neither can any country advance ignoring the spirit of the age."[20] In part this optimism was nurtured by the events of the day. The collapse of the Russian monarchy, the victory of the Allied powers in World War I, and the emergence of republican regimes in Austria and Hungary had convinced him that popular government was the wave of the future. It is equally important, however, that he also seems to have felt that a trend toward democratization was an element inherent in the character of industrial civilization. The spread of education and the development of closer communication within a country led to the gradual

[17] Ōyama, "Wagakuni kensei no zento," *CK*, XXXII:2, 19-22; "Yo ga yūkensha naraba" [If I Were Voting], *CK*, XXXII:3, 65-66.

[18] *Ibid.*, p. 66.

[19] Ōyama, "Kome sōdo no shakaiteki oyobi seijiteki kōsatsu" [A Political and Social Study of the Rice Riot], *CK*, XXXIII:10, 90-92.

[20] Ōyama, "Seiji shisō no konton jidai" [An Era of Confused Political Philosophy], *CK*, XXXII:11, 11-12.

levelling of differences among men in society.[21] In either case, he seemed to suggest that democracy was part of the "trend of the times."

Such optimism, though it doubtless comforted Ōyama, was hardly sufficient to convince others of the need to democratize Japanese politics. It was one thing to say that democracy was "the spirit of the age" or the "trend of the times," but quite another to say it was a good thing. What is inevitable is not always desirable. Indeed, there were many in Japan who regarded the advance of democracy throughout the world not as a sign of hope but as a sign that civilization was degenerating. Moreover, if the "trend of the times" changed or there emerged a new "spirit of the age," how could democracy stand proof against them? It was inevitable that Ōyama tried to justify political democracy as a positive good in itself.

Ōyama knew that many of the arguments advanced by early liberal democratic theory in the West did not apply to the Japanese case. He could not rely on the comforting theory of prescriptive rights ("rights as Englishmen" or "rights as free men") which often justified the extension of political liberties in the Anglo-American tradition. As he repeatedly pointed out, the mass of the Japanese people had not enjoyed "liberties" based on a long and complex historical development, and it was precisely this lack of a tradition of freedom that accounted for the "low level" of constitutional politics in Japan. At the same time, democratic theories based on the concept of natural rights or the myth of a primitive social contract were historically unverifiable, and hence empirically suspect. Indeed, Ōyama specifically dismissed such notions as "empty catchwords" or "idle theories" not worthy of serious consideration.

In the absence of other grounds for defending the value of

---

[21] Ōyama, "Seiji o shihai suru seishinryoku" [Politics and Spiritual Power], *Zenshū*, IV, 63-96; "Konji seihen no yūin, keika, oyobi kiketsu ni kansuru kōsatsu" [An Observation on Recent Political Change], *CK*, XXXIII:2, 39-40.

democracy, Ōyama chose to argue that democratic politics could be brought to the service of national unity and social harmony. At first, he suggested that democratic politics promoted the national spirit. Here he was doubtless pointing to the lessons of the European conflict. The people could not be expected to make sacrifices for the state, to give their lives for it and to pay taxes to it, unless they had some stake in political society. Democracy, by extending the right of participation and control to the people, strengthened their commitment to the state and its purposes. Democracy, in short, could be brought to the service of nationalism.[22] At other times, he suggested that democracy could promote social solidarity. In any society, he argued, there were two conflicting pressures at work—one the impulse of some men to dominate their fellows, and the other the need for all men to live together in harmony. The democratic mechanism, by reconciling these two necessities, prevented society from being plunged into a state of perpetual conflict.[23] Finally, toward the end of World War I, after the outbreak of rice riots in Japan, and more particularly after the October Revolution in Russia, Ōyama stressed the value of democratization as a barrier to the spread of radical ideas in Japan. For pragmatic reasons, as well as theoretical ones, it was urgent that the government undertake a program of social reform and democratization lest the people turn toward political extremism.[24] Only if Japan were democratized could the wounds of discontent be salved and the "privileged classes" and the common people live side by side in harmony.

The theme of social solidarity was the leitmotiv of most of

[22] Ōyama, "Demokurashii no seijitetsugakuteki igi," *Zenshū*, IV, 60-63.

[23] "Kensei sanjūnen no emono" [Progress during Thirty Years of Constitutional Government], *CK*, XXXIII:3.

[24] Ōyama, "Rokoku kagekiha no jisseiryoku ni taisuru kashōshi to sono seiji shisō no kachi ni taisuru kadaishi" [The Underestimation of the Power of the Russian Bolsheviks and the Overestimation of Their Political Ideology], *CK*, XXXIII:5, 1-16; "Kome sōdō no shaka-iteki oyobi seijiteki kōsatsu," *CK*, XXXIII:10, 77-92.

the Taishō liberals in their defense of democracy. Fukuda Tokuzō spoke of the need for a "true democracy" that would promote social stability through social justice for all classes in society, and Yoshino Sakuzō argued in favor of universal suffrage in order to give the people some stake in their political society.[25] This kind of appeal struck a harmonious chord with the residual Confucian ideas that permeated the political milieu, but it was different from the oligarchs' cry for "national unity" *vis-à-vis* the outside world, or the touting of "familistic solidarity" by social conservatives who conceived of Japan as "one great family." It recognized that social and political discontent could not be swept under the rug by appeals to patriotism or nostalgia for traditional values. Rather, it rested on the classical liberal argument that society would fly apart if it did not provide institutional outlets for discontent. At the same time, it also rested on a feeling that the claims of the individual were as important as those of the collectivity. Ultimately solidarity was possible only if the individual members of society felt they were getting their just deserts. The interests of the whole society were best served by recognizing the interest of its parts.

Ultimately this view rested on the assumptions that the reconciliation of conflicting interests in society was possible, and that the state was a neutral organ which would serve to mediate between such conflicting interests. As long as these assumptions remained unchallenged, the achievement of social harmony and stability through political democratization remained a likely prospect. But what if these assumptions proved incorrect? What if the "privileged classes" refused to make concessions to the people? What if the various interests in society proved irreconcilable? What if social conflict proved to be a permanent aspect of society rather than a passing phenomenon

[25] Sumiya Etsuji et al., comp., *Taishō demokurashii no shisō* [Taishō Democratic Thought] (Tokyo, 1967), pp. 140-48; Yoshino Sakuzō, *Yoshino Sakuzō Hakushi no minshushugi ronshū* [Collected Essays on Democracy by Yoshino Sakuzō] (Tokyo, 1948), II, 328-32.

which could be overcome by changing the rules of politics?
What if social revolution was inevitable? It was on questions
such as these that Ōyama's faith in the parliamentary process
began to founder.

Ōyama's Discovery of "Social Science"

Ōyama's belief that Japanese politics could be regenerated
through moderate democratic reform, the extension of the suffrage, and the establishment of party Cabinets did not long
survive the end of World War I. His "simple and vague cry
for democracy," as one young intellectual described it, began
to ring false.[26] Ōyama's disillusionment with the promise of
democratic reform sprang from his confrontation with class
antagonism in Japanese society. Before 1919 or so, Ōyama
tended to see politics in terms of the individual pitted against
the state or the "people" pitted against the "privileged classes."
These divisions within society, however, were political and
therefore could be dealt with by political means. But the
heightening of working class unrest at the end of the war left
Ōyama with the feeling that the capitalist economy produced
much more fundamental social cleavages.

Ōyama's view of class antagonism was neither very complex
nor very sophisticated. In his writings after 1918 he began to
draw a conventional contrast between "labor" and "capital,"
the "haves" and the "have nots," or the "bourgeoisie" and the
"proletariat." Such an array of terms suggests that his discovery of class differences was not Marxist in inspiration, but
simply reflected his observation of postwar social unrest. What
is significant about his discovery of class difference is that he
felt the gap between the classes was not merely political, but
involved styles of life as well. He drew the contrast between
the "haves" and the "have nots" in rather stark terms:

The present society is a paradise for the bourgeoisie just as
it is. In their eyes it is a rose-colored world. They have a

[26] Murofusa Takanobu, "Kaizō ron no ichinen" [On Democratic
Reform], *CK*, XXXIV:12, 50-52.

government that protects them, a Diet which represents them, a home which is the object of their affection, and a family to which they are fondly attached. In this society they can enjoy a rich life, they can receive the education they hope for, and they can have good health, enjoyment and love. By contrast, the present society is for the proletariat like a bleak plain, sere with winter. The government does not protect them, nor does the Diet represent them, and the whole of the good life which the bourgeoisie enjoy is denied to them. . . .[27]

The bourgeoisie, in short, benefitted as much from the existing social arrangements as the proletariat was alienated by them.

This social status quo aroused Ōyama's moral indignation because it violated the principle of equality to which he was so attached. From the end of the war on he began to fulminate about the "corruption" and "decadence" of bourgeois society. What he meant was not personal immorality or hedonism, but a pervasive social hypocrisy. The "culture of the bourgeoisie," though it touted the ideals of freedom and equality, was in fact based on the assumption of inequality, or as he put it, on a "sense of distinction" (*sabetsukan*). It was also manifestly unjust. The leisure class enjoyed most of the benefits of society, while the producing classes enjoyed very few. There was a radical imbalance in the distribution of rewards for purposive work and constructive activity. Any society where the leisure class dominated the productive class was topsy-turvy.[28]

The political implication of his new view of society were obvious. Just as it was no longer possible for him to think of Japanese society as a seamless web, so it was no longer possible to regard "national" politics as involving the whole na-

[27] Ōyama, "Minshū bunka no kisū to kyōiku" [The Future of Popular Culture and Education], *Zenshū*, IV, 333-34.
[28] Ōyama, "Rōdō mondai no bunkateki igi" [The Cultural Significance of Labor Problems], *Zenshū*, III, 289-92; "Minshū bunka no sekai e" [Toward a Popular Culture], *CK*, XXXV:1, 67-93.

tion. It was now clear to Ōyama that the politics of the Diet
were really the "politics of the capitalists." Political privilege
rested not simply on historical accident, but on economic
power. The defects of Japanese politics arose not from the residual strength of the hanbatsu nor from the weight of an authoritarian past. Rather, they were an expression of the control over
the Diet by the capitalists, the big landowners, and the aristocracy. The "politics of compromise," and all that they implied,
resulted from the alliance of these elements with the bureaucracy to defend their economic interests. The Diet was not an
instrument for dynamic change, but a buttress for the social
status quo.[29]

None of these themes in Ōyama's writings were strikingly
original. Many of his fellow liberals recognized the emergence
of class antagonism and also shared his feelings about the politics of the Diet and social injustice. What was peculiar to
Ōyama was that his discovery of social divisiveness did not
merely arouse his concern but led to a profound questioning
of his original assumptions about the nature of politics. Men
like Yoshino, who felt that social divisiveness could be rem-
edied within the framework of constitutional politics, continued to advocate measures to assure the "harmony of labor and
capital" and to enlarge the popular element of politics through
constitutional reform,[30] but Ōyama found this kind of discussion irrelevant. He began to feel that his earlier espousal of
democratic methods had rested on wishful thinking. He began
to feel that he had been talking about how politics *ought* to be,
and hence how he *wanted* them to be, rather than about how
politics *were*. Gradually turning away from such a "subjective"

[29] Ōyama, "Shakai-keizairyoku no hyōgen to shite no genjitsu seiji"
[Politics as the Expression of Social and Economic Forces], *Zenshū*,
IV, 139-69.

[30] Cf. *Kindai Nihon shisōshi kōza* [Lectures on Modern Japanese
Thought], I, 196-98, 200-203; Matsumoto Sannosuke, *Kindai Nihon no
seiji to ningen* [Politics and Men in Modern Japan] (Tokyo, 1966),
pp. 164-71.

and "sentimental" approach to politics, he sought instead to formulate a "scientific theory of politics," which would explain the fact of social and political inequality.[31]

The main influence which pushed Ōyama in this direction was his acquaintance with the Austrian school of sociology founded by Ludwig Gumplowicz and developed by his disciples Gustav Ratzenhofer and Franz Oppenheimer. While a student at the University of Chicago, Ōyama had come under the influence of two American adherents of this school, Lester Ward and Albion W. Small. Although its influence on Ōyama's thought had remained dormant during the early years of the Taishō period, by the early 1920's two aspects of this school seemed particularly relevant to him. One was its confident positivistic assumption that there were "social laws" or "social theorems" that could explain human social behavior. The other was its stress on conflict as the chief motor of social change and social evolution. Just as many younger men began to be attracted by the "scientific" character of Marxism in the early 1920's, Ōyama found in the Austrian school, as modified by the American optimism of Ward, an explanation of politics that was neither sentimental nor "metaphysical." His own sociology of politics leaned heavily on its tenets.[32]

At the base of Ōyama's political theory was the view that the evolution of human society was governed by "the social law of group struggle." Society was not an agglomeration of individ-

[31] Ōyama, "Seiji no shakaiteki kiso" [The Social Basis of Politics], *Zenshū*, I, 28-29.

[32] The most complete statement of Ōyama's sociological theory of politics is to be found in *ibid*. Amplifications of this theory may also be found in "Gendai Nihon no seiji katei" [The Political Process in Modern Japan], *Zenshū*, II, 1-152; and "Seijigaku genri no kaizō" [Changing Principles in Political Science], *ibid*., pp. 287-330. The theory has been summarized in Rōyama Masamichi, *Nihon ni okeru kindai seijigaku no hattatsu* [The Development of Modern Political Science in Japan] (Tokyo, 1949), pp. 137-50; Tabei, *op.cit.*, pp. 103-133; *Shakaigaku to Waseda Daigaku* [Sociology at Waseda University], pp. 77-91.

uals, as he had tended to think during his discussions of democracy, but rather was made up of competing groups, each tied together by a set of common interests, usually, though not invariably, of a material or economic character. In order to maintain itself intact each social group had to defend these interests, and since these interests often contradicted or infringed on the interests of others, each social group regarded every other as its enemy. In such a situation, social harmony, in either the Confucian or the liberal sense, was not possible. The chronic state of society was incessant social conflict or social struggle, which could be resolved only by the victory of one group over another. The struggle, in short, was Darwinian rather than Hobbesian, for it ended not with a social contract but with the triumph of the strong over the weak.

It was the triumph of one group over another that accounted for the origins of both political authority and social inequality. The victors in the struggle sought to establish their power over the losers in some institutional form. The result was the state, an "organization of power" that enabled "the stronger group to exploit the weaker economically." In primitive societies the establishment of political authority was accomplished by the simple conquest of one group by another, but in modern societies it took a subtler form. Legislation and law were substituted for physical force or conquest in maintaining the authority of the dominant social group. In either case, it was clear that the state was not a neutral organ to satisfy the interests of all or to mediate between interests, but rather an instrument for sustaining the interest of one social group at the expense of all the others.

This view of the state implied that politics was an extension of the social hostility and struggle inherent in any society, and conversely, that all social struggle found political expression. At base, politics was neither "the art of the state" nor "the adjustment of the means to the ends in the achievement of national policy." Rather, it was the struggle to seize power or political authority, either by covert or overt means, in order to perpetuate the interests of a particular group. Moreover, since the interests of one group were usually irreconcilable with the interests of other groups, political struggle took as its goal absolute victory rather than compromise or conciliation. Politics was therefore a kind of dialectical process. It sprang from the "group action of human beings, working affirmatively (defensively) or negatively (destructively) toward a certain fixed social organization or social order that takes as its goal control of society according to some fixed principle."[33] Implicitly, of course, the "fixed principle" would be the perpetuation of a particular set of group interests.

This view of politics was potentially relativistic. In Ōyama's theory it was possible to speak neither of fixed political forms nor of fixed political goals, since both were determined by the nature of the social group in control of the state and by the nature of those who opposed it. The only constant principle was the fact of struggle itself. Hence Ōyama freed himself of attachment to any particular set of institutions, democratic or otherwise. This implicit relativism was checked, however, by his passionate concern for the politics of his day. His analysis of the "social principles" that governed politics was not intended as an end in itself. His separation of political science or "social science" from discussions of political morality did not mean that he felt political action was aimless or that politics had been drained of its ethical content. On the contrary, he felt quite the opposite.

In Ōyama's mind what distinguished "social science" from idle speculation or abstract theorizing about society and the state was its applicability. It was the "practicality" of science that gave it value for human life. This was no less true for the study of society than it was for the study of nature. Like natural science, social science had its technology and though the applicability of this technology was not as great as that of

[33] Ōyama, "Musan kaikyū seitō no shakai shinkajō no igi" [The Significance of Proletarian Parties in Social Progress], *Zenshū*, IV, 198.

natural science, it could nonetheless establish an important link between thought and action. "Social science," he wrote, "provides knowledge about the facts of group processes and from these assembled facts reveals social principles. If it hopes to have some degree of social effectiveness, social philosophy must take as its role the discovery of goals for the ordering and controlling of the group process on the basis of this knowledge and these facts."[34] Theory and action were to be unified. Social science was to be a tool in promoting social change.

This belief in the applicability of social science meant that Ōyama did not have to adopt complete neutrality in the politics of his own day. On the contrary, it meant that he could act with great confidence in the "practicality" of his political involvement, for he was now armed with the certainty that came with "science." He felt he was guided not by a moralistic or sentimental theory, but rather by "social laws" derived from hard cold fact. However naive or spurious his scientism may seem to us, there is no question that Ōyama felt his thought and action rested on far steadier empirical grounds than his earlier advocacy of democratic reform. At the same time, "social science" suggested to him that parliamentary democracy, far from being a final doctrine, was rather a temporary phase of history. It merely marked the political ascendancy of the capitalist class. Intellectually, therefore, Ōyama had prepared himself for action outside the framework of conventional parliamentary politics. The problem remained, however, to find some satisfactory route for such action.

The Attraction of the Proletarian Party Movement

While he was formulating his "sociology of politics," Ōyama had been gradually drifting toward political activism. He was prominent in most of the liberal protest movements of the late Taishō period. In 1919 he became a member of the Reimeikai,

[34] Ōyama, "Gendai Nihon no seiji katei," *Zenshū*, II, 110-11.

organized by Yoshino Sakuzō and Fukuda Tokuzō to combat repressive government policies and reactionary ideas through public debate. In the years that followed he took to the public platform for a variety of liberal causes—the defense of Morito Tatsuo, the protest against the introduction of military training at the university, the movement against the passage of the Law for the Control of Radical Social Movements, the protest against the invasion of the Waseda campus by police during the first round-up of Communist party members in 1923, and so forth.[35] But all these efforts were largely defensive, directed against encroachments on freedom of thought and expression. They were not aimed at remaking Japanese politics and society, which was Ōyama's more basic concern.

Ever since the end of the war, Ōyama had spoken of the need for a rapprochement between the "intellectuals" and the mass of the people. At first he had seen the intellectual in the role of the impartial expert, perhaps like Yoshino's notion of the *tetsujin seijika*, able to stand above party and above class, yet willing to share his knowledge with the masses in order that they could better judge their own rulers. The intellectual had to be an instrument of enlightenment who would keep the uninformed or ignorant masses from disintegrating into "mobocracy."[36] But with his growing feeling that the cleavage between labor and capital was irretrievable, Ōyama began to see the intellectual not as a detached observer, but as a man inevitably involved in the class struggle. The intellectuals, he wrote, "have some degree of knowledge about society, consequently have some understanding of contemporary social problems, and accordingly are in a position to exercise some degree of influence on the fate of the society to which they belong. . . ."[37] They would have to exercise this influence

[35] On Ōyama's activism in the early 1920's, see Kitazawa et al., *op.cit.*, pp. 90-127.

[36] Ōyama, "Genka no waga seikai no katsuga" [A Vivid View of Our Present Day Political World], *CK*, XXXIII:2, 92-96.

[37] Ōyama, "Chishiki kaikyū to rōdōsha" [The Intelligentsia and the Laborer], *Zenshū*, III, 281-82.

either on the side of capital, the exploiting minority, or on the side of labor, the exploited majority. Neutrality was impossible since the failure of the intellectuals to act worked invariably to the advantage of the capitalists. Not surprisingly, Ōyama felt that the intellectuals should cast their "deciding vote" in favor of the working classes, who could become the motive force for building a new culture to replace the "decadent bourgeois culture."[38]

Ōyama was, however, at a loss to know what tactics to pursue. For all the vehemence of his attacks on the parties and "bourgeois culture," he was not quite able to abandon his attachment to the parliamentary mechanism. On the contrary, he remained conspicuously resistant to what he later called "easy solutions" to the problems of the plight of the "have nots." Though his own frustration with the parliamentary process as it operated in Japan made him sympathetic to the anarcho-syndicalist "rejection of politics," he could not agree that the only alternative was the extraparliamentary tactics of "direct action." His goal was not to destroy the state, but to rescue it from the monopoly of the privileged few.[39]

At the same time, however, he lost nearly all hope that the political parties might become an instrument of political reform. He began to feel that they were no more inclined to meet the needs of the people than "bureaucratic government" had been. The Hara Cabinet, the first party government since 1898, was not only unresponsive to demands for social legislation, but it also rejected the universal manhood suffrage bill in 1920 and dissolved the Diet on the issue. Indeed, the failure of universal suffrage sparked Ōyama to make increasingly virulent attacks on the parties. Although he had once thought their position not very different from his own, he now held

[38] *Ibid.*, p. 283; see also Ōyama, "Chishiki kaikyū no jikaku" [The Awakening of the Intellectual Class], *Zenshū*, III, 351-69.

[39] Ōyama, "Seiji no hitei no keikō" [A Tendency Toward Anarchism], *Zenshū*, IV, 170-81.

them in the same contempt he had once reserved for the hanbatsu bureaucrats. He wrote that he did not even feel like casting his "sacred vote" in the 1920 election.[40]

In taking this stand, Ōyama was caught in a poignant dilemma. He could neither accept the idea of working through the "established" political parties, nor could he accept the idea of working outside the parliamentary framework. About all he could do was to insist lamely on the need for universal suffrage without much conviction that it would be passed.

Ōyama was rescued from this dilemma by the organization of the proletarian party movement, which grew out of the Political Problems Study Association in 1924. Unlike the Reimeikai, which had no program of political action beyond the diffusion of ideas, the proletarian party movement came to grips with the question of how to organize a political party that would attract the support of the mass electorate created by the passage of universal suffrage. For Ōyama, as for most of the frustrated liberal intellectuals of the early 1920's who rejected the politics of the established parties, the proletarian party movement represented a "force to cleanse the corrupt and stagnant atmosphere of the present political world" and a "force to overcome the heavy feelings of ennui that are rampant in the political world."[41] Moreover, it offered an opportunity to act, not simply talk, about politics—to move from "the study to the streets," in the conventional phrase of the times.

Ōyama took a more radical view of the proletarian party movement than other liberal intellectuals. Although he continued to resist the idea of social revolution, his commitment to parliamentary tactics was placed in a rather different perspective from that of the days when he had advocated parlia-

[40] Ōyama, "Gikai no kaisan o ronjite" [The Dissolution of the Diet], *CK*, XXXV:4, 75-94.

[41] Ōyama, "Shin seiji ishiki no hassei to musan seitō no zento" [The Rise of a New Political Consciousness and the Future of Proletarian Parties], *Zenshū*, IV, 245.

mentary supremacy, an expansion of the suffrage, and responsible Cabinets. Having formulated his sociology of politics, he no longer regarded parliamentary institutions as important *per se*. The Diet was a battleground for social struggle, not an instrument for representing the people, and certainly not a means of achieving social solidarity. The proletarian party movement was therefore not simply an alternative to the "established parties," but part of the evolutionary "struggle of social groups." The immediate goal of the movement might be to secure representation of the "proletarian" class in the Diet, but its ultimate end would be the "reconstruction of society" in accord with the social views and interests of the proletarian class. In pursuing this struggle, moreover, the proletarian class need not confine its struggles to the Diet. Depending on the circumstances, it might also resort to "economic action," such as general strikes or work stoppages, to complement parliamentary tactics.[42] The proletarian party was thus only one string in the proletariat's bow.

It should also be noted that Ōyama's position was different from that of the early Japanese Marxists as well. He did not conceive of the "proletarian class" as simply the industrial working class, or even a highly unified entity. As he defined it it was "an enormous aggregate body" made up not only of factory workers, but also of agricultural workers, independent artisans, and what might be called the middle classes. In accordance with his pluralistic conception of society, each of these groups had its own set of common interests, but in order to overthrow the domination of the "bourgeoisie" they were willing to bury their differences. Hence the proletarian party was less a class party than a broad popular front of all society's discontents working to overthrow the present social order. This would not bring an end to politics, as the Marxists suggested, since the proletarian party movement would break up once it

---

[42] Ōyama, "Musan kaikyū seitō no shakai shinkajō no igi," *Zenshū*, IV, 182-87, 190-96; "Gendai Nihon ni okeru seiji katei," *Zenshū*, II, 44-45.

had paved the way for a new stage of historical evolution,[43] but it was no less important for that.

Despite his enthusiastic involvement in the movement, Ōyama did not think that the proletarian party would have any immediate or dramatic impact on Japanese politics. He felt that its successes would come only in the future. This caution, which was shared by many other participants in the movement, rested on an appreciation of the formidable obstacles in its path. First of all, the proletarian party movement lacked the "material resources"—the money and the manpower—that the "established parties" could command. Secondly, it was clear that the "established parties," after the passage of universal suffrage, would attempt to seduce the "innocent masses" with new slogans and programs intended to appeal to their interests. Doubtless many new voters would be beguiled by these tactics. Finally, as Ōyama had long been aware, the masses were subject to a kind of "psychological oppression." In order to keep the masses under their subjection, the bourgeoisie had foisted on them views of the state, society, and the world that rationalized bourgeois domination, and in the absence of alternatives the masses had accepted these views as their own. For all these reasons, it was obvious that the proletarian party movement was not likely to dislodge the "established parties" without considerable time and effort.[44]

Given these unfavorable circumstances, it was not possible to assess the political strength of the proletarian party movement in conventional terms. How then was it to succeed? For Ōyama its hope lay in the spread of a "new political consciousness" among the masses.[45] He was never very clear as to what

[43] Ōyama, "Shin seiji ishiki no rinriteki kiso" [The Ethical Basis of the New Political Consciousness], *Zenshū*, IV, 262; "Musan kaikyū seitō no shakai shinkajō no igi," *Zenshū*, IV, 202-203.

[44] Ōyama, "Shin seiji ishiki no rinriteki kiso," *Zenshū*, IV, 256-62; "Shin seiji ishiki no hassei to musan seitō no zento," *ibid.*, pp. 234-44.

[45] Ōyama, "Seijiteki kyūseiryoku e no saisho no ichigeki" [The First Blow to the Old Political Forces], *Zenshū*, IV, 286-309.

the content of this "political consciousness" was, but it was apparently predicated on a quickened sense of the masses' common interest. It implied on the one hand a growing awareness that the "established parties" were "instruments for the political expression of the interests of the bourgeoisie," and on the other, a decline in the old attitudes of political submissiveness and passivity. The immediate tasks of the proletarian party movement were therefore as much educational as political. It had to stimulate the growth of the new "political consciousness" by fostering the "political knowledge" and "political morality" of the masses, and by propagating among them "social theory" and "social thought" that was relevant to their lives.[46] Ōyama's conception of the proletarian party was thus much closer to the Leninist party model than it was to the liberal model of a parliamentary party.

In essence, Ōyama saw the proletarian party movement as an attempt to bring about the kind of "ethical revolution" or "moral revolution" that he felt had not taken place at the time of the Restoration. He was unwilling to abandon his gradualist position that violent revolution or political revolution was not likely to occur in contemporary Japan, and that even if it did, it was not likely to have much effect without a fundamental "change in the hearts of men." Moreover, in emphasizing the need to stimulate the growth of a "new political consciousness," he was reaffirming his voluntarist view of history. The ultimate "reconstruction" of Japanese society was not to come as the result of the inexorable working out of historical circumstances, but as the result of a conscious and creative act of men committed to a goal. Indeed he even suggested that the "new political consciousness" was necessary to make the masses capable of making sacrifices for the goal of social reconstruction.

The Appeal of Marxist-Leninist Thought

Ōyama's plunge into the proletarian party movement is hardly surprising, for it was a path chosen by many of the

[46] Ōyama, "Shin seiji ishiki no rinriteki kiso," *Zenshū*, IV, 268.

frustrated liberal intelligentsia of the 1920's. What is curious about Ōyama, in contrast to the other liberals, is his association with its extreme left wing. After the split of the movement in late 1926, Ōyama became the "shining party chairman" of the left-wing Labor-Farmer party. When the party was dissolved by the government in 1928, he was active in the Labor-Farmer League for the Establishment of Political Liberty, and in 1929 he attempted to reorganize the "legal left" through the formation of the "New" Labor-Farmer party.[47] In deed, and in word, he was an active sympathizer (some would say "puppet") of the Communist party, and as a political pamphleteer his rhetoric was larded with the slogans and cliches, if not the theoretical subtleties, of Marxist-Leninist thought.

Ōyama's turn to the extreme Left had much to do with his personality. Both his friends and his enemies were later quick to point out that he was a man easily led. Characterized as an "amiable robot," a "vest-pocket Saigō," and a man "perfect as a portable shrine," he was perhaps carried to the Left as much by his followers as by conscious choice.[48] From the mid-1920's, especially as a result of involvement in the movement against military encroachments on the university, Ōyama had been drawn into close contact with the radical student movement. He was an adviser to the Student Social Science Study Association, a Marxist organization whose name had been suggested by Ōyama's own writings on "social science." Attracted by and sharing in its youthful enthusiasm, Ōyama may have become its captive. But it would be an oversimplification to attribute Ōyama's turn to the extreme Left to these causes alone, for his conversion had been prepared for by his earlier intellectual progress.

Two other factors probably pushed Ōyama to the extreme Left. The first was his disagreement with the moderate liber-

[47] See Kitazawa et al., *op.cit.*, pp. 145-238, on Ōyama's activities in the proletarian party movement.

[48] Inomata Takeshi, *Shakaishugi yawa* [Socialism] (Tokyo, 1948), pp. 85-87; Aragaki Hideo, *Sengo jimbutsu ron* [Sketches of Leading Personalities in Postwar Japan] (Tokyo, 1948), pp. 220-22.

als and social democrats on the issue of whether or not to include the extreme left wing in the organization of a "proletarian party." The moderates opposed cooperation with the radical Left first of all because they were committed to a policy of social meliorism rather than revolutionary class struggle, and secondly because they correctly surmised that to work with the Communists and the radical Left was to invite government repression. By contrast, the extreme Left, and the Communists in particular, called for the creation of a "single national unified proletarian party," apparently confident that they could control such a party from within.[49] Ōyama's conception of the proletarian party movement made him more sympathetic to the latter point of view. Since he felt that it should be an all-embracing movement which would include in its ranks all those who were discontent with the existing social and political order, he was as ready to welcome the Communists as he was the middle class. Given the already considerable advantages of the "capitalists" and the "established parties," divisiveness within the ranks of the proletarian party movement could only weaken it. Proletarian unity, in short, was more important than doctrinal niceties, and repression was a risk that the movement ran in any case.[50]

The second, and perhaps more fundamental, influence that drew Ōyama to the extreme Left, was his sociology of politics. In his discovery of "social science," Ōyama had taken a giant stride closer to Marxism than men like Yoshino, who never really broke away from the idealistic framework out of which his political theory had grown. The conviction that social laws governed social behavior, the concept of history as evolutionary conflict, the characterization of politics as struggle, the

---

[49] George O. Totten, *The Social Democratic Movement in Prewar Japan* (New Haven, Conn., 1966), pp. 56-63; Rodger Swearingen and Paul Langer, *Red Flag in Japan* (Cambridge, Mass., 1952), pp. 29-30.

[50] Ōyama, "Tan'itsu musanseitōshugi no kiki" [The Crisis in the Unified Proletarian Party Movement], *Zenshū*, III, 16-26; "Rōdōnōm-intō no tanjō to sono seijiteki kankyō" [The Birth of the Labor-Farmer Party and Its Political Background], *ibid.*, pp. 27-34.

distrust of bourgeois intransigence, the vision of a "reconstructed" society in the future—all the themes that emerged in Ōyama's thought were echoed in the Marxist-Leninist synthesis. Marxist-Leninist thought confirmed many of his ideas and did so in a way that amplified them and gave them greater system. It took but a small shift to make them his own. However, unlike many younger men who came to the study of Marxism in the 1920's while still in school or at the university, Ōyama never felt constrained to swallow the system as a whole. He had little interest in its philosophical foundations or in its economic theories. Rather, he seized on those elements in Marxist-Leninist thought that confirmed his own convictions and paid scant regard to the rest.

There were perhaps two aspects of Marxist-Leninist thought that had special appeal for Ōyama—its conception of the role of the intelligentsia and its critique of "bourgeois democracy." Both permitted the amplification and completion of earlier themes in his thought.

The Marxist-Leninist conception of the political role of the intelligentsia helped Ōyama resolve his long-standing uncertainty about the relative importance of environment and consciousness in the historical process. There was a hidden contradiction in Ōyama's thought between his belief that conscious creative action could bring about social change and his discovery of "social laws" or "social principles" that underlay the course of social evolution. Marxist-Leninist thought let him keep a foot in both the determinist and voluntarist camps. On the one hand, it permitted him to come down emphatically on the side of those who said that the emergence of class consciousness and the awakening of the proletariat to their own interests was the result of the productive process. At the same time, he could retrieve his belief in human creativity by accepting the Leninist notion that the emergence of class consciousness and of the "scientific theory" that underlay it was uneven and that its propagation would primarily be the work of a "fighting intelligentsia" whose consciousness was more acute than that

of the masses. The intelligentsia might be the "historical product of the society in which they are acting," but they were not
mindless puppets of history.[51] The Leninist formula of an activist minority provided a measure of voluntary action which
could accelerate the forces of history if not alter them.

But perhaps more important, the Marxist-Leninist transval-
uation of the concept of democracy became for Ōyama a
weapon to turn against not only his old allies but also his own
earlier intellectual positions.[52] In his original political stance,
or what he had now come to call "bourgeois political theory,"
democracy was always defined in contrast to authoritarian government or dictatorship. Democracy was considered as the
"rule of the many" versus "the rule of the few" or as the "rule
of law" versus the "arbitrary will of the sovereign." Ōyama
now realized that such distinctions were purely formalistic,
touching only on externals without penetrating to the social
realities which underlay the forms. The real distinction was
between "proletarian democracy" (or, alternatively, "true democracy") on the one hand, and absolutism or "bourgeois
democracy," on the other.

It was against the latter, since it was the more immediate
and the more deceptive enemy, that Ōyama directed most of
his criticism. The bourgeois democrat demanded both freedom
and equality, yet it was clear that neither could be achieved in
a bourgeois democracy. First of all, the bourgeois democrat
assumed the continued existence of the state, and since the
state was coercive in character, its activities were necessarily in
conflict with the claims of liberty. As long as a mechanism for
imposing a general control over the society existed, freedom
would be curtailed. Furthermore, since the bourgeois democrat stood for indirect democracy or representative government,

[51] Ōyama, "Musan seitō ron" [The Proletarian Party], *Zenshū*, III,
333-92.
[52] Ōyama's recapitulation of the Marxist-Leninist attack on "bourgeois
democracy" may be found in Ōyama Ikuo, *Taishū wa ugoku* [The
Masses on the Rise] (Tokyo, 1930), pp. 129-202.

rather than direct democracy, it would also be difficult to achieve real political equality. In theory the principle of "one man, one vote" provided for the equal participation of all in politics, and in theory the principle of majority rule insured that the masses would have a decisive role in political decisions. But in practice, since this political equality had no foundation in social and economic equality, the capitalist minority would be able to control the votes of the exploited masses through oppression, seduction, and deception. The substantive economic power of the bourgeoisie, in other words, more than out weighed the weakness of their formalistic political power.

"Bourgeois democracy" which had begun as an attack on older forms of authority was thus reduced to a myth propagated by the bourgeoisie to justify their ascendancy. "In the period of its infancy, [bourgeois] democracy gives promise of an oasis filled with the spirit of liberty, equality, and fraternity for all mankind, transcending differences of sex, race, or nationality. But in the period of its maturity, it leads the world into a bleak desert."[53] Yet all this did not mean that "true democracy" was unattainable. On the contrary, the oasis was still there, but it was to be found in the Marxist vision of a classless society rather than in the bourgeois democratic state. With the creation of a classless society, general freedom would become possible because the state would vanish and with it the system of social control; general equality would become possible because the abolition of private property would bring an end to the social and economic inequality that prevented the operation of true political equality. The formula was simple, perhaps even pat, but it was compelling, and one can understand its attraction for Ōyama. Ironically, it was in the utopian Marxist vision of the stateless and classless world that he finally found fulfillment of the ideals of democracy he had espoused a decade before.

Yet for all his acceptance of certain elements of Marxist-Leninist thought, Ōyama never joined the Communist party.

[53] *Ibid.*, p. 188.

Indeed he was forced to break with his Communist supporters in 1929 when he refused to disband the newly reorganized Labor-Farmer party. It was not for lack of sympathy with the Communists, nor was it for want of courage.[54] Rather, it was due to his firm commitment to public political action. He had begun his career as a publicist, and it was on the podium haranguing the crowd or in the study drafting programs, statements, and pronunciamentos that he found his ambiance. Despite his denunciations of "bourgeois democracy" and his fulminations against the "established parties," he was never able to convince himself that parliamentary action was completely futile. It was perhaps this quality that led Kawakami to remark that he was a "frightful optimist,"[55] for he was unwilling to believe that an underground movement and extra-parliamentary resistance were the only effective weapons the masses had at their disposal.

Because he listened to the beat of his peculiar drummer, Ōyama was left in isolation by the early 1930's. After Kawakami and others left the reorganized Labor-Farmer party for the Communist underground, Ōyama succeeded in winning a Diet seat in the election of 1930, but his party never really prospered. Because of this Ōyama finally agreed to merge with the other moderate proletarian parties to form the National Labor-Farmer Masses party in 1931. Since he did not bring enough followers to the new party to justify a position as its head or even a position of importance, he chose instead to serve as a simple "rank and file member."

A renegade to the underground Left, a radical to the social democrats, and a harborer of "dangerous thoughts" to the Right, Ōyama was faced with political impotence. It was the realization of this, perhaps coupled with concern over his personal safety and exhaustion at the futility of his efforts in the

[54] Cf. Sumiya Etsuji et al., *Shōwa no hantaisei shisō* [Anti-Establishment Thought in the Shōwa Era] (Tokyo, 1967), pp. 193-96.
[55] Kawakami Hajime, "Jijoden" [Autobiography], in *Chōsakushū* [Collected Works] (Tokyo, 1964), VI, 260.

proletarian party movement, that made him decide to remain an exile in the United States after a trip there in 1932. Ironically, when he returned to Japan fifteen years later he came as a hero. Neither broken by prison, nor compromised by "conversion" or cooperation with the war effort, he ended his days as a radical elder statesman, championing to the finish the moral refurbishment of the Japanese people.[56]

The Dilemmas of Demokurashii

The career of a man like Ōyama Ikuo is likely to trouble those American intellectuals who feel that parliamentary democracy is the best (or at least most workable and just) of all possible forms of government. Rejection of the parliamentary process for some more radical political faith almost seems a personal affront, and like most such affronts calls for an explanation that comforts the offended and belittles the offender. It is therefore tempting to dismiss Ōyama with some *ad hominem* argument. One might characterize him as a victim of the political eclecticism common to many modern Japanese intellectuals, or one might condescendingly suggest that he lacked the maturity and patience needed for the difficult task of making democratic institutions work. Such appraisals, though not without a grain of truth, are fundamentally ahistorical, for they judge Ōyama without explaining him. In evaluating his career it would be more useful to consider the problems he felt himself to be facing, for these offer a key to his political behavior and to that of many members of his generation.

One should begin by pointing out that Ōyama's interest in democracy sprang less from an attachment to parliamentary government than from an interest in the uses to which it might be put. Even during his days as champion of *demokurashii*, Ōyama had been attracted by the larger goal of reforming Japanese society. As he wrote in 1918: "The demands for

[56] Cf. W. T. deBary et al., *Sources of Japanese Tradition* (New York, 1959), pp. 840-44.

the expansion of suffrage rights and the realization of responsible government are not ends in themselves. They are demands for the means needed to put domestic politics in order."[57] Like many of his peers, he called for a Taishō Restoration that would transform Japan's internal structure just as the Meiji Restoration had transformed her relations with the outside world.[58] He wanted a "rejuvenation" of politics to slough off the political conservatism and inertia that had settled on the country as the institutional structure created by the oligarchy became the bastion of an entrenched privileged class.

Such a rejuvenation involved a twofold task. On the one hand, Ōyama felt the need for a reform of the political and social structure to conform with the principle of equality, the guiding ethos of liberal institutions. This required a transformation of the attitude of the ruling classes who were in the best position to make such reforms. On the other hand, he also felt the need for a transformation in the political attitudes and awareness of the masses themselves. The people who had accepted for so long a passive role in politics had to be made active participants in the political process. The attraction of democratic reform was that it promised to kill both birds with one stone. By extending popular control the governors would be more responsible to the governed, and the governed more responsive to the governors.

Ōyama's disillusionment with *demokurashii* grew out of his realization that the rejuvenation of the country would be difficult to accomplish within the framework of conventional Diet politics. He discovered that the political parties were too complacent to be interested in promoting major social or political change. They were interested in using the parliamentary framework to acquire political power, not in bringing about a Taishō Restoration. The promise of the political parties, which had once seemed to stand for popular interests, had long

[57] Ōyama, "Seijiteki shinka to sono shakaiteki haikei" [Political Progress and Its Social Background], *CK*, XXXIII:1, 21.
[58] *Loc.cit.*

since dissipated. Save for a handful of mavericks the party politicians were more involved in log-rolling than in mobilizing
mass political enthusiasm or in developing a coherent political
ideology. By the mid-1920s, when Ōyama's desire for political
engagement grew stronger, participation in the established political parties had little intellectual or political appeal for him.
The only alternative was to opt for some other kind of political
activism.

In pursuit of such an alternative, Ōyama was not attracted
to the role of political extremist. During the early 1920's many
intellectuals in search of an active role in politics had embraced
anarchism and Marxism, but Ōyama was not one of them.
Excessive political utopianism had no more appeal for him
than excessive political pragmatism. The failure of the anarchists and the early Marxists to make any impact on politics
confirmed these feelings. The difficulty with men who took
such radical positions was that their enthusiasm outran their
capacity for rational calculation. Political action could not be
sustained by "boldness without forethought" or "enthusiasm
without reflection."[59] It had to be based on analysis and insight into the actual workings of society. Political action had
to be governed by the head as well as the heart.

The proletarian party movement, to which Ōyama committed himself with such enthusiasm, seemd to offer such a
route for political action. It sought achievable goals, yet it was
not enmired in the politics of compromise. Those who joined
it could act effectively without sacrificing their ideals or their
hopes for concrete results. For this reason Ōyama characterized
the proletarian party movement not as a "trend toward the
Left," but as a "trend toward practicality."[60] Moreover, since
the trend of politics in the rest of the civilized world was away
from middle-class liberalism and toward mass politics, the proletarian party movement could be fitted into a global pattern
of change. This heightened Ōyama's conviction that he was

[59] Ōyama, "Gendai Nihon no seiji katei," *Zenshū*, II, 13-15.
[60] *Ibid.*, p. 9.

acting "practically." He was increasingly convinced that he was sharing in the creation of a new political order that would someday replace bourgeois hegemony.

Participation in the proletarian party movement, however, did not mean that Ōyama had elected to reject liberal democratic values. On the contrary, he attacked not the goals of liberal democracy, but its institutional forms. He defined democracy less in terms of a concrete political system than in terms of the ideals a political system ought to embody. He did not regard the Diet as the best of all possible political systems, but merely as a convenient instrument for political action. At first he had thought it could be put to the service of the "people" as a whole, but when he discovered that this was not possible he came to regard it as a means for promoting the rise of a militant proletariat. As was true of many of his contemporaries, Ōyama's shift away from parliamentary liberalism came at the level of political practice rather than political values.

The detachability of the parliamentary process from the ends which it was supposed to serve perhaps helps to explain the moral vulnerability of party government during the 1920's. While professional politicians had come to appreciate the pragmatic usefulness of the Diet as a route to power, the intellectual community continued to be attracted primarily by the political ideals that the parliamentary process was supposed to embody. This fundamental dichotomy of outlook created an estrangement between intellectuals and politicians that grew wider as the decade wore on. It may have made it easier for many intellectuals, including those who joined the Shōwa Kenkyūkai, to adjust to the antiparliamentary mood of the 1930's with few pangs of conscience. They may not have been seeking to "escape from freedom," but they certainly did seek to escape from party rule.

PART FOUR

Comparisons and Conclusions

CHAPTER XII

Japan and Germany in the Interwar Period

KENTARŌ HAYASHI

Some Basic Similarities and Differences

I T IS generally acknowledged that there are many similarities in the modern histories of Japan and Germany. Both peoples achieved national unification and appeared on the stage of international politics about 1870. The comparative lateness of these events placed both of them in such a state of rivalry with the more advanced countries as to stamp certain common features on their modern institutions and politics.

In both Japan and Germany, for example, the power of the modern state was created not so much to accomplish the self-governing objectives of civil society as to concentrate the nation's strength to meet the felt threats from abroad. The result was that in both cases the state assumed a strong leadership role, thereby opening a gap between the "governors" and the "governed," and giving the state officials the character of a "ruling class." Germany was in fact Europe's typical bureaucratic state;[1] and, in this, Japan took Germany as her model, making the "exaltation of official life above private life" a conspicuous feature of the Meiji system.

In both countries, moreover, national unification was accomplished by military action. In Germany, the empire was born from the conquest by Prussia, a militarist state from the time of Frederick William I and Frederick the Great. The militaris-

[1] For a compact description of the German *Beamtenstaat* before World War I, see Th. Eschenburg, *Die Improvisierte Demokratie* (new edn., Munich, 1963).

tic character of Prussia was directly transferred to the new empire, the authority of the military being juridically assured by placing the supreme command of the army and navy in the hands of the emperor and by isolating military affairs entirely from the sphere of the civilian government. In Japan, the modern empire was not brought about by the army of an existing state, but the government which was formed after the Meiji Restoration did consist mainly of leaders of the two great clans, Satsuma and Chōshū, that had rendered distinguished service in the military victory over the Shogunate. Moreover, when a modern military system was adopted in Japan, it was the German model which was finally emulated, including the key institutions of the royal supreme command and the independence of the military from the civilian government. Victory in the Sino-Japanese War of 1894-95 and the Russo-Japanese War of 1904-1905 greatly enhanced the prestige of this new military establishment.

Finally, in both countries, the maintenance of such bureaucratic-militarist states inevitably required the supremacy of the imperial prerogative. In Japan it was codified by the Constitution of 1889, which proclaimed the emperor "sacred and inviolable." As is well known, Itō Hirobumi, who was responsible for the drafting of this constitution, spent over a year in Europe, during which time he listened to the advice of Lorenz von Stein and Rudolf von Gneist and observed the operation of the German constitution.

Differences in the modern societies and histories of Japan and Germany also are notable. There was, for example, much greater social mobility in Japan than in Germany. High civil and military officials in the German empire were drawn largely from the aristocracy, particularly the Prussian *Junkers*.[2] Superficially, the situation in Japan appears similar since the so-called "Satchō clique" almost monopolized the government during

[2] L. W. Muncy, *The Junker in the Prussian Administration* (Providence, R.I., 1944), is a detailed analysis although the subject of this book is quite limited.

the Meiji era. The truth is, however, that this clique derived its power from personal connections and had no special socio-economic base. Therefore, as the participants in the Meiji Restoration died, the Satchō clique gradually lost its dominant position. Itō Hirobumi, for example, who liked to be called "Japan's Bismarck," was no *Junker vom reinsten Wasser*: he was born into the family of a poor farmer, and it was only by adoption that he was raised to even the lowest samurai class.

This difference in social mobility was due to the difference between the *Reichsgründung* and the Meiji Restoration. The former was not a social revolution; it did not produce a new ruling class but strengthened the old one. The Meiji Restoration, on the other hand, although it was not accompanied by a popular upheaval as was the French Revolution, was a real revolution and did indeed overthrow the *ancien régime*. In its place was created a new ruling class, selected and promoted not on the basis of social class or status, but on the basis of merit as determined by performance in the new state universities (where students were admitted on the basis of merit from the public, compulsory system of primary and secondary schools) and afterward by performance on the job. It has been suggested that such a system could not guarantee mobility since in any society it is the stratum above the middle class that can best afford to send its children to the universities. Moreover, the record shows that in the Japanese case, the number of shizoku or former samurai among university graduates and therefore among government officials was disproportionately large. These facts, however, are somewhat misleading. The middle class in modern Japan was, after all, fairly large, and entry was not closed to those below. As for the continued predominance of the former samurai or persons from families of samurai origin, this is not to be explained by their retention of any special social privileges. Unlike the English gentry, for example, whom they resembled in certain other respects, except for a small number at the highest level, the samurai lost their property in the Meiji Restoration and thereafter were forced to earn their living like the commoners. That they remained the backbone of society was due not to their inherited wealth or status, but to their culture, their tradition of public service, and their aspiration for advancement. It was not their *Besitz und Bildung*, but their *Besitz durch Bildung* which gave them their strength.

The character of the Japanese monarchy was also different from that in Germany. In Germany, the Hohenzollern house was only one of several royal families, and it was neither the oldest nor the most legitimate of these. It was only its military achievement that secured for the Hohenzollern house the imperial crown; and thus, while it was generally acknowledged by the people, it did not enjoy the legitimacy that is attached to the wielding of traditional authority. In contrast, the family of the Tennō is the only family throughout Japanese history that has ruled as a legitimate monarchy; and, having remained aloof from the world of politics since the Middle Ages, it has not only been popularly acknowledged, but actually worshipped. Such worship has often been exploited by political leaders, but nothing has destroyed the national feeling that the imperial house or the emperor is the spiritual center of national unity.

It should not be forgotten that the constitutional development of the Japanese empire after the Meiji era also followed a course different from that of the German empire. In the latter, with the dismissal of Chancellor Bismarck, Germany is said to have fallen under the "personal rule" of Wilhelm II. Although historical research has shown that the Kaiser did not in fact rule his country "personally,"[3] it is undeniable that his personal influence was very great, his speeches and interviews creating sensations both at home and abroad.[4] Certainly prior to 1917 parliamentary government had not existed in Germany,

[3] E. R. Huber, *Deutsche Verfassungsgeschichte seit 1789*, Bd. III (Stuttgart, 1963), s.815.

[4] See Erich Eyck, *Das persönliche Regiment Wilhelms II* (Erlenbach-Zurich, 1948).

and party members had only rarely held seats in the Cabinet.

In form Japan was also an absolute monarchy after the Meiji Restoration; but four years prior to the promulgation of the constitution a Cabinet system was set up, and in the parliament that followed the promulgation of the constitution, political parties soon took shape. While the first prime minister, Itō Hirobumi, was at first opposed to such parties, he eventually saw the value of securing their cooperation and himself became the party leader of the Rikken Seiyūkai. Thereafter, the number of party men in the government gradually increased until in 1918, with the advent of Hara Takashi to the premiership, a pure party Cabinet appeared. This ushered in a period of two-party parliamentarianism from 1918 to 1932 which resembled that in Britain, but had no parallel in the history of the German *Reich* at all.

Weaknesses of Party Government

In the 1920's there were important similarities between Japan and Germany. Both countries experimented with party government, both experienced the rise of unsettling mass movements, both pursued conciliatory foreign policies while simultaneously trying unsuccessfully to suppress growing frustration at home, and both suffered from a breakdown of cultural values. The differences in this period also are important. It should be remembered that party government came to Japan in 1918 by an evolutionary process without breaking the framework of the constitution or the structure of traditional society, while it appeared in Germany only after defeat in World War I had discredited the old empire and its social order, and bloody revolution had set the stage. Although the parliamentary forces in both countries succumbed to rightist forces in little more than a decade, this difference in the circumstances of their advent had important effects on the details of their brief histories.

In the Weimar Republic, the danger of Communist revolution remained real even after the defeat of the Bolsheviks and Minority Socialists in 1919. In Japan, on the other hand, the danger from this quarter did not reach such proportions. To be sure, in the years following World War I, Japan too experienced an ascendancy of mass movements, for the wartime boom had not enriched all elements of the population equally. A disproportionately large share of the increment of income, "accrued to the well-to-do classes in the forms of rent, dividend, interest, and corporate savings,"[5] leaving the workers feeling under-rewarded. They also grew more and more dissatisfied with the conditions of their labor. The first Japanese Factory Act, for example, was not passed until 1916, and even then it had limited application. As told by Kawakami Hajime in his wartime work, *Bimbō monogatari* (Tales of Poverty), the more the working classes saw of the extravagance of the *nouveau riche*, the more bitter grew their discontent. Wartime economic prosperity thus awakened the class consciousness of the laborer. In the course of leading several industrial struggles, the Yūaikai, which was originally an organization for cooperation between the employed and the worker, became a trade union. More unions were formed; and when the inflationary bubble burst in March 1920, Japan experienced a wave of strikes under the guidance of union leaders now so radicalized as to be torn by internal feuds between Bolsheviks and anarchists. In 1922 an illegal Communist party was founded. Although the Communist party exercised little influence on the labor movement, the ruling circles, including the leaders of the conservative parties and the business circles with which they were intimately related, saw a great menace in the ideology of communism. When they granted universal male suffrage in 1925, they took care to enact at the same time the Peace Preservation Law, which aimed at the suppression of communism by outlawing the advocacy of any changes in the fundamental character of the state or the system of private property.

It might be supposed that the differences in the experiences of the two countries in World War I, Germany having been

[5] W. W. Lockwood, *The Economic Development of Japan: Growth and Structural Change, 1868-1938* (Princeton, 1955), p. 41.

defeated and Japan victorious, would have led to very different foreign policies in the ensuing years. The truth is that they were quite similar. In the initial postwar period, both Germany and Japan pursued policies of international conciliation. For example, Admiral Katō Tomosaburō, Japan's chief delegate at the Washington Conference, was a man of keen insight. He recognized the evil of the armaments race and overrode navy opposition to bring about acceptance of the naval limitation. After becoming prime minister in 1922, he achieved the evacuation of Japanese troops from Siberia and supported the Foreign Ministry's objection to military intervention in China. This same policy of international cooperation and nonintervention in China is identified even more strongly with Baron Shidehara Kijūrō, who served as foreign minister in Kenseikai and Minseitō Cabinets from 1924 to 1927 and 1929 to 1931. In many ways his policy in these years resembled that of the contemporary German chancellor and foreign minister, Gustav Stresemann.

At the same time both nations suffered from a feeling of frustration. Germany, of course, was humiliated by the Treaty of Versailles, which became the keynote in German politics throughout the interwar period. Japan too felt a sense of frustration, induced by the refusal of her fellow victors to recognize racial equality in the preamble to the Covenant of the League of Nations, and by their insistence at the Washington Conference that Japan evacuate Shantung. Feelings of hostility within the military found an outlet in the Seiyūkai Cabinet of General Baron Tanaka Gi'ichi, from 1927 to 1929, which prepared the way for the Manchurian incident by drafting a long-range continental policy at the Eastern Conference in 1927 and by sending troops to Shantung three times. Within the Navy General Staff frustrations deepened, and antagonism to the Washington Conference naval limitations erupted when the Hamaguchi Cabinet signed the London Naval Treaty in 1930.

Differences between the two countries in this period are more pronounced in the area of their domestic politics. The great change in European politics from the nineteenth to the twentieth centuries is, in the words of Max Weber, the change from *honoratioren* politics, that is, rule by socially prestigious individuals, to rule by the generality of men, or mass democracy.[6] In Great Britain this change was a gradual transition through successive enlargements of the suffrage and gradual enlargement of the power of Parliament. In Germany, while the way was opened for the masses to participate in politics by the granting of universal male suffrage in the nineteenth century, weight of the parliament was not correspondingly increased. Since the parties had not been given the right to form a government, they had had no opportunity to develop the capacity to govern. Moreover, they had not learned how to integrate the nation, each having evolved as the parochial representative of some particular class, region, or religion. Nor were they prepared to cope with the sudden enlargement of the electorate by the extension of the vote to women and the adoption of an electoral system of proportional representation, which served to cut the personal tie between the voter and the elected official. In short, when power was thrust upon them, they were not ready.

Recognizing these weaknesses of the parties, scholars like Hugo Preuss and Max Weber hoped to protect the democracy by devising a powerful presidency based on plebiscite. The president was not to intervene in politics in ordinary times, but was expected to show strong leadership should government find it impossible to reach effective decisions in time of emergency. But their expectations were unfounded. The election of the president by four million voters turned into an exercise in mass manipulation by symbols. A president thus elected could hardly be a sage. When crisis came in the early 1930's the president had in fact become nothing but a tool of the camarilla,[7]

[6] Max Weber, "Politik als Beruf," *Gesammelte Politische Schriften* (Munich, 1921), p. 369ff.

[7] Andreas Dorpalen, *Hindenburg and the Weimar Republic* (Princeton, 1964), pp. 447ff.

and his choice at the decisive moment destroyed the democracy.

In Japan, on the other hand, the advent of party government did not mean the rise of coalition politics. In contrast to the situation in Germany, Japan had enjoyed a two-party system almost from the beginning. Perhaps this was because of Japan's greater cultural and social homogeneity. The first two parties, the Jiyūtō and the Kaishintō, both aimed at a constitutional monarchy on the English model—at least after the establishment of the parliament—and had no major differences in viewpoint. Although they advocated a struggle against the domination of government by factions stemming from the old clans, so-called hanbatsu politics, the party leaders, Itagaki Taisuke and Ōkuma Shigenobu, both felt free to join hanbatsu-dominated Cabinets. In turn, clan leaders like Itō Hirobumi felt free to accept the presidency of the Jiyūtō's successor party, the Seiyū-kai. Thus, in personal as well as social relations, there was no decisive gap between the government and the parties; nor was there a decisive difference in their definition of the national interest.

This reflects another important difference from the situation in Germany: the advent of party government in Japan did not mean the rise of mass democracy. *Honoratioren* politics continued. The successors to the Jiyūtō and the Kaishintō, the Seiyūkai and the Kenseikai, even after securing Cabinet control, continued to draw their members from almost the same restricted social groups: rural notables and ex-officials.

From this it can be seen that the failure of party politics in Japan stemmed from different reasons from that in Germany. In Japan it might be said to be the result of the parties' premature participation in government. Unlike postwar party leaders in Germany, the leaders of the Japanese parties had already had experience as Cabinet ministers before parliamentarianism was established; and as parliamentarianism was not the result of constitutional change, it did not produce a new attitude in the minds of statesmen. Even after the Hara Cabinet, party leaders sought personal accession to power in preference to the establishment of a true party system. As a consequence, if compromise with nonparty bases of power were necessary either to secure a Cabinet position for oneself or one's party or to prevent a competitive party leader from winning that objective, most Japanese party politicians had long been accustomed to make such compromises. When the Takahashi Cabinet fell in 1922, the Seiyūkai allowed Admiral Katō to form a Cabinet composed largely of members of the House of Peers rather than permit the Kenseikai to come to power. In 1924 Viscount Kiyoura Keigo, president of the Privy Council, was able to form an otherwise unpopular Cabinet by the defection of the majority of the Seiyūkai to form the new Seiyūhontō. After the collapse of Katō Takaaki's three-party coalition "for the defense of the constitution" in 1927, the Seyūkai again turned to officialdom, electing General Tanaka as party president as an expedient for coming to power.

Even after the alternation of governments by each of the two parties became the rule, party behavior did not change. The Minseitō opposed the Tanaka Cabinet on the Kellogg-Briand Pact because the pact had been concluded "in the name of the people." When the Hamaguchi Cabinet ran into difficulties over the ratification of the London Naval Treaty, the Seiyūkai supported the Navy General Staff in its charge that the government had violated the prerogative of the supreme command. And the attack of the Privy Council which brought down the Wakatsuki Cabinet in December 1931, is reported to have been made with the encouragement of members of the Seiyūkai. In fact, it is owing chiefly to the decision of the genrō, Prince Saionji Kimmochi, rather than to the efforts of the parties, that parliamentary rule was established at all.

The corruption of the parties must also be mentioned. *Honoratioren* politics can be effective only when the notables who operate them share common objectives and a sense of *noblesse oblige*. In postwar Japan, the advent to power of party politicians in close association with the business world resulted in struggles for personal power that were corrupt to a wholly unprecedented degree. The secret fund of Tanaka at the time of his assumption of the party presidency is only the most flagrant example. Thus, whereas in Germany democracy was destroyed by the inadequacy of government by the masses, in Japan it was undermined by the failure of government by notables.

The Turn to the Right

In destroying the Versailles system, Japan was a step ahead of Germany. Two years before the collapse of the Weimar Republic in 1933, Japan precipitated the Manchurian incident; and in the following year a group of young radicals brought an end to the era of parliamentarianism by murdering Premier Inukai. These events, however, were neither accompanied by a "national revolution" as in Germany nor followed by dictatorship. One explanation is to be found in the differences in the cultural breakdown each country suffered during this period.

Friedrich Meinecke wrote in his memoirs: "Today we know that the era of civil society, the era in which the autonomous personality maintains and develops itself in the struggle with the superhuman power of life, was over with the outbreak of the war. Soon after 1914 I often monologized in remembrance of the words of Talleyrand in 1798. Those who lived before 1914 alone can truly know what it is to live." He also wrote on November 8, 1918, the day on which he heard Beethoven's Fifth Symphony in the Berlin Opera House: "I felt that I had just heard the last sounds of the sinking, beautiful world."[8]

Before the war, Europeans had lived in the belief that they were part of the stable order of a civilization that represented the human race. This belief was destroyed by the outbreak of World War I, and the end of the war forced them to feel the coming of a new age. It was, however, difficult to find new values to replace those which had been destroyed. This was

[8] Friedrich Meinecke, *Strassburg/Freiburg/Berlin, 1901-1919* (Stuttgart, 1949), pp. 133ff, and 257.

particularly true in Germany, where the people had to adapt to this new age in the midst of the utmost political and social confusion. It was in this atmosphere that Oswald Spengler's *Decline of the West* aroused a tremendous sensation. Karl Jaspers described this state of mind as follows: "The consciousness of the present is absorbed in the consciousness itself cut off from reality. Those who think in such a way feel themselves as naught." It was a time, according to Jaspers, when people turned to Kierkegaard and Nietzsche.[9]

A noticeable phenomenon in the spiritual history of the Weimar Republic is the so-called conservative revolution, identified with such names as Spengler, Moeller van den Bruck, and Edgar Jung.[10] This revolutionary or new conservatism was conservative in its denial of liberalism, democracy, parliamentarianism, party politics, and the class struggle, which were axioms of the Weimar Republic, but revolutionary in its negation of not only Weimar Germany but also *Wilhelminische* Germany as the final degradation of the nineteenth century. It was socialistic in its opposition to capitalism and in its application of the class struggle to the relations among nations. Moreover, it was revolutionary in international politics because it more or less sympathized with Russia as a young nation and called for a struggle against the Treaty of Versailles in alliance with the Soviet Union.

[9] Karl Jaspers, *Die geistige Situation der Zeit* (Berlin, 1931), p. 15.

[10] The name "conservative revolution" had been used in Hermann Rauschning's *The Conservative Revolution* (New York, 1941), but it was Arnim Mohler's *Die Konservative Revolution, 1918-1932* (Stuttgart, 1950) which made this word a historical term. Mohler, however, did not clearly distinguish between revolutionary and traditional conservatism. This distinction was left for Klemens von Klemperer's *Germany's New Conservatism* (Princeton, 1957). This "new conservatism" was later studied by O. E. Schüddekopf, *Linke Leute von Rechts* (Stuttgart, 1960); Kurt von Sontheimer, *Antidemokratisches Denken in der Weimarer Republik* (Munich, 1962); and others. Fritz Stern, *The Politics of Cultural Despair* (Berkeley, 1961), and H. J. Schwierskott, *Arthur Moeller van den Bruck* (n.p., 1962), are particularly important on Moeller van den Bruck.

This revolutionary conservatism played an important part in preparing the way for nazism, as is indicated by the fact that the name of the Third Reich originated with Moeller. Moeller himself disliked Hitler and is reported to have said, after he met Hitler for the first and last time, that he would rather commit suicide than see such a man in office.[11] Actually, Moeller committed suicide in 1925, and other new conservatives were eliminated after Hitler came to power.[12] Nevertheless, their philosophy was very important to nazism, for it provided a theoretical foundation for the wholesale denial of the existing state of things and offered new values to fill the vacuum of the postwar period. The Nazis, who caught the minds of the German people at the beginning of the 1930's, were very poor in theory, and except for anti-Semitism, what theory they had was largely borrowed along with the name of the Third Reich from revolutionary conservatism. It was, in short, this revolutionary conservatism that produced the myth which drove the dissatisfied masses to frantic action.[13]

Japan after World War I was characterized by confusion of thought. The Japanese intellectuals were always very sensitive to European intellectual trends, and new ideas were rapidly introduced into Japan. German revolutionary conservatism was not noticed, however, because it was too German to be easily transplanted to other countries. Be that as it may, Japan was not devoid of its own brand of revolutionary conservatism.

Japanese revolutionary rightists flourished, for example, in such secret groups as the Sakurakai or Cherry Blossom Society, which was formed among military officers in 1930 and which planned two coups before and after the Manchurian incident. Following the dissolution of the Sakurakai, other radicals under its influence executed the attempted coups of May 15, 1932,

[11] Stern, *op.cit.*, p. 237.

[12] In particular, Edgar Jung was murdered at the time of the Roehm affair. See Sir John Wheeler-Bennett, *The Nemesis of Power* (London, 1953), p. 323.

[13] Jean F. Neurohr, *Der Mythos vom dritten Reich* (Stuttgart, 1957).

and February 26, 1936. Revolutionary civilian rightists were also active, some participating with the military in these attempts and others carrying out assassinations independently. But while these groups have often been termed "fascistic," the truth is that they differed greatly from the Fascist or Nazi party.[14] The Sakurakai, for example, was a small, intimate group, and the officers who attempted the coups acted largely on their own. The radical civilian rightists also were divided into small groups, each with its own leader, and none large enough to be called a political party. If one makes a comparison with Germany, they resemble not so much the Nazi party as the numerous terrorist bands which existed in the early days of the Weimar Republic. True, these bands have been interpreted as the "vanguard of nazism,"[15] but they differed greatly from the Nazi party itself. That party's chief characteristic, distinguishing it from other rightist groups of the time, was its concern with organizing the masses, particularly after the failure of its putsch in Munich in 1923.[16] With such a party, the revolutionary rightists of Japan had little in common.

The ideology of revolutionary conservatism also found expression in Japan. Kita Ikki and Ōkawa Shūmei provided the rightist officers with theory, and both were involved in the attempted coups of May 15 and February 26. Their ideas were in many ways similar to German revolutionary conservatism. Kita Ikki's *Nippon kaizō hōan* (Plan for the Reconstruction of Japan, 1919) was the bible of the young rightist officers. It was conservative in advocating reform by imperial authority, but revolutionary in criticizing the emperor's position under the Meiji constitution, much as the German revolutionary conservative tracts were critical of prewar *Wilhelminische* Ger-

[14] Emperor Hirohito himself is reported to have said after the murder of Inukai, "I reject absolutely a fascist-type person." Harada Kumao, *Saionji kō to seikyoku* [Saionji Memoirs], II (Tokyo, 1950), 288.

[15] R. G. Waite, *Vanguard of Nazism: The Free Corps Movement in Post-War Germany, 1918-1923* (Cambridge, Mass., 1952).

[16] See H. H. Hoffman, *Der Hitlerputsch: Krisenjahre deutscher Geschichte, 1920-1924* (1961).

many. Kita's plan was socialist in repudiating capitalism and proposing the suspension of the constitution, the abolition of the nobility and the Upper House, and the prohibition of private property over a certain amount. It resembled the thought of Moeller in applying the idea of class struggle to international relations and in advocating the emancipation of the Asian peoples from Western imperialism. Ōkawa later broke with Kita, but his ideas were not greatly different; in particular, his *Kinsei Yōroppa shokuminshi* (History of Modern European Colonialism) contributed to the struggle against Western colonialism.

But in Japan, such revolutionary rightist thought encountered much heavier opposition from its rightist rival, traditional conservatism, than it did in Germany. In interwar Germany, traditional conservatism was represented chiefly by the *Deutschnationale Volkspartei*, or *DNVP*, the successor to the former *Konservative Partei*. Its aim was the restoration of the dynasty, but since the Hohenzollerns had little emotional appeal, it remained largely a local organization in the rural part of eastern Germany. By way of contrast, the Japanese traditional conservatives did not form a party or other unique political organization. They began as a small group of intellectuals and remained so, championing the uniqueness of the Japanese national character. Thus, they never challenged the existing organizations. Instead, they appealed to them and had great effect both on the organizations themselves and through them on the mass of the Japanese people. They seemed to offer change without violence at a time when there was a hunger for "renovation" (*kakushinshugi*), but little taste for the revolution which the national socialists like Kita and Ōkawa preached. They were thus useful tools for the reform-minded officers and officials. The fact is that, unlike the Germans, the Japanese, in spite of postwar confusion and unrest, had not lost faith in their prewar social order and value system. They were disillusioned, but they were not ready to "leap into the dark." The pull was to the past, not to revolution.

The Japanese were drawn, therefore, not so much to the revolutionary Left or revolutionary Right as to the traditional conservatives like Minoda Kyōki. In his organ, which he called *Genri Nippon* (The True Japan), Minoda attacked liberal scholars like Takigawa Yukitoki and Minobe Tatsukichi. His fanatic utterances found little support among intellectuals, but political leaders were soon caught up. In 1933 the Ministry of Education purged Takigawa from his professorship at Kyoto University. In 1935 Minobe was condemned by the House of Peers. A powerful campaign against liberalism was soon underway with the support of the army; and in 1936 when the army stepped up its intervention in Cabinet politics, it was Minoda who gave it the pretext it needed, the slogan he had long been trumpeting: *kokutai meichō* (clarification of the national policy).

The victory of traditional conservatism over revolutionary conservatism led not to dictatorship, but to a coalition structure resting on a balance of power between the army, the bureaucracy and the parties. With the failure of the coup d'etat of February 26, 1936, the political movement of the revolutionary conservatives was checked. In their place, the officers of the so-called Control faction (*Tōseiha*), who occupied the central organs of the army, increased in influence and began to direct politics.

The parties had already lost the courage to take over political power and produced many people who accommodated themselves to the army; the parliament, however, was not yet deprived of the function to criticize the government. The parliamentary speeches of Saitō Takao and Hamada Kunimatsu, delivered in 1936 and 1937, were famous philippics against the army. In the latter year, the Cabinet of General Hayashi Senjūrō, although it included no party members and was regarded as a puppet of the army, fell after only four months, because of its unpopularity in parliament. Again in 1939 the Cabinet of General Abe Nobuyuki, also a puppet of the army, resigned when a majority in the parliament signed a memorandum confessing no "confidence" in the government. The parties could no longer run the government, but they still retained the ability to overthrow puppet Cabinets. Throughout the 1930's the army was preeminent, but it could not dictate.

In October 1940, under the Second Konoe Cabinet, all parties were dissolved, and the Imperial Rule Assistance Association or IRAA (*Taisei Yokusankai*) was inaugurated as the only national political organization. It resembled a totalitarian structure, but it was basically quite different from the Nazi or Fascist party. The idea of the IRAA originated with Konoe and the renovationist bureaucrats and scholars who constituted his brain trust. Its aim was the canalization of the vital energy and interests of the nation at large, in view of the weakness of the parties. Some of its sponsors were inspired by democratic and socialist ideas of increasing mass participation in politics. On the other hand, others of its sponsors, like the chief of the Bureau of Military Affairs, General Mutō Akira, envisioned an instrument of mass mobilization similar to the Nazi party. Konoe himself was a person of some liberal attitudes, but he was also attracted by the new German regime and optimistically believed that these conflicting democratic and totalitarian conceptions could be united easily in the same movement.

Immediately after Konoe proclaimed the *shintaisei* (new regime) in June 1940, the Yonai Cabinet was overthrown by the army and, with the support of the army and the renovationist intellectuals, Konoe was named prime minister. Confronted with this new situation and fearful of being excluded from politics, the politicians dissolved their parties spontaneously one by one and scrambled for positions in the "new regime." Coming into existence this way, the IRAA was nothing but an aggregation of military people, renovationist bureaucrats and intellectuals, ex-party members, and civilian rightists. It is not surprising that it never became a true party or a political organization capable of any united action.

Although a totalitarian state did not develop in 1940, parties disappeared and Japan became a bureaucratic state controlled by the army in the name of Yokusan or "Imperial Assistance." In the election of 1942, the only one held under the Yokusan regime, the *Yokusan seijitaisei kyōgikai*, a specially appointed council under the chairmanship of ex-premier Abe, recommended candidates. Others could run, but they were greatly handicapped, so that this election seems analogous to that of a totalitarian state. On the other hand, it must be noted that this election was held during the Pacific War and in wartime completely free elections are rarely permitted even in democratic countries. Thus, Japan's quasi-dictatorial Yokusan regime differed greatly from the German Nazi dictatorship. It was in reality a kind of wartime structure not wholly unlike that of democratic states in a period of "total war."

The continuity of Japan's traditional culture and social structure has been stressed as an important restraint on Japan's turn to the Right. This was particularly apparent in the behavior of the senior advisers to the throne, the genrō and jūshin, and the emperor himself. Prince Saionji Kimmochi, the only surviving genrō at this time, strove to his last days to weaken the influence of the army on the government by recommending as candidates for the premiership such moderates as Saitō Makoto, Okada Keisuke, and Ugaki Kazushige. Yuasa Kurahei, Lord Keeper of the Privy Seal from 1936 to 1940, showed the same attitude. The role of Emperor Hirohito also was very important. He observed the principle of reigning without ruling, but always expressed his own beliefs in liberty and peace. The February 26th revolt was suppressed by his orders. He expressed strong dissatisfaction with the army on the occasions of the China war and the alliance with Germany. To the last he hoped to avoid war with the Western powers, and his role in ending the war is well known. The emperor followed the decisions of the government unconditionally, but when the government lost the ability to make decisions, he spoke with great weight,[17] surely revealing deeper political insight than

[17] Examples of the sagacity of the emperor are found very often in Harada Kumao, *op.cit.*; and the diaries of Honjō Shigeru, *Honjō nikki*

did President Hindenburg, who was in some senses his closest counterpart in the German system.

Rikugun and Reichswehr

If dictatorship by a single party is an essential characteristic of fascism, fascism never appeared in Japan. On the other hand, the thesis that the Japanese army played a role analogous to that of a fascist party, is not necessarily groundless. Certainly the Japanese *Rikugun* was very different from the German *Reichswehr*.

When the *Reichswehr* was newly established in the Weimar Republic after the fall of imperial Germany, it lost its independence. It was placed under oath to support the constitution of the Republic and the orders of the civil government. According to the Versailles Treaty, its size was restricted to 100,000 and compulsory military service was forbidden. It should therefore have become a democratic army. In reality, it became strongly antidemocratic and hostile to the Republic. The reason for this was that the task of constructing the new *Reichswehr* was assigned to leaders of the old imperial army. Their central figure, Hans von Seeckt, was a learned and able *Junker* and a dedicated monarchist opposed to the Versailles Treaty. Under the slogan of "political neutrality," he opposed government intervention in military affairs and through strict examination, he rejected persons who were considered to have social democratic or even strong liberal leanings. Prolongation of the term of service in order to compensate for the diminution of personnel made it easy to construct the exclusively professional army which Seeckt intended.[18]

In the confusion accompanying the early days of the Repub-

[Honjō Diary] (1967). The latter was the emperor's chief aide-de-camp.

[18] Gordon A. Craig, *The Politics of the Prussian Army, 1640-1945* (Oxford, 1955), pp. 394ff; F. L. Carsten, *Reichswehr und Politik, 1918-1933* (1964), pp. 115ff.

lic, the government could not but rely on the army to defend the state from revolutionary Communist and left-wing socialist movements. The army profited greatly from this situation. It could regain at once the influence which it had lost by its defeat and soon achieved the position of a "state within the state." The percentage of nobility among the officers increased in comparison with the last days of the empire,[19] and since, in spite of the revolution of 1918, the social status of the *Junker* did not change very much, the *Junker*-like character of the German army grew even stronger than it had been under the monarchy.

Such a body could have little sympathy with the ideal of middle class socialism which the Nazis championed, at least until the Roehm affair in 1934.[20] On the other hand, the *Reichswehr* could not ignore the Nazis any more than the Nazis could ignore it. Neither could win power without the support of the other. Accordingly, in the early stages of the Nazi movement, party leaders cultivated the Bavarian army; Hitler himself was active in this effort even after the failure of the Munich putsch. With the onset of the Depression, this effort met with some success, as was demonstrated by the Scheringer-Ludin affair in 1930.[21] Reciprocally, among certain high officers there was a group which urged that Hitler's approaches be exploited to strengthen the influence of the army in politics. Its representative was Kurt von Schleicher; and, although it was against his will, in the end he contributed more than anyone else to bringing the Nazis to power.

Schleicher was a peculiar soldier who aimed at a military autocracy based on a mass movement. Since the German army was of an essentially aristocratic character, he had to look for

[19] Wheeler-Bennett, *op.cit.*, pp. 98-99.

[20] A. Schweitzer, *Big Business in the Third Reich* (Bloomington, Indiana, 1964). A close study of the ideas and programs of the Nazis in the early 1930's shows that the Marxist definition of fascism as "a form of rule of monopoly capital" is clearly deficient.

[21] Carsten, *op.cit.*, p. 347ff.

another organization to provide a popular base, and he chose the Nazis.[22] Betraying his superior, Groener, he concluded a secret pact with Hitler; and when Hitler became his rival, he sought to split the Nazi party, subordinating half to himself. He failed, of course, but his attempt and failure are instructive of the differences between the *Reichswehr* and the Japanese *Rikugun*—the structure finally established by the latter being not too dissimilar from Schleicher's conception.

The social origins and ideology of the Japanese army were quite different from those of the *Reichswehr*. As mentioned earlier, there was no social stratum like the *Junkers* in Japan. In any event, Japanese officers were not drawn from the aristocracy as they were in Germany. The so-called Chōshū clique which once existed in the Japanese army had disappeared completely. On the contrary, the radical rightist officers who organized the Sakurakai were those people who represented the anti-Chōshū cliques. The Japanese officers came from the middle class just as did government officials; and the service schools, being free of charge, tended to be especially attractive to candidates from the lower middle class. Furthermore, the Japanese army and navy were always based on a system of conscription, so that most of the soldiers were sons of poor farmers, who suffered severely from the Depression.

The Japanese economy in the 1920's was in a state of chronic crisis. Not only did Japan not experience even moderate prosperity between 1924 and 1929, as did Germany, but in addition she suffered a severe blow from the earthquake of 1923 and plunged into the Great Depression two years earlier than did Europe. The effect of the Depression was greatest in the rural districts, which suffered especially from the fall in the prices of their two main products, rice and silk. Under the prevailing

---

[22] On the relations between the German army and the Nazis, and Schleicher's activities, see the works of Wheeler-Bennett, Craig, and Carsten; also Otto Ernst Schüddekopf, *Heer und Republik* (Hanover, 1955); and especially Th. Vogelsang, *Reichswehr, Staat und NSDAP* (Stuttgart, 1962).

system of tenant farming, characterized by high farm rentals, high taxes, and payments in kind, landowners sought to minimize their losses by raising farm rents and confiscating the lands of indigent tenants. Rural areas were further depressed by the migration of the unemployed from urban areas to their ancestral villages. Conditions became so desperate that farmers even resorted to "human traffic" in their daughters.

It is not surprising in these circumstances that the interwar period in Japan was plagued by conflicts between tenant farmers and landlords. Farmers unions grew up side by side with trade unions, and when a movement to form a socialist party occurred (at the time universal suffrage was realized) the farmers unions took the initiative. As the economic depression worsened in 1930, the misery of the rural districts deepened and the frustration of the farming poor grew more bitter as police intervention on the side of the landlords crushed their struggles.

In Germany, agrarian problems were not given much attention in Nazi ideology. The Nazis did advocate land reform, but it constituted only one item in their twenty-five article program. They were primarily city-oriented; the urban middle class, feeling itself deprived of its basis for existence by defeat and economic disaster, was the main support of the Nazi movement. In Japan too the urban middle class was impoverished by the Depression, but it did not fall into a psychology of complete despair as it did in Germany, except in the rural districts. If there was to be a middle class socialism in Japan, it had to come out of the distressed rural areas. Inevitably, the ideology of the Japanese Right was characterized by a trend toward physiocracy.

One might maintain that poor tenant farmers should not be called a middle class, but a part of the proletariat, and that had the influence of the Communist party been stronger in Japan, they would have been allied with the Communists as were the peasants in Russia. Indeed, as has already been pointed out, the farmers unions in Japan did work with the urban trade unions; the proletarian parties, however, were very weak and so bound by the theories of orthodox Marxism that they were far less able than the rightists to capitalize on the rural discontent.[23]

The Japanese radical rightist officers were very much impressed by the misery of the poor farmers, whose sons made up the bulk of their recruits; and it was largely with the aim of alleviating this misery that the young officers resorted to violence in the attempted coups of 1932 and 1936. Their concern was widely shared throughout the officer corps. Farm relief was taken up as an important subject, for example, in the "National Policy of the Army," drawn up under Army Minister Araki Sadao in 1933. One may reasonably say, therefore, that the army played a significant role, or at least tried to play a significant role, in the advancement of middle class socialism in Japan. Unlike the German *Reichswehr*'s vain effort to exploit a rising mass movement with which it had little sympathy, this attempt was more an expression of the Japanese army's own ethos, derived from its own proximity to the rural poor.

Although the Japanese army played a role perhaps more analogous to that of the Nazi party than to that of the German *Reichswehr* in championing middle-class socialism, it never became a totalitarian organization. A single personal leader did not head the Japanese army during the 1930's. Officially the leader was the army minister, but his authority was attached only to his position and was lost when he left office. Japan had ten army ministers during the 1930's. Among them, generals like Araki, Terauchi, and Itagaki Seishirō may be considered to have exercised some leadership, but they also acted only within the framework of the bureaucracy; even Araki, the most conspicuous, was no exception. A charismatic leader specific to fascism or totalitarianism never appeared in Japan. This meant that the civilian legal order was maintained to the last. The

[23] The situation was to some extent similar to that in eastern Europe. See David Mitrany, *Marx Against the Peasant* (Chapel Hill, N.C., 1951).

Ermächtigungsgesetz given to Hitler in 1933 had no counterpart in Japan. When the IRAA was formed in 1940, suspicion was voiced as to whether it was not a violation of the constitution, and it was permitted only as a "civil," not a "political," organization. Unlike events in Germany, no breakdown in the rule of law took place.

One explanation for the limited nature of the army's dictatorship in Japan in contrast to the Nazi party's dictatorship in Germany is to be found in the difference in intensity of the impact of outside circumstances. In both countries, all rightist groups were deeply convinced of the need for internal reformation and external expansion; and all rightist groups believed that reformation and expansion were indivisible. The difference was that in the international environment of Europe, it was impossible to attack the existing order without great risk; the creation of a dictatorial state, with its increased power of mobilization, was therefore felt to be prerequisite to any external expansion. But in the Asian environment, with China disunited and no other power prepared to act, the way was open for Japan to move—at least in the beginning—with little or no risk. Consequently, while the Japanese radical rightist officers planned an internal coup and an invasion of Manchuria simultaneously, the failure of the former did not prevent the success of the latter. A coup at home the genrō and jūshin could frustrate, for they could rally against it traditional sentiments of great power, but a military action abroad they could not reach: such actions had the support of an overwhelming chauvinism.[24]

The Japanese radical Right always insisted that the exaltation of national prestige was impossible unless accompanied by internal revolution, but in reality these two aspects did not develop equally during the Japanese drift to the Right. The Japanese invasion of China was bold and reckless, but the upset of the existing domestic political order was unsteady and in-

[24] The chauvinistic character of so-called mass democracy, which appeared at the end of the nineteenth century, is described in E. H. Carr, *Nationalism and After* (New York, 1945).

sufficient. F. J. Turner's frontier thesis in American history might be applied in reverse to Japan. China was the frontier in the minds of the Japanese renovationists, and the existence of this frontier helped to mitigate internal change.

We cannot overlook the fact that the Japanese invasion of China was not the planned action of the central organ of the army. It developed as an independent undertaking of troops dispatched to Manchuria or China proper; the center of the army only followed in their footsteps. Therefore, it is evident that the decision of the International Military Tribunal for the Far East, that there existed a conspiracy within Japanese governing circles, was incorrect. Moreover, the increase in the power of the army in internal politics, was not the product of long-range planning. The central organs of the army followed the situation created by the troops overseas and, accordingly, expanded their control over politics gradually, improvising as they went along.

Can Prewar Japan Be Called a Fascist State?

It is obvious that fascism in the Marxist definition of "a form of rule by monopoly capital" did not exist in Japan, but how about fascism in the definition of Maruyama Masao? Maruyama describes the basic elements of fascist ideology as follows: "the rejection of individualistic or liberal ideas, objection to parliamentarianism, the assertion of external expansion, a trend toward the glorification of armaments and war, an emphasis on national mythology and ultranationalism, the exclusion of class struggle on the grounds of totalitarianism, and especially the struggle against Marxism."[25]

It is undeniable that a similar ideology prevailed in Japan by the 1930's, but similarity of ideologies does not imply identity of social or political structures. These latter are most important, for, if we consider prewar Japan as fascist simply on the

[25] Maruyama Masao, *Gendai seiji no shisō to Kōdō* [Thought and Behavior in Modern Japanese Politics] (Tokyo, 1956), I, 36. I could not refer to the English translation by Ivan Morris (London, 1963).

grounds of ideological analogy, we shall fall into the error of overlooking the truly devilish nature of the Nazi dictatorship, which is to be found in the peculiar form of its political rule. That rule was characterized essentially by one party dictatorship, destruction of the civil legal order, and emphasis on the masses. None of these characteristics apply to Japan.

It is true that Communists were severely persecuted in Japan, but it was, in the end, according to legal procedures and the persecuted were released comparatively easily following *tenkō* or formal abandonment of their political creed. Although some people died under torture during Japanese investigations or as a result of maltreatment in Japanese prisons, there was no mass massacre in the darkness as in Germany. On this point, German totalitarianism can be compared only to Soviet totalitarianism under Stalin, not to the quasi-dictatorship of the Japanese military. An important element in Maruyama's thinking is his conception of fascism as "counterrevolutionary." Although Maruyama is not a Marxist, his view of social development follows that of Marxism. "The" revolution referred to is the Russian Revolution of 1917, and fascism is considered to be essentially a counterattack on it. However, if instead of "proletarian revolution," we take human rights and democracy as our standard of value, the similarities between communism and fascism appear more important than their differences, and each is recognized as a form of totalitarianism.

Emphasis on the masses was another essential element in nazism. This was also true in Italian fascism, but the function of the total state was made clear for the first time with the rise of the Nazi regime. Emil Lederer and Sigmund Neumann carefully analyzed this kind of state.[26] It is noteworthy, therefore, that at the end of the 1930's Lederer wrote with regard to Japan:

[26] Emil Lederer, *State of the Masses: The Threat of the Classless Society* (New York, 1940); and Sigmund Neumann, *Permanent Revolution: The Total State in a World at War* (New York, 1942).

If we recognize that a regime like the present one in Japan still has its social and psychological roots in the past, that it is still flexible enough to be transformed if the general situation changes, we shall see that it is fundamentally different from fascism. For fascism is the dictatorship by masses over the masses themselves and cannot be molded or transformed except by a revolution, which is not likely to break out unless there is a defeat on the battlefield.[27]

After the outbreak of the Pacific War, Japan did increase the "organization of society for war,"[28] but, as Lederer had predicted, it never developed a true fascist type mass structure.

In the end, the greatest difference between Japan and Germany in the prewar period is that, while in the latter mass society developed in the classical way as a result of the collapse of the empire, in the former the traditional framework of society was strongly retained and the "rule of amorphous masses" did not appear. The corresponding difference in the sphere of thought is also remarkable. Nazism is called a revolution of nihilism,[29] but in interwar Japan we find no such atmosphere. This difference seems to come from the difference in the roles of the "conservative revolution" in the two countries. Each produced an ideology of revolutionary conservatism that failed in practice; however, the effects of this failure were different in each country. In Germany the failure of revolutionary conservatism was remarkably successful in breaking down traditional conservatism and, following the bankruptcy of liberalism and democracy, produced a complete vacuum of values. It was this vacuum of values that gave nazism its chance.

No such vacuum of values occurred in Japan until after World War II. Then it came in much the same way as it had

[27] Lederer, *op.cit.*, p. 68.   [28] *Ibid.*, p. 67.
[29] Hermann Rauschning, *Die Revolution des Nihilismus, Kulisse und Wirklichkeit im Dritten Reich* (Zurich, 1938).

in Germany twenty-five years earlier: as a result of defeat, accompanied by the dissolution of the traditional social order and the sudden emergence of a mass society. Had Japan been simultaneously afflicted with sustained economic chaos, as Germany was following World War I, she might well have turned then to a dictatorship of fascism or communism. Fortunately, the circumstances were different: Japan's distress was less, no heavy burden of reparations was imposed, and the strains of high industrialization were eased by changes in the social structure, so that Japan soon came to enjoy the most extraordinary prosperity in her history. In this situation, Japan has been saved from the temptation of dictatorship, but she continues to face, in spite of her prosperity, the social and political instability and the spiritual imbalance which the onset of mass society engenders.[30]

[30] E. O. Reischauer, *Japan, Past and Present* (3rd edn.; New York, 1964), chap. 14.

CHAPTER XIII

What Went Wrong?

EDWIN O. REISCHAUER

DESPITE sharp disagreements among Japanese and Western scholars over the definition of "modernization" in general and the dynamics of Japan's own process of change during the past century, there is nonetheless wide agreement that, as Dore and Ōuchi put it, "something 'went wrong' in Japan in the late twenties and thirties of this century." The disastrous war that grew out of these years in itself seems adequate proof of this assumption, and most scholars, whether or not they have "value-free" definitions of "modernization," join in deploring the breakdown of political democratization that preceded and accompanied the war catastrophe.

No one would deny that the century between 1868 and 1968 witnessed great changes in Japan, many of which would fit most definitions of "modernization," but within this period the two decades between the mid-twenties and the mid-forties do stand out as a time of special troubles and of backsliding in at least some of the standards by which one might measure "modernization." It is the relationship of this time of trouble and setback to the secular trends of the century as a whole that is the subject of this volume and the conference that spawned it, as it has been of many previous studies.

As Morley points out, the International Military Tribunal for the Far East at the close of World War II judged that this seeming aberration in Japan's modern history was the product of a conspiracy by a specific group of "war criminals." At the other extreme, some historians of Marxist inclination have viewed it as the inevitable product of socio-economic forces set in motion by the nature of the initial change at the time of the Meiji Restoration. According to such a line of reasoning, the Restoration is to be regarded as having aborted a "true revolution" and thus inexorably produced conditions variously defined as "absolutism," the "Emperor System," monopoly capitalism, and imperialism, which in turn inevitably led Japan into its disastrous war experiences.

Any study of the manifold and complex interacting factors that lay behind actual historical developments in Japan, not only in the 1920's and 1930's but during the whole period since 1868, makes a simplistic explanation based on a conspiracy of individuals or on some unilinear socio-economic force seem implausible. While both personalities and basic trends within the society unquestionably helped shape what did happen, the story seems much too complex for any sort of monocausal explanation. The danger, however, is that in trying to accommodate all the varied and often conflicting data that seem relevant, one will become so lost in details that the only conclusion which can safely be drawn about what happened in the 1920's and 1930's is that it happened.

The title of this volume suggests a middle position, which I believe is a congenial one for all of the contributors. By phrasing the problem as "dilemmas of growth," it suggests that there may be a close causal relationship between the process of growth in Japan in the half century preceding the 1920's and 1930's and what happened during these two decades. By using the plural, it suggests that there were multiple and therefore interacting and presumably conflicting factors at work.

Whether or not the causal relationships discernible in modern Japanese history have a significance for other societies going through a parallel process of modernization is an important question but may be beyond our ability to answer at present. Hayashi's comparison of Japan with Germany, while helpful to our understanding of Japan, produces more contrasts than similarities. Perhaps closer parallels will be found with other non-Western societies as they "modernize," but at present our understanding of the causal relationships in the Japanese case is still too uncertain and the "modernization" process (or at least our knowledge of it) in other non-Western societies still too incomplete to permit clear comparisons.

Each of the several essays in this volume probes one of many areas in which significant causal relationships might be found. The purpose of this essay is to attempt to see how some of the findings of these studies may be related and what further studies would be helpful. It is as if we were diggers at some large and deeply buried archaeological site. Widely scattered probes have revealed some of the details of the site, and these suggest that its overall pattern is not a simple one. But we need to draw hypotheses as to what the pattern may be, so that we can guess where in the many unexcavated parts of the site it might be best to dig in order to find the most significant new clues.

We first need to define a little more clearly what we are looking for. The phrase "dilemmas of growth" and the statement "something went wrong" are both vague enough to hide very significant differences in the types of data we are trying to discover and analyze. It might be helpful to divide these into three theoretically distinct levels, while recognizing that no sharp dividing line can really be drawn between them, and that the three types of factors naturally interacted closely with one another. The first level might be defined as the objective difficulties Japan faced during the 1920's and 1930's, the second as Japanese perceptions of these problems as formulated during the period, and the third as what actually happened. These three levels need to be clearly differentiated and their relationships carefully analyzed before we can define what it was that did "go wrong." In attempting to untangle this problem, I have drawn heavily on the insights in the various essays and in the discussions which accompanied their presentation at the conference in Puerto Rico.

Objective Problems

Some of the major objective problems of the time are specifically studied in essays in this volume and others are merely alluded to as being already well known. Patrick clearly brings out the relatively poor showing of the Japanese economy in the 1920's (an overall growth rate of 33.4 percent as compared with an average of 57.3 percent for the three preceding decades). Within this broad economic problem, there was the more specific one of the growing gap in productivity between the modernizing and the more traditional sectors of the economy, to which Ohkawa and Rosovsky have called attention. This, together with the disastrous fall in agricultural prices in the late 1920's, produced a sharp decline in the relative economic standing and, to some extent, the absolute economic conditions of large segments of the agricultural community and parts of the labor force.

Such conditions helped produce considerable unrest among tenant farmers and urban laborers and a certain degree of subversive activity at both the extreme left and extreme right of the political spectrum. Probably a more important cause for these phenomena, however, was the rising political and social consciousness of these groups as a result of the spread of education and similar factors in the whole "modernization" process. Such unrest was part of an even broader sense of general malaise and dissatisfaction with what Japan was becoming, as she moved away from the uniformities and certainties of what had once been a more stable society and became less identifiable with the patterns and values of the past.

A third general area of objective difficulties can be perceived, at least in retrospect, in the decision-making process of the government. The relatively small and unified group of men (the original genrō and their early protégés), who had given reasonably clear, integrated, and flexible leadership to Japan during the nation's earlier stages of "modernization," had been replaced by the 1920's by a much larger and more complex leadership made up of a series of clearly differing elite groups (the military, the civil bureaucracy, politicians, businessmen, and "intellectuals" in the Japanese sense), which through more diversified careers had developed more deeply divergent values and policies. Through evolutionary processes, methods for balancing the conflicting attitudes of these elites had been worked out, but the growing complexity of the decision-making process and the expanding size of the decision-making groups, as Hosoya points out, had perhaps made it harder to achieve well defined and carefully coordinated policies than had been the case in earlier decades. As events were soon to reveal, there were also dangerous ambiguities and sharp disagreements regarding the whole process by which the top political leadership was to be chosen and crucial decisions made. In other words, in political decision-making the disintegrative tendencies of growth were outpacing integrative tendencies.

A final group of objective problems were those presented by new external conditions. The world-wide depression and rising tariff restrictions were major factors in the economic crisis Japan faced at the beginning of the 1930's. More important was the rapid rise of national consciousness in China, which presented Japan, by then the dominant military power in the area, with much more difficult problems than those faced by the British, French, or Russians in their earlier waves of imperialistic expansion in Asia. Growing American influence in East Asia and stiffening American support for its concepts of a moralistic international order, particularly as these applied to China, were also in a sense new external problems for the Japanese.

Perceptions of Problems

This is scarcely a comprehensive list of the objective problems Japan faced in the 1920's and 1930's, but it will suffice as a basis for comparison with the second level of our analysis, namely the perceptions of these problems as formulated by the Japanese at the time. As Patrick shows, the slowdown in the over-all rate of economic growth was rapidly overcome in the 1930's, in part because of increased government spending, not all of it for military purposes. Even during the 1920's the average annual growth in real terms had been 3.2 percent, a figure considered tolerable in many countries today, and during the

1930's the increase in real Net Domestic Product was 72.1 percent, the highest for any decade until Japan's postwar "economic miracle." These facts did not prevent many Japanese from believing that the country faced a grave economic crisis. As they saw it, the Japanese people, barred from emigration to salubrious climes in North America and Australia by hostile immigration laws and excluded from the markets and resources of much of the world by mounting tariffs and other bars maintained by hostile Western imperial powers, faced economic ruin in their own overcrowded islands unless they too could win a broad empire for economic exploitation. One can understand these fears during the time of crisis in Japan's foreign trade between 1927 and 1931, but the persistence and growth of these ideas, despite Japan's good economic showing and rapid increase in foreign trade after 1931, needs careful study.

The maldistribution of the nation's wealth did continue through the 1930's, but does not seem to have been perceived as a basically economic problem. At least, most of the correctives suggested for the situation appear to have been aimed more at political or moral than at economic objectives. On the extreme Left there were demands for a "dictatorship of the proletariat"; on the extreme Right there were yearnings for a return to an agrarian society of simpler and purer standards; in army circles there were serious worries about the health and physique of the peasant conscripts from depressed rural areas; and on all sides there was condemnation more of the political influence than of the wealth of the zaibatsu plutocracy. On the other hand, there seem to have been few real efforts, or even much discussion, of practical ways to redivide the economic pie more fairly. If this is true, then this is a surprising lack that deserves further study. In any case, the plight of the tenant farmers remained relatively unchanged for the American Occupation to solve; the problem of the gap in the "dual structure" of the economy remained to be ameliorated by postwar economic advances; and the zaibatsu system remained essentially intact to fall prey at the end of the war to American reformist zeal. As Tiedemann shows, the zaibatsu executives in the late 1930's, while no longer able to influence government policy through the old channel of the political parties and forced to take a cautious, circumspect attitude toward their critics, still exercised great economic power and considerable political influence.

Labor and tenant unrest as well as the subversive activities of the extreme Left and Right were recognized as problems but, quite rightly, do not seem to have been felt as really serious threats to society. Dore and Ōuchi clearly show that Japanese "fascism" cannot be explained as a conscious or unconscious reaction to a threat from the poor peasantry, and in any case both labor and tenant unrest melted away under the heat of rising chauvinistic excitement during the 1930's. Beckmann shows how minimal was the threat from the minuscule Communist groups, and the larger challenge of the more moderate Left, as organized in the Social Masses Party, was never great (the vote of the so-called proletarian parties never quite reached ten percent of the electorate) and was in time completely emasculated by patriotic war fervor. The extreme Right came closer to menacing the system but only in so far as its activities were tolerated by the public and used by elements in the leadership for their own purposes. The various putsch attempts before 1936 fell ridiculously short of success, and, when an uprising was carried out on a really dangerous scale that year, it was ruthlessly suppressed, and measures were taken to assure that there would be no repetitions.

The unrest of some of the less privileged classes and the subversive activities of a few extremists, thus, did not produce any clear defensive or corrective responses within Japanese society, much less force it into those actions which are meant when it it is asserted that "something went wrong" at this time. Instead they merged into the general sense of malaise and confusion of the period, which obviously drew more strongly from other sources.

495

I have mentioned the prevailing sense of malaise—the feeling that something was going wrong in Japanese society—as one of the objective problems Japan faced, which in a sense it was, but it fits even better our second category of perceptions of problems. The actual difficulties Japan faced during the 1920's and early 1930's, when compared with those of previous decades, do not themselves explain the rather sharp change in mood from the optimism or at least passive acceptance of the situation that had been the dominant attitude of earlier times. This profound change in mood deserves more study and analysis than it has received. Attention has been focused largely on the sharper expressions of discontent on the part of either the extreme Left or the extreme Right, but far more important are the reasons why and the processes by which those occupying the broad central spectrum of Japanese leadership and public opinion came to feel that things were so amiss that drastic changes might be necessary.

The broad and amorphous center of public opinion is always more difficult to analyze than the narrower and more clear-cut extremes. One clue, however, to the general sense of discontent that pervaded Japan at this time may be found in the types of solutions that were offered. A recurring theme in many of the essays in this volume is the call for unity and harmony and the stress on collectivist ethical values.

One is struck by the rather sharp contrast to the enthusiasm in the Meiji period for Smile's "Self-Help" and the emphasis on personal success (*shusse*), individual responsibility, and social Darwinism. During this earlier period, social critics had called for diversity and individualism in a society which they perceived to be still too bound by the traditions and collectivist ethics of the Tokugawa period. By the 1920's, however, Japan was no longer as strongly collectivist a society as it had been in the Meiji period and was in fact becoming decidedly pluralistic in that it was developing clearly divergent interests and attitudes among its various elites of leadership and social and occupational groupings. Now, however, the cry on all sides was for harmony and unity.

The growing complexity and urbanization of society, the capitalistic basis of the economy, the egalitarian but individually competitive educational system, the electoral and parliamentary institutions, which had by the 1920's come to occupy the center of the political stage, all pointed to a system of open conflict of interests and ideas, held together by accepted methods of achieving compromise rather than by any natural harmony of interests and attitudes. This developing system, of course, was still far from perfect. Both Cabinet responsibility to the Diet and universal male suffrage were only beginning to be achieved in the 1920's, and domination by the Diet and the Cabinet over some of the other organs of government, particularly the military, was far from secure. Japan thus faced serious problems of integration in political leadership and decision-making.

There seems to have been little perception of this problem, however. Instead there was a growing assumption that, because the system did not produce harmony and unity, it had failed even before it had been fully achieved. The widespread charges at the time of hopeless corruption on the part of the political parties and their zaibatsu financial backers seem in retrospect exaggerated, but, before we can really judge this point, we need studies of the actual level of corruption in Japan in the 1920's as compared to other societies at comparable stages of parliamentary development. The comparison may well prove to be in Japan's favor, and we may have to conclude that the great talk of corruption in Japan was more the product of high political standards than of high levels of corruption. As Patrick shows, the government was indeed inept in its handling of the economic problems of the 1920's, but this may have been less the fault of the system than of the level of economic understanding during the period. (The record of the Western countries is not impressive at this time either.) Otherwise, despite all the accusations of failure, the emerging parliamentary political system does seem to have done reasonably well even in the 1920's, and it has been proven a very decided success in postwar Japan.

Be that as it may, during the 1920's and 1930's Japanese public opinion seems to have turned away, either in disappointment or disgust, from the evolving system of balancing open conflicts of interest through parliamentary institutions. Attention became focused, not on completing and perfecting this system, but on recreating unity and harmony under some more orderly system. Duus' study of Ōyama Ikuo shows a one-time advocate of parliamentary democracy impatiently rejecting the system even before universal male suffrage had been achieved and espousing instead what was, at least at that time, the quixotic hope that "true democracy" could be more quickly achieved through a dictatorship of the proletariat. Najita shows how Nakano Seigō, an influential writer and member of the Diet, emphasized a traditional Ōyōmei (Wang Yang-ming) type of "individualism" which, far from recognizing the legitimacy of conflict between divergent views, served as moral justification for violent action and enforced conformity. Many others, including the "young officers" of the extreme Right, showed this same traditional, elitist philosophy and what Najita calls the "*hayato* personality," both of which significantly had been characteristic of the *shishi* activists during the earlier time of trouble in the Bakumatsu period. Still other extremists, such as Gondō Seikyō or Kita Ikki, advocated the return to a harmonious agrarian society or unity under the "imperial will."

No one should be surprised at the existence of these utopian and often backward-looking plans for a more harmonious society at this time of growing pluralism and a developing system of open conflict of interests in politics. They drew not only on the memory of the past but also on the traditional Confucian philosophy of the Tokugawa and on the more recently imported German idealism, which both posited rational, harmonious, unitary systems that lead more easily to utopianism than to the acceptance of diversity and pragmatic balancing of conflicting interests. They were also stimulated to some extent by new intellectual currents from the West, such as communism and fascism, which helped make these concepts of utopian uniformity seem more "modern" and respectable.

It does seem surprising, however, that there was not a more vigorous intellectual defense of the system as it was taking shape. This is a subject that needs much more careful study than it has received. Possibly there was more of a defense than we realize, because our attention has been drawn away from it to the extreme voices of protest. But one is struck by what seems to be the ambiguity and weakness of the defense of parliamentary government and the rather ready acceptance by its would-be defenders of the vocabulary of harmony.

The politicians themselves for the most part, having achieved power through practical compromises, attempted to retain it in the same way, instead of standing on principle, and as a result saw their powers steadily compromised away. Even a champion of democracy like Yoshino Sakuzō shied away from the usual word for democracy (*minshu-shugi*) as constituting a threat to the unifying imperial institution, and he showed an elitist distrust of rule by a popular majority. Minobe Tatsukichi remained a consistent and fearless supporter of his own cautious legalistic road to parliamentary democracy, but, when he was attacked by the proponents of a mystical concept of unity under the name of *kokutai*, he was deserted by those who might have been expected to stand by him and was allowed to be destroyed. There may have been a broader and much more effective ideological defense of the system as it was emerging in the 1920's than we now realize, but, if so, it needs to be made clear and, if not, its absence is really a more important and difficult question to explain than is the presence of the various proposals for unity and harmony.

It seems probable that society was becoming more pluralistic and conflicts of interest were becoming more apparent during the whole of the past century of rapid "modernization" in Japan. One wonders, therefore, why during this long process it was in the late 1920's and 1930's that this problem came suddenly to the fore in the consciousness of the Japanese and produced strong demands for either an atavistic return to the harmony of the past or a sudden leap to a new sort of utopian unity. One reason might be that by this time the divergencies in Japanese society had become too clear to be overlooked any longer—the great gap between a still heavily traditional countryside and the vastly changed cities, the growing disparity between the traditional and modern sectors of the economy, the increasing inequalities of wealth, and the sharpening clashes in interests and values between different social and occupational groups and between different professional elites of leadership. The now obvious lack of harmony and unity may have made these traditional qualities suddenly seem more desirable than in earlier decades when a good deal of harmony and unity inherited from the past could be taken for granted.

Another reason might be that the spread of education to the poorer peasants and workers had by this time not only helped produce conscious expressions of discontent on their part but had also brought the attitudes of such classes to the surface of Japanese politics for the first time. Agrarian Japan, which still constituted about half of the nation, had been much less affected by the trends of "modernization" than had the rest of the country and thus had remained a reservoir of the more traditional collectivist ethics. It is significant that so much of the talk of harmony and unity in the 1920's and 1930's was in one way or another focused on rural Japan rather than on the cities.

Both of these explanations are connected with the problem of divergent rates of change in Japanese society. The lag in rural Japan highlighted the growing discrepancies in society and also helps explain the powerful re-emergence of ideas and values that belonged to an earlier stage in Japan's history. The concept of divergent rates of change might also be applied in a broader way to the whole of Japanese society. The Meiji innovators forced technological changes on their countrymen as rapidly as they could and also forced a rapid pace of institutional change to create institutions they felt were superior to the old ones or were needed to accompany the changes in technology. Both technological and institutional change might be said to have achieved the "take-off" stage by the 1890's, as is shown by the continuing rapid development of the economy under business leadership and the rapid evolution of parliamentary institutions between 1890 and the 1920's under pressures from the politicians produced by the new system of elections and representative bodies.

What happened in the 1920's and 1930's and the quality of the debate at the time, however, suggests that the social habits and thinking of the Japanese as a whole had not kept pace with these technological and institutional changes. The value system seems to have remained basically collectivist, oriented more to harmony in a natural family or village unit than to the actual diversity and individualism of a modern industrialized society. In other words, by the 1920's the technology and institutions of Japan may have seriously outpaced the social, emotional, and intellectual attitudes of the Japanese, causing a dangerous imbalance between what actually existed and what people felt should exist. This would help explain the pervasive sense of malaise, even though the actual problems were no more critical than they had been in earlier decades. It might also explain why attention seems to have been focused not so much on meeting the specific problems of an industrializing society and on perfecting the obvious weaknesses of the developing political system as on broad moralistic correctives to the whole of Japanese society.

In discussing the general sense of malaise, I have already touched on the apparent lack of perception of the specific problem of the increasing complexity of the decision-making process in government and the sharpening disagreement over how it should operate. The framers of the constitution had left a dangerous ambiguity about the ultimate decision-making power. In theory, it was in the emperor's hands, but there was general recognition that he would exercise it only on the advice of others. At first, the Meiji genrō performed this function, but, as they died off and were not replaced by a similar group, the situation became decidedly ambiguous. A pragmatic, shifting balance of forces was achieved between the various elites of leadership, with dominance passing gradually into the hands of the Diet and the political leadership it produced. But this emerging system was open to challenge, as was shown by the army's refusal in 1928 to discipline the murderers of Chang Tso-lin in Manchuria, the navy's stiffening resistance to Cabinet control after the 1930 dispute over the London Naval Treaty, and the army's prosecution of its own war in Manchuria in 1931.

Japan thus faced the very serious problems of clarifying and stabilizing the method of choosing her top political leaders and making political decisions. The problem, however, does not seem to have been posed very effectively in these terms. Instead the prevalent demand was for a vague and unspecified "national unity" and "harmony." Such rhetoric tended to obscure the real problem of the growing divergence of interests and attitudes among the elites of leadership and the increasing complexity of the processes of decision-making. Behind the smoke screen of the concepts of unity and harmony that better fitted an earlier and simpler society, the actual mechanisms for the selection of leadership and the making of decisions became more obscure and in a sense more accidental than they had been before.

The end result, much aided by the nationalistic fervor of a period of foreign crises and wars, was the virtual monopoly of leadership and decision-making by one of the elites of leadership, the military bureaucracy. Centrist opinion of the 1920's and early 1930's would scarcely have approved of this outcome, but it may have contributed to it by failing to pose the political problems in truly relevant terms. But was this really the situation? Did the Japanese of the 1920's and 1930's fail to ask the right political questions or to develop cogent arguments in support of the parliamentary method of balancing conflicting interests? Or is this impression only the result of our having ignored those who thought in these terms because of our greater interest in more extremist opinion? We need more study of this problem to discover just how much clear analysis of the real political problem actually existed. If these attitudes were indeed weak or missing, then we face the further question as to why this was so. As I have already suggested, the concept of discrepancies in the speed of change in various aspects of Japanese culture may be one useful avenue of approach to this last problem.

Moving to the problems posed by conditions abroad, one is struck by the decided narrowing of the formulations of these problems between the 1920's and the late 1930's. I have already noted the growth of a sense of stifling economic encirclement in the 1930's despite Japan's clear economic success both at home and in foreign trade. The 1930's also showed a loss in the flexibility with which Japan had during the 1920's approached the problems of growing Chinese nationalism and American moralistic support for China. Such flexibility seems to have served Japanese interests well in the 1920's, and if it had still been operative in the 1930's would probably have continued to do so, especially after the outbreak of war in Europe, when, as during World War I, Japan would have had great opportunities for economic expansion. Instead, however, the Japanese international focus had become so narrow—it was now limited to a dream of a harmonious pan-Asian world dominated by Japan—that options had become progressively more limited, until Japan finally faced the choice between all-out war with a coalition of opponents or a complete backdown in China.

Thus the foreign policy crisis the Japanese faced in the 1930's may have been more the product of their own formulation of the problem than of the objective external situation. This narrowing of foreign policy options seems to have been closely associated with the failure to pose the problem in decision-making correctly and with the domestic political outcome that resulted from this failure. For example, the unilateral action of the army in Manchuria in 1931 produced the first serious reduction in foreign policy options for Japan, and, as Iriye and Hosoya show, Japan's foreign policy initiatives during the 1930's became limited to choices between the various perceptions the Japanese military had of the nation's external interests and strategic problems. The much broader range of perceptions of the 1920's, provided by businessmen, civil bureaucrats, politicians, and intellectuals, had for all practical purposes been eliminated.

Crowley's study of the Shōwa Kenkyūkai, in a sense, illustrates this point. This group of brilliant civilians seemed to think only within the narrow limits set by the dominant military formulation of the problem. While they rightly called attention to the significance of rising Chinese nationalism and the importance of avoiding a clash with this great new force, they seem to have been incapable of suggesting realistic ways of accommodating Japanese policies to it, because this would have necessitated breaking out of the policy strait-jacket imposed by the military interpretation of the problem. Instead they accepted the basic premises of the military and thus could only attempt to conjure Chinese nationalism away through the manipulation of words and theories.

What Actually "Went Wrong"

There may always be something of a gap between problems as they really exist and as people formulate them, but this gap seems to have been particularly great in Japan during the 1920's and 1930's. Our third level of analysis, what actually "went wrong," clearly was more a response to the formulations of the problems than to their actualities, but here too there was a considerable gap between the problems as posed and the eventual outcome. Economic problems, social unrest, a sense of malaise.

and difficulties in the decision-making process in government were merged into an ill-defined need for national unity and harmony. The end result, however, was scarcely a naturally harmonious, unified society, but rather a virtual military dictatorship with strong totalitarian overtones. The foreign problem was posed as a need for economic *Lebensraum*, but the outcome was a drive for imperial conquest that in retrospect is seen to have made little economic sense and in any case led shortly to military disaster.

When people speak of something "going wrong" in the 1920's and 1930's, these two end products are what is usually meant. The real question then is how the military was able to win control over the government and lead the nation into an ultimately disastrous war. Or, to reverse the question, why was there not a more effective opposition to military domination? And then, to return to our starting point, we have the question of how the military's winning of dominance was related to the objective problems the Japanese economy and society faced at the time and the contemporary perceptions of these problems.

It is not difficult to see why the military desired to control Japan's domestic politics and foreign policy. Military officers had a strong tradition of independence of the civil government and their own clear concepts of Japan's interests abroad, but during the 1920's they saw both eroding dangerously. Cabinets dominated by party politicians and business interests sharply reduced the military share of the budget (from 981,000,000 yen in 1919 to 437,000,000 yen in 1926) and of the nation's wealth (from 7.7 percent of Net Domestic Product in 1919 to 3.0 percent in 1925 and 1926). These business-minded Cabinets also followed more conciliatory policies toward the challenges of Chinese nationalism and American moralistic globalism than most military men thought wise. The latter, as inheritors of a centuries-old feudal tradition of contempt for nonmilitary men and especially for businessmen, were restive with a system that was giving increasing dominance to the representatives of taxpayers and of big business interests. Depending largely on rural conscripts for its manpower, the army was particularly responsive to the economic distress of the peasantry and even more to the physical weaknesses of the conscripts resulting from economic deprivation. As the chief custodian of the national interests in Manchuria, the army also stood in the front line of the clash with Chinese nationalism. For these various reasons, it is not at all surprising to find many military officers eager to take leadership into their own hands.

The clash of interests and policies between the military and other elements of leadership is illustrative of the diversification and disintegration of policy-making in a modernizing society that Hosoya points out. As we have seen, the disintegrative forces in decision-making in an expanding and steadily diverging leadership outpaced the development of an integrative system based on electoral and parliamentary procedures that could have accommodated the diversity of a modernized society. The latter was starting to take shape, but it was still far from perfected. Except for budgetary controls, the military, through the doctrine of the "right of supreme command," was still in theory completely free of the civil government and was joined to it only by the hypothetical though actually nonexistent control of the emperor. This permitted military defiance of the civil government, as in the Chang Tso-lin incident, and military determination of foreign policy through direct action abroad, as in the so-called Manchurian incident. Foreign crises and wars in turn created popular xenophobic responses, which then facilitated the further achievement of the foreign policy objectives of the military as well as their control over the civil government and domestic policy.

Viewed in this light, the key thing that "went wrong" was the usurpation of power by the military rather than any broader economic or social breakdown. This, however, was not the whole story. The other side of the coin was the lack of an effective resistance to the seizure of control over foreign policy by the military. This was perhaps more significant than the actions of the military itself. At the time of the Manchurian incident, some political leaders did favor a determined attempt to bring the military under control through a firm hold over the purse strings. Factionalism in the military, as shown by Hosoya and Iriye, and the tradition of permitting a high degree of autonomy in the field would have complicated such an effort, but it might have worked. However, the top political leadership backed away from such a course, apparently not understanding the nature of the problem; and in any case public opinion, aroused by military successes in Manchuria, might not have permitted it. Thus we see that the perceptions of the problems Japan faced and broad public reactions to the conditions of the time had an important bearing on the outcome, helping to account for the lack of a determined political stand against the military and also for the public tolerance of their acts.

The contrast between the still widely prevalent collectivist value system and the emerging parliamentary institutions of the 1920's also helps explain another important part of the story. As we have seen, assassination and putsch attempts were not a real threat to the system, but they were allowed to help push the government and its policies into the hands of the military. Reflecting the values of an earlier age, public opinion, instead of being outraged at each attack on the duly constituted representatives of the people and the officials of the emperor's government, tended to sympathize with the "pure motives" of the young assassins, who were permitted to turn their trials into fierce indictments of the alleged corruption and selfishness of the politicians, bureaucrats, and businessmen they had attacked. Each incident was interpreted not as evidence of a need for greater discipline in the military and for clarification of the processes of decision-making, but as proof that greater harmony and unity must be achieved in both government and society. In turn, the need for unity, instead of being interpreted as requiring a broader and more representative leadership, was used as justification for the reduction and eventually the total elimination of the politicians' role and subsequently for the diminution of the civil bureaucracy's share in leadership, as the military moved step by step toward control over the whole government. Thus the perceptions of problems on the part of the nonmilitary leaders and the general public figure at least as important background music for Japan's tragedy, even if they did not constitute the leitmotivs.

One interesting problem is why in this process of destruction of the emerging parliamentary system, the civil bureaucracy did not become a serious contender for power. It derived as much prestige from tradition as did the military; its higher ranks surrounded the emperor, the theoretical source of all legitimate authority; and it permeated the whole political process much more than did the military. But, as Spaulding shows, the civil bureaucracy remained divided among jealously competitive ministries. The bureaucrats, unlike the military, lacked unified goals and seem to have worked effectively together only to protect their own career interests against encroachment by outsiders. Those civil bureaucrats who took an active part in promoting the new policies of the 1930's, the so-called "revisionists," were essentially ambitious individuals willing to work across ministry lines in cooperation with the military and did not represent a coordinated bid for power by the civil bureaucracy itself. Spaulding's account is reassuring for contemporary Japan, because the civil bureaucracy is the part of the political system of the 1920's and 1930's that has survived least changed into postwar times.

An Overview

In this sketchy survey of a few of the factors in Japan's time of trouble in the 1920's and 1930's, I have not tried to provide any overall pattern. It is still too early to sort out all the manifold elements in the story or to define their complicated interrelationships. All that I have attempted to do is to show that, in analyzing the problem, it may be helpful to try to distinguish beween the three levels of objective problems, contemporary formulations of these problems, and what actually happened. There were, of course, complex interactions between these three levels, but there was not a simple and inevitable causal relationship between the three, with the first necessarily leading to the second and the second preordaining the third. In fact, the causal relationships between the three levels operated both ways. For instance, the army's seizure of foreign policy initiative in Manchuria in 1931 profoundly affected popular interpretations of the problems Japan faced and at the same time, by creating wartime conditions, greatly changed the nature of Japan's actual economic, social, and political problems.

This three-level analysis of the problems of the 1920's and 1930's may also help to show one underlying aspect of growth in Japan. This is the unevenness of the whole growth process. The 1920's and 1930's seem to have been a time of special trouble in modern Japanese history at least in part because the disequilibrium in the growth process had become severe by that time. I have in mind such factors as the sharp rural-urban split, the growing divergence in various sectors of the economy, the gap between relatively traditional social, emotional, and ethical attitudes on the one hand and rapidly evolving economic and political institutions on the other, and the greater speed at which the unity of leadership disintegrated than the new integrative processes of decision-making took shape.

This may be in part what Morley has in mind when he calls for a "pathology of growth." Growth in any society is likely to be uneven, thus producing new imbalances. This seems to be true even when growth has been a relatively slow, evolutionary process, but imbalances are more likely to become dangerously pronounced when growth has been artificially forced, as in Meiji Japan, by a strong leadership utilizing the experience and patterns of more developed societies. Japan's very success in changing her technology and institutions in the nineteenth century seems to have contributed to what had become dangerous imbalances by the 1920's and 1930's. The exact outcome, of course, was unpredictable. It was influenced by the interactions of a huge number of variables, including the accidents of individual personality and chance timing. But there seems to be a broad causal relationship between imbalanced growth and eventual instability. This is one conclusion to be derived from modern Japanese history that seems relevant for the many other countries which are undergoing rapid and usually forced change today.

The various chapters in this volume have probed some very important points in the story of the 1920's and 1930's, but their results, on the whole, are more suggestive than conclusive, indicating not so much why the history of the time unfolded the way it did as what we still need to know to have a better understanding of what happened. There is room for a great deal more digging at our rich archaeological site of prewar Japan.

CONTRIBUTORS

GEORGE M. BECKMANN, Dean of the College of Arts and Sciences and Professor of Asian Studies at the University of Washington, received his A.B. from Harvard in 1948 and his Ph.D. from Stanford in 1952. He is the author of *The Making of the Meiji Constitution* (1957), *The Modernization of China and Japan* (1962), and, with Kenji Ōkubo, *The Japanese Communist Party, 1922-1945* (1969).

JAMES B. CROWLEY is Associate Professor of History at Yale University. He completed his undergraduate work at the University of Connecticut in 1951 and his doctorate at the University of Michigan in 1960. He is the author of *Japan's Quest for Autonomy* (1966) and editor of *Modern East Asia: Essays in Interpretation* (1969).

R. P. DORE, Fellow of the Institute of Development Studies of the University of Sussex, has taught also at the University of British Columbia, the London School of Economics and Political Science, and the School of Oriental and African Studies, University of London. His publications include *City Life in Japan* (1958), *Land Reform in Japan* (1959), *Education in Tokugawa Japan* (1964), and *Aspects of Social Change in Modern Japan* (1967), the third volume in this series.

PETER DUUS is Associate Professor of Japanese History and Chairman of the Asian Studies Program at Claremont Graduate School, Claremont, California. Graduating from Harvard College in 1955, he received his M.A. from the University of Michigan in 1959 and his Ph.D. from Harvard in 1965, where he has also taught. His published works include *Party Rivalry and Political Change in Taisho Japan* (1968) and *Feudalism in Japan* (1969).

KENTARŌ HAYASHI is Professor of European History in the Faculty of Letters, Tokyo University. A graduate of Tokyo University in 1935, he is known for his contemporary criticism as well as for his numerous scholarly works on Western history, including *Kindai Doitsu no seiji to shakai* [Politics and Society in Modern Germany: A Study in the Prussian Reform, 1807-1815] (1952) and *Waimāru Kyōwakoku: Hittorā o shutsugen saseta mono* [The Weimar Republic] (1963).

CHIHIRO HOSOYA, Professor of International Relations in the Faculty of Law of Hitotsubashi University, was graduated from Tokyo University in 1945 and received his doctorate from Kyoto University in 1961. He is the editor of *Kokusai Seiji* [International Politics], the organ of the Japan Association of International Politics, and chairman of the Foreign Ministry's Diplomatic Documents Compilation Committee. Author of *Shiberia shuppei no shiteki kenkyū* [A Historical Study of the Japanese Intervention in Siberia] (1955) and co-author of *Taiheiyō sensō e no michi* [The Road to the Pacific War, vol. V] (1953), he also translated and edited the Japanese language edition of Marius Jansen's *Changing Japanese Attitudes toward Modernization*, volume 1 of this series, under the title, *Nihon ni okeru kindaika no mondai* (1968).

AKIRA IRIYE is Associate Professor of American Diplomatic History at the University of Chicago. A graduate of Haverford College (A.B., 1957) and Harvard University (Ph.D., 1961), he is the author of *After Imperialism: The Search for a New Order in the Far East* (1965), *Across the Pacific: An Inner History of American-East Asian Relations* (1967), and editor of *U.S. Policy in China* (1968). In Japanese his works include *Bei-Chū kankei no imēji* [Sino-American Relations: A Study in Images] (1966) and *Nihon no gaikō* [Diplomacy in Japan] (1966).

JAMES WILLIAM MORLEY, Professor of Government and Director of the East Asian Institute at Columbia University, received his A.B. from Harvard College in 1943 and his Ph.D. from Columbia University in 1954. His writings include *The Japanese Thrust into Siberia, 1918* (1957), *Japan and Korea: Amer-*

ica's Allies in the Pacific (1965), and, with Kuo Ting-yee, *Sino-Japanese Relations, 1862-1927* (1965). He is also editor of the forthcoming *Forecast for Japan: Security in the 1970's* (1972), *Japan's Foreign Policy, 1868-1941: A Research Guide*, and the translation of *Taiheiyo senso e no michi*, to be published in English as *Japan's Road to the Pacific War*.

TETSUO NAJITA, Associate Professor of History at the University of Chicago, received his B.A. from Grinnell College in 1958 and his Ph.D. from Harvard in 1965. Author of *Hara Kei in the Politics of Compromise, 1905-1915* (1967), which was awarded the John King Fairbank Prize by the American Historical Association, he has also published "Inukai Tsuyoshi: Some Dilemmas in Party Development in Pre-World War II Japan," in the *American Historical Review* (December 1968), and "Ōshio Heihachirō (1793-1837)," in *Personality in Japanese History*, edited by Albert Craig and Donald H. Shively (1970).

TSUTOMU ŌUCHI, Professor of Economics in the Faculty of Economics, Tokyo University, was graduated from that university in 1942 and received his doctorate there in 1961. He is the author of *Nihon shihonshugi no nōgyō mondai* [Problems of Agriculture under Japanese Capitalism] (1948), *Nihon keizai-ron* [Essays on the Economy of Japan], 2 vols. (1962-63), and *Fashizumu e no michi* [The Road to Fascism], which is vol. xxiv in the series *Nihon no rekishi* [The History of Japan] (1967).

HUGH T. PATRICK is Professor of Far Eastern Economics at Yale University, having received his A.B. from Yale in 1951 and his Ph.D. from Michigan in 1960. His writings include *Monetary Policy and Central Banking in Contemporary Japan* (1962); "Cyclical Instability and Fiscal-Monetary Policy" in the second volume in this series, *The State and Economic Enterprise in Modern Japan* (1965), edited by William W. Lockwood; "External Equilibrium and Internal Convertibility: Financial Policy in Meiji Japan," in *The Journal of Economic History*

(June 1965); "Financial Policy and Economic Growth in Underdeveloped Countries," in *Economic Development and Cultural Change* (January 1966); and "The Phoenix Risen from the Ashes: Postwar Japan," in James B. Crowley, ed., *Modern East Asia: Essays in Interpretation* (1969).

EDWIN O. REISCHAUER is University Professor at Harvard University. A graduate of Oberlin College in 1931 with his doctorate from Harvard in 1939, he served as United States Ambassador to Japan, 1961-66. His works include *Japan: the Story of a Nation* (1970), *The United States and Japan* (1965), *East Asia: The Great Tradition* (1965), *Beyond Vietnam: The United States and Asia* (1967), and *Wanted: An Asian Policy* (1955).

ROBERT M. SPAULDING, JR., Associate Professor of History at Oklahoma State University, received his doctorate from Michigan in 1965. He has written *Imperial Japan's Higher Civil Service Examinations* (1967), together with various articles, including "Amerikajin no mita Nihonkoku Kempō kaisei shoan" [Proposals for Revising the Constitution of Japan: An American's Views], in *Jiyū*, vol. 3, nos. 1-2 (1961); "Japan: Occupation and Foreign Relations, 1945-1960," in *Encyclopedia Americana* (1966); "The Intent of the Charter Oath," in *Studies in Japanese History and Politics*, edited by Richard K. Beardsley (1967); and "Japan's 'New Bureaucrats,' 1932-1945," in *Crisis Politics in Prewar Japan*, edited by George M. Wilson (1970).

ARTHUR E. TIEDEMANN, Professor of History at the City College of the City University of New York, received his doctorate from Columbia University in 1959. He is the author of *Modern Japan: A Brief History* (2nd rev. edn., 1962) and "Liberalism between the Wars" in *Sources of the Japanese Tradition*, compiled by Ryūsaku Tsunoda, Wm. Theodore de Bary, and Donald Keene (1958). He is also editor and contributor to a forthcoming text on Japanese history and civilization to be published by Columbia University Press.

INDEX